Nationalism in Asia

Nationalism in Asia

A History Since 1945

Jeff Kingston

WILEY Blackwell

This edition first published 2017

Registered Office
John Wiley & Sons, Ltd, The Atrium, Southern Gate, Chichester, West Sussex, PO19 8SQ, UK

Editorial Offices
350 Main Street, Malden, MA 02148-5020, USA
9600 Garsington Road, Oxford, OX4 2DQ, UK
The Atrium, Southern Gate, Chichester, West Sussex, PO19 8SQ, UK

For details of our global editorial offices, for customer services, and for information about how to apply for permission to reuse the copyright material in this book please see our website at www.wiley.com/wiley-blackwell.

Library of Congress Cataloging-in-Publication data applied for

HB ISBN: 9780470673010
PB ISBN: 9780470673027

A catalogue record for this book is available from the British Library.

Cover image: Jeff Kingston / It is handprints of veterans of the Sino-Japanese war 1937–45 at the Jinchuan Museum near Chengdu, China.

Set in 10.5/13pt Minion by SPi Global, Pondicherry, India
Printed and bound in Malaysia by Vivar Printing Sdn Bhd

1 2017

Contents

Acknowledgements

I would like to thank Temple University Japan's Dean Bruce Stronach, Associate Dean Alistair Howard, and Mariko Nagai, Director of Research, for their support of my research, fieldwork and writing, and Jonathan Wu, Assistant Dean for Academic Programs, for his deft scheduling of my teaching duties. I also want to thank Robert Dujarric, Director of the Institute of Contemporary Asian Studies, who recruits excellent research assistant interns. I am especially grateful to Chaninart Chunaharakchote, Sora Yang and Kimmin Jung for their extensive research assistance and to Eriko Kawaguchi and Mai Mitsui who have provided invaluable administrative support. Tom Boardman, our librarian, has been proactively helpful in tracking down material and alerting me to relevant publications.

I am grateful to the editorial crew at Wiley-Blackwell, especially Tessa Harvey for commissioning this book, and special thanks to Peter Coveney for picking up the baton when she retired and graciously shepherding the manuscript through the entire process before retiring. Kudos also to Brian Stone and Jayne Fargnoli for bringing the book out, Boston-based Katie DiFolco in marketing, UK-based Sarah Pearsall for copyediting and to the SPi Global production crew in India, making this a globe-spanning effort. I also want to thank anonymous reviewers and numerous colleagues who have shared their insights, offered suggestions and helped improve the final product. Finally, I would like to thank my wife Machiko for her unstinting support, and her father, Eichiro Osawa, who died at age 94 in early 2015 as this project was nearing completion. I trust he is singing with the angels on the sunny side of the street where he always seemed to be, perhaps walking with Rhubarb, our shibainu whose exuberance over 15 years (1999–2014) never failed to lift my spirits.

Maps

Glasgow
U.K.
Norwegian Sea
Svalbard
(NORWAY)
FRANZ JOSEF LAND
Arctic Ocean
Wrangel Island
North Sea
NORWAY
Oslo
SWEDEN
DEN.
Copenhagen
Stockholm
FINLAND
Barents Sea
NOVAYA ZEMLYA
Kara Sea
SEVERNAYA ZEMLYA
NEW SIBERIAN ISLANDS
Laptev Sea
East Siberian Sea
Bering Sea
Tallinn
Helsinki
RUS.
Riga
EST.
POL.
LITH.
LAT.
Warsaw
Vilnius
Minsk
BELARUS
Moscow
Kyiv
UKRAINE
Arctic Circle
S I B E R I A
RUSSIA
Sea of Okhotsk
KURIL ISLANDS
Occupied by the Soviet Union in 1945, administered by Russia, claimed by Japan.
Sakhalin
Black Sea
GEO.
Tbilisi
ARM.
Yerevan
Caspian Sea
AZERBAIJAN
Baku
Astana
KAZAKHSTAN
Ulaanbaatar
MONGOLIA
UZBEKISTAN
TURKMENISTAN
Ashgabat
Tashkent
Bishkek
KYRGYZSTAN
Tehran
Dushanbe
TAJIKISTAN
IRAN
AFGHANISTAN
Kabul
Islamabad
NORTH KOREA
Pyongyang
Sea of Japan
JAPAN
Tokyo
Seoul
SOUTH KOREA
Beijing
Yellow Sea
CHINA
East China Sea
Okinawa
RYUKYU ISLANDS (JAPAN)
Tropic of Cancer
Doha
QATAR
Abu Dhabi
U.A.E.
PAKISTAN
New Delhi
SAUDI ARABIA
Muscat
OMAN
NEPAL
Kathmandu
Thimphu
Taipei
Taiwan
BANGLADESH
Dhaka
INDIA
Hanoi
Philippine Sea
MYANMAR
Naypyidaw
LAOS
Vientiane
Hainan Dao
Luzon
Arabian Sea
South China Sea
Manila
THAILAND
Bangkok
VIETNAM
PHILIPPINES
LAKSHADWEEP (INDIA)
Bay of Bengal
ANDAMAN ISLANDS (INDIA)
Andaman Sea
CAMBODIA
Phnom Penh
Gulf of Thailand
SPRATLY ISLANDS
Mindanao
Sulu Sea
Laccadive Sea
SRI LANKA
Colombo
MALDIVES
Male
NICOBAR ISLANDS (INDIA)
Bandar Seri Begawan
BRUNEI
Celebes Sea
MALAYSIA
Kuala Lumpur
MALAYSIA
Borneo
SINGAPORE
Singapore
Sulawesi
Equator
Sumatra
Banda Sea
Scale 1:48,000,000
Azimuthal Equal-Area Projection
0 800 Kilometers
0 800 Miles
INDONESIA
Jakarta
Java Sea
Dili
TIMOR-LESTE
Timor
Java
Timor Sea
Indian Ocean
Boundary representation is not necessarily authoritative.
Cocos (Keeling) Islands (AUSTL.)
Christmas Island (AUSTL.)
AUSTRALIA

1 Asia

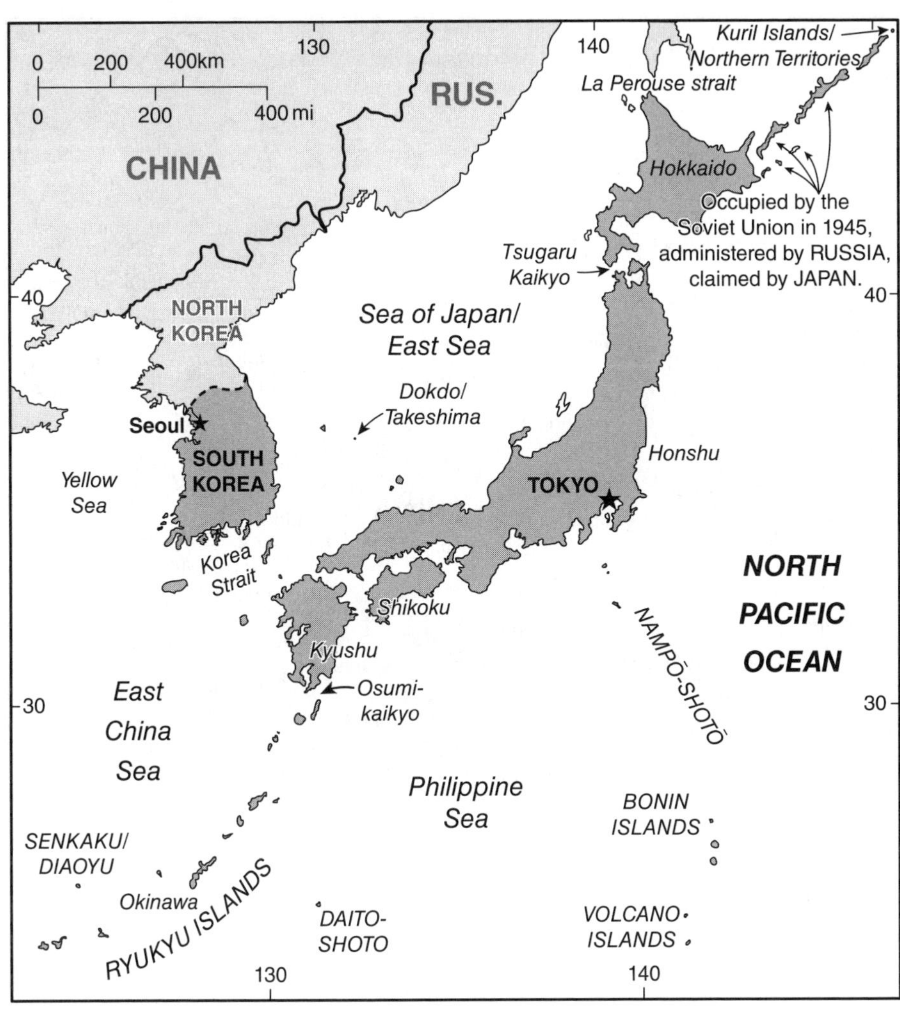

2 Northeast Asia

RUSSIA
KAZAKHSTAN
MONGOLIA
Heilongjiang
Jilin
KYRGYZSTAN
Urumqi
XINJIANG
Liaoning
NORTH KOREA
Neimongol
Beijing
Hebei
SOUTH KOREA
Gansu
Shanxi
Shandong
Qinghai
Shaanxi
Henan
Jiangsu
TIBET
CHINA
Anhui
Lhasa
Hubei
NEPAL
Sichuan
Zhejiang
Jiangxi
BHUTAN
Hunan
Fujian
INDIA
Guizhou
TAIWAN
BANGLADESH
Yunnan
Guangxi
Guangdong
Hongkong
MYANMAR
VIETNAM
LAOS
THAILAND
Hainan

3 China

4 Southeast Asia

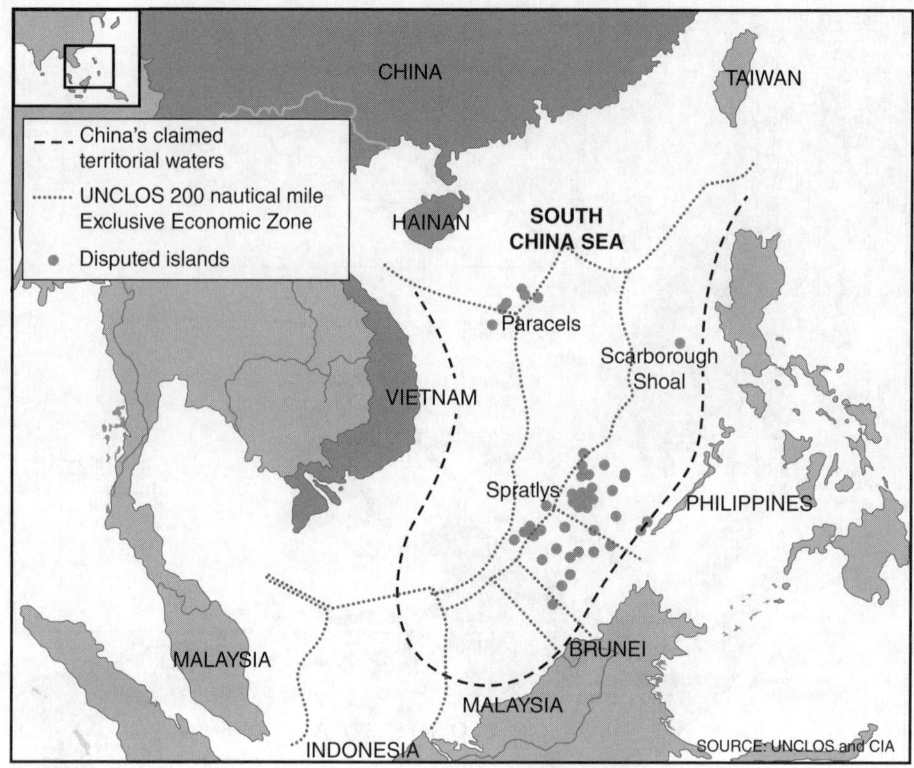

5 South China Sea: Disputed Claims

INDIA
Afghanistan
JAMMU & KASHMIR
Srinagar
China
HIMACHAL PRADESH
Simla
Chandigarh
PUNJAB
Dehradun
Pakistan
UTTARAKHAND
HARYANA
DELHI
New Delhi
Nepal
UTTAR PRADESH
SIKKIM
Gangtok
Bhutan
ARUNACHAL PRADESH
Itanagar
Jaipur
Lucknow
RAJASTHAN
Dispur
ASSAM
NAGALAND
Kohima
Patna
Shillong
MEGHALAYA
BIHAR
Bangladesh
Imphal
MANIPUR
JHARKHAND
WEST BENGAL
Agartala
TRIPURA
Aizawl
MIZORAM
Gandhinagar
Bhopal
MADHYA PRADESH
Ranchi
Kolkata
GUJARAT
CHHATTISGARH
Myanmar
Daman
DAMAN AND DIU
DADRA & NAGAR HAVELI
Silvasa
Raipur
ORISSA
Bhubaneshwar
Mumbai
MAHARASHTRA
Hyderabad
ANDHRA PRADESH
Arabian Sea
Bay of Bengal
Panaji
GOA
KARNATAKA
Bangalore
Chennai
PUDUCHERRY
ANDAMAN & NICOBAR (INDIA)
Port Blair
LAKSHADWEEP (INDIA)
Kavaratti
KERALA
TAMIL NADU
Thiruvananthapuram
Sri Lanka
INDIAN OCEAN

6 India

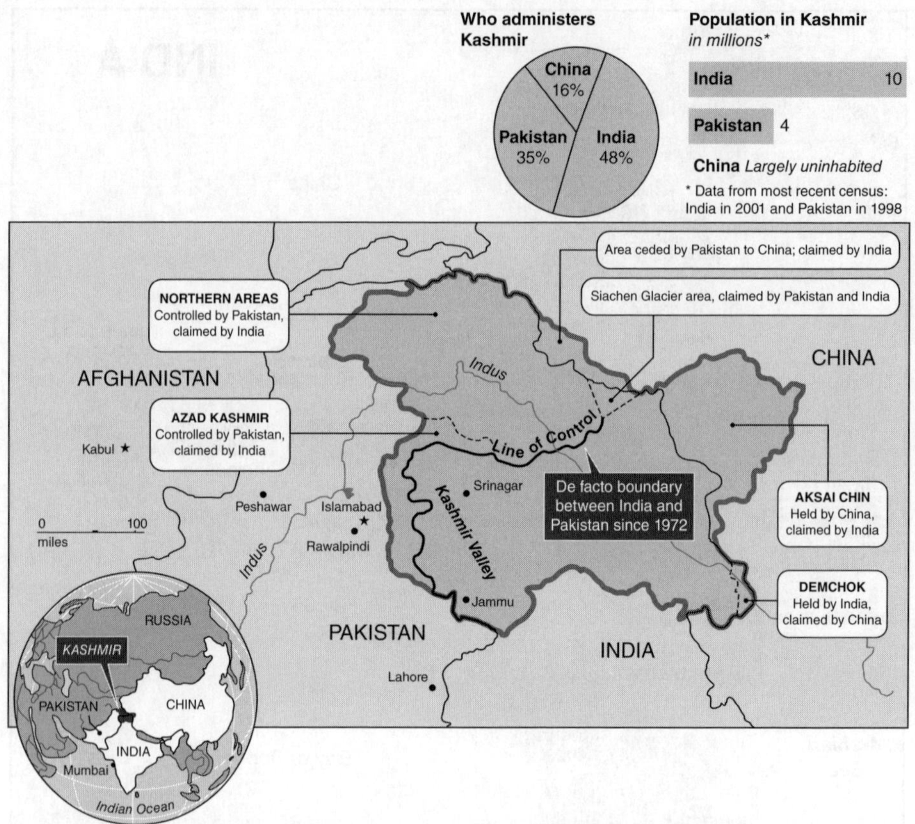

7 Map of Kashmir showing disputed regions

Introduction

If World War III ever breaks out, its origins will not lie in the Middle East, South Asia or Eastern Europe. It is in East Asia—where the strategic interests of China, the United States, and their respective partners intersect, that the geopolitical stakes, diplomatic tensions, and potential for a global explosion are highest.

Gareth Evans, former foreign minister of Australia, *Japan Times* (January 14, 2015)

Gareth Evans' warning about East Asia being the most likely site for a global conflagration is reason enough to probe deeper into the sources of regional tensions that are elucidated in the following pages. One need not be an alarmist or an economist to appreciate the increasing global importance of Asia. To understand the implications of the global geopolitical shift back to Asia after a two-century hiatus, it is critically important to examine the shared regional history and to appreciate how the end of colonial domination brought on by World War II, and legacies of that era, has shaped nationalistic attitudes. It is essential not to underestimate the power of the ghosts of the past to haunt 21st-century Asia and how they animate contemporary nationalism and influence national identity. Explaining this dynamic is one of the main goals of this book.

Nationalism

Nationalism is ever in search of an enemy. As such it is an abiding concern because it raises the risks of conflict, not just between nations, but also within nations. Nationalism is a modern ideology that draws on history, religion, beliefs, customs and traditions to establish a commonality and intense bonds of group solidarity that serve the purposes of the nation state (Smith 1995). Precisely because nationalism is so useful to the state, it involves myth-making, selective memories and dubious interpretations to construct the basis of a common identity and shared past that arouses and inspires. It involves forgetting that which divides or is inconvenient so that the Idea of nation can arouse "the feeling of the sacrifices that one has made in the past and of those that one is prepared to make in the future" (Renan 1882).

Nationalism is so useful because it justifies state policies, endorses leaders' aspirations and confers legitimacy on those who invoke it. By helping to construct unity based on shared identity, nationalism is crucial to establishing a sense of nation, an imagined community of affinity, belonging and communion that highlights distinctions between those who are part of the group and those who are not (Anderson 2006). Thus nationalism involves an intense "othering," drawing physical and psychological borders that exclude in ways that intensify a sense of belonging and solidarity among those who are included. Tensions that arise from nationalism can thus target other nations or those who reside within the national boundaries who are not part of the mainstream and are thus excluded or marginalized. The populist passions aroused, however, can careen out of state control, leading to unintended consequences, spreading like wildfire at the grassroots. Since the affairs of state and demands of international diplomacy often require compromises or concessions, nationalism can thus prove inconvenient and discrediting to those in power. Leaders often find that unleashing the genie of nationalism is easier than getting it back into the bottle.

There is also the risk of stoking what Ramachandra Guha (2012) calls "little nationalisms." This refers to the identity politics of groups residing within the national territory that feel excluded, mistreated, overlooked or overwhelmed by the mainstream nationalism. These threats or slights to minority identity can serve as the basis of autonomy or secessionist movements by political and diplomatic means, or in some cases insurgency, terrorism or other weapons of the weak. Like mainstream nationalisms, little nationalisms construct a common identity and shared history that is deployed to forge unity and advance agendas in their territory or community within the larger nation. To the extent that little nationalisms subvert the legitimacy of the prevailing mainstream nationalism, or resort to violence, they provoke a backlash because such subversion is an assault on the crucial idea of unity that is the foundation of the nation. This sabotage and treachery begets state-sponsored violence that inflames little nationalisms, strengthening solidarity in support of challenging the state and thereby igniting a cycle of violence. Guha also warns about the ugliness of little nationalisms, cautioning against glorifying or romanticizing what can deteriorate into sectarian thuggery and random violence in response to state repression.

There is a vast literature that specifies, complicates and interrogates theories of nationalism, but for our purposes, the succinct summary above can serve as a working definition/understanding that suffices for the narrative history that follows. This book focuses on how nationalism is embraced, expressed, contested, asserted and manipulated and how the confluence of these currents shapes national identity and destiny. In doing so, we explore the shackles of the past and how they influence contemporary attitudes and behavior.

Asian Five

Here the focus is on China, India, Indonesia, Japan and South Korea, five critically important nations in Asia that will play a key role in how the world's future plays out. Together they account for nearly 3 billion people, about 40% of the world's population, and account for about 25% of global GDP, with each ranking in the top 16 world economies. Four of the countries are in the top 10 for defense spending: China #2, Japan #8, India #9 and South Korea #10; and China and India are nuclear powers. China spends more on defense, $144 billion in 2014, than the other four focus nations combined. The ongoing modernization of the armed forces in each nation is increasing military capabilities across the region, one that is beset by various territorial disputes and lingering animosities related to previous conflicts and unresolved historical grievances. As we discuss throughout the book, there is no shortage of flashpoints in the region; hence a need to understand the basis and context for these disputes. India is the hegemon of South Asia; Indonesia dominates Southeast Asia; while China, Japan and South Korea are navigating the uncharted waters of a massive shift in geopolitical power in East Asia favoring Beijing at the expense of Tokyo, a process influenced significantly by the US alliances with Japan and South Korea. Indonesia, India, China and Japan also face significant internal tensions that arise from clashes of culture, religion or ethnicity within national borders and in some cases a backlash against the encroachment of mainstream nationalism on minority communities and their sense of threatened identity.

Framework

The target audience is university students and global citizens curious about understanding Asia in the 21st century. There is no attempt to add to the rich theoretical literature on nationalism as this project addresses the need for a narrative history and thematic analysis of nationalism in Asia. Rather than a series of nation-specific chapters, here the emphasis is on cross-national comparison of selected topics that illustrate the impact of nationalism in Asia since World War II and what this portends. In order to do so, nationalism is contextualized so that readers can understand how it fits into the wider mosaic of each nation's history. It is evident that past traumas cast a long shadow in 21st-century Asia that animates and sways identity politics relevant to comprehending nationalist sentiments and regional dynamics. The clinging to grievances, the selective amnesia and jingoistic swaggering are the basis of battles within and between nations on diverse battlefields ranging from textbooks and museums to territorial flashpoints.

The book is organized as follows. In the first section—National Identity—we explore the Idea of nation in each of the five nations that are the focus of this book: China, India, Indonesia, Japan and South Korea. Chapter 1 examines what these respective Ideas are and the leaders who played decisive roles in shaping their nations. Chapter 2 focuses on the legacies they bestowed and how these have been contested in recent decades as the Idea of nation has evolved. Chapter 3 focuses on national identity as represented in nation branding and soft power, while probing the gap between desired image and reality. The second section—Political Economy and Spectacle—shifts to examining nationalism and national identity in terms of economic policies (Chapter 4), democracy (Chapter 5) and sports (Chapter 6). This section imparts important context for understanding these societies, their varying trajectories and some key touchstones of national identity. Section III—Shackles of the Past—turns to the past and why it is relevant to understanding the present. Chapter 7 is about some of the key traumas that have shaped national identity and animate post-World War II nationalism. Chapter 8 examines museums as sites of collective memory and recrimination that provide insights on how the past is conveyed and wielded with an eye to contemporary purposes. Chapter 9 further develops this theme in focusing on textbooks. The fourth section—Flashpoints and Fringes—elucidates the implications of nationalism, internationally and domestically. Chapter 10 focuses on the origins and consequences of territorial disputes between nations, while Chapter 11 sketches some of the consequences of mainstream nationalism for domestic minorities and the backlash of 'little nationalisms" that contest their marginalization.

This overview of a wide range of themes spanning five nations introduces readers to the vast subject of nationalism in contemporary Asia, with the aim of stimulating curiosity in delving deeper into areas of specific interest. In order to assist in further research there is a subject-organized bibliography pointing readers to some key articles and books.

21st-Century Geopolitical Context

China's growing assertiveness in challenging the regional status quo and recalibrating it to serve Beijing's interests has sparked an arc of anxiety that stretches from Tokyo, Seoul, Hanoi and Manila to Sydney, Jakarta, Naypyidaw and New Delhi. Is this shared concern propelling a US-led containment policy in the region, targeting China? Beijing is convinced this is the case, pointing to the so-called Obama Pivot to Asia, involving a planned shift of US military assets that has yet to materialize and enhanced security cooperation with regional partners where many of the dominant 21st-century issues will be decided. Some analysts wonder if China's rise can be managed peacefully, while others counter that its track record is unthreatening and that its aspirations are about regaining the central role in regional affairs it exercised until the advent of western imperialism in the 19th century. And, isn't China acting just like other major powers? Problematically the US and Chinese governments have grown accustomed to getting their way, raising questions about whether the two dominant powers in Asia can continue to both compete and cooperate. Probably they can, but what if they can't?

India, the other Asian nation with a billion-plus population and impressive economic growth in recent years, is leveraging its position to maximum advantage, wooed by the US, Japan and Australia to offset China's growing regional power, while also seeking improved relations with Beijing for economic benefit and strategic reassurance on their shared border. India is also threatened by Beijing's "string of pearls" strategy of gaining access to ports in the Indian Ocean in order to project its growing naval power. While China promotes this as a maritime Silk Road, New Delhi sees an encircling initiative driven more by military considerations than commercial interests. Aside from a border war with China in 1962, India has fought four wars with Pakistan, three of them related to the disputed territory of Kashmir. Kashmir remains a volatile flashpoint, while Pakistani support for terrorist raids in India heightens the risk of retribution and the potential for skirmishing to escalate. Cozier relations between Beijing and Islamabad are evident in the Chinese-bankrolled and -built Gwadar deep-water port project in western Pakistan on the Arabian Sea, situated near the mouth of the Persian Gulf where much of China's imported oil and gas transits. This is a key link in China's string of pearls. India is also concerned about Beijing's increased support for weapons sales and nuclear energy projects in Pakistan, its arch-enemy.

Similar to India's nuclear standoff with Pakistan, Seoul faces an existential crisis across its border with nuclear-armed North Korea, where the imperatives of regime survival complicate hopes for reunification of the entire peninsula. But, one asks, on whose terms? China and the US have a common strategic interest in managing a soft-landing for the North Korean regime, but divergent views on how to proceed that are echoed in their respective client states. South Korea's growing economic dependence on China calls for a hedging strategy, but even if it is sensible to forge closer ties with Japan and thereby enhance the trilateral security alliance involving Washington, bitter enmities from the Japanese colonial era still resonate loudly in contemporary public discourse. Indeed, Beijing and Seoul have developed solidarity over their shared history with Japan and perceptions that Tokyo is again trying to whitewash this past. Indonesia, aside from squabbles with Australia, faces a relatively benign external environment.

There is a basis for cautious optimism that Gareth Evans' warning about East Asia, while valid, is an unlikely outcome. Of course that is what European diplomats, the so-called "sleepwalkers," were saying on the eve of WWI when it was assumed that strong economic ties between Germany and Great Britain made war unthinkable until the nightmare erupted (Clark 2013). Yet again the stakes are high and the losses would be incalculable, so the risk of regional or global conflagration seems very remote, or so we hope. Layered and extensive economic interdependence within Asia and between Asian nations and the US and Europe is a stabilizing factor that provides ballast in stormy seas. While the risk of conflicts within the region cannot be dismissed given the numerous flashpoints and tensions detailed in the following pages, the recent record on inter-state conflict is encouraging.

Peaceful Prospects?

Much of Asia has enjoyed a prolonged spell of peace since the late 1970s. To clarify, the East Asian peace refers to the lack of major violent conflicts between states over the past four decades. Two exceptions to this peace are the brief Indo-Pakistan war in 1999, a relatively small-scale conflict, and China's ill-fated 1979 incursion into Vietnam, also brief, but with heavy losses on both sides. Beijing learned the hard way what Washington already knew about Vietnamese tenacity.

While there are many competing theories about why the East Asian peace has prevailed and differing assessments about whether it will persist, there has been a significant degree of state violence directed within national borders (Kivimäki 2011; Weissmann 2012; Goldsmith 2014). Civil unrest, ethnic and sectarian conflict and secessionist insurgencies serve as a sobering counterpoint to the regional peace, and here it is argued that nationalism is a salient factor in domestic turmoil. Nationalism is one of many factors that have sustained antipathies, sabotaged reconciliation, limited governments' room for maneuver and judicious compromise, while amplifying anxieties that undermine trust and cooperation between fellow citizens, accentuating divides between communities. No country knows the costs more than Myanmar (formerly Burma) where multiple ethnic insurgencies have flared since the middle of the 20th century. The military justifies its outsized role in Myanmar in terms of preserving the unity of the nation, crushing those who seek independence or greater autonomy. Similar instances of endemic violence are evident in India and Indonesia, while China has also had to cope with restive frontiers.

How nationalism will influence Asia's future is a subject of considerable speculation. Predicting the future is not featured prominently here, but for what it is worth, it seems there are good reasons to expect that the Asian peace will persist and that cooler heads will prevail despite hotheaded nationalism. This doesn't mean everyone should assume complacently that there is nothing to worry about. Formal and informal mechanisms designed to help manage conflicts and prevent escalation provide a basis for cautious optimism that conflict will not engulf the region. But warnings by Evans and others serve as stark reminders that preserving the peace requires constant attention aimed at reducing risk factors, and that neglect to do so may prove destabilizing.

Nationalism is not one of the most urgent risks to regional peace, but it is a salient factor that complicates the task of conflict prevention and managing tensions. Strategic rivalry, and the inherent risks of a rising China challenging a status quo promoted and protected by the US, is the main threat to regional peace. History does not hold many inspiring examples of status quo powers ceding enough to accommodate the aspirations of a rising power or the rising power settling for much less than it expects. The most recent example in Asia involves Japan and its ill-fated efforts to join and modify the status quo in its favor from 1895 to 1945. Rebuffed by the western powers, feeling bottled up and treated with racist condescension, Japan embarked on war to achieve its aims. This ended in tragedy for Japan and the region, a nightmare that still resonates loudly even now. Inadvertently, however, Japan did hasten decolonization and unshackle the nationalisms that define the region and its tensions which we discuss in the following chapters. Although there are some striking parallels between 21st-century China and Imperial Japan, the differences are profound, as is the international system, cautioning against exaggerating the threat. Clearly, China's foreign policy has become more assertive, ratcheting up tensions with its extravagant maritime territorial claims, but it has also demonstrated restraint in pursuing its agenda, pushing forward and falling back in what amounts to a long diplomatic game in a situation where time appears to be on its side.

Cautious optimism on inter-state conflict in Asia is tempered by the relative fragility of peace between Pakistan and India and risks on the Korean Peninsula. Kashmir remains a potent source of tensions that could boil over again, and, given the nuclear option, a horrific scenario to contemplate. The tense standoff between the two Koreas could also spiral out of control, but China and the US have much at stake in averting such a scenario. Both nations also have much at stake in the East China Sea and South China Sea, a fraught situation of overlapping claims by China and its neighbors. Diplomatic and military maneuvering over these rival claims is driven and constrained by the Sino-US strategic rivalry and their respective interests. For the US, the stakes are arguably higher in the East China Sea because that involves Tokyo's worries that its security alliance with Washington might prove unreliable, unwilling to risk its extensive interests in China over the Senkaku/Diaoyu, as the disputed rocky islets are named by Tokyo and Beijing respectively. Meanwhile, China is constructing a military base closer to where any action might take place in this evolving flashpoint.

The risks of nationalism are arguably greater domestically than internationally. As noted above, Asia has enjoyed four decades of almost uninterrupted peace between nations, but the region has been beset by extensive internal conflict. Mainstream nationalism "others" minority groups inside the national borders, making them a target of discrimination, marginalization and sometimes violence, thereby alienating these minorities and sparking tensions that can escalate into communal clashes and insurgency. Whether targeting ethnic, religious or linguistic differences, or a combination thereof, the tendency of the state to acquiesce to or indeed actively promote mainstream jingoism and communal politics is destabilizing. Communities that are marginalized, find ambitions thwarted, feel they are treated unfairly or endure the indignities of discrimination have good reasons not to buy into the mainstream Idea of nation and are open to alternatives. As we discuss in subsequent chapters, identity politics, chauvinism and resource exploitation at the expense of minorities in China, India and Indonesia have provoked rioting, bloodshed and acts of terrorism. These problems will persist. In the far more ethnically homogeneous Japan, the situation is quite different, but identity politics among Okinawans has been mobilized against the extensive presence of the US military bases on their islands, and resentment towards Tokyo for foisting this on them. A recrudescent nationalism among Japan's conservative political elite generates other risks, notably hate speech targeting the large ethnic Korean minority in Japan, and orchestrated attacks on liberals and liberal institutions. These assaults spill over into international relations because the goal is to retract or dilute official Japanese admission of wrongdoing in the wartime and colonial eras and promote a valorizing and vindicating history that is unacceptable to those that suffered most from Japanese imperialism—Chinese and Koreans. In trying to regain national dignity, Japanese conservatives are trampling on that of Japan's past victims and in doing so tarnishing their own while roiling regional relations.

Nationalism has a checkered reputation for good reasons. George Orwell famously commented that it is "the worst enemy of peace." Nationalism feeds on grievance and unifies by recalling the shared struggle of overcoming past traumas. It is blinding and repressive, feeds on insecurities and appeals to primordial instincts. Problematically it also serves as the ideological basis for the modern state and thus shapes its agenda.

India's Nobel Literature laureate Rabindranath Tagore was also deeply wary of nationalism; thus it is ironic that a poem he wrote in 1911 and set to music in 1919 was adopted as the Indian national anthem in 1950, after his death. He wrote:

> Nationalism is a great menace. It is many countries packed in one geographical receptacle. They create huge eddies with their passions, and they feel dizzily inebriated with the mere velocity of their whirling movement, taking that to be freedom. (Tagore 1917, 144)

In a similar vein, Haruki Murakami (2012), a Japanese author with a 21st-century global cult following, also deplores nationalism writing:

> It's like cheap alcohol. It gets you drunk after only a few shots and makes you hysterical. It makes you speak loudly and act rudely … but after your drunken rampage you are left with nothing but an awful headache the next morning.

In his view, territorial disputes are an inescapable consequence of dividing humanity into countries with national borders. When such disputes are refracted through "nationalist sentiment," they become dangerous situations with no exit. As such, "We must be careful about politicians and polemicists who lavish us with this cheap alcohol and allow things to get out of control" (Murakami 2012).

Now let's turn to the Idea of nation and those who have distilled this powerful brew and bequeathed not only hangovers, but also shaped national identities on the anvil of history in the wake of World War II.

Part I
National Identity

Part I

National Identity

1

The Idea of Nation

Sketching the Idea of a nation is an audacious undertaking, particularly in Asia's plural and complex societies that are endowed with a rich ethnic, religious, cultural and linguistic diversity, where ideas are in competition and evolving, in a region that has experienced profound changes since 1945. Yet in broad brushes it is useful to delineate the shared conceptual framework that embodies a sense of national identity and speaks to the abiding question of who we are. Concepts of nation pre-date our post-1945 timeframe, but without straying too far into the distant past it is useful to examine the process of agitation and consolidation and how nation states in Asia came to be. Who projected what onto the broad canvas of nation and to what extent have their ideas held or been reevaluated and with what consequences?

I am inspired by Sunil Khilnani's, *The Idea of India* (1997), a *tour de force* that captures India's idea of itself and asserts that there is a broad and resilient consensus about what that idea is. Perhaps, but it does seem that the cultural wars we discuss later in this chapter and the next indicate that this broad acceptance is challenged in India, just as in all our focus nations where people are contesting, shaping and seeking 21st-century identities. With the exception of China where the Chinese Communist Party (CCP) under Mao Zedong was monolithic in power and scope, crushing dissent and any forces deemed counter-revolutionary, the nations have endured political competition and bouts of authoritarian rule, contexts in which longstanding fault lines have been a recurring source of tension and contestation. Defining a nation always raises questions about who is in and who is not, based on various criteria such as ethnicity, language, religion and customs that marginalize, divide and antagonize in ways that arouse nationalist sentiments.

The first step involves a strong leader—for better or worse. In our five countries, five leaders put their stamp on the idea of nation that emerged from the aftermath

Nationalism in Asia: A History Since 1945, First Edition. Jeff Kingston.

of war and revolution. Mao Zedong in China, Jawaharlal Nehru in India, Sukarno in Indonesia, Park Chung-hee in South Korea and, with some caveats, Shigeru Yoshida in Japan, were the architects of their post-1945 nations.

Secondly, in each of our nations a strong central state was key to the Idea of nation even if not always realized. Mao, Nehru and Sukarno had been leaders in their nation's struggle for independence and were keenly aware of the need to consolidate their power, and sought unquestioned authority to tackle the massive socio-economic problems they faced in trying to construct a unified nation with a strong and stable government. In addressing the pressing needs of the people, the legacies of colonialism in India and Indonesia, and imperial domination of China, contributed little to economic development or modernization. Japan already had a strong central state and the indirect nature of the US Occupation meant that it relied heavily on that state to remake Japan. This reliance reinforced the power of Tokyo's central bureaucracy. South Korea had the legacy of Japanese colonial rule and a relatively well-developed administrative structure and infrastructure to build on, although these legacies remain controversial among Koreans given the reluctance to credit Japan with any positive influences.

Thirdly, the nationalist resentments aroused by imperial humiliation powerfully shaped the Idea of nation. Japan is an outlier in this group because Japan was not colonized or subjugated by any imperial power and had already established a constitutional monarchy with a functioning democracy and representative government prior to 1945. It does share, however, the sense of humiliation and rancor stemming from having to submit to imperial domination. The unequal treaties imposed in the mid-19th century motivated Meiji-era (1868–1912) modernization efforts aimed at creating conditions that would enable Japan to revise the treaties by catching up with the West. The leaders who plunged Japan into war from the 1930s deeply resented entrenched western racism, a sentiment shared by nationalist leaders throughout Asia. Following defeat, the US Occupation of Japan from 1945 to 1952 was an intense period of reinventing Japan directed by an outside power, while China, India and Indonesia sought their own way forward from the debilitating consequences of imperialism. South Korea, like China, was baptized by a horrific civil war (1950–1953) and faced similar challenges to overcome the devastation. Unlike mainland China, the Korean Peninsula remained divided after its civil war, a division that persists until now. Like Japan, South Korea has been a client state of the US during and since the Cold War (1947–1989), and Seoul was also heavily dependent on, and influenced by, Washington in its formative years. The term client state means that security and foreign policy in both nations is subordinate to Washington's agenda and interests.

Subjugation and humiliation at the hands of imperial powers resonated powerfully among people in new nations who faced dire circumstances, ones that could be blamed persuasively on the former regimes. India had Great Britain, Indonesia had The Netherlands, while China and South Korea had Japan to blame. All of these nations could draw on shared traumas, while legitimacy was bestowed on the new leaders who provided a vision infused with hope. The Idea of nation also drew on powerful possibilities opened by realization of self-determination, overthrow of old orders and a sense of mission. Equally, perceptions of continued external manipulation and intervention remained resilient.

By contrast, Japan as the defeated aggressor occupied by the US was not in a position to blame anyone but its own military and political leaders. Nonetheless, it awkwardly embraces the narrative of "victim," awkward because it joined western nations in colonizing and subjugating Asia. The powerful discourse of Japan's victimization that has come to dominate wartime memories perturbs its former victims in East Asia (see Chapters 7, 8 and 9). During Japan's long war against Asia (1931–1945) it invoked past humiliations and resentment about a biased and racist international order, asserting unconvincingly that its invasions and occupation were part of a Pan-Asian crusade for liberation from western colonial rule, but after 1945 it was not able to tap these well-springs of identity because of all the devastation it inflicted in Asia. Yet in recent years this war has become contemporary Japan's chosen trauma and reactionaries have made headway in promoting the myth of Pan-Asian liberation and justifying the war as a defensive response to western hostility and encirclement. Thus in a triumph of chutzpah over history, one that only works within Japan's borders, the selective exhumation of the painful wartime past highlights suffering endured, overshadowing what its wartime leaders perpetrated.

Fourthly, the five nations split on the issue of ethnic identity as the basis of the Idea of nation. India and Indonesia celebrate diversity as intrinsic to their national identities, in contrast to Japan and South Korea which emphasize their relative homogeneity, while China tries to have it both ways, paying lip service to diversity while promoting a Han-centric identity. An Idea of nation based on common culture, language and ethnicity does not require quite the same tending and continual reinforcement. Diversity places an emphasis and burden on tolerance as a virtue, which is not always realized in China, India and Indonesia (or anywhere else). The ethnic Han in China have been inadequately attentive to minority sensitivities, especially the Muslim Uighurs and Tibetan Buddhists, as we discuss in Chapter 11. Other minorities that don't pose a threat because they lack the capacity to resist have done relatively better.

Nations also pick and choose which aspects of their past to celebrate. Mao Zedong sought to eradicate China's common Confucian identity, seeing this as one of the impediments to modernization, and replace it with Maoism, a cult of personality mixed with communism, but customs and traditions proved resilient and have made a comeback as the government now promotes Confucius Institutes around the world to nurture influence and project soft power. The convulsions under the banner of promoting a Maoist identity had an enormous impact on Chinese society in the second half of the 20th century, but the economic reforms unleashed by Deng Xiaoping since 1978 have marginalized Maoism as a source of collective identity even as he remains revered as a revolutionary.

Religion and language are another source of identity cohesion—and division. In Indonesia, ethnic Javanese hailing from its most populous island have dominated the state since independence, generating regional resentments against a Java-centric

Idea of Indonesia, but 90% of the population share an Islamic orientation, creating considerable common ground for understanding and empathy, if not always unity. The national motto is Unity in Diversity, a bold assertion that belies the inherent challenges in achieving this. The spread of the Indonesian language around the archipelago since 1945 has had a powerful unifying impact even as linguistic and ethnic differences remain powerful countercurrents. India is predominantly Hindu, but, as with Indonesian Islam, it is not practiced or embraced monolithically; while Hindi, the most widely spoken language, shares official status with regional languages; and English serves as a lingua franca. India also has a huge Muslim population that remains marginalized and poorly integrated, while the multitudinous ethnic and cultural variations in the sub-continent belie assertions of a shared vision. Yet, vibrant regional identities are subsumed within the inclusive Idea of India and portrayed as one of its strengths.

Each of our nations embraces a transcendent civilizational identity drawing on a rich and established heritage and history stretching back several centuries. In the context of this venerated and glorified past, the shocks of imperialism can be viewed as a prolonged and disruptive interregnum. This past is usefully malleable, accommodating various interpretations and lessons to be learned depending on the needs of the day. In some respects, all of our nations nurture a sense of a shared past and collective destiny that taps into this civilizational identity, while also brooding about the humiliations inflicted during the imperial encounter. The Idea of nation is embellished in reference to bygone eras of glory and splendor. Close scrutiny of the 'glorious past' in each of our countries yields inconsistencies and inglorious moments that are not part of the official story, but that is precisely the point; nationalism nurtures a convenient all-embracing history for contemporary use. The distant past can be invoked to ratify the current order, and if priorities shift, this can be recalibrated to match changing circumstances.

India's prevailing Idea involves tension between secular and religious values and between (and within) religions. Contemporary religious antagonisms are traced to Partition in 1947, involving the tumultuous movement of over 12 million Hindus and Muslims that ensued when the British presided over the hasty establishment of an independent India and Pakistan, thus dividing the sub-continent and sowing seeds of discord. Great Britain's rushed exit was to avoid becoming embroiled in civil war at a time when it had limited resources, faced difficulties in recovering from World War II and appetite for Empire had ebbed. During the upheaval as many as one million people were killed as newly displaced refugees moved across the new borders to join the presumed relative safety of majority religious communities. Following Partition, about 10% of India's population was Muslim, climbing now to about 15%, numbering almost 180 million, the world's third largest Muslim population. Overall, India's Muslims remain economically marginalized and poorly integrated. Islam is India's other great tradition (Mughal dynasty 1526–1707), but it is not monolithic and features various sects (Sufi, Shia, Ahmadiyya), caste divisions and stratification according to ancestry. India's national identity is inseparable from the concept, and still robust practice, of caste, the finely delineated social hierarchy that defines one's status from birth based on Hindu precepts. The large Sikh minority denies this caste hierarchy and has carved out a relatively successful place in Indian society, but was tragically targeted by Hindu violence in 1984, a stark reminder of the consequences of assertive majority nationalism for minorities, which we discuss in Chapter 11. The multitudinous ethnic and cultural variations in the sub-continent further challenge assertions of a shared vision or common heritage, which has been managed by elaborating and improvising an encompassing Idea of India that embraces immense diversity, if not always successfully.

Each of the national Ideas is fundamentally secular. In China, this was uncontroversial since the communists were eager to root out what it dismissed as feudal practices and superstitions. In secularism, Nehru and Sukarno saw a path to modernity, which was was threatened by religion and sectarian violence. Japan's secularism was born in the ashes of surrender when the US constitutionally separated the state from religion and Emperor Hirohito renounced his divinity. He had been the head priest of State Shinto, a Japanese animist religion that became intertwined with Japan's Holy War in Asia and goal of extending the Emperor's realm. As such it was implicated in and discredited by the wartime debacle. The American-led Occupation of Japan peeled religion away from the basic structure of democratic government that was hijacked by militarists in the 1930s. The Idea of South Korea is also secular, one liberated from the impositions of Japan's empire that is imbued with US influences and the modernizing policies of the state.

Forgetting

Forgetting is crucial to the Idea of nation in the sense of putting aside or burying whatever contradicts or undermines the core of the unifying and inspiring identity. Forgetting is expedient, artful and necessary, serving to bridge gaps, forge a shared consciousness and overcome divisive memories and experiences. But such concessions are difficult to sustain, festering within the nation, setting the stage for future battles. There are good reasons to put aside the unresolved and painful memories, but associated undercurrents also pull at the fabric of identity and generate tensions. Forgetting they were embarking on mission impossible was crucial to the nation-building projects of Nehru and Sukarno as they tried to stitch together sprawling nations out of unpromising colonial legacies. South Koreans also had a need for forgetting as many had collaborated with the Japanese and could thus be looked upon as traitors to the nation. But many of the collaborators had the skills, training, networks and wherewithal to help South Korea recover from war, and therefore gained positions of power and influence. Park Chung-hee, the general who took power in a military coup in 1961, served in the Japanese colonial army—an army that repressed Korean independence activists and supported Japan's empire. Park presided over an authoritarian state that imposed a collective forgetting because building Korea's future was considered more important than settling its past, and those in power had much to lose from historical scrutiny. Indeed, Park normalized relations with Japan in 1965, receiving $800 million in grants and loans from Tokyo to cover all compensation claims related to the colonial era; but because there was no apology, reconciliation has proven elusive. Sukarno also had dubious ties with the Japanese that were best forgotten. His collaboration involved actively assisting in the mobilization of romusha (forced labor), a program that claimed more than a million lives, and acquiesced to forced rice deliveries that drove many families to the brink of starvation. Throughout the war, however, he remained a stalwart cheerleader for Japan's Holy War, seeing this as Indonesia's best chance for ending Dutch colonial rule. Japan failed to reciprocate Sukarno's unequivocal support, infuriating and humiliating him by granting independence sooner to other Southeast Asian nations, but refusing Indonesia until it was clear the war was lost and Tokyo had no choice in the matter. This also was something to forget so that the nation could move forward.

Japan also had good reasons for forgetting, especially since the public had supported the war in Asia (1931–1945), at least until the consequences of the national folly rebounded, inflicting horrific devastation on Japan's cities and people. Also to be forgotten were the stunning continuities between Japan's wartime and postwar elite, embodied in Emperor Hirohito, senior political leaders and bureaucrats. The Americans rehabilitated the conservative elite that had planned and waged war because they could deliver a successful postwar recovery and political stability suitably deferential to US interests and their Cold War anti-communist agenda. The US also protected Japan from demands for a reckoning about its shared past with Asia and significant reparations that might slow recovery. Allying with the US, and relying on it for protection, also took a leap of forgetfulness as America had firebombed 66 Japanese cities and dropped atomic bombs on Hiroshima and Nagasaki, killing an estimated half a million civilians. Forgetting was thus central to the postwar Idea of Japan because remembering would raise too many awkward questions for those with much influence and lots to lose. A mere 12 years after the war, Nobusuke Kishi, a Class A war crimes suspect, became prime minister in 1957, a remarkable act of forgetting unthinkable in postwar Germany. His grandson, Shinzo Abe, subsequently became prime minister (2006–2007, 2012–) and seeks to rehabilitate Japan's wartime history while shedding constraints on Japan's military embodied in its pacifist Constitution.

Indeed, in 2015 Abe's statement on the 70th anniversary of the end of World War II elevated an exonerating revisionist narrative of history to Japan's official policy. The vague and ambiguous references to past misdeeds, the inadequate recognition of Japanese aggression and the horrors inflicted, the minimalist nods toward contrition, and putting an end to apology are now state policy. This is a major watershed in Japan's postwar history that digs a deep diplomatic hole and tarnishes the nation's significant and praiseworthy achievements of the past seven decades.

There was a very interesting contrast in the 70th anniversary commemoration statements by Abe and Emperor Akihito that highlights the ongoing political divide between the revisionists and most Japanese in their understanding of how the nation got to where it is today. Noting the deaths of more than 3 million Japanese during

Figure 1.1 The Hiroshima Dome Attests to the Folly of Nationalism. Photo © Jeff Kingston.

World War II, Abe asserted: "The peace we enjoy today exists only upon such precious sacrifices. And therein lies the origin of postwar Japan" (Abe Statement, August 14, 2015, Prime Minister's Office Japan). This assertion that wartime sacrifices begot contemporary peace is the revisionist conceit, one that Emperor Akihito clearly rejected on August 15, 2015. He said:

> Our country today enjoys peace and prosperity, thanks to the ceaseless efforts made by the people of Japan toward recovery from the devastation of the war and toward development, always backed by their earnest desire for the continuation of peace. (Address by His Majesty the Emperor on the Occasion of the Memorial Ceremony for the War Dead, August 15, 2015, Imperial Household Agency)

Peace and prosperity, in the Emperor's view, did not come from treating the Japanese people like cannon fodder during the war, but rather was based on their postwar efforts to overcome the tragedy inflicted by the nation's warmongering leaders. The Emperor has been a vigorous and popular advocate for a national identity based on pacifism that most Japanese support.

Like Japan's revisionists, Mao also embraced selective remembering. The Kuomintang (KMT) had done most of the fighting and, unlike the CCP, had grounds to claim credit for helping to defeat Japan. This too was forgotten for the time being as the CCP and People's Liberation Army (PLA) portrayed themselves as the saviors of the nation and the KMT were vilified as corrupt stooges of the US. Mao then proceeded to inflict a series of catastrophes on the Chinese, most notably the twin tragedies of the Great Famine (1958–1960) and the Cultural Revolution (1966–1976), traumatic events that also needed forgetting, facilitated by China's authoritarian state and repression of dissent. In 1972, when Japan and China normalized relations, Mao thanked the visiting Prime Minister Kakuei Tanaka for the invaluable assistance of the Imperial Armed Forces in helping the communists to victory by inflicting heavy losses on the KMT. Mao's gesture of reconciliation involved focusing blame on military leaders and absolving the Japanese people of responsibility for the horrific devastation inflicted on China, claiming an estimated 10–15 million lives from 1931 to 1945.

Forgetting, however, is challenged by those seeking to exhume the buried memories and experiences, drawing attention to what has been ignored. The reasons for remembering are as varied as those for forgetting, but it can be driven by personal loss, political agendas and changing geo-political considerations. For the Idea to prevail in the first place often required aggressive disremembering, leaving scars to be avenged. In a democracy, the Idea of nation can be hotly contested. Nehru's secularism prevailed over religious communalism, but not by much. Hindutva religious chauvinists never accepted defeat, never conceded, and so the battles have simmered and flared over the ensuing decades. Inclusiveness appeals to liberals as a fundamentally reasonable principle to defend, but for religious zealots this is a target, a sacrilege to be overturned. They have not forgotten Partition or other religion-based grievances and see no reason to support the compromise and concessions of forgetting. In Indonesia, Sukarno also managed to overcome zealous support for an Islamic state, establishing a government based on secular principles that were strongly supported by most nationalist leaders and, crucially, the army. But in an overwhelmingly Muslim nation, shifting religion to the side and asserting tolerance required constant vigilance. From the outset, Islamic leaders challenged the new Republic of Indonesia, claiming they had been betrayed by 'forgotten' promises of the Jakarta Charter of 1945 that elevated Islam to a central position in the Idea of nation. True or not, it was an effective call to arms that challenged Sukarno's Idea. Indonesian unity was threatened by separatist Islamic rebellions throughout the 1950s, forcing Sukarno to recalibrate the Idea by concentrating power in the executive and relying on his powers of persuasion and compromise along with the security forces. Sukarno visited Beijing in 1956 and was impressed by what he encountered, seeing what a stronger, less democratic state might achieve. Always ambivalent about western-style parliamentary government, Sukarno reconsidered the Idea of secular, representative democracy, siding with the military in moving to Guided Democracy, eschewing elections and serving as guide. Alas, as we discuss in Chapters 5, 7 and 8, he steered the nation into crisis, leading to his ouster and the ensuing massacres of 1965–1966. This required another collective forgetting under the New Order government that succeeded him.

The military assumed the reins of power under General Suharto and in 1967 the New Order was proclaimed, an authoritarian government that put the final nail in democracy, stamping out dissent and free elections, while also strengthening secularism. Sukarno's free-wheeling improvised Idea traded on his charisma, but was discredited by the prevailing sense of chaos and the growing despair of poverty. The New Order Idea of Indonesia was praetorian, espousing stability and development for a people who knew neither. It also drew on a conceit of selective memory, portraying the military as the saviors of the nation. The military had "saved" a largely Islamic nation from godless communism, then quickly moved to strictly control Islam's political role. The military, paramilitary and religious groups that carried out the bloody purges in 1965–1966 were never held accountable for the massacres of as many as one million people; responsibility for the slaughter was shifted onto the Partai Kommunis Indonesia, the Indonesian communist party, and its alleged plans to take power through a coup. The actual perpetrators were represented throughout the highest levels of the New Order government that ruled between 1967 and 1998, facilitating a collective amnesia, at least on the surface. But with the end of the New Order in 1998, that horrific chapter is currently being disinterred and subject to ongoing reconsideration. Incrementally, the organized forgetting of the mass carnage is receding, and there has been fitful progress in exhuming the painful memories, but accountability remains unfinished business. While passage of time matters—most of those responsible for the bloodbath have died—these events remain embarrassing for powerful institutions such as the military and religious groups who stand to lose considerable credibility if held accountable for the deep scars they inflicted on the nation, a burden they have shirked ever since.

For China, forgetfulness about policy bungling and unachieved targets was part of Mao's surreal style, but the Great Forgetting began after his death in 1976 with economic reforms in 1978 that abandoned Mao's bedrock communist principles. Deng hit the reset button because Maoism was an abject failure and his legacy risked dragging the CCP into the grave with him. Of course the official view now is that Mao was 70% right, but the other 30% includes some whopping megaflops. Mao's manmade disasters are not forgotten, but he remains almost universally admired by Chinese because they are continually reminded that he led the CCP to victory in the 1949 revolution. Like all of our founding fathers, Mao is a flawed figure, but perhaps the most egregiously so, and it is thus not surprising that the evolving Idea of China repudiates almost everything he stood for. Socialism with Chinese characteristics is the official euphemism for this stunning apostasy.

Legacies

The Idea of nation was sown in the poisoned soil of imperialism, colonial subjugation and humiliations that bred resentments. These same resentments were subsequently nurtured during the Cold War. What happened in the first half of the 20th century left an indelible imprint on the leaders and the ideas they projected onto their nations. The poverty and scars, physical and psychological, which lingered in the postwar era could be attributed persuasively to imperialism and war. China and

South Korea had both suffered from Japanese subjugation while India and Indonesia had endured British and Dutch rule. Japan had also felt pressured by western imperialism in the 19th century and in response embarked on rapid state-led modernization and industrialization. In doing so it became like the other imperial powers, aggressively expanding its power in Asia through a series of conflicts stretching over half a century from 1895, that eventually led to confrontation with the US and defeat in 1945. Alone among the five countries, it was a marauding imperial power in Asia and thus has had quite a different legacy to come to terms with in crafting its new Idea, under US guidance.

Subsequent efforts at nation-building in our focus countries were shaped by this imperial past, but also by the Cold War and the tensions generated by this global contest for power and influence between Moscow and Washington. China was a US adversary squarely in the Soviet camp, while India and Indonesia tried to steer a middle path and launched the Non-Aligned Movement at the 1955 Asian-African Conference in Bandung, Indonesia, with like-minded leaders who did not want to be pawns in the superpowers' rivalry. In the feverish Cold War context, such machinations earned the ire of Washington. The Central Intelligence Agency (CIA) intervened in Tibet and in regional rebellions in Indonesia, provoking anti-Americanism, while Nehru leaned towards the Beijing/Moscow axis, at least until 1962 when a border war erupted with China. The Cold War helpfully established a credible US bogeyman for China, India and Indonesia that could be used to mobilize support while providing handy reasons for domestic failures.

In contrast, the US was in charge in Japan and South Korea and could impose its agenda. The example of Germany rebounding from defeat in World War I only to launch World War II inspired the American mission in Japan; a harsh peace would be counterproductive. In Cold War Japan, the US demilitarized and democratized on its own terms, imposing a pacifist constitution, prosecuting a handful of wartime leaders in a show trial with foreordained verdicts, while letting Emperor Hirohito off the hook for a war waged in his name. It established a network of military bases and a military alliance while embracing the wartime conservative elite in a bid to fast-track Japan's recovery from war devastation so it could be a shining triumph and showcase of the superiority of the US system. Clearly, the US Occupation of Japan from 1945 to 1952 gave it a key role in shaping the Idea of Japan, establishing the guidelines for the postwar order as it promoted a series of extensive political, economic and security reforms aimed at ensuring Japan would never again be a threat to the US. To regain sovereignty, Japan had to do so on US terms and accept a liberal Constitution that enshrined civil liberties and universal human rights, forgoing a military, while acknowledging unequivocally its war responsibility in the 1951 Treaty of San Francisco. In the hothouse of the Cold War, the CIA also intervened to help fund and launch the Liberal Democratic Party (LDP) that has dominated Japanese politics since 1955.

Thus, the Idea of Japan that held sway until the 21st century was a hybrid, partly made in the USA, generating a backlash across the political spectrum. Shigeru Yoshida, premier from 1948 to 1954, was less the architect of this Idea than its exponent. Previously a diplomat, Yoshida's incarceration during the war bestowed legitimacy in the eyes of the US, while his impeccable conservative credentials reassured powerful domestic constituents in business and politics. Americans were impressed that they had a pragmatic leader with whom they could do business and who could deliver. But he was not an American stooge and is remembered for the Yoshida Doctrine in which he deflected US pressure during the Korean War (1950–1953) to rearm and ignore the military- and war-renouncing Article 9 of the Constitution the US had imposed on Japan. He declared that Japan needed to focus on rebuilding its economy and thus would not divert scarce resources to a defense buildup, instead relying on the US for its security. In this way Yoshida indigenized the Idea of Japan foisted on the defeated nation by the reformist victors. His articulation and embrace of "GNPism" (emphasis on economic growth) and pacifism have been defining aspects of the postwar Idea of Japan, as is the ceding of autonomy in security. He took the American template and made it Japan's Idea, championing what the US Occupation had insisted on and then defying Washington's pressure to rearm, paradoxically asserting nationalism within the confines of dependence. This "clipped-wing" nationalism was the grand bargain that subsequent leaders had to swallow, a client state relationship that has been an irritant in bilateral relations. Ironically, nationalism is usually associated with the right wing, but the demands of alliance management required Japan's conservatives to downplay their nationalist inclinations, especially on any issue related to the US alliance. Lobbying for return of Okinawa to full Japanese sovereignty should have been a right-wing issue, but left-wing agitation played a leading role in pressing for the 1972 reversion, arguably the most important assertion of Japanese sovereignty in the postwar decades, while the right-wing government agreed to host the US bases that remain concentrated in Okinawa. The ongoing anti-base movement among Okinawans commands overwhelming local support, while the conservative LDP continues to support the US military presence. In signing the 1951 Treaty of San Francisco, the right wing also had to swallow its pride about war responsibility and agree with the judgments of the International Military Tribunal for the Far East (IMTFE) that pinned full blame on Japan's right-wing wartime leaders. Yoshida played a central role in promoting the democratic, demilitarized, war-perpetrator- and economic-growth-oriented Idea, but was ambivalent about democracy, invoking the pun "demokureshi," which sounds like how Japanese pronounce democracy, but also means, "it hurts."

South Korea owes its existence to the US intervention from 1950 to 1953 in the civil war initiated and nearly won by Pyongyang until US forces under the command of General Douglas MacArthur turned the tide of war at Incheon. Eventually this provoked Beijing's massive counter-intervention against the US-led forces operating under a United Nations mandate, creating North Korea. Three million people, about 10% of the peninsula's total population, were killed, and the war devastation was extensive, creating grim circumstances for a new nation dealing with the mixed legacies of nearly four decades of Japanese colonial rule. Like Japan, South Korea became a US client state and had little leeway, accepting the ineffectual, corrupt and authoritarian Syngman Rhee as president because Washington chose him. In doing so, Washington discredited the democratic principles it was trying to foster, and promoted bad governance, facilitating the subsequent rise of a military authoritarian regime led by Park Chung-hee.

China faced overcoming the legacy of the western imperial powers from the mid-19th century, the depredations of Japan (1931–1945) and the civil war (1945–1949) against the Kuomintang. The war against imperialism and the internecine struggle for power in China were the crucible in which Mao conceived his Idea of nation, one that drew not only on communism, but also on China's longstanding quest for a modernizing state. He was at the end of a long line of would-be reformers who sought inspiration in China's humiliations, and consequent need to become strong to regain what had been lost—power, status, dignity and influence. Mao, like Nehru and Sukarno, tapped into a sense of civilizational grandeur, invoking the past to legitimize this ambitious agenda of reform aimed at restoring China's greatness.

Indonesia had to overcome the relatively neglectful Dutch colonial presence, one that maximized profits and minimized outlays for education and other social welfare policies. Sukarno had been jailed and exiled by the Dutch colonial government for his role in the national struggle for independence and knew well their repressive ways. He also knew about the dire consequences for Indonesians stemming from the Great Depression and the collapse of global capitalism. Nehru had similar anti-colonial struggles and experiences that made him and Sukarno soulmates of a sort, both controlling their nations' destinies for most of the formative two decades after independence. They relied on personal charisma to convince others that their vision was the only way forward, even if many resolutely disagreed.

Partition was a particularly divisive crucible for Indians, not one that could be forgotten, but one that Nehru did his best to set aside and overcome by vigorously promoting secularism in a context primed for religious fanaticism. The Idea of India stripped to its essentials owes most to Nehru's vision of the nation. Mahatma Gandhi was the only Indian leader who could claim greater moral authority, but his Idea of India was rooted in tradition and the village sphere, the antithesis of Nehru's modernizing vision. His Idea is based on a secular, inclusive constitutional democracy espousing tolerance, with a strong central state committed to promoting modernization and striving to eradicate poverty while helping and protecting the vulnerable. Establishment of an independent India was the goal of the Congress Party and anticolonial swadeshi agitation that gained momentum from the 1920s, and both Gandhi and Nehru were outsized figures in this movement. Following Gandhi's assassination in 1948 by a disgruntled Hindu zealot, Nehru was left to improvise a nation from decidedly inauspicious circumstances. He ruled India from its birth in 1947 until his death in 1964, putting his stamp on modern India and establishing the foundation for the Idea. The Indian elite, led by Nehru, bestowed a Constitution and nurtured what has become a vibrant—and the world's largest—democracy, at least during election campaigns when parties vie for support from over 800 million voters.

The Idea of Indonesia is succinctly encapsulated in the Panca Sila, the five core principles of the nation's basic ideology: (1) Belief in the one and only God; (2) Just and civilized humanity; (3) The unity of Indonesia; (4) Democracy guided by the inner wisdom in the unanimity arising from deliberation among representatives; (5) Social justice for all. Also emerging from inauspicious circumstances, Sukarno's Indonesia was improvised from this philosophical foundation, passing on an encompassing vision that enthralled the people and stoked pride in nation even as his erratic policymaking undermined the agenda of nation-building and economic development.

Each of our nations is secular, features a strong central state, has drawn on the humiliation and traumas inflicted by imperialism to forge unity and nationalism, has engaged in organized forgetting of certain inconvenient trauma, and draws legitimacy by promoting development and improvements in living standards. The Cold War (1945–1989) profoundly influenced each of the nations, but nowhere more dramatically than the Korean Peninsula, as the proxy war fought there from 1950 to 1953, involving China, left it divided into two nations. China, India and Indonesia were targeted by US machinations during the Cold War, while Japan and South Korea were allies, hosted US military bases and experienced considerable political intervention by Washington. Only China is not democratic, but all have experienced authoritarian or prolonged one-party rule that facilitated coherent policymaking, even if not consistently pursued, that boosted economic growth. Each has also made a transition towards more market-oriented economic policies, even as there is an abiding distrust of unfettered market forces and inclinations favoring strong government intervention.

In the next chapter we examine more closely how the Idea of nation nurtured in the second half of the 20th century has been reconsidered and revised in the early 21st century. Much remains the same, as the appeals of forgetting and humiliation remain strong. China remains an authoritarian one-party state and India, Indonesia, South Korea and Japan remain secular democracies, but prevailing norms and values confront evolving realities, while the state copes with economic, social and international challenges that influence national identity and status. Nationalism is a powerful binding force of shared identity and common purpose, but also unleashes contemporary culture wars that resonate at home and overseas.

2

Contemporary Culture Wars and National Identity

As discussed in the previous chapter, the original Idea of each nation elaborated by the respective leaders has not gone unchallenged or unchanged over the intervening years. By and large, the big Idea of nation has persisted, and continuities abound, but there has been considerable evolution in fundamental aspects of the Ideas. By examining ongoing culture wars in each society it is possible to understand in what ways the Idea is being recalibrated and the implications thereof. These culture wars speak to issues at the core of national identity: What kind of society are we? What is it that defines us? This is a propitious time to examine the evolving Ideas and ways in which they are being reconsidered as there have been striking changes in political leadership in recent years: Japan in 2012, South Korea and China in 2013, and India and Indonesia in 2014. In all of our nations, the new leaders took office promising good governance and sweeping changes in economic policies. Shinzo Abe, Park Geun-hye, Xi Jinping, Narendra Modi and Joko Widodo all espouse a more muscular nationalism. This externally projected nationalism also feeds a more strident domestic nationalism that plays out in a variety of arenas, ranging from textbooks and economic policy to conservative socio-cultural agendas. Early on, there is growing skepticism about whether these leaders can deliver on promised reforms, but they remain important symbols of the yearning for change and powerful agents in 21st-century identity politics.

Japan

Japan remains a secular constitutional democracy where pacifist sentiments and constraints still impose limits on security capabilities and where there is more focus on economic issues than politics. Broadly it remains a society with strong egalitarian

Nationalism in Asia: A History Since 1945, First Edition. Jeff Kingston.

norms and values, and citizens enjoy a broad range of civil liberties. Since 1945 Japan has sought redemption, and largely achieved it, because it has recovered from the war, both economically and politically, contributing significantly to regional peace and prosperity through aid programs, technical assistance, trade, loans and investment. The second half of the 20th century is thus a source of considerable pride among Japanese and its achievements are intrinsic to the Idea of Japan that the US and Yoshida bequeathed. And yet, there are reactionary forces that are gaining ground in the 21st century that challenge this postwar consensus in dramatic ways.

In 2012 Shinzo Abe began his second term as prime minister, and he is credited with undertaking bold policy actions, dubbed Abenomics, that belie the nation's reputation for cautious consensus. After two decades of relative stagnation, Abe's monetary easing and fiscal stimulus restored confidence and a national swagger. But, as in his first term as premier in 2006–2007, Abe and his supporters are waging an aggressive culture war that targets the postwar consensus on Japan's war guilt and responsibility. Abe instituted changes in textbook guidelines to support his revisionist views about Japan's wartime history, and openly calls for overturning the postwar order that most Japanese are proud of. In Japan, the term "revisionists" refers to conservative pundits, politicians and historians who argue that Japan has been unfairly singled out for war crimes and maintain that it fought the 1931–1945 war to liberate Asia from the yoke of western imperialism. The postwar consensus in Japan that they challenge has been shaped by the judgments of the IMTFE concerning Japan's war responsibility. Article 9 of the 1951 Treaty of San Francisco signed by Japan requires it to respect these judgments. This acceptance has been intrinsic to Japan's rehabilitation and reentry into the community of nations, based on US sponsorship. The culture wars mounted by revisionists thus represent an attack on the basis of Japan's reintegration into the postwar international order. They seek to exonerate Japan of allegations regarding comfort women (sex slaves), the Nanjing Massacre, the human experiments of Unit 731, etc., and refocus attention on Allied war crimes such as the atomic bombings of Hiroshima and Nagasaki, as well as the firebombing of Tokyo that incinerated an estimated 100,000 civilians overnight. They argue that the IMTFE was a cover-up for the Allies and a frame-job on Japan, noting a widespread consensus that the judicial proceedings were deeply flawed and biased. Until the 21st century such arguments were definitely not mainstream, although ranking members of the ruling LDP would occasionally voice such an opinion and then be forced to retract their remarks and face sacking from the cabinet under a torrent of criticism. Thus, some elements of the conservative elite that ruled postwar Japan long harbored such thoughts, but rarely expressed them, and did so at grave peril to their political careers.

In 21st-century Japan conservatives are more forthright in voicing their revisionist opinions, and even if they do attract considerable criticism, they are no longer automatically removed from high-profile positions and win some plaudits for standing up for Japan. Nationalist sentiments have flowered since the millennium because China is seen as a grave threat and there are growing doubts that the US would protect Japan's interests if it meant sacrificing US interests and ties with

China. China's rapid rise, and intensified vilification of Japan by China and South Korea over the shared past, have generated a backlash among Japanese, especially the younger generation. Polls indicate that Japanese still remain attached to their Peace Constitution, are leery of lifting military constraints on the Self-Defense Forces and repudiate revisionist views on history, but it appears that a certain degree of perpetrator's fatigue has set in and more Japanese now wonder why they continue to shoulder the burdens of the 1930s and 1940s.

The US government criticized Shinzo Abe's visit to the Yasukuni war shrine at the end of 2013, turning it into a diplomatic disaster. As former Ambassador Kazuhiko Togo pointed out, "Through the single act of visiting Yasukuni, Abe has allowed the creation of an international coalition against Japan related to historical recognition among the United States, China, South Korea and Russia" (*Asahi*, January 19, 2014). Abe may have scored points with his reactionary base, but at the cost of alienating those who wish Japan well in Washington. Abe says he visits to promote peace and understanding, but something gets lost in translation since Yasukuni serves as a talismanic symbol for an unrepentant view of Japan's wartime aggression. Abe's revisionist views are on display at the adjacent Yushukan Museum. There the Nanjing Massacre didn't happen, there were no comfort women, there were no gruesome vivisection or biological war experiments conducted by the infamous Unit 731, indeed there was no Japanese aggression claiming the lives of 10–15 million

Figure 2.1 Tokyo's Controversial Yasukuni Shrine Honoring War Dead. Photo © Jeff Kingston.

Chinese and displacing 100 million refugees. Degrading treatment of Koreans during the colonial era, 1910–1945? No mention. Japan's wartime leaders blamed for starting and prolonging a war they knew they could not win, causing the deaths of nearly 3 million Japanese (and some 20 million Asians) for vainglorious dreams of empire? Incredibly, these dubious leaders are depicted as martyrs.

Japan's culture wars rage over reactionary efforts to undermine liberal values and 21st-century norms. Inevitably these domestic battles have spilled over into the global arena, pitting Japan against its neighbors and liberal democracies around the world. At the 2014 World Economic Forum in Davos, Abe compared the current situation between Japan and China with Europe on the eve of World War I, pointing out that everyone then thought war unlikely because of strong economic ties between Great Britain and Germany. It was a useful reminder that nobody should be complacent about current tensions in Asia. Japanese conservatives were dismayed that the global reaction was uniformly critical of Abe, but only weeks beforehand he had reinforced his hawkish image by genuflecting at Yasukuni where 14 Class A war criminals are enshrined. In doing so, he invited criticism and isolated Japan within the region and among liberal democracies usually sympathetic to Japan. Ironically, after a year of China militarizing conflicts in the South and East China Seas, Abe managed to come out looking like the warmonger by diverting attention from China's contemporary bellicosity to Japan's inglorious wartime past.

In 2014, NHK, Japan's quasi-national broadcasting company, was engulfed in a scandal related to Abe's appointment of reactionaries to the board of directors. These are figures that rationalize the comfort women system, deny the Nanjing Massacre, deify the Emperor and criticize career women. In early 2014, Abe's pick as the new NHK Chairman, Katsuto Momii, trivialized the comfort women system and showed little appreciation for press freedom and journalistic ethics. In a Pyongyang moment, he insisted that NHK's job is to serve as the government's mouthpiece: "When the government is saying right, we can't say left."

In contrast, the vast majority of Japanese value their open society, and many fear that the forces of darkness are descending. In 2013 a local school board moved to restrict students' access to Barefoot Gen, the iconic anti-war manga about the horrors of Hiroshima. The public outcry denouncing this demagoguery forced the rightists to retreat and sparked a surge in sales. Apparently Barefoot Gen's criticism of Japan's wartime leaders and military atrocities still resonates uncomfortably for rightists eager to reclaim that era. They also condemned Haruo Miyazaki's 2013 anime *The Wind Rises* about the development of the wartime Zero fighter, deeming it antipatriotic because the lead engineer cared more about producing an elegant design than about winning the war. Indeed that was exactly Miyazaki's point and it proved to be a blockbuster at the box office.

Another 2013 film on the same fighter plane, *The Eternal Zero*, also became one of the top ten grossing Japanese films of all time. It is an unequivocally anti-war film, one that laments the wasted lives of the young kamikaze pilots. The protagonist of the film is a reluctant warrior more eager to stay alive for his family than to sacrifice his life for the Emperor, trying to protect students drafted into the kamikaze corps from meaningless sacrifice. The patriots in the movie are depicted as angry psychopaths whose devotion to winning the war at all costs, and insistence on fighting it after it was lost, betrayed the people and nation. Ironically, the film is based on a best-selling book by a reactionary author, Naoki Hyakuta, infamous for glorifying Japan's wartime past.

Anti-Korean demonstrations in Japan are another manifestation of 21st-century Japanese jingoism, as small groups of marchers make nasty threats and intimidate shoppers in Korean enclaves and students at Korean schools. This thuggery has been red-carded in the courts and repudiated by counter-demonstrations, but is a reminder that in the Abe era, ugly nationalism is coming out of the closet. In this context, in 2014 the Tokyo Metropolitan Art Museum forced sculptor Katsuhisa Nakagaki to remove a sign on his work that read:

> Let us protect Article 9 of the Constitution, admit the stupidity of visiting Yasukuni Shrine, stop the rightward tilt of the current administration and seek political leaders who are more intellectual and thoughtful.

In Abe's era of reactionary fanaticism, even artists are not allowed to be subversive or edgy. This is certainly not the idea of Japan that was nurtured and valued in the second half of the 20th century.

China

The Idea of China has gone through an even more profound rethink. Since China embraced economic reforms at the end of the 1970s, the socio-economic consequences have been sweeping and tumultuous and nobody then could have anticipated just how much it would transform. There is little about contemporary China that evokes Mao's China. The glitzy celebration of Mao's 120th birthday at the end of 2013 highlighted exactly how far social values and norms have evolved as the nation has grown wealthy and living standards for many have soared. The garish materialism that animates China today has come at the expense of Mao's egalitarian vision, while the CCP can no longer claim persuasively to be the protector of the poor and weak. The Tiananmen Square pro-democracy demonstrations of 1989 that ended in brutal repression forced the CCP to cast about for new sources of legitimacy. Rapid economic growth was lifting tens of millions out of poverty, but also raising aspirations and nurturing discontent among those who were not benefiting. Widespread reports about corrupt party officials and military leaders lining their pockets and abusing their powers at the expense of the people are making the CCP resemble uncomfortably the 'traitorous' Kuomintang Nationalists it defeated in 1949 and has vilified ever since.

China today is defined by its multifaceted contradictions. Every luxury brand from watches to cars is piling into the nation, and doing very well, although "luxury" is a word the Party tries to ban from advertisements. This nominally communist nation boasts two of the world's leading Internet companies and a vast reservoir of state censors working overtime to stamp out free expression. Yet even as the empire of censorship expands, there is increasing freedom of expression. China is about to overtake the US as the world's leading economy, but few Chinese seem to believe it, or at least they can't seem to find compelling evidence in their daily lives. Throughout the region, China is seen as a regional threat, while it dwells on its vulnerabilities.

One of the most prominent slogans during the Mao era was "Never forget class struggle." In a country of shared poverty, the Party rooted out landlords, capitalists and other counter-revolutionaries in the name of class struggle, but at that time everyone was a pauper and material shortages prevailed. So even though there were no classes to speak of and no real class conflict, the Party enjoined the people to "never forget the class struggle." Since Mao died in 1976, classes have emerged as disparities have widened, generating class conflict and widespread resentment. As Yu Hua (2014) wryly notes,

> China has, over the past thirty years, gone through tumultuous changes. Its abnormal development has generated a huge gap between rich and poor, and pervasive corruption has ignited conflict between officialdom and the population at large. These days, Chinese society is riddled with contradictions, but "Never forget class struggle" has been replaced by "harmonious society" and stability overrides all other considerations.

The Xi government has cracked down on corruption and even started limiting the number of meal courses that can be served at feasts attended by high-ranking government officials and military officers; and with considerable fanfare has tried to curb lavish displays and conspicuous consumption by government officials. In 2013 alone it charged more than 27,000 officials with corruption, involving nearly $1 billion; but most observers believe this is the tip of the iceberg. Indeed, since 2012 the western media has exposed the vast assets accumulated by the families of top officials, including populist ex-Prime Minister Wen Jiabao (2002–2012), fueling perceptions that the rot at the top is all-encompassing, including President Xi's family and cronies, and that corruption charges reflect power struggles between rival factions more than any commitment to principled governance and shift towards the rule of law. Now that there are obvious class differences fueled by venality, Chinese officials are sidelining class struggle, consigning it to the ash heap of history in favor of purging blatantly corrupt Party cadres.

Efforts to promote transparency by anti-corruption activists are another barometer of this struggle: Yuan Dong and three other activists calling on all officials to make a public accounting of their financial assets were arrested in 2013. Yu (2014) reminds us that,

> That earthshaking slogan of "never forget class struggle" has vanished from the scene, absconding to another world and seeking refuge with Mao. For our current leaders even to mention class struggle would be tantamount to digging their own graves.

From the early 1990s the CCP played the history card, invoking the atrocities committed by the Japanese in the 1930s and 1940s as a means to reinforce the "century of humiliation" narrative and promote patriotism. Mao and the first generation of Chinese leaders downplayed Japan's rampage, partly because the CCP had a relatively small role in the anti-Japanese war compared to the Kuomintang. Mao also wanted Japan to break away from its alliance with the US and thus, rather than focusing on the humiliation inflicted by imperial Japan, Mao emphasized the triumph of the CCP over the Kuomintang and acknowledged that Japan had contributed to that victory by weakening KMT forces.

From the early 1990s, in the wake of the Tiananmen Square crackdown, Japan emerged as the great adversary in popular culture and history textbooks. The Party tried to bolster its legitimacy by nurturing a strong sense of victimization at the hands of the Japanese and lauding the Party's role in vanquishing the enemy. Along with this shift towards a stridently anti-Japanese narrative, the previously vilified KMT has been rehabilitated and its contributions to the patriotic victory over Japan acknowledged. This new nationalism sparked a backlash in Japan and in the 21st century mutual vilification and increasingly angry relations have prevailed. Japan's conservative turn in the 21st century feeds on growing anxieties about China, and these reactionaries make comments and pursue policies that stoke China's aggrieved nationalism. It is an interesting lesson in how nationalist passions are orchestrated by ruling elites to regain lost legitimacy.

Yet China is not comfortable with what it has become, or rather, Chinese are questioning the new values and norms that have accompanied growing prosperity. There was a famous episode of a game show where a young woman was asked whether she would prefer to ride on the back of a bicycle pedaled by the man she loved or in a BMW sedan with a man she didn't love. By choosing the comfortable car and the wealth it denotes, she held up a mirror for China, exposing the ugly reality of materialism run amok. Many thought she made the right choice, pragmatically putting feelings aside for a better life, while many others wondered what kind of society they lived in where love was betrayed for baubles. Officials suspended the popular show for sparking a debate that confronted approved values with China's new realities.

In part, China's cultural wars are generational, dividing a younger urban middle class, and those who aspire to that lifestyle, from an older generation raised on Maoist orthodoxy, embracing a survival strategy of always being careful to keep heads down, not attract attention or envy, and accepting a grim, monochrome lifestyle. For a generation that came of age in turmoil and poverty, a stable and boring life is enough. The younger generation cares a great deal about being stylish, about consuming and accumulating, about crafting a cool lifestyle. Engaging in politics, openly criticizing authorities, promoting freedom of speech and expression remain risky. So it is in the material realm that the government delivers and is judged, while civil society activists, human rights campaigners, artists and bloggers walk a tightrope. There certainly is space in China at think tanks and universities to voice opinions, criticize the government and stray from orthodoxy, but this is risky and subject to the whims and sensitivities of authorities; professors are still dragged away and detained for what they think or say. Thus China's culture wars are circumscribed, carefully channeled away from threatening the Party's interests and power, but with increasingly less effectiveness. The economic success has unleashed powerful social forces and desires that censorship and repression can't quell entirely.

Increasingly liberal Chinese sexual attitudes and practices stray beyond the vestiges of official puritanism. The drab and stultifying norms of the Mao era are but a distant echo as the young explore sexual freedoms and divergent lifestyles. Old taboos linger, but have been steadily eroded as Chinese in the 21st century enjoy greater tolerance and more personal freedom in their private lives. The Party seems increasingly clueless about changing social attitudes, sparking disbelief tinged with anger, and subjecting itself to widespread ridicule, as in 2015 when it censored a period drama for showing too much cleavage. Urban migration has freed many from watchful eyes in tight communities and unleashed many from the relentless indignities of poverty. Prostitution, nightclubs, massage parlors, escort services, all repressed as social evils under Mao, have mushroomed in contemporary China, although subject to periodic ritual crackdowns. According to Richard Burger's *Behind the Red Door: Sex in China* (2012), Chinese are more sexually promiscuous than the government cares to recognize. In 1989, surveys showed that 15% of women engaged in premarital sex, while in 2013 this had increased to over 60%.

Mao is famous for promoting gender equality by noting that "women hold up half the sky," but Chinese society remains deeply patriarchal and gender inequalities are significant. Even so, in contemporary China urban women find much more leeway to put off marriage and pursue an active single lifestyle. About 20% of managers in China are women, compared to less than 10% in Japan. But tolerance has its limits, as women in their late twenties face heavy family pressure to marry before the age of 30. The mass media reinforces this pressure, popularizing the pejorative term "leftover" women (*sheng-nu*). (In Japan the equivalent expression, now fallen into disuse, was loser dog-—*makeinu*.) Ironically, it was the All-China Women's Federation that identified sheng-nu as a social problem requiring a public program to encourage women to sacrifice careers in favor of marriage. Problematically, China's one-child policy led to many selective abortions, so there is a stark gender imbalance featuring a shortage of women that dims male marriage prospects; the male/female ratio is 120:100. There are orchestrated media campaigns accusing women of having too high expectations and stigmatizing unmarried women over the age of 27 as being unable to find a husband; but in reality this lifestyle appears to be a matter of individual preference.

Expanding career opportunities for university graduates help many women overcome the state shaming campaign. As in other nations, men at the bottom and women at the top have the most difficulty in finding a suitable partner. Low earning men are much more likely to be single because they can't fulfill the role of provider, while men tend to shy away from women with a higher status, making it difficult for accomplished women to find suitable partners. What governments across Asia don't seem to appreciate is that many modern single women are comfortable with their lifestyles, enjoy their independence and are in no rush to marry on a tight timeline, even as they age. Similar pressures confront others too as people explore identities that don't jibe with national norms and values. Unrealized aspirations for gender equality are thus challenging and redefining national identities across the region.

Being openly gay remains difficult in contemporary China and is still widely stigmatized. Despite all the new social freedoms and tolerance, being gay remains taboo. Even so, it is certainly evident and tolerated implicitly by official and social indifference. Certainly China has a long history of accepting same-sex relationships, but not in Mao's China. Even today the lesbian, gay, bisexual and transgender (LGBT) community is subject to harassment—the organizer of a gay pride march was arrested in 2013—and same-sex marriage is not yet legal, entailing the usual indignities and disadvantages. Being gay, however, is not illegal, as it was decriminalized in 1997 and subsequently removed from the list of mental illnesses. There is no religious notion of immorality in China, but there are no laws preventing discrimination. Moreover, gay websites and pageants are routinely shut down, while social pressures to marry, bear offspring and continue the family line remain strong. This is partly due to the one-child policy, but also because social acceptance remains low. Thus most gays remain in the closet, only coming out to a small circle of close friends. Gays' preference for invisibility helps limit workplace discrimination, but also means that they have to hide their sexuality and same-sex relationships. It is estimated that 80% of China's gays get married to appease their families and blend into society. To the extent the media covers homosexuality, it tends to portray it as a disease that can be cured or link it with HIV/AIDS, reinforcing prejudices and an overall stigma. It appears that younger urban Chinese are indifferent about same-sex relationships, but limited and biased public discourse indicates a very restricted official tolerance. Certainly contemporary China's acceptance of homosexuality is increasing, but this remains a far cry from its courtly celebration as recently as the Qing dynasty (1644–1912). Sexuality is yet another realm where freedom of expression in authoritarian China remains limited and at the state's discretion.

More broadly, China's culture wars subvert the Party. Getting rich is a powerful ambition, but as more people become affluent and want a say in shaping the world around them and addressing the evident problems such as pollution, corruption and destabilizing disparities, the Party struggles to surf the wave it has generated. It falls back on the need for stability above all and darkly warns about the chaos and dire consequences that came in the wake of the dissolution of the USSR and Yugoslavia. Its legitimacy is thus increasingly defined in negative terms—things are not perfect now, but imagine the catastrophe that would ensue if the Party was not in charge to guide and maintain a firm hand. And it is an appealing argument to an older generation that knows all about instability. The quest for a strong state is an abiding one in China precisely because it has always been deemed crucial to modernization, strength, unity, stability and prosperity (Schell and Delury 2013). Yet, now that it has become firmly entrenched, a stable state is taken for granted, especially by the majority of Chinese who were born after Mao's disasters. Nobody really expects a sudden collapse although more than a few would welcome the Party's demise.

The CCP's monopoly on political power is central to Mao's Idea of China, and his successors make no concessions or apologies for maintaining this monopoly. The slaughter and incarceration of pro-democracy protesters in 1989, the imprisonment of democracy activist Liu Xiaobo, the 2010 Nobel Peace Prize laureate, and harassment and jailing of other activists and dissidents promoting transparency and accountability suggest that new ideas are swirling around that raise uncomfortable questions about the Party's legitimacy. In responding to these political consequences of rapid economic growth, the CCP has been ruthless in stamping on those with views that threaten its position and Idea; but eradicating such views, and alternative ideas, is an impossible dream.

Dreaming

Nothing better underscores the problems facing the Party than President Xi Jinping's call for Chinese to articulate and embrace a new Dream. But what is the Chinese Dream in the 21st century? Certainly Xi has sparked vigorous sloganeering about desired ideals and hopes for how China should evolve. Ironically, *New York Times* columnist Thomas Friedman is credited, at least in the western media, with popularizing the concept in China with his 2012 commentary, "China Needs Its Own Dream." He attributes the concept to an environmental non-governmental organization (NGO) that conducted 100 interviews with upwardly mobile Chinese and published *The Chinese Dream Book* (2010) about sustainability. The book draws attention to "affluenza," the social malaise of growing prosperity, and the need for China to balance the dictates of growth with responsible management of scarce resources. The CCP is probably also thinking of its own sustainability and wondering what will define the Chinese Dream and how will it differ from the American Dream. Commentary suggests a vague mixture of traditional values with technology, innovation and creativity to achieve sustainable development and national glory, but it's not exactly a blueprint.

The sudden spike in interest in clarifying the Chinese Dream is a window on a nation in search of an identity and rethinking the Idea of China, one that people seem to think needs rejuvenating. In Party-speak, Xi explained that it means to "cherish the glorious youth, strive with pioneer spirit and contribute their wisdom and energy to the realization of the Chinese dream" (Xinhua, May 14, 2013). This must have been on the minds of youthful pro-democracy demonstrators in Hong Kong after they were pepper-sprayed by security forces in October 2014. Xi also calls it a process of "national rejuvenation, improvement of people's livelihoods, prosperity, construction of a better society and military strengthening." Easier said than done. Essentially, like the American Dream, it means to have a better life and to ensure the next generation has an even better life. It means upward mobility in a society where aspirations and ambitions can be realized. It is about prosperity, sustainability, modernization and national resurgence.

The Chinese Dream is clearly emblematic of Party-orchestrated nationalism, the idea of a society collectively moving onward and upward, regaining its proper place in the world as the Middle Kingdom, commanding respect and calling the shots. The Dream deliberately elides the fact that China exhibits even greater inequality than the US and jails Chinese who call for greater transparency about inequalities of wealth and lobby for asset disclosure by public officials because they threaten to expose the sham of socialism and subvert and tarnish the Idea of China (Link 2014). Posting such information on a website invites swift deletion by vigilant authorities. This less appealing side of the rising China narrative is an inconvenient truth that speaks volumes about the Chinese system and the diverting Dreams it sponsors.

The rub is whether this is a collective monolithic dream or a society where individuals define and pursue their own dreams (Osnos 2013). Is the dream oriented towards individual satisfaction or collective benefits? The Idea of China has been defined collectively, an egalitarian model that is increasingly at odds with growing disparities and the aspirations of upwardly mobile urbanites seeking the good life based on their individual achievements and fulfilling their individual ambitions. But individualism is seen to be western and not rooted in the ideals of Chinese civilization. It is often portrayed as selfish and irresponsible.

Again, the Idea of China is a contemporary battleground as society experiences a tumultuous transformation that gnaws at the foundations of Mao's China and generates pressures to recast national identity. It is a struggle about renewal and reform with sweeping economic, social and political implications that are still being thrashed out. Ultimately, the people's and China's destiny are being negotiated within the confines of the Party's commitment to "socialism with Chinese characteristics," the euphemism for the essentially contradictory nature of state-directed, market-oriented reforms that embrace hard-nosed capitalism. Problematically, the Dream betrays the Party's insecurity and suggests that it still remains haunted by the nightmares of the 1989 pro-democracy uprising even as it outwardly projects confidence (Wasserstrom 2014). In overreacting to the limited threats it confronts in Hong Kong, Xinjiang and Tibet, the Party seems as paranoid as it is powerful.

Incredible India?

William Dalrymple, one of the most astute observers of modern India, quips that one should never underestimate the capacity of old India to embarrass the new India. He means that the newly affluent, upwardly mobile and aspirational India seeks to distance itself from the flawed image and backward mores and traditional values associated with the India that has been left behind, psychologically, materially, spiritually and in terms of what is called lifestyle. In the early 2000s the rapid growth of the Indian economy spawned a nationalistic hubris about prospects for wealth and power that have largely been unrealized. Campaigns to promote the national brand embraced the slogan "Incredible India," but it's impossible to sloganeer away the stark realities of widespread poverty, growing inequalities and endemic corruption. But the nation whetted its appetite for greatness and from this gathering disappointment elected Narendra Modi, a man whose life trajectory embodied can-doism, overcoming disadvantages and allegations about his role in an anti-Muslim pogrom in 2002, to reach the nation's highest office.

Prime Minister Narendra Modi made a rousing speech about reforming national character on Independence Day, August 15, 2014, lamenting that his countrymen only do something if there is something in it for them and calling for greater civic-mindedness. He also shared some less grandiose practical dreams such as everyone having bank accounts, insurance and access to toilets; it is estimated that over one-half of India's 1.2 billion population have no toilet at home—more people have access to a cell phone than to a toilet. The prevalence of open defecation undermines public hygiene and impedes achievement of longstanding sanitation goals. Thus, Modi has confronted the India Rising story, and ambitions to emulate China's growth trajectory, by reminding everyone that some very basic needs remain unaddressed. Modi even issued his own "bucket challenge," disseminating a video showing him sweeping the streets in a bid to encourage Indians to become more fastidious. "Made in India" is Modi's slogan, calling on investors and entrepreneurs to make India a manufacturing hub—currently manufacturing accounts for only 15% of GDP. Modi responded to criticisms that his Bharatiya Janata Party (BJP) has condoned communal violence and downplayed the nation's rape epidemic, condemning both. He also dismantled the Planning Commission, terminating Nehru's creation that put technocrats in charge of economic policy-making, signaling his dream of downsizing the License Raj, by all accounts one of the most unfortunate Nehruvian legacies.

Figure 2.2 The Red Fort Is a Mughal-Era Architectural Gem Where Indian Leaders Celebrate Independence Day. Photo © Jeff Kingston.

Nehru's Idea of India nonetheless remains resilient in the early 21st century even as it shows signs of wear and is slowly evolving. India still values Nehru's vision of modernizing the nation, one rooted in a secular, constitutional and inclusive democracy. Nehru's improvised concept of India, a triumph of vision and personal charisma over stark realities prevailing in 1947, still faces challenges from Hindu chauvinists who seek a religious-based state and national identity. The culture wars over Nehru's secular model have persisted over the decades, and perhaps this too is part of the Idea of India—an ongoing battle. The struggle for constitutional democracy, secularism and inclusivity is never won, never finished and as such is a dynamic foundation of the Idea of India.

Narendra Modi campaigned in 2014 to uphold that vision, positioning himself as the more efficient torchbearer of that Idea of India, rather than the Congress Party that Nehru once ruled. Modi embodies Hindutva (Hindu chauvinism), but in the campaign he downplayed his party's religious and sectarian agenda to broaden its appeal, perhaps because everyone understands where he is coming from and imagined what they could expect. Many intellectuals remain skeptical and worry that the BJP has been emboldened by victory and remains intent on tearing down the Nehruvian legacy of tolerance and secularism, but the fact that Modi felt compelled to distance himself from Hindutva to broaden his electoral appeal speaks volumes about the resilience of the original Idea.

Indian liberals have good reason to despair the power of Hindutva to gain mass support and fear that the ongoing struggle to maintain a modern liberal democracy is threatened by the rise of the BJP (Mishra 2014). In 2014 parliamentary deliberations were suspended as opposition groups demanded that Prime Minister Modi condemn forced conversions of Muslims and Christians to Hinduism by extremists associated with the Rashtriya Swayamsevak Sangh (RSS), a massive Hindu nationalist organization with strong links to the BJP that is often implicated in communal violence. Modi was once a member of the RSS, but has tried to publicly distance himself from its extremism, even as many suspect that he condones its actions. Certainly under Modi the RSS feels emboldened and is aggressively promoting its chauvinist agenda. Pankaj Mishra argues that the "vengeful nativism" of the RSS carries ominous implications, reflecting a wounded civilization's sense of inadequacy, espousing a nationalist dogma inconsistent with the Idea of India, one that could come unhinged by dreams of vengeance and aggrandizement. It is an exultant Hindutva that finds enemies at home—Muslims and Christians—and abroad—Pakistan and China. Modi the statesman has done little to rein in such impulses.

The BJP is also associated with an accentuation of communal divisions resulting from the system of "reservations." These reservations are based on the principle of helping disadvantaged groups, an affirmative action policy to alleviate evident hardships. However, since the 1980s Congress has extended this system for political gain, trying to cultivate voter banks among designated communities based on targeted subsidies, tax incentives and job quotas. This proliferation of reservations creates enormous disincentives for assimilation and encourages groups to differentiate themselves and lobby for recognition and attendant benefits. India was never going to be a melting pot, but this sharpening of divisions and identity politics does place strains on the shared idea of India and is not what Nehru had in mind.

Modi challenges this distorted Idea of India. In the run-up to the 2014 elections, Modi threw down a gauntlet to the ruling Congress, articulating his own Idea of India. It is striking that the leader of the party that represents Hindutva presented an Idea of India that is also secular without any reference to a religious agenda. Modi has never been able to shrug off allegations of complicity in the deaths of over 1,000 Muslims in 2002 on his watch as chief minister of Gujarat, and is often pilloried for his communalist sympathies. Yet he understands the power of the Idea of India and thus set aside religion to focus on development, equality and special privileges. He presented himself as the ultimate outsider with a vision for reform and like any good politician managed to be all things to all people. Reactionary Hindus saw him as a cultural warrior, industrialists saw him as a supporter of big business, the middle class saw him as a facilitator of their aspirations, while others hoped he would crack down on corruption and impose discipline. Policy wonks imagined a bold reformer while disaffected Congress voters abandoned their feckless party in droves, giving up hope that it could tackle India's enormous problems.

Raising so many contradictory expectations carries risks of disappointment, but Modi is in a better position than anyone since Nehru to put his stamp on the Idea of India. He managed to extend the BJP's electoral appeal beyond states in northern India and won a parliamentary majority. Yet, the BJP won only 32% of the national vote, so Modi does not enjoy a massive mandate. Much owes to the fumbling governance of the Congress Party over the preceding decade and the lackluster campaign by Rahul Gandhi, the designated dynastic heir. The big question mark hanging over Modi is whether he will sustain an inclusive India or tear apart its secular fabric. Liberal skeptics and non-Hindu minorities are concerned about whether existing checks and balances, including the media and judiciary, will be sufficient to prevent Modi from dismantling the democratic liberal order. Given his reputation and background, he has much to prove.

Modi's Idea shuns the reservations that Congress has presided over, calling for an end to privileges and sectional giveaways, arguing that assistance for the vulnerable should be based on need rather than category. There are shades of Nehru in Modi's proposal for an inclusive, non-discriminatory Idea shorn of special privileges. In the battle to control the high ground, Modi portrayed himself as the more reliable caretaker of the Idea while painting Congress as hopelessly corrupt and incompetent. Voters agreed. A self-made man whose parents ran a tea stall, his "embrace" of the Idea enjoyed enough credibility to catapult him to victory even if liberals doubt his sincerity. It is borrowed credibility because it restates the core principles of Nehru's original Idea, since betrayed by his successors, notably his daughter Indira Gandhi and her son Rajiv Gandhi who trampled on Nehruvian ideals in the 1970s and 1980s. Distancing himself from community-based appeals offered a contrast to voters accustomed to Congress's pandering, but naturally there are doubts that he and his party will remain true to the Idea. Critics suspect he merely pays lip service for electoral advantage to counter charges that he is a polarizing figure favoring religious chauvinism.

Free speech and a free press have been essential to the concept of India and a functioning democracy. These freedoms are at risk from the Hindu chauvinists Modi represents. They take exception to criticism and anyone who strays from their orthodox interpretations of Hinduism. Ananya Vajpeyi (2014), a young Indian intellectual, laments that the Doniger affair, discussed below, reflects a right-wing ascendance in Indian politics and society that is gathering momentum. She points out that Modi heads the most right-wing government since India became independent and that his victory represents the culmination of decades of Hindu nationalist activism, one that poses a significant threat to Indian liberalism and tolerance.

It is a sign of the times that in 2014 an Indian publishing house bowed to intimidation and the prospect of losing a lawsuit by withdrawing and promising to pulp all copies of *The Hindus: An Alternative History*. This proved an alternative too far, as the acclaimed academic study, authored by Wendy Doniger, a University of Chicago professor, angered Hindu nationalists and the self-appointed guardians of religious orthodoxy. Colonial-era laws that are still valid in the contemporary penal code make it a crime to outrage the religious feeling of Indians, a sweepingly vague concept that has facilitated criminal and civil lawsuits that overwhelmingly favor the plaintiff. This law undermines the freedom of speech and expression guaranteed in the 1949 Constitution and puts all writers on notice. Hindus and Muslims invoke this law to ban books they deem offensive. The Indian government also amended the Constitution in 1951, granting it the power to curb free expression and ban books, while libel laws are a further source of intimidation and means for powerful interests to suppress critical books and articles. In the end, no copies of Doniger's book were pulped because they sold out as Indians reacted to the scandalous accusations by rushing out to buy the book; and in any event people have access to Kindle versions. Thus the book-banning campaign backfired spectacularly, underscoring that there is widespread tolerance and belief that people should get to decide what they read rather than have ill-informed vigilantes invoke blasphemy laws in order to impose their blinkered views.

The Doniger affair focused on her "heretical" interpretations of eroticism and sexuality in Hindu traditions, and the norms that right-wing Hindu groups seek to enforce. Doniger pointed out that accusations in the lawsuit that her book is "filthy and dirty" represent false advertising since her scholarly exegesis of Hindi scriptures is anything but smutty (Doniger 2014a). She chides contemporary Hindu chauvinists for making common cause with Victorian Christians, who early on sought to repress and expunge the sexual aspects of these scriptures. Ironically, Doniger writes: "In my defense, I can tell you there is a lot of sex in Hinduism and therefore a lot of puritanism in Hindutva; where there are lions there are jackals." Her mistake lay in trying to resurrect the vital traditions of earthy mythology and spirited mockery of the gods, emphasizing the way that Hinduism was practiced and celebrated before it was hijacked and purified by an upper caste, male elite eager to "rescue" Hinduism from its popular manifestations (Doniger 2014b).

India's free speech crisis is not only a judicial matter. Threats of violence are aimed at authors, employees of publishing houses, social activists and public intellectuals who tread on sacred taboos, annoy the powerful or reveal what some prefer to keep hidden (Dalrymple 2005). The abuse of laws in order to curtail free expression, backed up by harassment and credible threats of violence, is nurturing a climate of fear, rendering writing a more dangerous occupation than it ought to be in a free society. In 2013, India ranked 140th out of 180 countries for free speech, an alarmingly low rank for a nation that prides itself as a vibrant democracy. Apparently, journalists are warned off reporting certain stories and, in a climate of intimidation, need to exercise self-censorship in covering groups embracing Hindu chauvinism, or face nasty consequences. The culture wars in India are thus fought with a dangerous ferocity and emboldened groups seek to make further inroads on the free press.

Sexuality, and sexual violence, are critical elements of ongoing cultural wars. The domestic media engaged in a feeding frenzy of self-mortification about the rash of rapes that suddenly became part of the news cycle after a particularly grisly rape on a New Delhi bus in 2012. Since then society has taken notice, and registered outrage at something that was not new or uncommon. The veil of silence fell quickly, and what had long been tolerated, ignored or quietly endured, was seen to be barbaric and out of touch with contemporary norms. Pundits, politicians, prosecutors and police scrambled to adapt to the new climate, condemning mishandling of rape cases and the insensitivity towards victims that had prevailed. Not everyone, though—some conservative politicians still blamed the victims and downplayed the issue.

The international media also took notice, reinforcing the image of India as a "rape state" where antediluvian patriarchal attitudes still prevail and women are widely mistreated. Nobel Prize-winning economist Amartya Sen examined crime statistics and gender birth ratios, finding a striking correlation between incidence of rape and areas where sexual selection by parents has created an excess of males. Certainly it is a far more complex situation and there must be a range of factors, but it seems India may have reached a turning point. Sexuality, however, poses various problems other than sexual violence.

In 2013 the Supreme Court overturned a law that legalized homosexuality on constitutional grounds. Whatever the legal merits of the case, the highest court of the land sent a chilling message to the gay and lesbian community that they do not enjoy equality and the full protection of the law. This move outlawing homosexuality seems even more absurd considering that a few months later, in 2014, the Supreme Court moved to recognize *hijra* (transgender) as a third gender with legal rights to the full range of government social services and welfare programs that help marginalized groups overcome the disadvantages of entrenched discrimination. Now hijra can identify themselves on official documents as transgender and claim the same civil rights as men and women. The court ruled that, "The spirit of the [Indian] constitution is to provide equal opportunity to every citizen to grow and attain their potential, irrespective of caste, religion or gender." The 2014 national elections were the first in which all voter registration forms allowed a third gender choice—"other"—and a total of 28,000 voters out of some 815 million declared as such. It is estimated that the ruling affects some 3 million hijra nationwide, many of whom work irregularly and precariously in entertainment and prostitution.

This takes care of the T in LGBT, but gays, bisexuals and lesbians deplore the rights that they lost in 2013 when a different bench of the Supreme Court upheld Section 377 of the Indian penal code, a colonial legacy, which criminalizes "sex against the order of nature," a provision that apparently applies exclusively to consensual gay sex while overlooking paid sex with hijra. Why the different rulings? In general, hijra tend to be poor while homosexuals are regarded as having middle- and upper-class roots. The latter thus represent more of a threat to mainstream Hindu family values and are targeted accordingly. Hijra, in contrast, occupy a sacred space of sorts in Hinduism and are invited to births and weddings because of their imagined magical powers.

In recent years the LGBT community has become increasingly visible in India, and widely accepted, so the contradictory judicial rulings seem like a setback. But perhaps this is an accurate barometer of changing Indian values and norms in transition, a period when some cling to old established ways as others adjust to new realities regarding identity, sexuality, dignity and freedom. In 2015 the BJP government of Goa, a Mecca for foreign tourists that boasts a hedonistic image, launched a counseling program aimed at helping youth overcome "same-sex feelings" so that they can lead a "normal life," conducting these sessions at special camps. As in all of our Asian nations, India's sexual identities are no longer as repressed as they once were, but they still remain marginalized and unacceptable to many in this socially conservative society.

Indonesia

In the summer of 2012 Lady Gaga canceled her sold-out show in Jakarta because of threats made by Islamic fundamentalists. These self-appointed guardians of public mores claimed that her revealing clothes and provocative dance moves would corrupt the nation's youth so they threatened to disrupt the show by violent means. The police refused to issue a permit to concert organizers because of these threats, essentially caving in to the demands of thuggish zealots representing an extremist minority. The "Born This Way Ball" was not to be, even though fans snapped up tickets for the 52,000-seat stadium hoping to see the global icon's live performance. The Islamic Defenders Front called Lady Gaga a "messenger of the devil" and vowed to block her arrival at the airport and wreak havoc at the concert. When she canceled the show, Islamic hardliners exulted in their "victory" while dozens of Little Monsters, as her fans are known, dressed up like the pop diva and performed a mob flash dance to her hit songs at a Jakarta shopping mall.

Given Indonesia's reputation for tolerance and freedom of expression, the specter of Islamic fundamentalism is casting a shadow over the secular idea central to Sukarno's idea of Indonesia. Indonesia, a nation of 240 million, is usually held up as a shining example of a pluralistic moderate Islamic nation with a functioning

Figure 2.3 National Monument Known as Monas in Central Jakarta Commemorating Indonesian Struggle for Independence. Photo © Jeff Kingston.

constitutional democracy, confounding those who assert that Islam and democracy are incompatible. Since Suharto stepped down in 1998, human rights have improved while democracy in Indonesia has blossomed, with free and fair elections, regular changes of power and direct presidential elections. In 2014 Joko Widodo became the first of the nation's seven presidents to come from a humble background, espousing a clean, accountable and secular agenda. A striking aspect of Indonesian democracy in a nation where 90% of the population are Islamic is the relatively poor showing of political parties that emphasize a religious agenda. While Islam is certainly a key ingredient of national identity, zealotry does not poll well among Indonesian voters.

There is a troubling trend, however, of Islamic fundamentalists in 21st-century Indonesia pushing their agenda by other means, relying on intimidation and violence to impose their values. Apparently they are not worried about the corrupting consequences of violence because they believe they are carrying out Allah's will, and are intolerant about allowing other Muslims to act based on their own beliefs. Religious minorities, women and anyone deemed immoral are fair game. Islamic vigilante groups have taken to patrolling some towns and abusing women they accuse of dressing indecently or being out after dark. Islamic fundamentalists have also succeeded in persuading local governments to adopt ordinances on proper moral conduct and pressuring police to raid bars, nightclubs and massage parlors. Paradoxically, it is a moral campaign often waged by thugs and gangs enjoying tacit support from politicians and elements in the security forces who know a lucrative protection racket when they see one.

In 2013, President Susilo Bambang Yudhoyono (2004–2014), or SBY as he is commonly known, finally expressed concern in parliament about growing religious intolerance after enduring criticism for averting his eyes from the growing menace, not condemning it and doing nothing to rein it in. On his watch, incidents of religious extremism and violence skyrocketed, and he did little to defend the rights of religious minorities despite the constitutional guarantee of freedom of religion. SBY's sad legacy of a decade in power is one of eroding freedom of religion, growing intolerance and unchecked violence targeting minorities. This toleration of intolerance under SBY emboldened hardliners and sowed insecurity while undermining Indonesia's pluralist foundations and the national slogan, "Unity in Diversity."

Radical ideologies represent a threat to these pluralist principles and the bedrock of tolerance that lies at the heart of the Idea of Indonesia. Since 2002, Islamic militants associated with Jemaah Islamiyah, a terrorist group associated with al-Qaeda, have carried out a number of bombings, most notably in the tourist resort island of Bali and Jakarta, the nation's capital. Security forces, however, have been successful in disrupting terrorist networks and arresting militants, reducing this threat significantly. Meanwhile Islamic fundamentalist groups wage their war of harassment and sporadic violence with impunity, and indeed were linked to members of SBY's cabinet. There are increasing numbers of violent incidents fueled by religious extremists. Muslim mobs have openly attacked Christians and burned their churches while police have stood by. Security forces have also witnessed violent clashes between the majority Sunni Muslim vigilantes and the Shiite and Ahmadiyya minority sects without intervening. Increased frequency of sectarian violence is a disturbing sign of the times and a barometer of Indonesia's culture wars. The intensification of this campaign of intimidation owes much to government complicity and inaction as politicians pander to vocal minority groups and find little electoral advantage in sticking up for constitutional rights or tolerance. SBY's religious affairs minister asserted that religious minorities bring the attacks on themselves and criticized women for dressing provocatively. His information minister lashed out against homosexuals while the justice minister failed to use his powers to stop the violence.

Indonesia's reputation for a tolerant form of Islam, heavily influenced by Sufism, mysticism and syncretism, is somewhat misleading. There are good reasons why Indonesians are not known for being fervently devout, but such sweeping generalizations overlook the heterogeneous nature of Islam in modern Indonesia. Religion and religious practice are not monolithic and there are different strands of Islam in Indonesia and wide variations in practice and devotion. Mainstream Islam in

Indonesia has a history of tolerance and inclusiveness, but practices vary in this vast archipelago. The Dutch waged long wars against Islamic militants in 19th-century Sumatra and western Java, encountering there a more rigid and radical Islamic Wahabism introduced and sustained by a relatively higher rate of pilgrimage (Haj) to Mecca, the global heartland of Islam. Hajis returned to Indonesia seeking to "purify" religious practice and root out syncretistic practices that drew on local traditions and customs. So across time and location, there have long been variations and divergences in Indonesian Islam and what it means to be a proper Muslim.

Soon after achieving independence, the secular, tolerant and inclusive Idea of Indonesia espoused by Sukarno was challenged by regional Islamic rebellions in west Java, Sulawesi and Aceh under the banner of Darul Islam (House of Islam). Leaders of the rebellions felt betrayed by the new Republic of Indonesia that they had hoped would be more resolutely Islamic (Elson 2010). There has been considerable controversy over the omission of the requirement that Muslims live according to Islamic law (shariah) from the final draft of the 1945 Constitution, especially among fundamentalists who chafe under the nation's secularism. The Darul Islam movement was aimed at creating a non-secular Indonesia and in 1949 Islamic militia units in west Java under the leadership of the charismatic cleric Kartosuwirjo established the Islamic State of Indonesia based on shariah. Kartosuwirjo led a powerful rebellion against the central government throughout the 1950s, drawing support from other regional rebels in Sulawesi, Aceh and Kalimantan, which challenged the limited capacity of an ineffectual central government. This open flouting of the central government's authority, and an attempted assassination attempt on President Sukarno, led to the declaration of martial law in 1957. The rebellion was a significant factor precipitating the subsequent imposition of Guided Democracy in 1959, circumscribing democratic rights, wherein Sukarno moved to strengthen his powers and overcome chronic instability and fractious parliamentary politics (see Chapter 5). By 1960, the government had negotiated an end to the conflict in Aceh by agreeing to respect its autonomy and confer special accommodations for applying Islamic law. The insurgencies in Java and Sulawesi were crushed by 1965, but veterans of the Darul Islam militias continued sporadic attacks as Komando Jihad into the 1980s. Current extremists hail from this strand of fundamentalism in Indonesian Islam, one not known for tolerance or a commitment to pluralist principles.

South Korea

Lady Gaga also drew protests from South Korean Christians appalled by her sexual ambiguities and risqué show, accusing her of promoting pornography and licentiousness. But her shows have not been blocked and in 2014 she toured with a K-pop girl group and did a summer show with global pop icon Psy, famous for the megahit "Gangnam Style," coinciding with Pope Francis' visit to Seoul. It was a marked contrast with her 2012 concert that attracted throngs of Christian protesters, perhaps benefiting from the Vatican distraction.

Christian protesters have also disrupted gay pride celebrations in South Korea. The 15th Korea Queer Festival in 2014 drew some 10,000 participants with the usual displays of exuberance, rainbow flags, and risqué and eccentric outfits. But conservative religious protesters heckled and denounced the marchers, stepped in front of parade vehicles and lay down in the street to block the procession. Same-sex sexual activity is legal in South Korea, but is subject to organized condemnation by religious groups, and same-sex couples do not enjoy the same rights as heterosexual couples.

Koreans have long valued and reinforced the idea, and virtues, of a mono-ethnic society, but unlike Japan, have adjusted more rapidly to changing realities in the 21st century. While foreign-born constitute about 2% of Japan's population as of 2014, they represent over 3% of South Korea's population. The government had long touted the advantages of mono-ethnicity, drawing on tropes of uniqueness and superiority familiar to Japanese. However, in the early 2000s, the government began to change its tune, pivoting towards the advantages of multi-ethnicity and mounting a vigorous public campaign to encourage citizens to welcome and assimilate foreign immigrants. Given South Korea's demographic time bomb, with a steep drop in numbers of children relative to elderly, very much like Japan and China, it faces potentially serious economic and fiscal consequences. In the context of labor shortages and the plunge in fertility, welcoming more immigrants makes sense, but it is not the only society leery about the problems of a larger foreign community. Public discourse here and in Japan overlooks the dynamism of immigrants and how they have been engines of growth and innovation in the American economy, instead focusing on the problems of coping with diversity and promoting assimilation. In 2014 the government imposed a language test for spouses that will make it more difficult for Korean men to import brides. This is not entirely a xenophobic response of pulling up the drawbridges as there are justified concerns that many of these wives are abused and isolated in Korean society, and, as parents, put their children at a disadvantage in one of the world's most intensely competitive educational systems. But jingoism is never far from the surface.

Pop Culture Wars

Identity politics in contemporary South Korea is not exclusively rooted in anti-Japanese nationalism, but it remains a powerful factor. Strange as it may seem, the realm of cartoons and pop culture is another fiercely contested battleground in the history wars. At the War Memorial of Korea in Seoul, there is a placard at the entrance to the plaza proclaiming, "Freedom Is Not Free." The irony became apparent just three days before a special exhibit was to open on the premises on July 12, 2014, with newspaper headlines announcing that the One Piece manga/anime show from Japan was canceled. Why? Because in this Japanese manga/anime series featuring the adventures of pirates and other outlaws searching for treasure there are some sketchy depictions of the Rising Sun flag—a red center with lines representing sun rays extending outward—which Koreans associate with Japanese militarism and the painful experiences of Japan's colonial rule, 1910–1945. It was an absurd overreaction because there are very few scenes in the manga in which this Rising Sun flag is displayed and, more importantly, it is the flag of the protagonists' enemy and therefore not glorified. Interestingly, the manga is a best-seller in South Korea and hundreds of televised episodes of One Piece dubbed in Korean have been aired in South Korea since 2003, with uncut and edited versions appearing on different channels and, until 2014, no controversy over its very few scattered images of Rising Sun flags.

In contrast, the same show, staged simultaneously during the summer of 2014, was a huge hit in Taiwan (also a former Japanese colony, 1895–1945), attracting 100,000 visitors in the first week alone. The promotional campaign emblazoned the Taipei metro with One Piece cartoons, something unthinkable in Seoul's subway given the prevailing sensitivities about the two nations' shared history. After all, it wasn't until 1998 that South Korea began to incrementally ease the blanket ban on Japanese cultural products that was imposed following independence in 1945. In fact, satellite broadcasts and the Internet had facilitated considerable cultural seepage before then, and Korean translations of Japanese manga were widely available and extremely popular, a grassroots rejection of state policy that helped propel the state-sanctioned cultural opening.

There is no denying the popularity of Japanese popular culture among young Koreans, who are avid fans of manga and anime and disinclined to see them through the prism of historical animosities or state-promoted narratives of victimization because that is not what they are about. This hasn't prevented the South Korean government, however, from deploying popular culture in a global battle to win hearts and minds. In January 2014, soon after Prime Minister Shinzo Abe's controversial visit to the Yasukuni Shrine in Tokyo on December 26, 2013, which serves as ground zero for an unrepentant, glorifying view of Japanese imperialism, the South Korean government requested that the annual Angouleme International Comics Festival in southwestern France exhibit Korean *manhwa* (cartoons) about comfort women, the euphemism for women forced into sexual slavery between 1931 and 1945 to provide sex for Japanese soldiers—many were teenage Korean girls. Among Koreans, Abe is associated with revisionist history that downplays, justifies, valorizes and shifts blame for Japanese imperialism. In his first stint as premier, Abe drew ire in 2007 when he quibbled about the level of coercion used to recruit Koreans to serve as comfort women, on March 1, the day when South Koreans commemorate their anti-Japanese uprising in 1919 and celebrate Independence Declaration Day.

Netizens in Korea, one of the most wired societies anywhere, have become guardians of public mores and the thought police of the 21st century; some seem to have an obsession with the Rising Sun flag and pressured the War Memorial to cancel the One Piece show over the flag. The back-story of the One Piece saga is that recently there have been a number of cases where K-pop artists have been attacked online for displaying or wearing Rising Sun flag images. Whether as a backdrop for a music video poster, or on designer hoodies and hats, the Rising Sun flag, which conjures up images of Japanese imperialism and brutal subjugation among many Koreans, seems to have become the East Asian swastika. Just as punk bands once cultivated a bad boy, transgressive image by dabbling in Nazi imagery, the Rising Sun flag has become a merchandizing strategy guaranteed to draw attention in a highly competitive field.

Figure 2.4 Comfort Woman Statue across from Japanese Embassy in Seoul. Photo © Jeff Kingston.

Given how assiduously K-pop bands are marketed and the extent to which coordinators choreograph everything about their dance routines, appearances, clothing, diet and private lives, it is unimaginable that such displays are unwitting. But the Rising Sun flag is good copy and, after the attention-grabbing ritual apology, the show goes on, hopefully accompanied by rising sales.

Although there were no Rising Sun flag images among the many items in the proposed show, and advance ticket sales had been brisk, War Memorial management abruptly decided to cancel the show at the last minute. Organizers, however, took the case to court and won speedy justice, the judge ruling on July 17, 2014 that the government-run facility was contractually obligated to host the exhibit since it had agreed to rent the space to the organizers. The court also ruled that One Piece does not glorify Japanese imperialism, perhaps the first legal opinion about the politics of any Japanese manga anywhere.

The delayed show finally premiered on July 26, 2014 and proved a big hit with Korean fans of Japanese pop culture who flocked to the exhibit whipping out smartphones to take pictures of the life-size models of the characters on display. So in the end, this tempest in a teapot proved to be good PR, with no protests and South Koreans embracing both the rule of law and Cool Japan. Alas, the two countries don't have many of these happy endings to brag of.

In the next chapter we examine how national identity is expressed in and shaped by soft power and branding campaigns.

3

Nation Branding Confronts Troubling Realities

The collective Idea that shapes a nation and unifies its people by articulating a common purpose and shared values is not necessarily the same as the projected image, the Brand, although there may be considerable overlap. Images often draw on misleading stereotypes and may not reflect reality, but they influence perceptions and, as such, nations work hard to improve their images while contending with undesired impressions. A nation's global brand is defining and thus governments work hard to make it dazzling and attractive. It's a competitive market as nations vie with one another to get attention, attract tourists and investors, and establish a collective identity appealing to their own citizens. What is projected outward can also be useful in terms of inculcating desired values. CNN often carries advertising spots for countries that allow them to project a simplified, positive image embodied in a snappy slogan—"Incredible India," "Remarkable Indonesia," "Malaysia—Truly Asia." Japanese officials push Cool Japan—anime, manga, cosplay and cute mascots—while those in tourism tout Yokoso (Welcome to) Japan, emphasizing *omotenashi* (warm hospitality), innovation, high tech and wondrous natural beauty. And then there is "Imagine Korea," the 2014 slogan chosen out of thousands of entries aimed at building a trendy and innovative image. There is even a South Korean Presidential Council on Nation Branding that has overseen promotional campaigns such as "Korea, Sparkling," "Korea, Be Inspired" and "Hi, Seoul."

Branding, obviously, is not an exact science and it is hard to measure the impact on perceptions, but that doesn't mean governments don't relentlessly try to market the product and buff the image. In some circles, branding is considered an important aspect of soft power, a way to gain international political influence. So instead of relying on the hardware of military power, nations can promote the national interest by convincing others to follow their example and want the same things.

Nationalism in Asia: A History Since 1945, First Edition. Jeff Kingston.

Soft power can also be a way of remaking a nation's image and sparking overseas interest in studying the language and culture. China has launched Confucius Institutes, South Korea has King Sejong Institutes, while Tokyo is launching Japan House and operates the Japan Foundation, all distributing scholarships, research funds, seed money for universities and sponsoring conferences in a bid to win hearts and minds and exert influence on international public discourse and attitudes. It is a high-stakes game featuring lavish government backing. There are over 400 Confucius Institutes worldwide and 80 in the US alone, all based in universities where they cover the costs and provide books and teachers for Chinese language instruction, and provide research money to selected faculty. They also pay yearly dues that warm the hearts of administrators who are also taken on lavish junkets in China where curricular matters are no doubt hammered out over banquets. This is part of a concerted effort by Beijing to extend its influence, a campaign that has sparked a backlash among American academics who worry that it is encroaching on academic freedom while exporting censorship and imposing taboos regarding sensitive subjects like Tibet, the Dalai Lama, Uighur separatism and Falun Gong. China is discovering the hard way that it is not easy to buy soft power even if strategies of cooptation have some effect.

Soft power also encompasses promotion of cultural exports. Cool Japan captured fans and markets worldwide based on the appeal of manga and anime, with Doraemon, Hello Kitty and Pokemon emerging as iconic characters with far higher name recognition than Japanese leaders. Japan's trendsetting fashions and exquisite cuisine add to the allure of a nation admired for meticulous attention to detail. It is a matter of national pride for governments to boost the brand, but it is also lucrative, and none has better organized the synergies than South Korea. Cultural exports are big business, amounting to $5 billion in 2013, and the government targets a doubling of this figure by 2017. South Korea has become the trendsetter in Asia, with global audiences for its television dramas and K-pop music. From the 2 billion views of "Gangnam Style" and popular films to consumer electronics, cosmetics and fashion, the global appeal of Korean culture is stunning. South Korea has come a long way from the dour military culture of repression that prevailed until the late 1980s. The *hallyu* (Korean cultural) wave emerged from the 1997 Asian financial crisis as the government opened up the market, reducing somewhat the stifling dominance of the big conglomerates (*chaebul*), especially in IT and media. In 2005 the government launched a $1 billion investment fund to promote the pop industry and, by any measure, it has been a financial success. Less well-known is that video-game industry revenues dwarf K-pop revenues by a factor of 12.

Branding, soft-power and creativity are coordinated with the same precision and determination as K-pop singers' dance moves in what Euny Hong (2014) describes as, "a full-on amphibious attack." The synergies come from promoting Korean tastes and preferences and stimulating curiosity about things Korean in overseas markets. Actors, actresses and singers are often then hired as "pitchmen," pulling in viewers and listeners to buy Korean consumer products, generating a Korean cool buzz that feeds the export machine of Korea, Inc. Little is left to chance and consumer whims as officials organize flash-mobs and work the international media and festivals to sustain the marketing momentum for Korea's considerable cultural charms. Tokyo has taken note and established its own $500 million incubator fund to boost Cool Japan, but there are doubts about whether colorless and stodgy bureaucrats are really the best people to promote an image of cool that draws on creative talents. In fact, Japan's image probably got its biggest boost from the quiet dignity displayed by those displaced by the horrific events of March 11, 2011 when a huge tsunami pulverized communities on Japan's northeast coast and three reactor meltdowns in Fukushima forced an exodus of nuclear refugees. People around the world looked on in admiration at the social cohesion on display and the plucky perseverance of people who lost everything, while politicians and bureaucrats appeared fumbling, indecisive and overwhelmed by the disaster.

Nation branding ties into promoting the official self-image embodied in the Idea of nation. This Idea of nation is how political leaders would like their nation to be perceived. As we discussed, this Idea is subject to intense domestic contestation because the main purpose is to conjure up a collective sense of nation based on a shared vision. But, whose vision? In general, the international community does not have a direct stake in the Idea, or the contests over it, but certainly the international media express preferences. Mainstream western media generally promote secularism, democracy, and good governance based on transparency, accountability and the rule of law, human rights, sustainable development and market-oriented economic policies. This short list does not exhaust the issues and priorities, and is not meant to suggest that western nations all live up to these ideals. But they are a baseline for how nations' images are refracted through the lens of western media, influencing not only international perceptions, but also bouncing back to shape domestic perceptions; what the world thinks matters. It matters because it is like a report card on those who govern, and in terms of generating support for those who seek reforms in line with international perceptions. International criticism is often unwelcome and incites a prickly nationalistic backlash and defensiveness, but can also be handy to break through domestic impasses or overcome vested interests blocking reform. Nationalism can be invoked to protect and prolong the status quo, but can also be mobilized to justify reforms that will show the world a nation's capacity to overcome, improve and excel according to international yardsticks. Intrinsic to national identity is a desire to measure up and be accepted on equal terms, and here image is reality.

When people think about nations, certain images leap to mind, drawing on stereotypes often reinforced by media coverage. More often than not these images, seared into the global brain, are contrary to branding, symptomatic as they are of a nation's shortcomings. For example, everyone knows about the 2014 Sewol ferry disaster in South Korea that claimed the lives of nearly 300 students and exposed lax safety practices due to cozy and collusive relations between regulators and the ferry company, seen by Koreans as a microcosm of larger socio-economic problems. This was followed by the "nut rage" case later in the year, involving an arrogant executive of Korean Airlines, symbolic of privileged business elites from family dynasties that wield incredible power, who are seldom held accountable. In the unforgiving mass media, headlines suggest that India has become the "rape nation" of religious zealots; China is the corruption and smog superpower; Japan is known for nuclear disaster and Abenesia; while Indonesia is associated with terrorism and the death penalty. Such inglorious global moments constitute an agenda for branding campaigns—what needs to be overcome. These images become part of a nation's identity and often spark a nationalistic backlash that is defensive towards external critics, while at home, criticism and anger target those deemed responsible for tarnishing that identity and abusing power. This inward/outward pressure generates pressures to rectify or mitigate the problem. Here we gauge the image of our five countries based on key common problems, what I term the five "P"s—Pollution, Payola, Press, Poverty and Patriarchy. How do our nations measure up on these metrics?

Pollution

China and India have the unenviable image of being pollution superpowers. In the midst of rapid economic growth, their problems will get worse before they get better, but citizens in both countries are campaigning for more sustainable policies—a movement that is growing as the smog thickens and rivers and lakes grow ever more noxious. China is the world's leading producer of carbon emissions, having overtaken the US in 2006, while India is number three, with Japan (5), South Korea (7) and Indonesia (11) further highlighting Asia's major dilemma. As hundreds of millions more Chinese come to adopt more affluent, energy-intensive lifestyles and start driving cars, the challenges are immense. India, which like China relies extensively on coal as a source of energy, is also in the early stages of galloping pollution; currently less than half of India's 1.2 billion population are connected to the electricity grid, and as this figure rises, so will carbon emissions. Global warming is thus strongly influenced by the rising Asia story and the countries of the region are reaping what they sow, with increased risks from devastating storms and environmental degradation.

Japan and South Korea complain about Chinese toxic smog drifting into their environment and blame China's industrialization for increasing acid rain and disrupting regional weather patterns. Trilateral efforts to tackle this problem carry the potential for greater regional cooperation, but have had little impact. This is unfortunate because Japan has a lot of experience in coping with environmental degradation, and boasts cutting-edge technologies in reducing carbon emissions. It is encouraging that Japan has exported its scrubbing systems to China that reduce emissions from coal-fired plants, but much more could be achieved if both nations could dial down the nationalist demonizing that scuttles cooperation. For example the Japanese government pledged to clean up the wartime chemical weapons dumpsites it left behind in northeast China, but progress has been slowed due to red tape and stonewalling which have prevented Japanese experts from completing their task. One wonders who benefits from this nationalistic posturing.

Rapid industrialization in Japan during the 1950s and 1960s had dire environmental consequences, epitomized in what the world knows as Minamata Disease, an affliction of the central nervous system caused by ingestion of methyl mercury. Chisso Corporation dumped untreated industrial effluent into Minamata Bay, which was absorbed by fish, causing a horrific outbreak among those who ate the tainted seafood. This grisly saga and others led Japan to establish stricter environmental regulations from the 1970s, leading to significant improvements of air and water quality, at considerable expense. South Korea's industrialization drive in the 1970s mirrored the Japanese experience of growth at all costs, meaning little regard for the environmental consequences. It has also made significant progress in cleaning up its environment, but China's pollution problems have become Seoul's and Tokyo's due to proximity and prevailing weather patterns.

Environmental protests have skyrocketed in China in recent years as local residents try to shut down or prevent the building of factories that pollute the environment. Beijing's smog problems have grown so legendary that critics have coined the evocative term "airpocalypse." In 2014 the government began publishing data on polluting factories, signaling that it sees the need to respond and giving both ammunition and official sanction to environmental activists. These activists have highlighted the role of corrupt Party cadres selling off town land for factories and pocketing the money while they are left with a degraded environment and prospects of severe health consequences. The CCP permits these demonstrations of public anger to the extent that they focus on local actors and don't implicate central government authorities. For example, in 2013 local protesters successfully stopped the construction of a uranium processing facility in southern China, a significant victory given the government's emphasis on promoting nuclear energy. This is consistent with belated efforts to cope with China's gathering environmental crisis by heavily investing in renewable energy. It has become the world's largest producer of renewable energy, as part of an effort to enhance energy security and cut carbon emissions. China has a long way to go to become a green superpower, but it is an official aspiration, as evident in the bilateral climate deal reached with the US in 2014.

Indonesia, as the least developed of the five nations, is in the process of increasing harmful emissions and pollutants as it develops. Anyone visiting the main cities on the island of Java will come away convinced that Indonesia is racing toward environmental disaster, while its destruction of rainforest through the deliberate setting of fires to clear land in Sumatra and Kalimantan for palm oil plantations is devastating the environment and subjecting citizens of Singapore and Malaysia to high levels of unhealthy smoke. Given Indonesia's economic growth trends and high population density on the main island of Java, the current severe situation is rapidly getting worse.

Beijing and New Delhi are in the unenviable position of leading the world's capitals in PM2.5, a hazardous form of air pollution that often leaves them enveloped in noxious smog fed by increasing numbers of vehicles and factory emissions. PM2.5 refers to hazardous particulate matter measuring less than 2.5 microns, or 2.5 thousandths of a millimeter, in diameter, which can be absorbed by the lungs and lead to heart disease and lung diseases such as asthma, bronchitis and lung cancer. Panasonic announced in 2014 that it would pay a pollution premium to its expatriate employees in China, a form of hazard pay that is embarrassing to China. Many Indians believe that their nation is an environmental basket case, citing air and water pollution, disappearing forests, declining water tables and increasing volumes of untreated waste. Alas, Indonesia is not far behind and actually emits more carbon dioxide per capita than India. Japan can claim to have provided global leadership with the 1997 Kyoto Protocol, but it fell short of its emission reduction targets. The Kyoto Protocol was doomed by the refusal of the US to join and developing countries' refusal to accept reductions at the expense of growth. In recent negotiations under UN auspices the global community has not demonstrated a strong enough commitment to making the sacrifices necessary to slow climate change, and Asian governments are no exception.

Payola

This smog-sodden image inflicts reputational damage, as do reports of endemic corruption in India, Indonesia and China. On this payola scorecard, Transparency International's corruption perceptions index ranks Indonesia as the most corrupt among our five nations. In 2013 Japan was ranked 18 out of 177 nations, South Korea 46, China 80, India 94 and Indonesia 114. Authorities in China, India and Indonesia episodically crack down on corruption with some high-profile convictions, but overall there is a stunning degree of tolerance of malfeasance as anti-corruption initiatives dissipate and laws are watered down or ignored. It is considered a cost of doing business in these countries, and for many people in these nations it is a source of resentment and national shame.

According to Columbia University economist Jagdish Bhagwati (2014), not all corruption is equal. He contends that in the case of China and India,

> A crucial difference between the two countries is the type of corruption they have. India's is classic "rent-seeking," where people jostle to grab a cut of existing wealth. The Chinese have what I call "profit-sharing corruption": the Communist party puts a straw into the milkshake so they have an interest in having the milkshake grow larger.

Either way, this is not exactly the basis for chest-thumping nationalism.

In China, since 2013 President Xi has conducted a sweeping anti-corruption campaign that has accomplished far more than his predecessors in prosecuting venality at the highest levels, although it does not appear to mark a shift towards the rule of law. Xi's campaign looks more like a purge of his rivals and bid to consolidate power, but it is riveting political theater targeting a vast audience disgruntled with inequalities and a slowing economy. "Cleaning House" is also an effort to rid China of a structural problem that dims growth prospects, tarnishes the nation brand and discourages foreign investment. President Jokowi (Joko Widodo) is also associated with anti-corruption crusades in previous government posts, while Prime Minister

Modi campaigned on delivering good governance, demonstrating the electoral appeal of cracking down on graft. In South Korea influence peddling has also emerged as a source of public discontent, as the investigation into the 2014 Sewol ferry disaster revealed dubious ties between regulators and businessmen that compromised public safety. Similar findings about collusive relations between Japan's nuclear regulators and the operators of the Fukushima nuclear plant have also spurred controversy about the extent of regulatory capture in an industry where the culture of safety was alarmingly lax before the three meltdowns.

A handshake away from corruption, cronyism enables well-connected businessmen to gain favorable access and treatment by governments. Tycoons are able to leverage their networks in ways that have enabled them to disproportionately benefit from rapid growth, adding to their fortunes through rent-seeking activities such as creating cartels or securing favorable regulatory regimes that benefit their firms at the expense of competitors, consumers and the public interest. Asia's crony capitalism has produced a high concentration of wealth based on connections rather than entrepreneurial innovation. The *Economist* magazine's 2014 crony capitalism index places all of our focus economies in the top 22: South Korea (22), Japan (21), China (19), Indonesia (10) and India (9). Since 2007 India and Japan have become less crony-friendly, falling from 6th and 17th place respectively, while Indonesia has become more crony-friendly, rising from 18th place (*Economist*, March 15, 2014, 54–55). The rankings of China and South Korea have remained stable, with the latter the least crony-ridden of our focus group. Worldwide the *Economist* asserts that cronyism has probably peaked, as regulatory oversight improves, and market forces and investors punish such practices. Perhaps, but in Asia, cronyism is deeply embedded and likely to persist, accentuating insider advantages and creating destabilizing disparities that shape international perceptions accordingly. It is also something that attracts ridicule and as such is downplayed by the elites most likely to benefit from such practices.

Press

International reputation also relies on the degree of press freedom. Countries where journalists get a hard time tend to be given a hard time in the international media, as a professional courtesy and show of support. Governments and those with secrets to keep and reputations to protect are tempted to muzzle the media. Curbing press freedom often occurs through censorship and other legal restrictions that circumscribe freedom of expression or limit access to information. In addition, laws may fail to protect journalists or their sources from arbitrary government restrictions and penalties, or leave media organizations and writers legally vulnerable to judicial harassment by vested interests. Censorship is also enforced through extrajudicial intimidation and brutal violence, making journalism a dangerous profession. The annual press freedom index prepared by Reporters without Borders assesses government intentions and attitudes towards media freedom.

In 2013, out of 179 nations, South Korea ranked 50th, Japan 53rd, Indonesia 139th, India 140th and China 173rd. Japan dropped from 22nd in the 2012 survey due to perceptions of informal censorship, lack of transparency and restricted access regarding the Fukushima nuclear disaster. The passage of a new state secrets bill in Japan at the end of 2013 gives bureaucrats new sweeping powers to designate a wide range of information "special secrets" that can be kept under wraps for 60 years. There is no independent oversight mechanism and penalties for disclosure of such information are severe. Moreover, there is no right-to-know provision that privileges the public interest and protects whistleblowing when it is endangered. As such the government doesn't recognize the public's right to know. This legislation erodes freedom of the press as journalists are also subject to lengthy imprisonment for merely trying to solicit such information and have no right to protect their sources.

India may be the world's biggest democracy, but ranks low on media freedom due to impunity for escalating violence targeting journalists and greater Internet censorship. State security and non-state actors in India routinely threaten journalists and discourage investigative reporting about sensitive issues, ranging from Kashmir and the Naxalite insurgency (some 20,000 insurgents are active in large swathes of central India) to corporate malfeasance and unsavory ties between politicians, businessmen and organized crime.

China is the unsurprising laggard of Asia, just ahead of North Korea, due to state intimidation of the media and extensive censorship. The mainstream media essentially serves as a mouthpiece for the government and treads carefully on sensitive issues, knowing that offending the wrong powerful people can have nasty consequences. It is certainly an exaggeration to talk about the Big Brother Orwellian nature of Chinese censorship in the press and academia, but equally there is no denying the limits on freedom of expression. Even in the blogosphere the authorities devote considerable resources to monitoring, deleting, banning and stifling open discourse on taboo topics. Bloggers push the limits and play a cat-and-mouse game with state security, but remain vulnerable to its discretionary and arbitrary powers. Many journalists and Netizens remain imprisoned, while authorities continue to censor the Internet and otherwise curb access to information and transparency. As we discuss later in Chapter 11, problems involving Tibet and the Uighur minority in Xinjiang represent some of the taboos the government imposes on reporting. In 2013 the government courted global ridicule by requiring all domestic journalists to undergo Marxist indoctrination sessions, in a nation that, aside from empty ideological rhetoric, has all but abandoned communism.

South Korea, only a quarter of a century after ending authoritarian rule, has a relatively vibrant, diverse and innovative media and press freedoms are somewhat respected in line with constitutional guarantees. Freedom House reports that during the Lee Myung-bak era (2008–2012), the government infringed on editorial independence and 180 journalists were penalized for writing critical reports about government policy and advocating press freedom. Staff at two television networks went on strike to protest political interference, an act that attests to the strength of professionalism and commitment to press freedom. Defamation is a criminal offense, and this law is used by the powerful to intimidate critics, while extensive corporate influence over the media appears to soften critical coverage of the chaebul giants like Samsung. President Park Geun-hye's government has arrested local and international journalists for critical coverage and satire, and has significantly undermined media freedoms in other ways. The Internet, however, remains relatively unrestricted, with the exception of North Korea-related news, to which draconian laws still apply for anyone expressing sympathy towards the regime. An estimated 84% of the population have Internet access and thus tap a rich array of online sources that enable them to bypass mainstream media gatekeepers, but the government keeps tabs on critical bloggers, who can be subject to legal measures if they cross powerful figures.

Indonesia has drawn criticism for not taking effective action against intimidation and violence targeting journalists operating in the Papua region implicating the nation's security forces (see Chapter 11). Press freedom has also suffered in the general climate of growing intolerance and impunity for vigilantes and groups seeking to impose Islamic values as they define them. The courts have sided with the government that outlawing blasphemy is necessary for promoting religious harmony, undermining freedom of reporting on the increasing number of cases where Islamic organizations intimidate or attack others for blasphemy. Moreover, Indonesia criminalized the leaking of state secrets in 2011 and broadened the State Intelligence Agency's authority to gather and monitor information in ways that potentially threaten press freedom, thereby undermining the 2008 Law on Public Information, designed to promote transparency. In all of our nations, efforts to promote transparency have been stymied by governments under various pretexts, including national security, arousing public suspicions that officials have reasons to be anxious about accountability.

Poverty[1]

The pathologies of poverty in Asia are a human disaster of epic proportions, depriving people of basic needs and leading to social exclusion. It is also a black mark on national identity, a troubling reality that fits uncomfortably with the onward and upward narratives of national success that stoke nationalism. Limited access to social services and education condemns many families to a cycle of poverty with little hope of escaping. Poverty remains endemic in India and at high levels in Indonesia and China. South Korea and Japan are also confronting surprisingly high levels of relative poverty and increasing poverty among the elderly.

In Japan, poverty was long a taboo subject in a nation that proudly embraced egalitarian values and achieved rapid economic growth without a significant widening of income disparities. It was not until 2009, however, that the government made

---

[1] In general, relative poverty refers to households living on less than the national median income. Absolute poverty is defined as having income insufficient to buy what are deemed basic daily necessities.

public poverty data that it had been collecting, showing that Japan's relative poverty rate was 16%, not far below the US. In addition, nearly 14% of Japanese children are raised in conditions of relative poverty, and it is apparent that in a society that eschews class differentiation there is a self-perpetuating underclass. In 2008, when Lehman Brothers went bankrupt due to the sub-prime mortgage debacle launched on Wall Street, the global economy imploded. This had serious consequences for the Japanese economy and led to the dismissal of a quarter of a million contract workers, who were suddenly out of jobs and literally on the streets as they were kicked out of company dormitories. These were uncomfortable facts in terms of the nation's self-image and played a significant role in the ouster of the LDP in the 2009 elections, because it was blamed for presiding over the expansion of the precariat—contract workers in low-paid, dead-end jobs with no job security—along with growing income disparities and poverty.

Abenomics has entered the global lexicon as an ambitious set of three policy arrows—monetary expansion, fiscal stimulus and structural reforms—but none of these arrows targets poverty. Wages are not keeping up with inflation, leaving most households worse off, and changes in labor laws are plunging more workers into the precariat and relative poverty. The precariat, nearly 40% of the entire workforce, numbers more than 20 million workers and half of them are defined as the "working poor," earning less than 2 million yen a year ($16,000 at $1 = 120 yen). The doubling of the precariat over the past two decades has had a number of adverse consequences, including the derailing of career ambitions for younger workers and working mothers, who are disproportionately represented in their ranks. Because this is a contingent workforce subject to dismissal, firms invest less in training, depressing Japan's already relatively low level of productivity, estimated as being one-third lower than the US overall. In addition, the precariat are worsening Japan's social welfare deficit because most don't contribute to pensions or social insurance, but are more likely to need government assistance. The precariat also contribute to deflation, identified by Abe as the key problem of the Japanese economy, because they can't buy much with their low incomes. Moreover, the precariat are far less likely to get married and have families because they can't afford to, depressing Japan's already low fertility rate and worsening Japan's demographic dilemma of a rapidly aging population. Finally, the relatively high suicide rate for younger men is attributed to derailed careers and bleak futures for the precariat. It is difficult to make the transition from non-regular employment to a regular full-time job because there are fewer of these as firms opt for greater flexibility. All of these problems are also evident in South Korea—the two nations, dubbed "frenemies," share much in common.

South Korea is a poverty success story. In the mid-1950s over one-half of Koreans lived in absolute poverty; by 2001, the proportion had declined to less than 2%, benefiting from sustained, rapid economic growth and egalitarian policies. Relative poverty (half of the national median annual income of about $20,000) also declined, but, similar to Japan, has risen in the 2000s to about 15%. Surprisingly, in light of Confucian reverence for the aged, more than half of South Korea's elderly live in relative poverty, the highest percentage in the member countries of the Organization for Economic Cooperation and Development (OECD). The high incidence of relative poverty is partly because social welfare spending is relatively low in South Korea, about 8% of GDP versus an OECD average of 19%. It is also symptomatic of Korea's dual labor market, with about one-third of workers engaged in non-regular employment. As in Japan, this precariat works for relatively low wages with few benefits and little job security. Moreover, Korean firms retire their workers at a relatively young 55 years of age, meaning the elderly have to rely longer on their own savings and meager pensions. Government social policies have long assumed that families would take care of their own, but there has been a precipitous decline in co-residence of three-generation families, and children are much more likely to let their parents shift for themselves—a generation that invested heavily in their children's education and is now left with few resources to fall back on. As in Japan, the government tends to overlook or downplay the issue of poverty, relying on the family as the safety net rather than ramping up social programs and training schemes to help displaced workers find rewarding careers.

Nehru and all of his successors have identified eliminating poverty as an urgent priority, but far too many Indians are born and die poor, as numerous government initiatives have made little impact. Politicians argue endlessly about whether poverty has declined appreciably since independence in 1947, but it is apparent that the fruits of economic growth, or government programs, have not trickled down to the needy. In contrast, "Incredible India" now boasts nearly 15,000 multi-millionaires, placing it eighth in the world table.

The extent of India's poverty remains uncertain because the calculation of poverty is politicized and thus highly contentious. Governments are accused of fiddling the methodologies to lower or inflate the numbers to suit political agendas, and there is a cascade of assessments and reassessments that produce widely divergent results. In this case, "widely divergent" means headcounts that can vary by over 250 million. Recent Indian estimates of absolute poverty in 2011–2012 ranged from 270 million to 363 million, both marking a significant decline from estimates in 2005. In 2014 the World Bank weighed in with a calculation that the number of "extreme" poor was 99 million in 2010, about 8.1%, down by 300 million people from 2005. That is remarkable progress, but unconvincing to many Indians who attribute this incredible improvement to statistical legerdemain. Much depends on where the poverty line is drawn. The World Bank uses its global standard of $1.25 a day, adjusted for purchasing power parity (PPP) which takes into account variations in the prices of daily necessities. In contrast, a 2014 estimate by an affiliate of the Brookings Institute finds that the number of extremely poor is 180 million, using a poverty line of $1.55 a day, indicating considerable sensitivity at the margins. Indeed, the government's Rangarajan Committee used $1.94 as the poverty line and estimated that 363 million Indians live in extreme poverty, almost one-third of the population.

There were hopes that liberalization of the economy in the 1990s would boost growth and thereby lessen poverty, but the hype did little for the poor. A majority of Indians still work in agriculture and 90% are employed in the informal sector, while the benefits of "modern" India are narrowly distributed. Crony capitalism has bypassed the poor, who can only read about the mammoth scandals involving sales of billions of dollars of natural resources and telecoms concessions for a fraction of their value. One of the problems is the "license-Raj," a variety of restrictions and rules that confer extensive discretionary power on the bureaucracy, generating lucrative opportunities for corrupt officials and politicians to shake down businesses seeking permissions. This is a factor in the disproportionate rise of income at the upper end of the scale, leaving the poor farther behind.

The tens of thousands of farmers who have committed suicide in recent years are one barometer of poverty's consequences in India. The "Incredible India" narrative must also contend with the fact that Bangladesh, which is only half as rich as India, measured by per capita income, now exceeds India in life expectancy, child mortality, and immunization. Nearly half of all Indian children are underweight, health care is inadequate and the caloric intake of the poor has been declining. According to the Asian Development Bank, India spends less than Nepal and Timor-Leste—only 1.7% of its GDP—on health, education, and various forms of social protection. The pro-business bias of Modinomics seems likely to accentuate this neglect.

Optimists contend that there are six factors that might endow India with a comparative advantage over China: democracy, rule of law, demography, domestic demand, the private sector and civil society. But this depends on getting policies right, and implementing them effectively. India's poor record on poverty alleviation, a perennial rhetorical priority, is reason for pessimism.

China's record on poverty is relatively enviable, having pulled several hundred million citizens out of dire circumstances over the past few decades, during an era of stunning growth, recording annual double-digit increases in GDP since the early 1980s. From 1981 to 2004 about 500 million people climbed out of poverty as the percentage of those living below the poverty line dropped from 63% to just 10%. Absolute poverty (defined by the government as living on less than $1.25 a day) dropped precipitously from 85% in 1981 to 13% as of 2008, but even so, that means 172 million people were living in poverty. If the bar is set at $5 a day, according to the World Bank the number of poor as of 2008 was 948 million. And at $2 a day, about 36% of the population live in poverty, numbering about 468 million people as of 2009. As in India, there is great sensitivity on the margins, meaning that many people not officially counted as poor are uncomfortably close to being so and thus vulnerable to minor economic fluctuations.

By most counts, about 300 million out of China's 1.3 billion enjoy a middle-class lifestyle with attendant improvements and rising aspirations. From 1990 to 2005, per capita income growth averaged 8.7%, fueling unprecedented speed in poverty reduction. Declining poverty, however, has been accompanied by growing disparities, and unequal access to education and health services, that are especially pronounced between urban and rural populations. There has been some easing of the *hukou* household registration system that curbed rural to urban migration, but these restrictions on residential mobility persist and curtail opportunities for upward mobility for most Chinese living in the countryside. In addition, rural farmers have not been able to sell or leverage their land to borrow, keeping them tied to what represents their principal asset, one that is subject to the whim of local party officials who have often been implicated in land grabs, selling off parcels to businessmen and pocketing all the proceeds.

In 2009, according to China's Bureau of Statistics, urban per capita income was about triple rural per capita income. It is thus good news in some respects that China is going through rapid urbanization, with over 100 cities having a population of more than 1 million, of which 16 exceed 5 million residents, although congestion, smog, sprawl and anomie are other less desirable consequences. About 54% of Chinese live in cities, less than the 70% that urban planners anticipate based on China's per capita income, meaning that significant exodus from rural areas will continue. By 2030, some 1 billion Chinese will live in cities, amplifying existing problems, especially insufficient water and shrinking aquifers.

There is an urban bias to economic policies and social services that sustains and widens the gap between city dwellers and those living in the countryside; the World Bank estimates that 90% of Chinese poverty is rural. But the ranks of the urban poor have also swelled as a large "floating population" of more than 200 million migrant workers has flooded cities in search of better wages and living conditions; but many of these rural migrants fail to land stable jobs with good wages. In addition, the government has cut back support for state-owned enterprises, meaning an increase in unemployed or laid-off workers who depended on their employer to provide them the full range of social services, from housing to health care, the so-called "iron rice bowl." Persistent poverty in rural areas is creating a cycle of poverty and contributing to growing disparities, developments that take some of the shine off of China's phenomenal growth record. Just to highlight those disparities, the number of Chinese billionaires has risen from three in 2004 to 354 by 2014, compared to 492 in the US, up from 274 in 2004.

Indonesia reports that poverty has declined from 17.8% in 2005 to 11.5% in 2013, meaning that by official reckoning nearly 30 million of the nation's 250 million citizens live in poverty. During the Suharto era (1967–1998) rapid economic growth and social welfare policies helped reduce poverty that afflicted about half the population, featuring an extensive agricultural support program, a rural electrification program and reduction of family size through population planning. This progress, however, proved fragile as the 1997–1998 Asian financial crisis wiped out many gains in poverty alleviation, with the poverty rate climbing back to 20% by the end of 1998. The current 11.5% poverty rate means that Indonesia has only managed to return to the pre-crisis situation under the Suharto government.

Statistics can be misleading. The Indonesian government calculates the poverty rate based on a monthly per capita income of $25 (in a country where GDP per capita exceeds $3,000 a year), an extremely low threshold even considering the relatively low cost of living and prevalence of in-kind barter arrangements in rural areas that help families get by with fewer cash outlays. The World Bank calculates that about half the population live on less than $2 a day, while various domestic media estimate that 25% of the population live in poverty. Government subsidies play a key role in capping rice and fuel prices, but budgetary pressures have forced the government to cut such subsidies, with adverse consequences for poor families.

By whatever standard, poverty remains a huge problem in Indonesia, but varies considerably within the sprawling archipelago and between urban (8.5%) and rural (14.4%) areas, as of 2013. About half of all Indonesians live on the island of Java, but relative poverty is concentrated in the eastern provinces and is especially high in Papua (31.5%) and West Papua (27.1%), areas of political instability. In these rural areas, indigenous farmers engage in subsistence agriculture, but their communities have not benefited from national development schemes; out-migration is the only path of upward social mobility. In contrast, absolute poverty is most evident in Java, partly owing to extremely high population densities. In general, rural poverty is higher than urban poverty, although both are declining. One of the significant developments in Indonesia is the rapid urbanization of the population, from about one-third in the mid-1990s to about one-half today. This means that the cash-based economy has expanded, with fewer people able to resort to the rural bartering mechanisms and informal village safety nets that help families get by. Moreover, increases in food and fuel prices have a more significant impact on urban household welfare. Overall, wage increases have not kept up with inflation, leaving more people less well-off and fueling resentments about growing disparities. This is the Indonesia lurking behind the "Remarkable Indonesia" branding campaign.

Patriarchy

If the *Economist* glass-ceiling index is anything to go by, Japan and South Korea have a lot of room for improvement in terms of gender equality in the workplace. This index is based on a weighted average of nine indicators (including higher education, labor force participation, wages, child-care costs, maternity rights, business school applications and representation in senior jobs). Out of 27 countries, South Korea and Japan came in 27th and 26th respectively, with Norway leading the pack with a score of 80 and Japan scoring only 20 (*Economist*, March 8, 2014). The World Economic Forum's 2013 Gender Gap Report ranks China 69, Indonesia 95, India 101, Japan 105 and South Korea 111, out of 135 countries. Only India marked improvement over its 2006 ranking, while the situation in Japan, South Korea and Indonesia worsened. Thus none of the Asian nations stand out on gender equality as none are in the top half of the global rankings.

Prime Minister Abe has set a 2020 target of 30% for the proportion of women managers in Japan, but this seems little more than an empty gesture as he has done little to address the underlying reasons why women are so poorly represented in the upper echelons in Japan, Inc.—only 8% as of 2014. In South Korea, the percentage of female managers is 12%. Women there are as likely as men to graduate from university, but the nation ranks last in the OECD for employing female graduates. It is also the only OECD member where women with university education don't have a higher employment rate than women with basic compulsory education. In addition, South Korea also has the highest gender wage gap in the OECD, earning on average 44% of what men earn (compared to 57% in Japan); and 28% of women workers are engaged as part-timers, compared to an OECD average of 12.5%.

Globally women hold approximately 24% of senior management positions, as of 2013, up from 19% in 2004; while in China this figure is 51% and in India 19%. The benefits of gender parity and diversity in terms of economic growth, company performance and life satisfaction are well established, but patriarchal attitudes and insufficient corporate and government support mechanisms continue to marginalize too many women from managerial careers. This is not just Asia's issue, but it is an especially glaring problem in all of our focus countries with the exception of China.

In 2014 the OECD published a study indicating that men in Japan and South Korea spend 31 minutes a day on caring for household members and routine housework, compared to spouses who log 125 and 186 minutes respectively; the OECD average is 90 minutes for men and 208 minutes for women (OECD 2014). In China, men spend 61 minutes and women 188 minutes on these tasks, while in India, men spend 27 minutes and women 335 minutes a day. This division of labor contributes to Asia's shared identity as a region of deeply entrenched gender inequality. Mao's famous aphorism that women hold up half the sky appears to short-change them in all of our countries.

Women are also underrepresented in Asian political systems. The Inter-Parliamentary Union reported in 2014 that out of 147 nations surveyed in terms of women representatives in national politics, Japan ranked 128th, India 112th, South Korea 92nd, Indonesia 83rd and China 62nd. In 2015 China arrested five feminist activists on the eve of International Women's Day to prevent them from campaigning, inadvertently highlighting how serious the gender problem in China remains despite its relatively high ranking.

Patriarchal attitudes also contribute to sexual violence against women, by ignoring or condoning it, or blaming the victim. Rape and harassment are problems in each of our focus countries, but India has become the most notorious. In Indonesia, self-appointed religious vigilantes have harassed and intimidated women into staying home at night and dressing more conservatively. Islamic groups are lobbying for legislation to require women to not only cover their heads, but also wear more conservative attire than is the prevailing fashion. Tight jeans, for example, are deemed too provocative by the "fashion Taliban" in a society that has long been more permissive and tolerant than such radicals prefer.

India has developed an unenviable global reputation as a "rape state." Indian media have played a crucial role in uncovering numerous cases of sexual violence against women, a norm that has been a taboo subject, known but rarely made public. Indian women have protested about systematic harassment, what is called Eve-teasing, while conservative men assert that by dressing and acting provocatively women are encouraging rape. But it was not until an especially horrific gang rape of a medical student on a New Delhi bus in 2012 that suddenly the eye-averting Establishment went into action and the media began reporting sexual violence that previously went unremarked. This led to a greater willingness to speak about rape and other sexual crimes, ones that often involve caste discrimination, and put pressure on police to stop covering up such crimes. Parliament created a fast-track court for rape cases and introduced legislation that makes especially brutal rapes subject to capital punishment. Rapists have long operated with little fear of police action because police are often complicit with the perpetrators and fail to protect their accusers. Moreover the criminal justice system fails the nation's women because the courts are inefficient and corrupt, systematically failing to deliver justice to women who have been raped. Will the current moral panic translate into more convictions and fewer rapes? Probably not, but Indian women surely hope so.

Japan too is coping with the unenviable reputation of being a rape state, based on the wartime conduct of its military in occupied areas and former colonies. Iris Chang's *Rape of Nanking* (1995) focused on Japanese soldiers' war crimes, including widespread rape and the indiscriminate slaughter of civilians and prisoners of war following the invasion of Nanking in December 1937. From 1932 until 1945 the Imperial Armed Forces operated so-called "comfort stations" throughout Asia that used young women to provide sexual services to their troops. Many of these *ianfu* (comfort women) were recruited by deception and coercion in colonial Korea, often relying on local brokers, and subjected to sexual slavery. The Japanese military started this system in China in 1932, where it became widespread during the ensuing war because China had the highest concentration of Japanese troops. Although there was a concerted effort by Japanese government authorities to burn relevant documents in the aftermath of surrender, archival research, and testimony by comfort women, clarify that the military was involved in recruiting women, transporting them to comfort stations and carefully supervising these facilities. Soh (2008) explains that it was not a monolithic system and points out that there was coercive recruitment of women by soldiers in battle-front areas on local initiative, not state policy. While Japanese revisionist historians and politicians seek to dismiss such claims and evidence, in his 1978 memoir former Prime Minister Yasuhiro Nakasone inconveniently recalled his own wartime experience in the navy as a lieutenant setting up a comfort station in Kalimantan, Indonesia (then known as the Netherlands East Indies) and his role in recruiting local women.

It was only after 1992 that this controversy erupted in Japan and the region. Before then, the Japanese government denied its existence, while the military authoritarian government in South Korea, reinforcing Confucian and patriarchal norms, stifled the voices of former comfort women and civil society in general. With the emergence of democracy in South Korea from the late 1980s, and in cooperation with Japanese researchers and civil society organizations, the story emerged and led the Japanese government to investigate, and issue the 1993 Kono Statement acknowledging responsibility and apologizing for the comfort women system. As a result, the Japanese government established a non-governmental organization, the Asia Women's Fund (AWF; 1995–2007), for the purpose of providing compensation to former comfort women, including Dutch abducted from an internment camp in Java, and apology letters signed by the prime minister. This was Japan's first attempt at reconciliation with individual victims of wartime excesses, but it was a failure because it was an attempt to resolve the issue at arm's length without accepting legal responsibility. This carefully calibrated initiative fell short of the grand gesture required to restore dignity to the comfort women and indeed Japan. Advocacy groups in South Korea castigated the AWF as a flawed gesture of contrition that sidestepped government responsibility, and pressured the former comfort women not to accept the offered compensation. Before it was wound down in 2007, only 364 women received compensation from the AWF, a tiny fraction of the tens of thousands of comfort women, and it served mostly to reopen wounds and arouse animosities. While victims were disappointed, Japanese reactionaries and revisionists were outraged that their government admitted responsibility and provided compensation. They continue to insist there is no archival proof of the military using coercion to recruit women, and indeed mounted a concerted campaign in 2014 to vilify the relatively liberal *Asahi* newspaper for its forthright reporting on the issue. Out of the myriad sources the *Asahi* relied on for its reporting only one former soldier's testimony was discredited, sparking conservative media organizations to try to use this as reason for a disingenuous blanket denial. Prime Minister Abe has publicly supported the campaign against the *Asahi*, signaling that it is more about politics than journalistic standards.

There is considerable controversy about exactly how many women were involved in the comfort women system (0–200,000), how and under what conditions they were recruited and by whom, and why Japan's response to this gross violation of human rights has ranged from sincere contrition to downplaying and denial. The domestic battle over the Kono Statement and the AWF highlights the fundamental post-World War II political fault-line between reactionaries, who seek to rehabilitate and justify Japan's wartime actions, and liberals, who argue that militarists derailed Japanese democracy in the 1930s and feel it is imperative that Japan take responsibility, and atone, for its war crimes. As discussed in subsequent chapters (see Chapters 8 and 9), this battle is fought in textbooks and in museums and is a major source of tension between Japan and its neighbors—China and Korea. Prime Minister Abe was not elected for his views on history, but he has ensured that northeast Asia's shared past resonates divisively in the 21st century. In 2014 his colleagues in the Diet mounted an investigation designed to undermine the Kono Statement, and he has often voiced skepticism about its conclusions, thereby impeding efforts towards reconciliation. For Japan's neo-nationalists, much is at stake, especially the nation's honor and reputation. But the backlash against their denials in South Korea and China has attracted unwanted attention elsewhere, as the US Congress condemned Abe's prevarications in 2007 and towns in the US have erected memorials to the comfort women. In this sense those nationalists who seek to rewrite wartime history have undermined Japan's national interests and complicated its future by trying to rehabilitate a shabby wartime past. Many Japanese, including Emperor Akihito, disagree with such efforts and understand that Japan can only regain its dignity by restoring dignity to its victims; but Japan's revisionists currently wield political power. Akihito's New Year comments in 2015 drew attention to the 70th anniversary of the end of World War II and urged the nation to learn the lessons of Japanese aggression in 1931 and the whirlwind of carnage and destruction it unleashed, precisely not the lessons that reactionary nationalists and revisionists are eager to propagate.

In the next chapter we turn to examine the economic taproot of nationalism and how it has shaped policymaking and national identity.

Part II

Political Economy and Spectacle

4

Economic Nationalism

The taproot of economic nationalism in Asia is imperialism. The domination and exploitation that engulfed Asia with gathering momentum from the 17th century bequeathed a deep reservoir of nationalist resentment and suspicion directed towards a western-dominated global order. Post-1945 economic policies adopted by our focus countries, and underlying attitudes towards the norms, practices and values of capitalist industrialized nations, remain influenced by the age of imperialism—when economic subordination was intertwined with direct military oppression. In the 21st century there has been a convergence of policies towards the prevailing market-oriented model based on capitalist tenets, but this remains contentious within these nations, in large part because it is viewed through the prism of anti-imperialism. Globalization has lowered barriers between nations and fostered greater interdependence. Yet the expanded opportunities for collaboration and cooperation have also generated concerns about domination and exploitation in nations where imperialism and colonialism remain scars on the national psyche. Market-oriented reforms are often touted as the solution to promote increased productivity, efficiency and economic growth, but are also contested because they are seen as a manifestation of neo-imperialism. They are also criticized for increasing risks, especially for those who are made more vulnerable by such changes. Skeptics about the market as panacea point out that neo-liberal reforms tend to accentuate income disparities and reduce protections for workers and producers while exposing them to the risks of international market forces and competition. In many cases powerful international companies have enormous advantages over local firms and thus government intervention is seen to be a sensible way to mitigate disruptive changes and to level the playing field.

Nationalism in Asia: A History Since 1945, First Edition. Jeff Kingston.

Overall, our focus economies have been relatively successful by global standards, recording significant growth and improvement in economic conditions and living standards compared to the mid-20th century. They pursue a mix of liberalization and state control and tend to blame external forces for negative consequences while often courting foreign investors and selectively adopting market-friendly reforms. In each, the state plays a critically important role in managing markets and embracing nationalist economic policies, even though there has been a significant shift towards market-oriented policymaking. Economic nationalism is advocated and embraced as a means to promote local interests through various forms of protectionism. This can involve a variety of export and import restrictions such as quotas, tariffs, local content rules, government procurement restrictions, or regulatory regimes that exclude or limit foreign entry into specified sectors. Governments invoke national interests to justify such strategies, but in many cases specific policies are supported by local vested interests that benefit from such policies. These are rationalized in terms of resistance to foreign domination, protecting jobs, promoting development and growth, generating a trade surplus, cultural preferences, or health and safety concerns. These arguments are persuasive domestically, and paying higher costs for lower-quality domestically produced products is justified in terms of helping the home team.

Governments may require increased local value added in processing of natural resources with the goal of enhancing domestic economic benefits from such exports. Since large drilling and mining companies are international firms with powerful connections and exert influence over global markets, they are viewed with suspicion and treated accordingly. But in most cases where there are alternative options to obtain the same resource from another country, these firms leverage their capital and technology to resist compliance, water down demands or gain exemptions.

In negotiating international liberalization of trade in goods and services, governments are attracted to the opportunities for increasing market access overseas and boosting exports, but are less enthusiastic about opening their own markets to intensified foreign competition. Governments are thus constrained by domestic political and economic considerations precisely because the perceived national interest is at stake, and domestic lobby groups can mobilize public opinion and use their access to politicians and officials to protect their turf.

In summary, economic nationalism is thus evident in protectionist policies including: (1) tariff barriers; (2) quotas; (3) subsidies and tax breaks; (4) exclusionary cartels; (5) various non-tariff barriers; (6) restrictive public tenders for goods and services excluding foreign vendors; (7) regulations that discourage foreign investment; (8) setting product standards that favor domestic firms; (9) stipulating increased local value added in processing of natural resources; and (10) discriminatory enforcement of rules, regulations and laws. The list could be much longer, but clearly, if governments have a will, there is a way to protect the domestic market. Increasingly, harmonization with the international trading system according to the rules of the game established in the World Trade Organization (WTO) is reducing the scope for such practices, and the big challenge to free trade remains implementation and enforcement. The Doha Round of multilateral negotiations between WTO member states that began in 2001 aims to further reduce trade barriers, but has lurched from crisis to crisis, and may prove to be a missed opportunity due to nations wanting to concede as little as possible while protecting as much as possible from unrestrained market forces. Developing nations believe that free trade favors more advanced nations, and thus that it is another strategy of domination and exploitation reminiscent of imperialism.

In the aftermath of World War II, our focus countries were all impoverished, and thus cutting imports and promoting local production made virtue out of necessity. Without sufficient capital and technology all were dependent, and thus gaining autonomy, and not being at the mercy of outside powers, animated efforts to develop local industries. In considering the context, it is important to bear in mind that Japan, Korea and China suffered considerable war devastation: China from 1931 to 1949, Japan from 1941 to 1945, and Korea from 1950 to 1953. In addition, Indonesia, Korea and India endured lengthy periods of colonial rule when their economies were developed/exploited in the interests of the colonizing power.

China too was subject to informal imperialism from the mid-19th century, whereby western nations (and Japan from 1895) forced the Chinese government to accept what are called unequal treaties. These unequal treaties dictated commercial relations, providing access to the Chinese market and its resources while taking away China's tariff autonomy. This not only gave unfettered access to foreign firms, which undermined local producers and stymied growth in local manufacturing, but also weakened the finances of the Chinese government since it received relatively low revenues from increased trade. It is crucial, therefore, not to underestimate the pre-1945 influence over post-1945 developments and a lingering wariness about the dangers of global capitalism for nations that have seen themselves as vulnerable "have-nots." Economic nationalism is seen to be a survival strategy and more recently a competitive edge, spawning a web of vested interests that have proven hard to dismantle.

Japan

Japan's economic nationalism can be traced back to the Meiji era (1868–1912) of rapid modernization that involved extensive state support and intervention. Japan's industrial revolution was compressed into a few decades at the end of the 19th century. The Meiji government established state-owned enterprises by importing plant, equipment, technology and advisors, and paid for this expensive undertaking by raising tax revenue from the agricultural sector. The guiding slogan of the day was *fukoku kyohei* (rich nation, strong military). The acceleration of western imperialism in the 19th century represented a serious threat and in response Japan quickly promoted industrialization to avoid being colonized and to gain the power and standing requisite to end the humiliating unequal treaties that were a sign of Japan's second-class status among world powers. From the outset, the state played a dominant role, and its economic policies were inspired by the German neo-mercantilist economist Friedrich List who argued that backward economies like Japan required protectionism in order to catch up and become competitive with more advanced economies. Until the early 20th century, Japan was subject to unequal treaties that facilitated commercial access by foreign firms, and, like China, did not enjoy tariff autonomy. This caused extensive problems for Japan's uncompetitive producers and political risk for the government. But by working with foreign firms and buying their expertise and equipment, the state established the foundations of Japanese manufacturing. It moved to sell off these state enterprises from the late 1880s at low prices to domestic entrepreneurs, many from the former samurai class, and also to large established family companies called *zaibatsu*.

Economic nationalism dominated Japan's pre-1945 economic policies, not only in jumpstarting its industrial revolution, but also in driving imperial expansion. Its first overseas war was in 1895 against China, and following victory, Tokyo claimed a huge war indemnity, seized Taiwan and some smaller islands, while imposing an unequal treaty on China. In 1905 it defeated Russia, and in the aftermath secured access to Chinese resources in Manchuria and colonized Korea from 1910. Imperial aggression accelerated in the 1930s with the seizure of Manchuria in 1931 and western colonies in Southeast Asia from 1941, which was justified in terms of Pan-Asianism, the idea that Japan was the natural leader of Asia and was liberating the region from the yoke of western imperialism. This idea resonated to a degree among some Asian leaders, but as we previously discussed, it was also viewed with suspicion and skepticism by others such as China's Sun Yat Sen and India's Rabindranath Tagore who saw Japan emulating western ways of might over right, predicting the violent cataclysm that ensued as Japan plunged Asia into war (Mishra 2013).

Japan's industrial production capacity proved inadequate to sustain prolonged war against China and the US, but established a strong base of technology and knowhow that helps explain why Japan recovered so quickly from the war. Certainly post-1945 US support in the form of preferred access to the world's largest market and cutting-edge technologies helped tremendously, but economic nationalism also proved beneficial. As the Cold War with the Soviet Union heated up from 1947, the US occupation forces were keen to transform Japan into a showcase of the superiority of the US capitalist system and did whatever it took to make this happen. It revived what the Japanese called the 1940 system, granting sweeping discretionary powers to government officials, the antithesis of a free market system. This was the system that enabled Japan to maximize production during wartime and it also proved a winning strategy in the post-World War II era. Government planners moved to promote certain sectors, known as industrial targeting, providing low interest loans, subsidies and infrastructure that facilitated the emergence of a manufacturing powerhouse. The government also negotiated favorable technology licensing agreements with foreign firms that provided cheap access to cutting-edge technologies that meant avoiding the cost and delays of research and development programs. The US believed that zaibatsu, family-owned industrial conglomerates, had been supportive of Japan's wartime aggression and thus held them responsible. Some of these conglomerates were initially broken up and put under professional management, but America's trust-busting rhetoric was not backed up by resolute action. Japanese industry advocates lobbied the US Congress to water down punitive policies, warning that breaking up the conglomerates would worsen the economy, help communists and require additional financial assistance from the US, for which there was no support in America. After the US Occupation ended in 1952, the zaibatsu conglomerates were reconstituted as *keiretsu*, related firms centered on banks under professional management rather than family control, creating a significant postwar continuity in Japan's industrial sector.

Government promotion of domestic winners, including the keiretsu, was a successful policy and supported by a variety of protectionist measures designed to insulate them from foreign competition. Tariff and non-tariff barriers limited imports of foreign products and kept them relatively expensive. Predatory trading practices included foreign exchange controls that allowed the government discretion over what got imported. Japanese trading firms had to apply for an allocation of foreign exchange (since the yen was not convertible) to purchase imports and the government could control such purchase through its allocations (or refusals). Foreign firms were also barred from repatriating profits made in Japan, meaning they had to reinvest them, a significant disincentive that kept many firms from operating in Japan. Inspection procedures for imported products were convoluted, lengthy and costly, while Japan's distribution system was geared in favor of domestic producers, limiting market access for foreign products. Large companies tended to buy products from their affiliated firms rather than import from overseas, a preference that also prevailed in government procurement. For example, bidding rules on public works projects effectively steered contracts to domestic construction firms, while it was a matter of course to purchase stationery or furniture from domestic makers, even if prices for imported products might be lower.

In all these ways Japan pursued economic nationalism and achieved what is dubbed an "economic miracle" of double-digit growth from the late 1950s through the end of the 1960s. It became a leading manufacturer of automobiles and electronic devices, known for high quality and advanced technologies, and began to amass huge trade surpluses by the late 1970s, generating friction with leading trading partners, especially the US. Throughout the 1980s and into the 1990s Japan came under intense US pressure to abandon nationalist economic policies and to facilitate market access to goods and services for foreign companies. Chalmers Johnson's *MITI and the Japanese Economic Miracle* (1982) detailed how Japan was rigging the system to its own advantage at America's expense. There were also US accusations of Japanese free-riding on the American military, taking US protection for granted while contributing little to its own defense. This put strains on the US–Japan alliance and prompted a nationalist backlash among some Japanese who felt that they were being targeted because they had done so well through hard effort and sacrifice.

Nationalist politician Shintaro Ishihara gave voice to these frustrations in a book he co-authored with Sony Chairman Akio Morita entitled *The Japan That Can Say No* (1989). American bullying and Japanese kowtowing had come to characterize

Figure 4.1 Trans-Pacific Partnership Stokes Anxieties in Japan. Photo © Jeff Kingston.

bilateral relations, but Ishihara suggested that the client state relationship should end and Japan should develop the capacity to defend itself. He pointed out that US weapons systems depended on Japanese semiconductors and technology, hinting that Japan might trade secrets with the Soviet Union and withhold certain components needed in US missiles. Ironically, his threats were issued just as the Berlin Wall fell and the Soviet Union was unraveling. He criticized US scapegoating of Japan for its own shortcomings, accusing the US of Japan-bashing and racism. He also asserted that Japan produced better products and benefited from a superior work ethic, education and culture. Not all Japanese agreed with his combative stance, but his views did strike a chord, as Japan in the late 1980s seemed like it was on top of the world, and some pundits predicted a Pax Nipponica. Economic nationalism appeared to work quite well, at least for Japan.

Then Japan's asset bubble collapsed in the early 1990s, as land and stock prices imploded by more than 60%, leaving a trail of misery and bad debts. This was the so-called Lost Decade when Japan's banking system was on the verge of collapse due to bad loans and the entire economy stagnated. Suddenly the Japan, Inc. system that had spread unprecedented prosperity among Japanese and seen Japanese firms rise to dominance seemed deeply flawed (Katz 1998). But the economic distress did not lessen nationalistic tendencies in economic policy. The nation's businesses remain the state's business and even if barriers have been dismantled and regulations revised, there is no abiding belief in the virtue of market forces.

Shinzo Abe was elected prime minister in 2012 and unveiled Abenomics, a set of three main policy measures: massive monetary easing, fiscal stimulus, and structural reforms aimed at overcoming deflation and boosting productivity and economic growth. Part of this strategy depended on a competitive devaluation, lowering the value of the yen in order to boost exports. Structural reforms aimed at deregulation, promoting and improving women's careers, relaxing restrictions on the labor market and immigration, among other initiatives, have been more difficult to achieve. Abe has also been slow to liberalize the agricultural sector due to the strong farm lobby of small producers who arouse nationalist sentiments by raising the alarm about the negative consequences for a way of life that still resonates powerfully in the national psyche. But the political influence of the farming vote is receding as depopulation of the countryside gains momentum; in 2010 the average age of full-time farmers had reached 65 years. Prime Minister Abe is an ardent nationalist in terms of politics, security and history, but in the economics sphere he is an advocate of economic liberalization and can count on the support of large businesses that benefit from such initiatives. However, with about 80% of the Japanese workforce engaged in less competitive small and medium-size enterprises, there are widespread concerns that market liberalization is a risky strategy.

South Korea

Korea was colonized by Japan between 1910 and 1945. This shared history remains a powerful source of contemporary tensions as grievances over forced labor and the comfort women remain unresolved. Koreans remember the colonial era for harsh political repression and economic exploitation for good reasons, but the Japanese colonial administration did contribute to development and significant levels of economic growth. Japanese ventures established mining and manufacturing enterprises, disseminating technology, while the colonial government expanded education and infrastructure vital to industrialization and economic growth. Koreans tend to downplay the benefits of colonial rule and this remains a controversial subject.

Many Koreans worked in the colonial government, gaining knowledge of policymaking and administration, putting a Japanese stamp on institutions and business practices that represent a significant post-1945 continuity. Koreans have emulated Japanese economic policies, emphasizing the role of the state in promoting development and shared suspicions about the virtues of market forces. Korean family-controlled industrial conglomerates, known as chaebols, are closely modeled on Japanese zaibatsu/keiretsu and dominate the economy.

Japan's defeat meant liberation for Korea, but the celebrations were short-lived as the US and Soviet Union divided the peninsula at the 38th parallel in 1945, taking responsibility for their respective zones in the south and north. This was intended as a transitional phase prior to the newly established United Nations supervising elections over a united peninsula. But growing Cold War tensions between Washington and Moscow axed reunification plans as both sides installed leaders supportive of their ideological stances. In 1948 the division of the peninsula into two independent states was formalized, with US-backed Syngman Rhee elected president of South Korea (1948–1960), while Kim Il-Sung assumed the premiership of the North Korean regime (1948–1994). Kim Il-Sung launched a full-scale invasion of South Korea in June 1950, plunging newly liberated Koreans into a devastating civil war fought as a proxy battle between the communist camp (Soviet Union and China), and mostly American troops under UN auspices. Mao dispatched several hundred thousand troops to support North Korea and turn back the US advance, leading to a bloody stalemate.

After three years of war, an armistice was signed in 1953 between the combatants that preserved the previous division at the 38th parallel. During the conflict, an estimated 3 million people died, of whom 2.5 million were Korean civilians. At the time, the combined population of the entire Korean Peninsula was only 30 million. Those that survived faced destitution as the peninsula's infrastructure was almost completely destroyed, and shelter was scarce with the destruction of about half of all residences. The newly created South Korea was thus baptized by war and ruin, an impoverished nation with per capita GDP rising to only $79 in 1960 under an authoritarian government given to corruption and brutal repression. South Korea was highly dependent on US foreign aid, and living standards were low and didn't begin to improve significantly until the 1980s.

It is important to bear in mind this tragic start in assessing South Korea today, the fifteenth largest economy in the world. Clearly, South Korea's remarkable development was not inevitable and few people surveying the ruins of what was left of Seoul at war's end could have imagined the vibrant capital that Seoul has become. Nor would many have imagined that the chaebols such as Samsung, Hyundai and LG would launch brands with global appeal and help propel an economy that has achieved a massive improvement in living standards, and a rise in life expectancy from 54 years of age in 1950 to 80 by 2011.

In 2012 South Korea became the seventh member of the "20-50 club"— nations with a population of at least 50 million and a per capita income exceeding $20,000. How was it possible that this resource-poor overcrowded nation managed to triple per capita GDP between 1980 and 2010 and graduate from being a major recipient of aid to become a significant donor of Official Development Assistance by 2008? What went right?

The repressive, unpopular and corrupt President Rhee was forced to flee the country in 1960 due to popular protests against a rigged election. In the ensuing turmoil, General Park Chung-hee seized power in a military coup in 1961. President Park helped launch the so-called "Miracle by the Han." The Han is the major river in

Seoul and the miracle refers to the average annual GDP growth of 8% between 1962 and 1989. During this period, the manufacturing sector expanded from 14% of gross national product (GNP) in 1962 to 30% by 1987. South Korea adopted an export-led growth model based on labor-intensive manufacturing, where it had a competitive edge due to low wages. Given the small domestic market, poor resource endowment and shortage of capital, this model made sense and was actively supported by the government through subsidies, infrastructure projects and encouragement of foreign capital inflows. This outward-looking strategy proved crucial to rapid growth of industry and enabled South Korea to benefit from global growth and liberalization of trade under the auspices of the General Agreement on Tariffs and Trade (GATT).

The Miracle on the Han was made possible in 1965 when South Korea and Japan normalized relations and Seoul received $800 million in grants and soft loans that served as compensation for colonial-era abuses. This money was invested in infrastructure and heavy industrialization projects and was a catalyst for South Korea's era of rapid growth. Given the smoldering bilateral tensions that prevail, Japan gets little kudos for its contributions.

Park overcame his dislike of businessmen, but not before subjecting them to public humiliation soon after he came to power. He was incensed by the crony capitalism of the 1950s when businessmen close to President Rhee were allowed to buy up abandoned Japanese factories at low prices. The founder of Samsung, Lee Byung-chul, was accused of acquiring massive amounts of illicit wealth, but he struck a deal by paying large fines and donations to the government and agreeing to promote Park's economic policies among other businessmen, as head of the newly established Korean Federation of Industries, a large business lobby group.

Park needed their help to realize his ambitious industrialization plans aimed at lifting people out of poverty and, more importantly, to strengthen the country *vis-à-vis* North Korea, where many of the colonial-era mining and manufacturing ventures had left behind a stronger foundation for industry. The fines paid by the wealthy cronies to the state provided seed money for an impressive array of projects ranging from steel, shipbuilding, cement and chemicals to oil refining, fertilizer and textile factories. Preferential interest rates on loans targeted the government's priority sectors and helped spur development under state guidance, a system modeled on Japan.

Park continued the established practices of economic nationalism, corruption and collusion, while supporting extensive protectionism to boost local champions. Once a domestic firm started producing something, imports from overseas competitors were blocked. Import substitution and infant industry protection went hand in hand, but the government also directed the beneficiaries of protection to boost exports to help pay for imports of natural resources. This guidance did not really mean voluntary compliance, but was more like an order. Giving Korean firms domestic monopolies while nudging them to compete in international markets proved successful, forcing them to become more efficient and competitive and thus avoiding the hazards of protectionism whereby high-cost, inefficient local producers stagnate, to the detriment of other producers who rely on their inputs, and consumers who buy their products. Moreover, the Korean model accommodated a degree of market discipline and bankruptcy was common; firms that could not cut it were allowed to fail. Thus, the Korean government provided generous support, but did not saddle itself with loss-making enterprises.

Chaebol capitalism shared some features with Japanese postwar keiretsu, including significant political influence and close working relations between business and government policymakers. Chaebols also embraced a strategy of protecting the domestic market and export promotion. These vertically integrated organizations worked to boost group interests and that meant procurement as much as possible from affiliated firms, keeping outsiders at bay even if it meant paying a bit more. Consumers in both countries paid a price for economic nationalism as high tariffs and distribution barriers kept foreign products out or priced them beyond reach of all except the wealthy. The lack of competition at home meant consumers had less choice and paid more than if policies had been more market-oriented, but this was justified in terms of supporting these enterprises and the jobs, and tax revenues, they represented. There was also an expectation that companies would adopt paternalistic employment practices, assuring workers' job security while training them. Since the end of the 1990s firms in Japan and South Korea have shed many of the tenets of this corporate welfare-ism, and paternalistic management practices have faded under the intense global competition and the need to reduce costs. The core workforce in both nations' firms remains relatively well-paid and enjoys job security, but the percentage of workers in non-regular jobs, the so-called precariat, has risen dramatically in both countries since the early 1990s, exceeding 35% of the workforce as of 2014.

Paradoxically, the support for national champions has stifled innovation and the benefits of competition. Samsung products are cutting-edge in global markets and esteemed for their innovation (although accused of reverse-engineering of technologies developed by competitors such as Apple), but the dominance of large firms throughout the economy has created high barriers to entry. In short, South Korea is not an environment conducive to entrepreneurship because business start-ups face formidable challenges and the educational system doesn't encourage thinking outside the box.

One of the major developments in the 2000s has been the shift of South Korea into China's economic orbit. It has long been closely intertwined with the Japanese economy, but China is now South Korea's leading trading partner, a development with strategic implications. Given the fractious relations between Tokyo, Beijing and Seoul, this shift in economic relations makes South Korea somewhat less beholden to Japan, but at the same time anxious about Chinese domination. There has been a considerable warming of bilateral relations with China, a nation long viewed with antagonism for its support of North Korea and its communist ideology. South Korean industry, however, wants to tap the benefits of a rising China, while the government seeks Beijing's help in dealing with Pyongyang and its program to develop nuclear weapons. Yet there is abiding nationalistic wariness about China's regional hegemonic ambitions and the vulnerabilities that arise from becoming overly dependent on China economically. This deepening economic relationship amidst continued frictions with Japan complicates the US alliances with Seoul and Tokyo, and Washington's desire to promote more robust trilateral security cooperation.

Indonesia

Indonesia achieved independence in 1949 after four years of intermittent armed clashes and negotiations with the Dutch, who were eager to resume control over the resource-rich archipelago. The nationalist movement that had gathered strength since the early 20th century finally succeeded in gaining independence and ousting the Dutch overlords, but this did not erase memories of brutal repression or the severe socio-economic dislocations that accompanied the Great Depression of the 1930s, when Indonesia's commodity export-oriented economy plunged amidst a global economic collapse. Tens of thousands of migrant workers from Java employed in Sumatra's vast rubber and tobacco plantation sectors lost their jobs and income. Most returned to their home villages in Java, burdening families who were also suffering from similar consequences, especially those working in sugar plantations and coffee production. Indonesia, or at least the Dutch, had benefited considerably from booming commodity exports, but this also made the economy vulnerable to prices decided in distant global markets. Living standards also worsened, pushing many households to the brink, while the Dutch responded by incarcerating nationalist leaders, fearful that the economic dislocation might trigger political unrest.

The Japanese invasion in 1942 ended Dutch colonial rule, but continued the economic exploitation of that era. The forced labor and rice requisition policies proved disastrous and quickly exposed the grim reality of Japanese Pan-Asianism. Cut off from European markets and products, the Indonesian economy deteriorated further under Tokyo's rule, while the Dutch scorched earth policies limited Japan's ability to extract resources to support its war effort. In the wake of Japan's defeat in August 1945, the Japanese-trained army and militias rose up in resistance to Dutch plans to resume colonial rule, eventually forcing the Netherlands to capitulate and agree to independence in 1949.

The Republic of Indonesia nationalized Dutch plantations and factories, effectively seizing ownership and control without compensation. Colonial exploitation under Dutch rule since the 17th century provided ample justification for expropriation, at least in the minds of Indonesians. The Dutch tried to retain some of their former empire in Indonesia, including West Irian on the island of New Guinea (see Chapter 11), providing a handy target for Sukarno's nationalism and a pretext for nationalization of Dutch assets and the expulsion of tens of thousands of Dutch nationals residing in Indonesia. The loss of foreign expertise combined with the shortage of suitably trained Indonesians added to Indonesia's economic woes. In addition, foreign capital became wary about doing business in what was seen to be a hostile operating environment.

This grim experience influenced the attitudes of Indonesia's early postwar leaders who shared suspicions about globalization and the inordinate influence of advanced capitalist nations over the world economy. Sukarno, the leader of the nationalist movement and founding father of the nation, sought to consolidate control over a sprawling archipelago and transform the Netherlands East Indies into the Republic of Indonesia. Widespread poverty, local insurrections and persistent Dutch meddling complicated his task. Sukarno was an inspirational and charismatic leader with grandiose visions, but he was not an astute administrator or policymaker. He conjured up the idea of Indonesia, but his economic policies did little to advance development or alleviate poverty. His economic nationalism was visceral and he boldly told the US that it could "go to hell" with it's economic aid.

Resource nationalism is common as nations seek to maximize the benefits from their resource endowments. This often pits governments against large multinational companies that exert powerful influence over global markets and have the capital and technology needed by less developed economies seeking to tap the potential of their resources. Around the globe, in the post-World War II era, local leaders sought to rectify what they perceived as unfair arrangements whereby most of the export earnings from resources disproportionately benefited multinationals at the expense of local interests. This resource nationalism carried political consequences. For example, Iranian Prime Minister Mohammad Mossadegh was ousted in 1953 by a CIA-orchestrated coup because he advocated nationalization of a British-owned oil company. His stance sparked fears of a contagion effect in the Middle East harmful to other oil companies. Similarly, Chilean President Salvador Allende threatened multinationals' interests, including a major copper mine, and was killed during a 1973 military coup that enjoyed the backing of the Nixon Administration. The Congo has been victimized by similar foreign intrigues over the decades, leaving it little to show for all of its mineral wealth.

Indonesia, as the most populous nation in Southeast Asia, strategically located astride major shipping lanes between the Indian Ocean and South China Sea, connecting Middle East oil and gas producers with energy-hungry Asia, is also richly endowed with a wide range of natural resources valuable to advanced industrialized nations. As such Indonesia was an important battleground during the Cold War. Sukarno's flirtation with Indonesia's Communist Party, the world's third largest at the time, posed a further threat in the context of the Cold War, and a military coup in 1965 led to his ouster. General Suharto assumed power and installed a team of technocrats mostly trained at the University of California-Berkeley, the so-called "Berkeley Mafia," who implemented various economic reforms at the behest of the International Monetary Fund (IMF) and World Bank from the late 1960s. This marked a dramatic shift away from Sukarno's economic nationalism, integrating Indonesia more closely with the global capitalist economy he distrusted. Doing so opened the spigots of foreign aid loans and investments that contributed to Indonesia's subsequent development and put it firmly in the western camp.

Suharto's version of crony capitalism relied on the skills of ethnic Chinese entrepreneurs resident in Indonesia, who were handsomely rewarded with contracts, kickbacks, monopolies and access to the top. Suharto's family also benefited and his wife, Tien Suharto, was nicknamed Mrs. Ten Percent in reference to the standard rate of contract skimming in this highly centralized system of one-stop influence peddling. Despite these distortions, economic growth was impressive and, owing to a green revolution launched in the 1970s, Indonesia became self-sufficient in rice production.

The government also pursued large-scale import substitution projects in various industries such as steel, cement, shipbuilding and aircraft. The idea was to use resource revenues to establish an industrial base, but these projects were plagued by cost overruns, delays and inefficiency—"white elephants" that never became competitive and relied on government subsidies. While nationalist policies aimed at transforming Indonesia from a resource-dependent nation subject to the vagaries of global commodity markets into an industrialized manufacturing hub were politically appealing, they never proved viable. Japan provided some assistance to these projects to counter anti-Japanese sentiments among Indonesians, who in 1974 greeted the arrival of Prime Minister Kakuei Tanaka with rioting—the so-called Malari Affair—that targeted Japanese-affiliated businesses. The protests were driven in part by nationalist perceptions that Japan dominated the Indonesian economy and was profiting handsomely while contributing little to Indonesia's development. In the aftermath, the Japanese government subsequently unveiled ambitious plans to help Indonesia (and other Association of Southeast Asian Nations (ASEAN) members) industrialize, but these goals were never met.

Developing, resource-rich nations like Indonesia seek to generate growth by pursuing value-added production and improving their deals with international mining and resource extraction firms. In recent years, Indonesian politicians have promoted nationalist policies that appeal to voters, even if the consequences have been mixed. Nonetheless, advocates stress the advantages of promoting domestic industry rather than just selling resources at low prices to foreign firms who produce the final product and make most of the profits. For example, rather than export unprocessed logs, the Indonesian government has required processing of logs for exports as timber, plywood or furniture, building up these industries and generating employment while boosting export revenues. Extensive logging has reduced the size of Indonesia's vast tropical forest over the past few decades, sparking concerns about the environmental and economic impact. As a result, the government has introduced regulations that promote sustainable logging practices and replanting. Of course, with large profits at stake, illegal logging continues and not all companies comply with the new rules, bribing officials to look the other way.

The Indonesian government also seeks to improve production-sharing agreements in the oil and gas sector, meaning Indonesia retaining more of the production from oil and gas fields developed by international firms. As Indonesia's demand for oil has surged with economic development, it has now become a net oil importer and reserves are declining. Problematically, the government's initiative to improve production-sharing arrangements has led to a decrease in exploration activity by international firms because exploration and drilling to locate new reserves is costly and the new arrangements reduce incentives. Indonesia's unexplored oil basins are in relatively hard-to-drill deep waters and extraction requires expensive technologies. Without exploration of Indonesia's considerable hydrocarbon potential, proven reserves may be exhausted by the mid-2020s. The politics of resource nationalism has put the government on a collision course with foreign firms in the oil and gas sector as politicians seek to score points and bolster local interests to attract voters. Balancing investor interests with economic nationalism is tricky, but with output down by half from the mid-1990s and dwindling reserves, combined with a pressing need to attract foreign capital and technology, the government is in a weak bargaining position.

In 2009 the Indonesian government threw down the nationalist gauntlet in the mining sector in a bid to increase local value added in ore exports while also promoting domestic ownership of mining ventures. To force mining firms to build smelters in Indonesia for processing ore, in 2014 the government issued a decree banning exports of unprocessed raw mineral ore in an effort to promote its own smelting capacity and boost value added. Although the government had second thoughts about the wisdom of doing so, politicians blocked changes, mindful that nationalist economic policies have a populist appeal and thus are useful in the theater of politics.

The ban covers nickel, bauxite, tin, gold and some types of coal, but at the last minute copper was exempted under pressure from two mining giants, Freeport and Newmont. But there is little value added in smelting copper and much more in other minerals such as nickel, so there is logic to the exemption for copper. The copper mining firms will pay higher export taxes on the unprocessed copper ore and promise to expand local smelting capacity. Given Indonesia's massive presence as an exporter of various mineral ores, the new restrictions attracted widespread interest and generated a backlash; ore shipments and revenues plummeted.

The new nationalistic measures affecting mining were announced in 2009 amid a commodity boom, but with China's economy slowing down, commodity prices slumped, changing the economics of smelting. Smelters are expensive—in the US$1 billion range—so commodity prices have to be at a certain level to justify the investment. Moreover, the poor commercial prospects of smelting make it hard to negotiate (and service) the loans that typically provide more than half the financing of a smelting project. Weaker commodity prices mean that new local smelters and refineries are not cost-effective; and not all ores are equal: smelting only adds 10% to the value of copper, but adds 80% to the value of nickel. To some extent, customers can shift to other producers, but mining firms are captive since they have large existing investments and need to work with the government. Imposing new regulations on ore exports, however, carries its own costs, as mining firms cut thousands of jobs, and production, to pay for the new smelters that employ relatively few workers. This, along with sagging revenues from mining exports, generates pressure on the government to relax the regulations. Thus, nationalist sentiments and policies enacted to nurture national economic interests can have unintended consequences, especially when battling with powerful multinational firms that are used to getting their way.

India

In 1914, after returning from two decades in South Africa, Mahatma Gandhi became a leading figure in India's nationalist movement, and is remembered for his campaigns of civil disobedience, hunger strikes, economic boycotts and promotion of spinning and weaving. He understood how to pressure British colonial authorities and arouse public opinion through *satyagraha* (passive resistance). He also understood the emotional appeal of self-reliance, promoting homespun cloth as a way to cut British textile imports, undermine colonial power and revenues, and remind people that Indians could regain what had been lost under colonial rule. Only wearing simple dhotis made from homespun cloth woven from homegrown cotton, Gandhi endowed spinning and weaving with a powerful symbolism, and thus bequeathed a legacy of economic nationalism that resonated powerfully in independent India. Indeed, the spinning wheel was an iconic symbol once featured on the Congress Party flag, a potent reminder of the *swadeshi* movement (self-sufficiency) and the aspiration for *swaraj* (self-rule).

Congress was split between Gandhians and industrializers, those who sought to preserve village ways and those who looked to industry and land redistribution in rural areas as the only way to address poverty. Gandhi warned of the perils of industrialization and was dismissive of its potential benefits. In his view, the goal of swaraj was to free India from ensnarement in the imperialist system and the need to emulate the West. The answer to poverty, he argued, was not in following the dictates of western economics, but rather in relying on handiwork, craftsmanship and local industries. He believed in austerity as a lifestyle and saw no compelling reason to imitate western production and consumption excesses, and no redemptive possibilities in industrialization, in some ways foreshadowing contemporary environmentalist concerns. In contrast, Nehru believed that industrialization would promote development, raise living standards and have a transformative impact on social relations and caste.

But translating such plans into effective economic policies was never going to be easy given the grim realities of a cash-strapped government suddenly left to its own devices, with a largely agrarian economy that had been oriented in favor of British economic interests. The government embraced import substitution and tried to build up heavy industries, but with modest success. Swadeshi in this context took on a new form, focusing on industrialization under state direction in a succession of five-year plans. Emerging from two centuries of colonial exploitation and confronting competition with advanced capitalist economies, the policymakers Nehru entrusted acted on their belief that infant industry protection was the only reasonable option.

For the first 17 years following independence in 1947, Jawaharlal Nehru ruled India and promoted economic nationalism and socialist economic policies as he pursued autonomy. India's 1949 constitution, after all, declared India to be a secular, democratic and *socialist* republic. Nehru believed that decolonization was an opportunity to restore dignity to India, and thus the scars of British colonial rule required policies that pulled the nation out of London's orbit and addressed the crushing poverty that prevailed. For nationalist leaders around the world, achieving political independence in the wake of World War II sparked a yearning for economic independence and that meant protecting their economies from foreign capital. Nehru was also mindful that colonial rule had saddled independent India with an underproductive agricultural sector, a weak industrial base, and extremely low levels of literacy (27% for men, 9% for women). Endemic poverty and lack of human resources hampered efforts to achieve economic autonomy and improve living conditions. One of the institutional legacies of British rule was a relatively well–developed civil service, a source of technical expertise that Nehru entrusted with economic policymaking.

Planned industrialization was not the only option for newly independent India and Congress was not committed to any cohesive economic strategy. In the late 1940s India was the world's tenth largest manufacturing economy, so there was a foundation to build on. But the nationalist movement had focused on gaining political power rather than practical means to generate wealth, and its leaders were more concerned with poverty, the specter of famine and yawning disparities. But economic deprivation would not fade on its own and the model of western industrialization appealed to Indian leaders precisely because it had delivered prosperity and power. This was a time when development economics promised to distill the lessons of the western trajectory of progress and offer a universal set of policy lessons that could help developing nations achieve "take-off." There was also a palpable suspicion that an open, internationalized Indian economy would be prey to the more powerful trading nations.

The emphasis was on "mother" industries like steel that were deemed crucial for nurturing other industries and Indian military capacity. This meant, in practice, neglecting development of light or consumer-oriented industries. India's industrial future and economic independence would be based on heavy industry under state ownership, to ensure redistribution of benefits and national security. The emphasis on heavy industrial development under five-year plans suggests that Nehru was rolling out the Soviet model in India, but Nehru's main goal was economic independence. He was taken with the idea of heavy industry and import substitution and, in the midst of the Cold War, found generous support from the Soviet Union. He was influenced by Marxist analysis of the fundamentals of the colonial relationship, but was more Keynesian in terms of his view on the state's role in a mixed economy of public and private enterprise, mitigating the impact of business cycles with countercyclical spending and promoting redistribution. Given constitutional constraints on agricultural taxes, the industrial sector had to be the main source of revenues for redistribution.

Democracy, economic development and redistribution were seen to be mutually supportive, but in practice Congress relied on rural vote banks mobilized by those who stood to lose most from land redistribution, a necessary reform to address poverty. It was this electoral dependence that curbed land redistribution throughout most of India and ensured that poverty would remain entrenched whatever happened in the industrial sector. This was the great dilemma Nehru faced: democracy slowed reform and development, but development without democracy was anathema in Nehru's scheme of things. Nehru turned to technocrats to help make his modern vision come to fruition, establishing the powerful Planning Commission, lumbering along until Modi dismantled it in 2014, to oversee bureaucratic efforts and institutionalize rational planning. This removed economic development policymaking from the purview of parliament and fractious public debate, concentrating powers in a technocratic elite who shared Nehru's social democratic ideals, market skepticism, economic nationalism and preference for extensive state planning. The Planning Commission, however, proved a failure because it could not deliver on the promised social and economic revolution, a failure Gunnar Myrdal's *Asian Drama* (1968) attributed to institutional obstacles and inadequate social reforms.

Nehru bequeathed an unrealized vision to his daughter and successor Indira Gandhi, and, even if his inclinations remained influential, from the 1970s economic policymaking was no longer the preserve of a benevolent nationalist elite in tandem with technocrats. The politicization of economic policies intruded, driven by electoral considerations more than development imperatives. Nehru presided over the creation of a modern state but was unable to translate this into his vision of economic development where the fruits of growth would be widely shared. Basically, he wanted the state to serve as a vehicle of political and economic transformation, reconstituting India and putting it on the trajectory of what he took as universal historical progress. His audacious dreams, however, went unrealized.

Nehru was the first leader of Congress, the party that ruled India without interruption from 1947 to 1977. Indira Gandhi succeeded him and ruled until losing elections that saw voters repudiating her suspension of democracy during The Emergency (1975–1977). She regained power in the 1980 elections and remained in power until her assassination in 1984. So in the initial three decades Indian economic policy was heavily influenced by Nehru's socialist inclinations. Rajiv Gandhi succeeded his mother in 1984 and introduced market-oriented reforms that have gained increased momentum since the 1990s and have a strong advocate in Prime Minister Narendra Modi (2014–).

The Nehru vision was largely abandoned with the economic crisis of 1991. There are various factors that contributed to this acute fiscal crisis, including sharp increases in military spending that followed wars with China and Pakistan. Moreover, the democratization of economic policymaking and the temptations of attracting voters with various subsidies and social programs aimed at poverty alleviation put rising demands on the budget, while tax revenues failed to keep pace. The problems snowballed from the mid-1960s when India faced the bleak consequences of two successive failed monsoons. The IMF and World Bank provided emergency aid on the condition that India devaluate the rupee, reinforcing a sense that the international system was rigged against developing nations. Indira Gandhi, who became premier in 1966 amid the crisis and endured the humiliating terms dictated by the international financial institutions, resented India's vulnerability to external pressures. This experience reinforced her view that the World Bank and

IMF were less interested in promoting development than in promoting US global interests. She also became more convinced that protectionist policies were crucial to protect Indian interests and that the state should do more to boost development and alleviate poverty, an economic policy that was principally aimed at building political support.

Under Indira Gandhi, Congress wooed rural voters and regional parties with various subsidies and other carrots, providing electricity, fuel, fertilizer, water and loans at subsidized rates, meaning the state treasury was picking up the tab. But no new taxes were imposed. State coffers also confronted the demands of unionized public sector workers, the need to keep loss-making state enterprises running, and pressures from small enterprises and traders for various concessions and protection. On top of this, Gandhi abandoned her father's austerity and caution by nationalizing banking, coal, insurance and even textile companies teetering at the edge of insolvency. All of this bloated the public sector and helped precipitate fiscal crisis. At the same time, protecting national sovereignty meant keeping foreign investment at bay. Ironically, Gandhi's populist socialism raised expectations that she could not meet, generating a political backlash that led her to declare The Emergency and suspend democracy. But authoritarian politics did not enable her to rescue economic policymaking from the politicization she had overseen, or growing fiscal imbalances.

Unlike many other newly independent nations, India managed to avoid bouts of hyperinflation and did not accumulate massive foreign debts, but the new demands placed on the treasury by Gandhi's grandiose expansion of the public sector and role of the government in the economy represented a time bomb that finally exploded in the 1990s. Meanwhile, the economy kept growing at a steady but lackluster pace, averaging about 3.5% from the 1950s to the 1980s, which has been disparagingly termed the Hindu rate of growth. However, this growth rate had less to do with religious fatalism or cultural inclinations than with a nationalist economic program of protectionist policies and the "license Raj," a reference to excessive regulations that stifled entrepreneurship and institutionalized red tape and bribery. This practice extends from petty clerks to government ministers, who have the power to ignore, frustrate or accommodate because regulations and discretionary authority enable them to do so. Fundamental suspicions of capitalist market-oriented policies, combined with concerns about promoting welfare and curtailing inequalities, nurtured an anti-business environment. Population increases meant that lackluster growth translated into average annual per capita income increases of 1.3%. Villages remained poor and isolated due to an inadequate infrastructure, and few rural households enjoyed access to education or electricity, living in feudal circumstances where local leaders dominated. Too little has changed or improved, even now.

Unlike authoritarian China, India was democratic, meaning that its policies were a product of compromise and thus more gradualist because wrenching change is disruptive and often unpopular with voters. India's economic policies were underwhelming, but less devastating for the people compared to Mao's disastrous experiments discussed below. Subsequently, China swerved to market-oriented reforms from the late 1970s under Deng Xiaoping that have unleashed China's massive economic potential, while India's incremental liberalization commenced in the 1990s. In 1991, facing a balance of payments crisis that led to another IMF bailout, the government enacted sweeping reforms and liberalization measures that reversed substantially the regime of economic nationalism and populist socialism that had prevailed since independence. This involved dismantling import controls, lowering customs duties, currency devaluation, abolishing regulations on private investment, lowering tax rates, and privatization of state enterprises. In contrast to China, where reforms boosted the manufacturing sector, India's reforms produced a surge in the services sector. The overall share of manufacturing in the Indian gross domestic product (GDP) has languished at about 16%, helping to explain why India's 1.4% share of world trade lags behind China's 15% share. The surge in services has made some Indian firms global IT brands, but they have not generated enough jobs for the growing number of job seekers, while foreign investors remain wary of India's regulatory regime, corruption and infrastructure bottlenecks.

There is also the legacy of the Bhopal disaster to contend with. In 1984 a Union Carbide pesticide plant leaked toxic gas that killed about 4,000 people, permanently disabled a similar number and injured some 500,000 others. The cause of the accident is a source of controversy, with Union Carbide contending it was an act of sabotage, while in the court of public opinion and in the Indian courts the company is guilty of negligence. The company agreed to a $470 million settlement to resolve all claims for compensation. In addition, several Indian executives were found guilty of negligence and imprisoned, while the American chief executive officer of the company was charged with manslaughter and declared a fugitive from justice for failing to appear in court. Bhopal has become shorthand for corporate negligence and reckless practices by foreign firms operating in India, while for multinationals it is a cautionary tale of political risk in a nation where nationalist sentiments leave the public predisposed to believe the worst. It is a major reason why India has a strict liability law in the nuclear industry that makes producers accountable for accidents, not just the plant operator, as is standard elsewhere. This law has been a major impediment to building more nuclear plants in India, as most reactor producers, excluding Russia, shy away from what is one of the most promising nuclear energy markets in the world.

India's economic liberalization measures since the 1990s also remain a source of controversy as questions persist about how inclusive they have been. Skeptics point out that the fruits of growth have not been widely shared, pointing to widening income disparities. They liken the reform measures to a Ponzi scheme, arguing that the IMF-driven, Washington consensus on economic policy is not addressing the pressing needs of India's poor, where 68% of people get by on less than $2 a day (Goswami 2013). The tens of thousands of suicides amongst farmers in recent years, often overwhelmed by heavy debts, suggest the scale of the misery unaddressed by reforms. Privatization is portrayed as handouts to the wealthy as state assets are sold at low prices to well-connected business groups. High growth in the 2000s is attributed to favorable global economic conditions rather than domestic policy changes. Moreover, GDP growth has not led to the spread of better jobs, as employment

Figure 4.2 Indian Activists Condemn Rich Countries' Fleecing of the Poor to Maintain Affluent Lifestyles. Photo © Jeff Kingston.

remains concentrated in low-paid, low-productivity informal sectors. Despite cheap wages and government subsidies and tax breaks, India's exports have also fallen because Indian manufacturing is not competitive, and India's current account deficit has widened as a percentage of GDP over the past two decades of reform. Moreover, poverty has not declined appreciably despite higher GDP growth. A small, well-educated white-collar workforce has benefited from rising salaries, but on the underside of India's dual economy, wages and productivity in agriculture and the informal sector have been relatively stagnant. In contrast, wages in China's booming manufacturing sector have grown by 12% since 2000, compared with 2.5% in India.

India's reforms are credited with accentuating disparities. India's 100 wealthiest people boast a combined net worth of $300 billion, a quarter of the country's GDP (Mishra 2013). As Mishra argues,

> corruption scandals involving the sale of billions of dollars' worth of national resources such as mines, forests, land, water, and telecom spectrums reveal that crony capitalism and rent-seeking, rather than entrepreneurial dynamism and innovation in a free market, are the real engines of India's economic growth.

Rather than pro-market, he argues that India's economy is more of a pro-business rigged market of collusion. And all at enormous environmental cost, as New Delhi has far worse smog levels than Beijing, rivers throughout the nation are choked with pollution, forests are disappearing, and massive mining ventures displace villagers and devastate their habitat. This imbalanced growth and the lack of a social infrastructure are disruptive to many, while the benefits are enjoyed by very few. Comparing Asia's giants, China's economic miracle is lauded for catapulting one-quarter of its population into the middle class, but no such claims are made about India.

The green revolution in the 1970s meant that India became self-sufficient in food, an important achievement in a country with far too much experience of famine. Food self-sufficiency may have nurtured a sense of security, but it did not translate into significant improvements in farming households' welfare. The absence of land redistribution ensured that most farmers were born and died in penury and reared children with similar prospects. The situation remains dire in contemporary rural India, where in recent years there has been a rash of suicides concentrated among small-holders raising cash crops, who easily fall into debt and do not have the resources to weather fluctuations in global markets (Kennedy and King 2014). They are prey to moneylenders and as pressures and harassment for repayment mount, for many, death is the only escape. Even now, over 800 million Indians, some 70% of the entire population, live in rural areas, so problems besetting the agricultural sector are a crucial issue. While urban India has enjoyed impressive growth in the 21st century, this has not spread to rural areas. The scaling back of government support for farmers and economic liberalization have sparked an agrarian crisis, especially among small-holders engaged in cash crop production on plots of less than 1 hectare. Periodic droughts spell doom and desperation as farmers become ensnared in a vicious cycle of debt from which many are unable to escape, one bad harvest away from ruin, making it difficult to provide for their families. Suicide rates among farmers were 47% higher than the national average in 2011, averaging nearly 17,000 a year since 2001, and have risen from levels in the 1990s. As Sunil Khilnani (2003, 11) concludes: "Economic possibilities have indeed rapidly changed for many Indians, yet the majority still find themselves waiting, some expectantly, most with no hope at all."

Prime Minister Modi was elected in 2014, promising to revive growth, and pledging to further streamline regulations, accelerate privatization, ramp up modernization of infrastructure, rationalize government subsidies and attract foreign investment. Proponents argue that unleashing the "animal spirits" of industry will raise growth, generate jobs and boost average living standards. Expectations for Modinomics are exuberant, based on what he achieved in the state of Gujarat where he served as chief minister (2001–2014). But does his record justify the hype? The *Guardian* thinks not, pointing out that per capita income growth was not quite as spectacular as Modi's supporters assert (*Guardian*, March 13, 2014). It is also evident that the gains of growth were unevenly distributed, as inequality became higher than the national average.

Early signs suggest that Modinomics will embrace a more nationalist economic agenda than betokened by his market-friendly reputation. Modi opposes opening India's retailing sector to international firms, preferring to protect small local shops from global competition. In 2014 Modi faced off with the World Trade Organization, only agreeing to sign a landmark Trade Facilitation Agreement (TFA) after India was given permission to continue food stockpiling. This program is criticized as a food subsidy that contravenes the new trading regime, but Indians maintain this is a food security program for the poor. Modi took considerable criticism for nearly scuttling the TFA, but in sticking to his guns he emerged as a resolute leader on the world stage able to effectively secure national interests.

Modi's nationalist agenda is also evident in boosting the defense budget by 12% to $38 billion in 2014, and approving weapons purchases worth $45 billion in his first year in office. Despite pledging to "Buy Indian," however, in 2015 Modi opted to buy 36 "ready to fly" French-made fighter jets for $7 billion to speed up delivery, ensure reliability and lower costs, highlighting the problems plaguing the local aerospace industry. India is the world's largest arms importer and the government hopes to nurture domestic manufacturing, but understands this is a formidable long-term challenge. Modi's move to buy French reflects his alarm at the pace of China's military modernization and urgent need to upgrade India's defense capabilities to counter Pakistan. He has also eased foreign investment restrictions in the domestic weapons industry to lure increased foreign investment, raising the ceiling from 26% ownership to 49%, in the hope of promoting technology transfer. Overall, it appears that bolstering national defense has trumped boosting national champions due to pragmatic considerations.

Modi is also eager to spur foreign participation in nuclear power plant deals in order to address growing energy shortages. A strict liability law enacted in 2010 that requires suppliers to pay compensation for accidents has deterred investment by major global nuclear power suppliers who insist that the onus should be on plant operators. The Modi government proposed an insurance scheme that would indemnify nuclear suppliers against liability, striking a balance between nationalistic concerns about irresponsible multinationals, stemming from the Bhopal tragedy, and the expectations of international business.

China

China has been the world's fastest growing economy over the past three decades. Chinese exulted when their economy overtook Japan's to become the world's second largest in 2010, and feel a strong sense of pride in projections that suggest it will overtake the US as the world's largest economy by 2030. Using another measure of GDP, based on purchasing power parity, the IMF estimates that China has already overtaken the US. Of course realities on the ground in China provide a sobering counterpoint to such Sino-phoria.

Whatever the global ranking, this unprecedented growth trajectory has lifted some 300 million of China's 1.3 billion population into the middle class, and unleashed a torrent of migration from inland areas to urban centers. China has become the workshop of the world, producing and assembling products at cheap prices that are available everywhere. The costs of rapid development are evident in the smog that enshrouds China's cities, the pollution of waterways, traffic congestion, and growing disparities. Corruption has become a national epidemic and, along with land grabs by the well connected, a source of political unrest that indicts the Chinese Communist Party. The CCP has abandoned its founding ideology, but has retained power and legitimacy because it has delivered on economic growth and can rely on extensive powers of repression.

China's meteoric rise is a source of great national pride and widespread global admiration. It is also vindication of the bold economic experiments enacted in the late 1970s under Deng Xiaoping. While its success is held up as a model for emulation in India, Africa and elsewhere in the developing world, China's increasing economic power also poses a threat as it builds up its military power and diplomatic influence. As of 2015, China is the largest holder of US Treasury bonds, and runs a massive trade surplus with the US, generating a sense of vulnerability in Washington. The US sees Asia as crucial to its interests, but is concerned about China's aspirations to modify the status quo in its favor. The clash of interests between the US and China and the ongoing geopolitical power shift in China's favor in Asia generate tensions beyond the bilateral relationship. In Asia, China's economic rise has made it more assertive in dealing with neighbors, most prominently sparking tensions with Japan and Southeast Asian nations over unresolved historical grievances and disputed territories in the East China and South China Seas. These tensions cast a cloud over economic prospects and trigger worries about how to cope with the surge in Chinese nationalism. To allay such fears and to gain influence, Beijing has spread massive loans and investments around the region.

Before Deng's reforms, China was an economic basket case. Mao Zedong led the communists to victory and established the People's Republic in 1949, taking over a war-devastated nation. There was no heavy industry, very little manufacturing capacity, no capital and scarce expertise. The challenges were gargantuan for an impoverished nation subject to isolation by the US bloc and dependent on the Soviet Union for technology and equipment. Domestic "capitalists" were squeezed with fines, exploited for what they could contribute and inevitably denounced and eliminated. The communists centralized all economic policymaking under a succession of five-year plans that were based more on wishful thinking than rational policies and plausible targets. Land reform was accomplished in two years, eliminating landlords and redistributing their holdings. In practice, anyone not desperately poor and landless could be denounced as a counter-revolutionary and stripped of any property. Neglect of the nation's transport system further slowed economic development.

In 1958, Mao launched the Great Leap Forward, aimed at reorganizing agricultural collectives into communes subject to strict party discipline. Ambitious targets were established and party cadres competed to exceed their quotas, all at the expense of the peasantry. The government also urged citizens to establish backyard furnaces to boost steel production and help the nation become an industrial giant. Not surprisingly, the Great Leap Forward was a monumental catastrophe, and caused the Great Famine, which claimed an estimated 45 million lives between 1958 and 1960 (see Chapter 7).

Following that upheaval, there was a brief interlude of stability, but in 1966 Mao unleashed the Cultural Revolution, mandating destruction of the "Four Olds" (old thoughts, culture, customs and habits). The closing of universities, persecution of intellectuals, and practice of sending Red Guards to the countryside so they could develop their revolutionary fervor and expose counter-revolutionaries, generated a maelstrom of violence and anarchy detrimental to economic development. Mao was more concerned with his enemies, real and imagined, and purifying the nation through revolutionary zeal than with promoting economic growth.

Mao favored typical nationalistic economic policies such as import substitution, and promoted self-reliance through bizarre initiatives such as the backyard steel furnaces. But throughout the Great Famine, China was sending grain to other communist nations, a gesture of solidarity at a time when Chinese peasants were dying by the millions. He created an economic system that was based on mountains of imaginary statistics, because nobody wanted to acknowledge the grim reality and risk being held responsible for thwarting the revolution. The state-owned enterprises established during this era served not only as industrial units, but also as social agencies responsible for workers and their families. Workers obtained housing, daycare, health care and education from their work units, and the security of stable employment, a system known as the "iron rice bowl." Certainly China's economy under Mao developed considerably between 1949 and 1976, but this was often despite his policies and owed much to relatively efficient central planning. It is revealing that there is nobody left trying to defend Mao's economic policies as the nation lurched from one Mao-made crisis to the next, part of his continuous revolution that prioritized retaining power above all else.

Mao's excesses underscored the virtues of pragmatism. Deng Xiaoping, a victim of Mao's erratic governance, made a political comeback after Mao's death in 1976. He is known for quipping, perhaps apocryphally, "Who cares if a cat is black or white, as long as it catches mice." The message was that pursuing economic growth was the priority and thus ideological inflexibility was no longer tenable. He promoted a series of reforms and policy experiments designed to help the nation recover from Mao's nightmares and the devastation they had inflicted. Rather than ideology, Deng relied on what worked and increasingly this meant introducing capitalist reforms, combining central planning with market-oriented reforms, boosting exports, and seeking investments and technology from overseas. The goal was to improve the welfare of Chinese citizens and thereby regain legitimacy for the CCP.

The key aspect of Deng's revolution was that he created special economic zones in coastal areas where regulations were pared back, policy experiments were launched and risk-taking and mistakes were seen as part of the learning curve. Resource allocation and pricing were increasingly left to market forces, and local entrepreneurs suddenly found space to operate without worrying that success would be held against them, as in the Mao era. China's special economic zones focused on labor-intensive manufacturing and assembly geared towards export markets. The state then took what worked and disseminated the policies and ideas that transformed China into an economic powerhouse. Deng also unleashed the agricultural sector, breaking up rural communes and allowing farmers to sell surplus production and retain profits. This fueled dramatic production increases and boosted rural incomes.

China's opening under Deng was a recognition that China could not develop on its own. Deng knew that for China to become stronger it would have to rely on its former enemies and adopt their ways. After normalizing relations with Japan with the 1978 Treaty of Peace and Friendship, China became the largest recipient of Japanese foreign aid, involving over $30 billion in loans, grants and technological training between 1979 and 2007. These government programs also facilitated private sector investments, helping make Japan China's largest investor, setting up low-cost offshore production facilities. This massive infusion of Japanese financing and knowhow played a critical role in China's development, one that is rarely given the credit it's due. Officially China renounced any claims to war-related reparations, but unofficially, the massive aid program served as war redress. Much of the influx focused on developing China's infrastructure, a cardinal principle in Japanese development philosophy.

China's growing economy has spurred a degree of nationalistic hubris and leverage. The government also encourages consumer boycotts that arise from international disputes, usually targeting Japan, but also France in 2008 in reprisal for the Olympic torch relay protests; Carrefour retail operations in China suffered dramatically at that time. The government also encouraged a series of boycotts targeting Japan in 2005, 2010 and 2012, knowing that this hurts the Japanese economy and induces business leaders in Tokyo to pressure the government to moderate its stance. But this hardball strategy is risky, triggering a sharp drop in Japanese foreign direct investment since 2014 and stoking anti-Chinese attitudes among Japanese. The Chinese government orchestrates anti-Japanese nationalist sentiments to gain diplomatic leverage, pressing for concessions to appease the public anger that it has sown and fanned. But, in playing this game so often, Beijing has poisoned popular sentiments. The government can quell demonstrations or turn boycotts on and off at its discretion, but grassroots anger and resentment linger. In this febrile atmosphere, it doesn't take much to ignite nationalist passions.

Crisis and Economic Nationalism

In 1997–1998 a financial typhoon swept through Asian economies. The crisis began in Thailand and spread through the region, with Indonesia and South Korea also suffering severe consequences. The value of the Thai baht collapsed after the government no longer had sufficient foreign currency reserves to maintain the stable US dollar peg. This was a debt-driven crisis as overleveraged private companies, many in real estate, borrowed heavily overseas, sparking a run on national currencies as market confidence ebbed and speculators saw opportunities. The crisis also hit regional stock and land prices and sparked fears of a global contagion.

Exactly what triggered the panic remains a matter of controversy, but at the time many Japanese banks refused to rollover their loans to regional borrowers due to ongoing domestic economic problems and reports of massive bad loans that plagued the entire Japanese banking sector throughout the 1990s. Clearly, regulatory authorities in the affected economies had not monitored the risk of surging short-term borrowings denominated in foreign currencies used for long-term projects and speculation in real estate. Asian economies at the time were attracting huge capital inflows because of annual GDP growth rates ranging from 8 to 14% and seemingly good prospects. This inflow of investments and loans pumped up asset bubbles, but it was "hot money" in search of a quick profit, and external developments triggered rapid outflows. Rising US interest rates from the early 1990s boosted the value of the US dollar and thus the value of many regional currencies since governments pegged their currencies to the dollar. This made Asian exports more expensive and less competitive, while capital flows shifted to the US, attracted by higher interest rates and political stability. These developments led to worsening current accounts that eventually unnerved foreign investors and banks, leading to a credit crunch. The sudden panic of investors trying to cash out drove currencies downward, forcing central banks in the region to raise interest rates in a bid to diminish capital flight. This strategy did not work as foreign exchange reserves plummeted and local businesses could not afford to borrow at the higher interest rates, exacerbating the credit crunch. The sharp devaluation of the Thai baht, Indonesian rupiah and South Korean won also meant that servicing debts denominated in US dollars or Japanese yen became more onerous for borrowers in these countries, causing a cascade of defaults and bankruptcies that further undermined business confidence. As currencies imploded, prices exploded, sparking inflation and rioting by many who could no longer afford daily essentials.

The IMF mandated fiscal austerity as a price of bailouts and a cure for the crisis, actually making circumstances worse as governments cut spending and subsidies, contributing to the downward spiral. Protesters around the region carried placards denouncing the IMF measures, an abbreviation that came to stand for "I'M Fired." In Indonesia, GDP declined by 13.5% in 1998, a crucial factor contributing to the finale of the New Order and President Suharto's departure from office after three decades in power. While most Indonesians welcomed his ouster at the time, the role of international financial institutions in toppling a dictator that they had long propped up, precisely because his technocrats had heeded advice on economic policy, did touch a nationalistic nerve. Reports of massive illicit wealth stashed in overseas accounts by Suharto's family and cronies also implied a degree of international collusion and led some to call for repudiating Indonesia's large public debts. Surely, the argument went, the lenders had known that the money borrowed would be skimmed and squandered so why should Indonesian taxpayers be forced to repay reckless lenders?

The crisis led to suspicions that international financiers and speculators deliberately sparked the crisis for their own benefit. Malaysian Prime Minister Mohammed Mahathir, for example, accused George Soros and Jewish bankers of profiting from the region's woes. Iconic pictures of the IMF President Michael Camdessus towering like a colonial overlord over President Suharto and dictating harsh terms in exchange for rescue packages clarified power relations for those predisposed to suspect the worst of globalization, and anti-western sentiments spread throughout the region.

Japan's Finance Minister Kiichi Miyazawa proposed an Asian Monetary Fund, implicitly criticizing the IMF's insistence on one-size-fits-all austerity and structural adjustment packages that pushed many companies and individuals into insolvency. Miyazawa called for providing credit and currency swaps aimed at reducing volatility and vulnerabilities. This proposal was dismissed peremptorily by the IMF and drew strong criticism in the western financial press at the time, but subsequent developments have vindicated the wisdom of the proposed arrangements. President Bill Clinton has acknowledged this as one of his administration's major policy blunders. In 2010, China, Japan and South Korea in cooperation with the Association of Southeast Asian nations launched the Chiang Mai Initiative designed to insulate the region from financial volatility by managing short-term liquidity problems through a multilateral currency swap mechanism worth $240 billion as of 2012. This is what Miyazawa had in mind.

The economic impact of the 1997–1998 crisis on Japan was significant, as 40% of Japan's total exports went to Asia and its banks had significant exposure; GDP growth declined from 5% to 1.6% in 1997 and contracted in 1998, although this was prompted more by a hike in the consumption tax and fiscal austerity rather than the "Asian flu." China was relatively insulated from the crisis although growth slowed sharply in 1998 and 1999. China's currency, the renminbi, was also pegged to the US dollar, but it was not convertible. In contrast to capital inflows to Southeast Asia, foreign capital in China was concentrated in factories, limiting possibilities of capital flight. But the lessons of the crisis were not lost on Chinese policymakers who felt vindicated in retaining a mix of central planning and market-oriented reforms, and remaining wary of globalized financial markets.

South Korea was hit harder by the crisis than Japan, but it is credited with adopting countermeasures more quickly, as Japan, Inc. adopted slow-motion reforms. South Korea saw its currency fall by one-third, while its 1997–1998 GDP contracted by a staggering 34.2%. South Korea's US dollar GDP per capita declined by 18.5%, compared to a massive 42.3% in Indonesia. Not wanting to let a crisis go to waste, the South Korean government and corporations enacted sweeping reforms, promoting improved corporate governance and cracking down on corruption. Companies also adopted structural reforms, shedding staff, boosting non-regular employment and lobbying government to weaken labor protections. The crisis also caused numerous bankruptcies, 25 chaebols in one year alone, and consolidation, as heavily indebted corporations foundered, including carmaker KIA and Daewoo, a chaebol that enjoyed strong government backing during the Park era and had been a global leader in shipbuilding. But the stronger chaebols weathered the storm and still dominate the economy and retain extensive political and media influence.

Under the circumstances, and given the nationalistic backlash among ordinary Koreans feeling the painful adjustments, it is remarkable that the Korean government embraced further liberalization of the economy, and continued to reduce tariffs and dismantle trade barriers while signing Free Trade Agreements (FTAs) with leading trading partners such as the US and the European Union. However, one can still sense a high degree of economic nationalism among Koreans and two favored targets are Japan and the US. Korea is not alone in invoking food safety in the service of imposing import restrictions. Given the importance of beef in the Korean diet, it is not surprising that consumers are especially sensitive to any reports raising alarms about beef imports. Washington pressured Seoul to relax a ban imposed on imported beef from the US that began in 2003 due to a case of mad cow disease, but imports did not resume until 2008. The US beef industry complained that the import ban was an overreaction and an unjustified protectionist measure aimed at protecting Korean beef producers. Despite protests, the ban was lifted and as of 2010 South Korea became the third largest importer of US beef.

Repercussions of the Lehman Shock

The next global economic crisis started in Wall Street in 2007 and spread to the rest of the world. It started off as a panic instigated by a collapse in the value of derivatives linked to sub-prime mortgages and inadequate risk assessment, driving some major global financial institutions to the edge of the abyss, and the venerable investment bank Lehman Brothers into insolvency. But this crisis was not restricted to financial markets and morphed into a global systemic crisis that saw sharp declines in trade that hit exporting economies like those in Asia very hard. The credit crunch and loss of confidence meant shrinking consumer demand, fewer orders and higher unemployment, a vicious downward spiral that sideswiped Asian economies where it was initially assumed there would be limited contagion effect because exposure to the hybrid financial products that sparked the crisis was relatively limited.

The crisis stoked nationalistic resentment throughout Asia that "cowboys" on Wall Street could bring the global economy to its knees. This crisis reinforced skepticism about the wisdom of unfettered markets and also triggered accusations of hypocrisy as Washington bailed out troubled firms. Naturally, schadenfreude (German for taking joy in others' misfortunes) was a particularly powerful sentiment throughout Asia since Washington had long been lecturing about the need for market-friendly policy reforms, touting deregulation as the tonic of growth and prosperity. It seemed that state intervention in markets is undesirable and counterproductive except when it isn't. And, it was not lost on Asians that Washington resorted to massive fiscal stimulus and expansionary monetary policy to prop up the economy, disregarding the austerity prescription Asians were dispensed a decade earlier.

Thus a succession of global economic crises in 1987, 1997 and 2007 has heightened wariness about the wisdom of embracing market fundamentalism and reducing the state role in the economy, the so-called Washington Consensus. Before the 2007 global economic crisis and meltdown of large international financial institutions, the US, World Bank and IMF promoted a set of neo-liberal policy prescriptions embracing a market-based approach to development that depends on privatization, reining in the role of government and labor unions, eliminating trade barriers, welcoming foreign direct investment, ending subsidies, cuts in government spending and social programs, and allocating resources according to efficiency and productivity. But unleashing intensified competition carries ominous implications. As Thomas Friedman, the *New York Times* columnist, explains, "if you are a little too slow or too costly ... you will be left as roadkill before you know what hit you" (quoted in Mishra 2013).

The World Bank and IMF now disavow the standard package of reforms they once assertively imposed. The failures of the Washington Consensus have spurred criticism of globalization and accusations that the First World has been imposing terms and setting rules that are advantageous to advanced countries and harmful to developing nations, sparking a nationalistic backlash. In countries like India and Indonesia, poverty remains staggering and endemic, with all the grim consequences that entails, raising questions about who actually benefits from globalization. Market-opening measures are seen as a mechanism that nurtures a small indigenous elite that benefit disproportionately from the reforms and serve as influential advocates of globalization despite the evident risks and harm to their economies. Market fundamentalism also can't explain the success of Asian economies that have systematically violated these precepts while recording tremendous growth. There have been significant political consequences of this growth as increasingly affluent citizens across Asia seek a greater say in government, nurturing democratic aspirations, which we discuss in the next chapter.

5

Democracy and Nationalism

In this chapter we look at democracy and democratization and how this influences contemporary nationalism and identity politics in China, Japan, India, Indonesia and South Korea.

Democracies seemingly lurch from crisis to crisis, but manage to survive by showing a great capacity for adaptability and piecemeal, incremental changes that accomplish just enough to sustain the system as it hurtles to the next crisis. Yet for all of the problems and risks inherent in democracy, it remains, as Winston Churchill famously suggested, the least bad option. Democracy represents an audacious political experiment that has repeatedly defied the doomsayers, its spread and survival marking an impressive achievement. The semi-permanent state of crisis that bedevils democracy is one of its strengths because it thus requires ever renewed commitments and compromises that are based on the assumption that democracy always survives, the so-called confidence trap (Runciman 2013).

Democracy is usually seen as the system that best promotes individual liberty, tolerance and social pluralism, but this is not necessarily so. There are longstanding doubts about the wavering and equivocal relationship between democracy and liberal values. Democratic governments that are complicit in violence against religious and ethnic minorities, allow intimidation of the press and intolerance to flourish, impede transparency, or accommodate endemic corruption, violate liberal values. But each democracy strikes its own balance between a government with strong powers and individual liberties, a source of dynamic tension that also generates considerable risk. Hence democracies can be quite illiberal even if they involve regular elections, open competition for power and a free press. Rule by an elected majority does not in itself exclude the possibility that liberal values and personal freedoms will be violated or denied. It is precisely the ambivalent relationship

Nationalism in Asia: A History Since 1945, First Edition. Jeff Kingston.

between majority rule and liberal norms and values that spurs nations to develop rules that protect rights and freedoms of speech, assembly, media and minorities. The tyranny of the majority is an ever- present danger of democracy and is the reason why liberal democracies have developed various safeguards, such as constitutional constraints on the state, checks and balances to guard against excessive concentration of power, and electoral rules that facilitate democratic transitions. But such legal restraints are no guarantee against government infringement on the entrenched rights of minorities and individuals. There is also a risk that democracy is reduced to perfunctory, formal exercise of electoral democracy without promoting civil liberties or greater accountability of the state and those who govern. Campaigns and tallying votes represent an important barometer of democracy, but don't necessarily translate into good governance. If the expectations raised by elections are not met, or voters feel their voices are not heard, there is also a risk that democratic norms and values can be subverted by cynicism, neglect and apathy. This risk is heightened to the extent that governments privilege religious or cultural values over the principle of freedom.

In democracies, nationalism is frequently invoked and manipulated by politicians to boost their broader agendas. Nationalist symbols, rhetoric and gestures are a powerful way for candidates to connect with the masses and to generate electoral support. Nationalism appeals to something primordial, a shared sense of loyalty,

Figure 5.1 Indian Activists Seek to End Corruption because It Undermines Democracy Throughout Asia. Photo © Jeff Kingston.

community and nativistic feelings that trump careful analysis of policy options. While the ins-and-outs of tax or administrative reform might be quite important, these are difficult to communicate about in the sound-bite world of political campaigns. It is much easier to stage-manage patriotic campaigns drawing on national history, culture and trauma. There is a risk that in playing the nationalist card politicians are tempted to use one-upmanship, stoking emotions with more radical stances. This can be directed domestically at non-majority groups and/or internationally, usually involving disputed borders and overlapping territorial claims. The danger is that nationalistic rhetoric can light grassroots fires that rage out of control and constrain political leaders' options, making sensible compromise and conciliatory gestures more difficult. In this way democracy incentivizes politicians to grandstand on nationalist issues that carry dangerous implications for minorities and foreign policy.

Democracy is one of many influences on, and sources of, nationalism in contemporary Asia. Much is at stake in shaping the national historical narrative because it gets to the core of how a nation sees itself and how it seeks to project itself. Nationalism is much more than the layered stories that a society tells itself about who we are as a people and nation, but these stories are key foundations of nationalist consciousness and as such contested because they can lend legitimacy and confer power on those who can control the story. Who are the heroes and villains? What were/are the achievements and successes and, perhaps more importantly, what were/are the failures and shortcomings? What aspects of the past are invoked in the present and how are events connected, with what implications? What is marginalized or erased from the national narrative? And, what are the talismanic symbols of a nation and key characteristics of national identity? These questions help define the political stage on which nationalism is contested, orchestrated and projected.

Democracy and Asian Values

"Democracy in India," B.R. Ambedkar famously warned, "is only a top dressing on an Indian soil, which is essentially undemocratic."

Ambedkar's concerns about the undemocratic nature of India resonate across Asia, but perhaps not in precisely the way he intended. Ambedkar (1891–1956), a prominent leader of low-caste Hindus (the Untouchables or dalits), played a key role in drafting India's 1949 Constitution that laid out the ground rules for a secular, inclusive democracy. His warning was intended to promote a deepening of democracy because he strongly believed that it was the only option for such a diverse, sprawling continent which had suddenly gained independence accompanied by the traumas of Partition. In contrast to Ambedkar's hopes for democracy, some regional politicians and pundits, most prominently Singapore's founding father Lee Kuan Yew, have invoked Asian values to suggest that enlightened authoritarianism is the most appropriate form of government in Asia given its traditions, history, culture and philosophy. In this view, democracy is too alien and unstable to provide strong state-led development and an efficient mode of improving social welfare. Advocates of Asian values believe that governments beholden to the vicissitudes of public opinion are unable to make the tough and sometimes unpopular decisions that leaders need to make along the path of progress. Furthermore, democracy is seen to be overly confrontational and divisive in fragile multi-ethnic societies where there is a longstanding tendency towards deference to state authority and general acceptance of the proposition that good governance requires a strong state.

Perhaps all this is true, but casting an eye about Asia it would seem that democracy is doing just fine in what is said to be inhospitable soil, precisely because Asians have made it one of their core values and cornerstones of good governance. As we discuss below, democracy is a key element in national identity politics and embraced as a system in tune with the needs of Asia's diverse societies. There is of course the risk of tyranny of the majority, but democracy is also a way for minorities to get a voice in government to look after their interests.

Ambedkar's concerns, shared by many at the birth of modern India, served to inspire many Indians to nurture representative government and tend its ways and means in the world's largest democracy. As prominent Indian intellectuals remind us, India has not perfected democracy, and beyond vibrant campaigns and high voter turnout at elections, democracy remains attenuated in substance, but there is no doubt that democracy has become a central feature of the Idea of India. It is often deafeningly cacophonous, but Indians exercise their freedom of expression with gusto and round on those who try to censor or suppress their ideas or opinions. Hindu chauvinists and corporate titans are known to attack in print, and in person, those who tread on taboo topics, but their attempts to stifle such discourse are sabotaged and have not prevailed. The Constitution, Ambedkar's handiwork and legacy, has sunk deep roots and Indians consider democracy an inalienable right, something they deem essential despite the many flaws in governance and policy-making by their elected leaders.

Similarly across Asia it appears that most Asians have not allowed the Asian values promoted by authoritarian elites to get in the way of their democratic aspirations, and have challenged the forces of suppression. People have taken to the streets on numerous occasions throughout the region in support of democratic values and to hold governments accountable. During the 1980s, at great personal risk, citizens participated in the Gwangju uprising in South Korea (1980), People Power in the Philippines (1986), the 8/8/88 student movement in Burma/Myanmar (1988) and demonstrations in Tiananmen Square in China (1989) to protest tyranny and promote democracy. Subsequently, in Black May 1992, Thais took to the streets in massive numbers to topple an illegitimate military government, with the helpful intervention of King Bhumibol. Since then the extra-parliamentary politics of the street have figured prominently in Thai politics to counter, and sometimes support, the military's periodic interventions. Tragically during the 2007 Saffron Revolution in Myanmar, troops slaughtered numerous unarmed monks marching in the streets of Yangon in protest against the military government, an event that helped trigger the subsequent moves towards democracy. Their brave defiance of the military gives weight to the assertion of Aung San Suu Kyi, the 1991 Nobel Peace Prize Laureate, that democracy and human rights are essential Asian values and consistent with Asian traditions.

Which Asian Values?

In the 1990s the term Asian values was invoked to justify the authoritarian practices and inclinations of Asian governments that were often targets of criticism. Advocates portrayed democracy and universal human rights as western values incompatible with Asian norms, based on Asia's unique cultural, institutional and historical context and experiences. Asian values were said to place greater emphasis on collective interests over individual rights, and prioritized social harmony and consensus. Accordingly, the Asian authoritarian state draws legitimacy and inspires loyalty by delivering economic growth and improving socio-economic welfare. Asians, it is argued, are deferential to state authority, and the government reciprocates through paternalistic practices. It is also asserted that Asia has a cultural predisposition to stable, single-party rule, and Asia's economic success is ascribed to its ostensibly shared values and cultural attributes.

Critics of Asian values question the notion that Asians share a common heritage, pointing out that such assertions overlook the region's rich cultural and religious diversity (Sen 1999). Problematically, the concept of Asian values draws heavily on Confucian precepts that are largely confined to East Asia. The Asian values thesis provided an ideological counterpoint to western critics of authoritarian governance and one-party rule, but was undermined by the Asian financial crisis in 1997 as many of the cultural attributes deemed positive were suddenly seen to be contributing factors to the economic implosion that rocked the region. Critics have long asserted that Asian values are a convenient construct cynically invoked by repressive governments and their apologists to justify repression and curtail civil liberties and freedom of expression by their citizens. Many proponents hailed from countries where authoritarian, one-party rule has prevailed, such as China, Singapore, Malaysia and Indonesia. Asian dissidents and human rights activists point out that universal values such as a desire for democracy and accountability and freedom from arbitrary arrest are embraced by Asians and not viewed as western impositions. While the absence of democratic pluralism and the strong role of the state in promoting development had fairly positive consequences in Asia, this does not mean that Asian values are inconsistent with democracy or that liberal values are antithetical to Asian values.

Democratization

Anyone witnessing the fair and free elections held in India and Indonesia during 2014 understands just how vibrant their democracies are and how democracy is an entrenched and indigenized Asian norm. Since the end of military rule in the late

1980s, South Korea has enjoyed a series of peaceful political transitions; and the 2012 elections were also vigorously contested in a dramatic campaign. Although Japanese may take their democratic rights for granted, and complacency is evident in low voter turnout, democracy is also intrinsic to their identity.

China, however, bucks the trend of Asian democratization and the CCP has demonstrated that it will do whatever it takes to prevent the emergence of a multi-party system. Many Chinese, not just the tens of thousands of Hong Kongers demonstrating in the autumn of 2014, also aspire to democracy, but the Party's grasp on power is not seriously threatened because it has been adept at manufacturing consent by brainwashing, coopting and intimidating enough of the people to ensure that many have a stake in ensuring the system's survival.

India is the world's biggest democracy, but beyond this headline, Indian intellectuals such as Sunil Khilnani (2003) note that it has become something of an empty shell despite entrenched liberal values and practices. In juxtaposition to the liberal values enshrined in the Indian Constitution, illiberal practices have flourished that call into question the quality of the largest democracy. Instead of a tyrannous majority, India seems more at risk from an irreconcilable minority of Hindu chauvinists who abhor liberal values, but manage to mainstream their message and broaden their constituency. Their party is the BJP which won a landslide victory in 2014 under Narendra Modi by downplaying Hindutva ideology while promising reforms and a revitalized economy. But, will the religious groups that helped catapult Modi into power allow him to continue in this fashion, and will various socio-economic problems create a temptation to promote a more ideological agenda rooted in Hindu chauvinism?

Japan has practiced democracy since the end of the 19th century, so democratic norms and values are well-established despite the wartime hiatus during the 1930s and 1940s when militarists dominated the government. Under the Meiji Constitution there was a high concentration of power accorded the Emperor that was exercised by an unelected elite that worked to keep democracy on a short leash and insulated from the popular will. Under the new 1947 Constitution, written and imposed by the US, various safeguards on freedoms, checks and balances, and curbs on state power have become entrenched, even if sometimes honored in the breach.

Japan's democracy seems relatively sclerotic by regional standards, as prolonged one-party dominance by the LDP under what is dubbed the 1955 system has sapped its vitality and campaigns are not substantive or issue-focused, thus provoking voter apathy. The LDP led by Abe won a so-called "landslide" victory in 2012 with 2 million fewer votes than it won in getting trounced in the 2009 elections, while turnout marked a post-World War II low of 59%, a record that was broken in the 2014 parliamentary elections, also won by Abe, when voter turnout sank to 52%. The legitimacy crisis has been amplified by the Supreme Court's ruling that Japan's electoral system is in a state of unconstitutionality because of voting disparities that over-represent rural constituencies.

South Koreans have memories of authoritarian governments under Japanese colonial rule and US-sponsored dictators in the post-World War II period, and perhaps because of that are deeply attached and passionate about the liberal democracy that activists struggled to establish in 1987. The flowering of democratic dreams in the 1990s, however, has given way to growing disillusion with democracy, owing to the unedifying spectacle of fractious politics, political opportunism and disappointments about flawed leaders and the state of Korean society. Even so, democratic norms and values have quickly sunk deep roots in South Korea and are also intrinsic to national identity.

Indonesian democracy has gone through distinctive phases since independence in 1949, involving western-style parliamentary government in the early 1950s, followed by Guided Democracy under the firm if erratic grip of Sukarno, the nation's founding father, until his ouster in 1966. His successor, General Suharto, presided over the New Order praetorian democracy from 1967 to 1998 until the financial crisis forced his resignation. During that period, democracy was more ritual than substance, and a repressive government curtailed civil liberties and worked to depoliticize Indonesia, partly to impede accountability, but also in reaction to the turmoil of the early 1960s. Since then Indonesia has been in a transitional phase of consolidating democracy after three decades of authoritarian rule. Indonesians have embraced democratic norms and values, and as the New Order fades in the collective memory, democracy has become a touchstone of national identity in the 21st century.

Odd State Out

China is not a democracy in any meaningful sense of the term. It is a modernizing, authoritarian one-party state that does not allow open competition for power or freedom of expression. It is illiberal regarding individual freedoms and liberties and spends more on keeping an eye on Chinese citizens, censoring and incarcerating them, than it does on national defense.

The Party's priority is to sustain its grip on power and to do whatever it takes to do so. Well-honed survival instincts enable it to convince enough people that the Party's interests are the nation's interests while intimidating the rest. Delivering rapid economic growth has bolstered its legitimacy as it nurtures a growing number of stakeholders in the system, helping it reposition itself as the force of stability, and distancing itself from its revolutionary origins. The effective mix of carrots and sticks—growth and propaganda combined with ruthless repression—has worked, but even if the new China has impressive laurels to rest on, it is more feared than admired. The great risk is that sustaining high growth gets ever harder, raising the probability of disappointing popular expectations. Keeping a lid on discontent will be that much harder in the future because of these higher expectations, and because the growing middle class desires more of a say in government. Manufacturing their consent combines propaganda extolling the virtues of the current system and depoliticizing the public, distracting them with material gains and the Chinese Dream while sending unmistakable warnings through harsh treatment of dissidents.

Economic development and growing wealth have raised living standards, but this also generates vulnerability. People know more, want more and feel frustrated that they have little say about the world they live in. The Party has thus far delivered, meeting the demands of the majority and coopting the elite by making them fabulously rich, but can it continue to do so given prospects of ebbing growth? Democracy provides a pressure valve for societies in crisis that autocracy does not have, creating a dangerous dynamic. The ruthless pragmatism of China's autocracy may well prevail, but there are many signs of discontent, ranging from local protests over land grabs by Party officials to bloggers naming and shaming those with lavish lifestyles. China is the only country in the world where a Nobel Peace Prize Laureate (2010), Liu Xiaobo, languishes in jail, suggesting that the Party views democracy as an ideological threat. Lu's sin is his advocacy of a multi-party, competitive democracy and thus an end to the Party's monopoly of political power.

Tiananmen Square's Long Shadow

On June 4, 1989 in Beijing the Chinese government cracked down on pro-democracy demonstrators occupying Tiananmen Square ("square of heavenly peace"), adjacent to the Forbidden City, who were hoping to create a pluralist society by challenging the legitimacy of the Party's monopoly on political power. In the following months and years, the "butchers of Beijing" crushed dissent throughout the nation and proved resilient in adapting to the restiveness and ultimately strengthening the Party's grip on power. The Party leadership was purged of moderates sympathetic to the demonstrators and reluctant to resort to harsh methods.

Tiananmen Square is the largest public open space in the world and sacred territory for the government, the symbolic heart of power and political legitimacy in China. Students, and workers who joined them in solidarity, tapped into widespread grievances about corruption, nepotism and inequalities, some even resorting to hunger strikes to demonstrate their sincerity and to pressure the government into making concessions. During the protests a 10-meter-tall statue of the Goddess of Democracy was placed in the square, facing a large portrait of Mao Zedong displayed at Tiananmen Gate, symbolizing aspirations that drew widespread support among Beijing's citizenry. But they didn't know that Deng Xiaoping, China's leader at the time, was prepared to unleash the military on the peaceful demonstrators and, unlike East German leaders after the fall of the Berlin Wall, engage in brutal repression to remain in power. Throughout the Cold War (1947–1989) the Soviets never shied from resorting to violence to stifle dissent and retain power. After Mikhail Gorbachev assumed power and embraced *glasnost* in the mid-1980s, there was a loosening of restrictions that inevitably undermined communist rule as disgruntled citizens vented grievances that discredited the Party, growing bolder in the absence of a crackdown. In 1989, the Soviet Union began to unravel without a shot being fired and Gorbachev became indelibly associated with the collapse of communist power.

During the Tiananmen Square student protests, Soviet leader Mikhail Gorbachev visited Beijing for summit talks as the two communist superpowers normalized relations after a three-decade-long chill. His presence seemed to inspire student leaders who wanted to emulate what Soviet-bloc citizens had achieved. The students, however, badly misread the situation, and there was to be no Chinese Gorbachev and no final curtain for the CCP. Instead, the CCP leadership, under paramount leader Deng Xiaoping and Premier Li Peng, declared martial law and authorized a military crackdown. Security forces killed and beat many in the streets near the square while arresting many others, displaying a ruthlessness that was repeated elsewhere around the nation, although official sensitivity and censorship make it difficult to determine accurate figures, with the death toll ranging from several hundred to a few thousand (Brooks 1999; Lim 2014).

The CCP quelled the democracy movement in 1989, but did not succeed in eradicating democratic yearnings that target its legitimacy. As mentioned above, Liu Xiaobo, the Nobel Peace Prize Laureate in 2010, was incarcerated in 2009 due to his call for an end to single-party rule and involvement in writing the Charter 08 manifesto that promotes political freedoms, civil liberties and human rights. Charter 08 is modeled on the anti-Soviet, pro-democracy Czech dissident document Charter 77, and is thus viewed as a serious threat to the CCP's authority and legitimacy. Clearly, some Chinese are eager to recast national identity in terms of a pluralistic political system and move beyond the current authoritarian system, but the lessons of the Soviet Union are taken to heart by the CCP. The Party views the incremental concessions made by the Soviet government under Mikhail Gorbachev, and his reluctance to resort to repression, as serious mistakes and a cautionary tale. There is no risk of a repeat in China where Xi has made it clear that Lenin and Stalin remain more inspirational in the realm of power politics (*New York Times*, January 4, 2015).

The anti-democratic principles and policies of post-1949 China under Mao draw on a longstanding desire for a strong state and a concomitant concern that democracy is an inappropriate political system for China. Mao embraced a "guerilla policy style," characterized by opportunism, improvisation and constant upheaval dedicated to keeping Mao on top (Heilmann and Perry 2011). In the process of leading the communist revolution in China before and after assuming power in 1949, Mao set about reinventing the nation and resetting the foundations of national identity. For example, in the new China, Confucianism was suppressed as a feudal legacy and counter-revolutionary doctrine. In this and myriad other ways, the remaking of China and the Chinese people was a wrenching experience, but Mao reveled in turmoil, seeing it as crucial to his continued rule and an effective means to counter his opponents, real and imagined. China's aspiring modernizers had long believed that democracy was unsuitable to China due to the risk of instability and weak governance, instead advocating enlightened despotism (Schell and Delury 2013).

Whether Mao qualifies as enlightened depends on what one is prepared to overlook. He transformed China, but at great cost to tens of millions of people who were sacrificed as he pursued perpetual revolution. Was this a necessary stage in China's evolution, one that laid the foundations of modern China and made possible its meteoric rise at the end of the 20th and early decades of the 21st century? This is a hotly debated issue among Sinologists and the Chinese people, but there is no compelling evidence to suggest that the damage Mao inflicted on China, or his brutal methods, were necessary or contributed to the nation's economic modernization.

In contemporary China, Mao's mistakes are acknowledged, but downplayed. His official score is seven out of ten, meaning Mao supposedly got it right 70% of the time; informally Chinese will confide they rate him lower. Mao is still revered officially as a national hero and lauded as a visionary whose accomplishments exceeded his mistakes, but he is also an awkward legacy for the CCP because his despotic rule was erratic and harmful. He represents constant upheaval while the CCP has positioned itself as the best guarantor of stability and a better life. It warns that loosening its grip on power might lead to a Yugoslavia nightmare scenario of chaotic unraveling. From this perspective, full-blown democracy is portrayed as a recipe for anarchy. Economic growth and stability win considerable support for the CCP, but those not benefiting are angry that they are not sharing the prosperity and dreams that so many others are enjoying, while younger middle-class Chinese are finding it increasingly difficult to land good jobs and purchase housing. Thus when the Arab Spring erupted in 2012, public security officials grew anxious that the Jasmine Revolution might spark the kindling of discontent, and snuffed demonstrations, censored blogs and made mention of jasmine a taboo.

The Internet and social media have opened up considerable space for Chinese to probe the extent of state tolerance while questioning state narratives. This has created space for Netizens to exploit the political possibilities of nationalism and to invoke it in support of wider agendas of dissent. The rapid spread of blogs and social networking platforms makes it much harder for the state to control information. Scandals, abuses or protests that until recently could be easily ignored, denied or downplayed can now be disseminated across the nation instantaneously. The government works hard to keep the disruptive technology of social media on a tight leash, but these efforts are routinely circumvented. In some respects, blogs and social networking platforms are democratizing China despite government efforts to block and censor. They may well be havens for subversion, irony and dissent, but they are also a forum for ultra-nationalism and generate pressure on the government to stick to hardline positions, especially regarding history and territorial issues with Japan.

The Internet is creating a propaganda crisis for the CCP because it is getting much more difficult to manufacture consent and control the narrative (Mengin 2004; Brady 2008). Party control of the media facilitated dissemination of its views and it could control what information was disseminated. But since 1997 when online bulletin board services arrived, more and more Chinese have gotten ever greater access to alternative information and analysis that subverts Party propaganda. When China Central Television (CCTV) and the *People's Daily* were the dominant news sources, perhaps trusted by the Chinese as authoritative when there were no alternatives, manufacturing consent was not so complicated. The post-1989 erosion of the Party's legitimacy also undermined the credibility of the mainstream media, and this gathering loss of trust coincided with the emergence of the Internet and online alternative news and information sources. Previously people may have been quietly skeptical, but quite a few didn't know any better because the Party deliberately kept them in the dark. It also promoted negative views of western media outlets as anti-Chinese so that the public was inclined to dismiss critical analysis from such sources as being biased and controlled by the hostile forces of depraved capitalism, part of a wider imperialist conspiracy. So older Chinese were conditioned to believe they were living in a socialist paradise surrounded by enemies eager to discredit China's successes, and some may still feel this way, at least regarding the enemies. But many younger Chinese who are savvy navigators of the Internet easily bypass the Great Wall of censorship erected by the state, and the scales are falling from their eyes as they can see for themselves more reliable and accurate reporting about the world they experience and see. Many Chinese confess that they have lost faith in state-controlled media because they know it disseminates propaganda and downplays stories that discredit the Party and officials, and covers up heinous crimes. Murong Xuecon, a novelist and blogger, dates his apostasy to 1999 when he started to read about the Great Famine 1958–1962 (Xuecon 2014). He found accounts that contradicted CCTV versions of this tragedy and claims that the famine was caused by natural disasters. The CCTV's portrayal of the pro-democracy demonstrations at Tiananmen Square as "counter-revolutionary riots" also contradicts what people know and what they can read. The state media has also been silent about arrests of dissidents and activists and has done little to explain why so many Tibetans have been setting themselves on fire in recent years. The silence on various taboo topics is an eloquent indictment of the state media's credibility and has eroded public trust. People's eyes have been opened, and even though the truth might not be setting them free, it is spreading discontent and skepticism such that there is now a natural inclination to question state sources and to wonder about hidden agendas. Mockery is perhaps the strongest symptom of spreading distrust as Internet postings lampooning the Party line have become ubiquitous. Netizens, for example, draw attention to the policy errors that led to the Great Famine and criticize the media for disseminating lies and disinformation about this horrific Mao-made tragedy. They openly wonder why there has been no apology or retraction by CCTV of its erroneous reporting, clearly pointing the finger at the Party. The Party seeks to depoliticize the masses and keep them ignorant, but the corollary of that is that the reality of increasing access to knowledge carries political consequences. George Orwell's *1984* is a source of inspiration, as the government's Ministry of Propaganda (yes there is one) is now sarcastically referred to as the Ministry of Truth. The Party seems to be losing control over what people think even as it tries to tighten controls over what information they can access.

The CCP understands it has a propaganda crisis and is innovatively responding by diverting attention away from the fundamental problems and creating distractions such as the 2008 Olympics, space travel and its territorial disputes with Japan (Brady 2011). It is also drawing attention to Party campaigns to crack down on corruption and the sex trade, protect the environment and promote stability. Stability is the Party's trump card as it positions itself as the only institution able to safeguard the nation and guide it through tumultuous times. To some extent it acknowledges its shortcomings, allows some criticism as a way to shore up its tattered credibility, while at the same time emphasizing that there is no viable alternative. It has concentrated efforts on cultivating the urbanized well-educated youth because they pose the most potential danger. So even if there is a propaganda crisis the Party is still managing to nurture consent, diverting and distracting public discontent. It concedes some space for dissent, but ring-fences this space and determines what to allow, reserving the right to abruptly change its mind, flexibly adapting to circumstances with the one overriding goal in mind: maintaining Party power. The blueprint for democratic reforms laid out in Liu Xiaobo's Charter 08 is precisely what the Party is working to prevent, with considerable success.

Xi Jinping has moved resolutely since coming to office in 2012 to consolidate power by launching a sweeping anti-corruption campaign aimed at catching "flies and tigers," meaning everyone is fair game including the elite. He has backed this up by bringing down powerful potential rivals on corruption charges, including a top military general, a security chief who was also a member of the Politburo, and Bo Xilai, a contender for power. He understood that shoring up the CCP's dwindling credibility required more concerted action on the public's main grievance—corruption. Promoting accountability and cracking down on malfeasance plays well in the theater of politics, and promotes Xi's political agenda, but he is dead set against democratizing China. Rather than the low-key style of "government by committee" under Hu Jintao (2002–2012), Xi is showing himself to be an authoritarian strongman with no tolerance for dissent, amassing more power than anyone since Deng stepped down.

National identity is vigorously contested in all of the nations we are examining, but the state-controlled limits on this battle and debate are most evident in China, precisely because it is not democratic. Thus, compared to the other four nations, China's national narrative and identity are subject to extensive state control and intervention. This doesn't mean that all Chinese embrace a monolithic nationalist identity according to Party dictates, but this is far more the case in China than in the other nations. Certainly in private, Chinese express a range of perspectives and subversive views, but in the public space of mainstream political discourse people remain wary of not crossing the blurry line between tolerated dissent and taboo, erring on the side of caution. Strict limits on media and academic freedom mean that the state can control the terms of discourse to an extraordinary degree, while vigilant censorship of the Internet also circumscribes this forum for dissent, even if there are edgy blogs. Here too the state is clamping down, snooping, monitoring and policing subversive or potentially destabilizing posts. And now all online bloggers and posters are required to register online with national identity cards, subjecting all Internet users to the whims and abuses of the cyber-security services.

Under President Xi Jinping, the blade of censorship has sharpened as the state tries to rein in social media. These expanding restrictions on free expression betray the Party's growing anxiety about widespread social grievances and the dangers of a post-Soviet-style color revolution (Yu Gao 2015). In doing so the Party forfeits what little trust it commanded and risks mockery and a popular backlash. Back in 2000, former US President Bill Clinton dismissed China's Internet censorship as akin to nailing Jell-O to the wall, but these efforts have been unrelenting while muffling voices and curbing freedom of expression. In 2015 authorities disabled virtual private networks (VPNs), the siege towers that enabled Netizens to peek over the Great Firewall that blocked access to forbidden sites. In this cat-and-mouse game, censorship appears somewhat farcical, but it also has real consequences, enabling authorities to construct an unchallenged parallel reality. In these times, scholarly commentary and media reportage about nationalist issues manifest a startling degree of brainwashing as discordant voices that challenge or criticize the government vie in a tightly monitored and circumscribed space that exists, and is withdrawn, at the authorities' discretion.

Democratization and Nationalism

Democratization is a process that generates temptations for political parties to play the nationalist card. In appealing to voters, political parties tap into and amplify identity politics, domestic grievances and international disputes, in the process defining what are the key nationalist issues. Political competition over defining national identity, and constructing an identity that cultivates voter support, means embracing and expressing nationalist aspirations. This raises the stakes over crafting an identity that can be communicated simply and effectively, often in emotive ways. For parties seeking to displace incumbent parties, there are countervailing tendencies. Adopting more extreme positions highlights the alternatives to the status quo and underscores why that status quo should be overturned, while adopting more moderate positions responds to perceptions that more radical stands are reckless and/or endangering the national interest.

The politics of nationalism, however, is not usually a simple competition between overtly extremist and moderate positions. The opponent is portrayed as engaging in dangerous posturing or insufficiently heeding the will of the people or protecting the national interest. Extremism and moderation are thus in the eye of the beholder and complicated by ethnic or religious appeals that transform positions into deeply felt convictions rather than bargaining chips or negotiable options. It is always useful to portray opponents as being controlled by vested interests, and to depict the status quo as stagnant and government as inept. Certainly this is not only over nationalist issues or identity politics, but they are an especially volatile part of the mix.

Such efforts to nurture loyal constituencies spark competition between politicians and parties to define nationalism and project an identity that arouses voters. Hot-button issues such as ethnic antagonisms, religion, language, discrimination and territorial disputes are given prominence and thrust into mainstream public discourse. Democratization is ostensibly about giving voice and power to people, and parties and politicians respond accordingly, and often opportunistically, because it is in their interest to do so. Sometimes taking certain stands on these issues is a mixture of shrewd calculation and deeply felt convictions, but there are incentives for whipping up public emotions and creating crises to gain attention and support from voters. Electoral competition often involves contesting what is important to national identity and helping to define that identity by wielding symbols, tapping into grievances and demonstrating a party's claim to be the most reliable or ardent in pursuing a nationalist identity.

Democracy provides political space to contest national identity and articulate nationalist discourse. With the exception of China, our focus countries are all democracies where nationalist issues are not projected unilaterally or monolithically by state authorities. Certainly each of the governments espouses and promotes nationalist narratives, but Indians, Koreans, Japanese and Indonesians also enjoy freedom to embrace, question, disparage or reject such narratives. This is not to argue that Chinese citizens do not have any recourse, but their room for maneuver in challenging official narratives is more limited, and doing so runs the risk of harassment, surveillance and arrest. Challenging or exposing nationalist narratives and myths in China puts citizens on a collision course with authorities in an authoritarian system where police powers are extensive and routinely used. It was similar in Indonesia until the late 1990s and South Korea until the late 1980s. Certainly in India, as journalists and academics can attest, there are risks in challenging cherished Hindutva myths, but this has not been systematically orchestrated by the state, even if it may be complicit. In Japan too there are clashes over national identity between jingoistic conservatives and more liberal elements, and many of the latter complain that the police fail to act against right-wing thugs and patriotic organizations that enjoy close ties with the ruling Liberal Democratic Party. And there is state intimidation of teachers and activists who question the myths and prerogatives of the Imperial System, so such intimidation is not only China's problem.

Japan

The US priority in occupying Japan from 1945 to 1952 was to democratize and demilitarize its World War II enemy. To this end, the US Occupation authorities wrote Japan's new Constitution and enshrined strong respect for civil liberties and democratic freedoms. It is therefore ironic that Japan's Constitution and democracy were imposed from above at the behest of Americans. Moreover, the US Occupation authorities practiced strict censorship, not allowing the media to cover the atomic bombings or any consequences thereof. It was also taboo to report about the many crimes and misdemeanors of the occupying soldiers. But the Japanese people embraced democracy enthusiastically, especially women, who were finally given the right to vote. As the nation was recovering from war devastation, most citizens blamed the militarists for the debacle, and learned from reporting on the International Military Tribunal for the Far East (1946–1948) about the extensive war crimes committed by the Imperial Armed Forces throughout Asia, contrasting sharply with wartime reports about glorious victories and Pan Asian brotherhood. With a death toll exceeding 3 million, and most of Japan's cities damaged by extensive firebombing, the Japanese knew all they needed to know about the folly of war and were especially keen about the constitutional constraints on Japan's military expressed in Article 9. This feature of what is known as the Peace Constitution quickly became a vibrant and popular symbol of Japan's democratic postwar identity, one rooted in pacifism.

Oddly enough, the US Occupation authorities embraced the wartime conservative elite and enlisted their support in rebuilding Japan. Due to the onset of the Cold War in 1947, the US was determined to make Japan into a showcase for demonstrating the superiority of the US system *vis-à-vis* the Soviet Union. US Occupation authorities were alarmed at the stark economic conditions prevailing in Japan and increasing labor unrest and support for left-wing unions and political parties. This helps explains why the Americans worked with the conservative elite, because their hopes of transforming Japan into a calling card for the American system depended on eliciting their cooperation in reviving the economy, efficiently administering the nation and steering it away from a leftist political program inimical to Washington's geo-political interests.

The Liberal Democratic Party has been the dominant party in Japan since it was established in 1955 with CIA funding. It is a conservative party that asserts a strong nationalist identity while also supporting Japan's role as a client state to the US. In 1957, only a dozen years after the war ended, the party elected Nobusuke Kishi as its leader and he served as prime minister until 1960 when he ignored strong political and public opposition in ramming through parliamentary approval of the US–Japan Mutual Security Treaty. He had been a Class A war crimes suspect due to his wartime role in slave labor, but was never prosecuted at the IMTFE, popularly known as the Tokyo Trials. Kishi symbolized the awkward continuities in prewar and postwar leadership and the shift of the conservative elite to supporting the US, a country that they once waged war against. The Tokyo Trials led to the conviction of 25 Japanese wartime leaders and the hanging of seven of them, but aroused lingering controversy due to deeply flawed judicial procedures. Instead of a fair trial, the defendants got "victor's justice," while war crimes committed by Allied forces such as the atomic bombings of Hiroshima and Nagasaki, and the firebombing of Tokyo and dozens of other cities, that claimed an estimated half a million civilian lives, were overlooked.

During much of the latter half of the 20th century, the LDP and the Socialist Party dominated Japanese politics. The LDP has supported a more vindicating and unrepentant view of Japan's wartime conduct, while the Socialist Party and most Japanese have opposed this whitewashing of history. The two parties also clashed over security policy and the emperor system, with the LDP supporting the alliance with the US and retaining the Emperor, and the Socialists opposing. During the 1950s companies engaged in union busting with the implicit support of the LDP government, while the 1960s was a time of fierce clashes over security issues and the Vietnam War. The Socialists relied heavily on unions for funding and votes, and bitterly opposed the US–Japan Mutual Security Treaty, making it the centerpiece of its campaigns against the LDP.

The LDP delivered strong economic growth—the so-called "miracle"—from the late 1950s until the late 1960s, boosting incomes and political support. After Kishi resigned, his successor, Hayato Ikeda, announced his Income Doubling Plan in response to the bitter divisions over security policy and to woo voters. The target of doubling income was reached in a phenomenal seven years, three years ahead of schedule, earning the LDP considerable kudos. The LDP also has a track record of reinventing itself—for example, in the 1970 Diet adopting a series of environmental initiatives aimed at addressing the horrific environmental impact of the pell-mell, unregulated growth that it had been promoting. Minamata disease, caused by ingesting methyl mercury, affecting the central nervous system, became a global symbol for this growth-at-all-costs mentality. Victims in Japan struggled from the 1950s to stop the dumping of untreated effluent into Minamata Bay and to win compensation, while the government was complicit in Chisso Corporation's cover-up and attempts to evade responsibility. But working through the courts and with media support, victims relentlessly pursued their case and won compensation, a process that took nearly half a century. It was a belated, and many argue inadequate, victory for democracy (George 2001). The story of Japan's lepers followed a similar trajectory, demonstrating that democracy can help defend the weak and vulnerable. In both cases, international attention exposed Japan as being out of touch with global norms and values, and in this way democracy served as a mechanism for reforms aimed at removing stains on the nation's image.

Over the decades, the LDP has been plagued by numerous money scandals, reflecting the close and cooperative ties between the party, the bureaucracy and big business, often referred to as the Iron Triangle or Japan, Inc. Despite these improprieties, the LDP has ruled continuously, with the exception of two interregnums, one in 1993 when voters kicked it out of office over mismanagement of the economy and yet another major money scandal, that linked party leaders with a transport firm (Sagawa Kyubin), illicit construction contracts and *yakuza* (organized crime).

The second hiatus was in 2009 when the Democratic Party of Japan (DPJ) won a landslide victory owing to growing concerns that deregulation measures prompted by the LDP were creating widening income disparities at odds with a national identity rooted in egalitarian norms and values. But the DPJ proved ineffective in promoting its agenda of social welfare reforms, alienating bureaucrats by trying to trim their powers, and Washington by seeking to revise an agreement regarding US military bases in Okinawa and making overtures to China. In addition, the DPJ was blamed for the government's fumbling response to the March 11, 2011 triple disaster (earthquake, tsunami and nuclear reactor meltdowns), even though bureaucrats and the LDP were also culpable. Additionally, growing tensions with China over disputed islands in the East China Sea were poorly managed by the DPJ, and the economy remained stagnant, helping the LDP roar back to power in 2012 with Shinzo Abe at the helm. This marked a stunning political comeback for Abe after he had resigned in 2007 for his fumbling performance. The new Abe campaigned on economic recovery measures, dubbed Abenomics, keeping under wraps his ideological agenda that voters remain wary of. This agenda involves lifting constitutional constraints on Japan's military, ramping up Japan's military capacity, and overturning the postwar order based on pacifism and acceptance of war guilt that Washington imposed.

While the LDP has provided continuity and strong leadership, many observers worry that prolonged one-party rule has created a democratic deficit and that voters lack viable alternatives. There are also questions about the powerful influence of the bureaucracy in Japan's polity as some observers believe that it dictates to, rather than does the bidding of, elected officials. Thus widespread perceptions about the inevitability of LDP rule, the lack of options and a paramount bureaucracy have led to increasing voter apathy because the government seems well insulated from their voices and concerns; a system that is democratic in form but technocratic, unresponsive and high-handed in practice.

In 21st-century Japan, the LDP owns the nationalist card and its leader, Prime Minister Abe Shinzo, promotes a more vigorous nationalism through patriotic education and gestures. When he reinterpreted Article 9 of the Constitution in July 2014 to enable Japan to engage in collective self-defense, he aroused strong opposition, because he had done so without following democratic procedures for revising the Constitution and had trampled on the deeply engrained pacifist identity among Japanese.[1] He has also raised liberal hackles by pushing through a new state secrets law that threatens to muzzle the media and erode transparency; ended self-imposed curbs on arms exports; and promoted a revival of nuclear energy despite majority public opposition. With the opposition weak and divided, there is concern that under Abe democracy is in crisis and he is imposing an agenda that most people reject but are powerless to stop. In his 2015 New Year message, Emperor Akihito gave voice to these concerns, urging the nation to reflect on the abject plight of Fukushima's nuclear refugees, implying criticism about Abe's support for restarting the nation's fleet of reactors. Noting that 2015 marked the 70th anniversary of the end of World War II, the Emperor also recalled the suffering and devastation of war, and repudiated revisionists like Abe who assert that it was a war of Pan Asian liberation by drawing attention to Japanese aggression against China in 1931 that ignited the wider conflagration. His remarks also seemed aimed at Abe's agenda of expanding security cooperation with the US, which most Japanese oppose because they worry that Japan will be dragged into a war at Washington's behest. Known as the "people's emperor," Akihito is constitutionally banned from any formal role in politics or government, but the aging monarch continues to play a key role in promoting democratic values and reconciliation with regional nations that suffered from Japanese aggression.

---

[1] Collective self-defense refers to Japan's right to deploy its military in support of allies even when it is not under direct attack.

India

Secular democracy is the pride of India, the world's largest democracy, where struggles with communal violence, religious bigotry and caste-driven inequalities divide the polity and infuse it with the most bitter sectarian enmities within our focus group. At the time India became independent in 1947, there were considerable doubts that it could become a viable state let alone a vibrant democracy. But India has become a plural and inclusive society conducting free and fair elections that often enough oust incumbent governments, though getting there was a struggle and not foreordained. From the outset Prime Minister Jawaharlal Nehru put his stamp on Indian democracy, insisting on secularism and fighting to suppress communal politics. In the awful aftermath of Partition in 1947, it was Nehru who steered the nation away from a descent into Hindu communalism, against considerable opposition from within his Congress Party and various Hindu nationalist parties and groups. Mistreatment of Hindus in post-Partition Pakistan inflamed the Hindutva movement and gave impetus to its agenda of transforming Indian democracy into a nation run according to the dictates of Hindu chauvinism. Nehru, however, would not allow it.

Nehru had a quest to modernize India and establish a firm foundation for secular democracy. He saw Hindu bigotry as the main enemy of the plural, inclusive idea of Indian democracy he espoused, and acted accordingly. His success in doing so in a nation where 80% of the population is Hindu is a testament to his powers of persuasion, steely political will and a wily sense of brinksmanship. To secure secularism he staked his political career, offering to resign from the premiership if others did not pledge support.

The Indian Congress Party under the Nehru/Gandhi dynasty has dominated Indian politics since independence. It has often been criticized for assuming that political power was its birthright and ruling fecklessly. Nehru passed away in 1964, prompting a brief crisis, but then his daughter Indira Gandhi took over and plunged the party and the nation into a deeper crisis. Due to widespread political unrest, fractious parliamentary politics and incessant media criticism, Gandhi declared an Emergency in 1975 and suspended democracy for 19 months. Democracy in shackles allowed her to rule by decree, suspend civil liberties and censor the press. This democratic hiatus was a colossal mistake, and perhaps the most positive legacy was in proving that India could and should only be governed democratically. An estimated 140,000 people were detained without trial, nearly 5 million more were subjected to forced sterilizations, while the Emergency inflicted lasting damage on the institutions of democracy Gandhi's father had nurtured by curbing their autonomy and subjecting them to partisan machinations. The Akali Dal, a Sikh party based in Punjab, became a force of organized dissent, mounting "A Campaign to Save Democracy." About 40,000 Sikhs were arrested, accounting for nearly one-third of all political prisoners during The Emergency even though they represent only 2% of the national population. Punjab agitation for autonomy, defiance of Gandhi and a low-level insurgency put Sikhs on a collision course with the central government, with tragic consequences.

Gandhi's humiliating defeat in the 1977 elections was a repudiation of her dictatorship and a reassertion of Indian's democratic national identity, but she returned to power in 1980. She was assassinated in October 1984 by a Sikh bodyguard in retaliation for the Indian Army's assault on the Golden Temple in Amritsar, the holiest shrine for Sikh devotees, in June 1984. Following the assassination, anti-Sikh mobs went on a rampage while security forces stood aside as they killed an estimate 8,000 Sikhs in Delhi. Congress and Rajiv Gandhi, the son who succeeded her, are accused of complicity if not active involvement in this pogrom. As the extent of the massacre emerged, Rajiv Gandhi callously commented, "When a big tree falls, the earth shakes." Subsequently, during the 2014 election campaign when Congress kept reminding voters about Modi's links with the 2002 anti-Muslim riots, the BJP reminded them of the 1984 massacre for which nobody has been held accountable.

The Bharatiya Janata Party is the torchbearer of Hindu chauvinism in mainstream politics and seeks to replace secularism with Hinduism. It has relied on ethno-religious mobilization, but, to enhance its electoral appeal, the BJP has moderated some of its more extreme positions (Jaffrelot 1999). It maintains, however, close ties with more ardent and unequivocal proponents of Hindutva (a political movement advocating Hindu nationalism and the establishment of an exclusively Hindu state). The Rashtriya Swayamsevak Sangh, the Vishwa Hindu Parishad and the Bajrang Dal, along with a variety of associated organizations, rail against secularism and

Figure 5.2 Ink Mark Indicates Voter Has Voted in India. Photo © Jeff Kingston.

promote Hindutva. This religious movement ramps up the threat of the Other, usually Muslim, but Christians will do, to whip up animosity and intolerance that is at odds with the values enshrined in India's Constitution and its secular, inclusive and liberal democracy.

The Hindutva movement wields powerful symbols and harps on various historical grievances, mounting public spectacles that arouse frenzied support among the masses. The campaign to reclaim a sacred Hindu site in present-day Ayodhya demonstrates the popular appeal of such manifestations and the deadly consequences. The archaeological evidence is fragmentary and inconclusive and there are good reasons to doubt that contemporary Ayodhya corresponds to Ram's birthplace mentioned in the Ramayana, the legendary Hindu epic (Jaffrelot 1999, 91–94). Ram is considered one of the most important and popular deities in Hinduism, and some devotees regard him as the Supreme Being. He embodies duty and sacrifice and unwavering devotion to religious values. For purposes of ethno-religious mobilization, agitation to reclaim this sacred site of Ram's birth from Muslims for the Hindu community resonates powerfully among many devout Hindus. It is argued that a Mughal ruler destroyed a Hindu temple on the site and replaced it with the Babri Mosque, in effect stealing this sacred site from Hindus. Jains assert that they were there first, back in the 6th century, showing that the complex layers of religious contestation in modern India extend to archaeological battles.

The struggle over Ayodhya, however, was never a search for incontrovertible evidence. Instead it became a symbol of Hindu victimization at the hands of Muslims, invoking past wrongs to justify contemporary reprisals. Post-independence agitation focusing on this injustice began in 1949 when Hindu idols were placed in the mosque and declared a "miracle" by Hindus, and regarded as sacrilege by Muslims. Shortly thereafter Muslim tombs in the vicinity were desecrated, and Hindu organizations held mass rallies in the area. In the 1980s, Hindu chauvinists campaigned to reclaim the site and BJP leader L.K. Advani, accompanied by activists bedecked in saffron and religious paraphernalia, embarked on a 10,000 km journey, riding a chariot-like vehicle with great fanfare, drawing massive crowds, designed to demonstrate popular support. The religious fervor and militancy aimed to boost Hindu solidarity and ethno-nationalist sentiments in support of the Ayodhya project. Rapturous press coverage of this spectacle generated a "Hindu wave" that threatened communal harmony and indeed the secular state ruled by the Congress Party. The 1990 arrest of Advani sparked widespread outbreaks of communal rioting and violence, while the BJP launched a mass protest movement seeking to topple the government, to no avail. Subsequently, the destruction of the Babri Mosque by a massive crowd of Hindu fanatics in 1992 sparked rioting across the nation, and further eruptions of political violence generated by religious chauvinism have become a destructive and divisive staple of Indian democracy.

Narendra Modi manifests the 21st-century remaking of the BJP's image from a party capitalizing on and politicizing communal relations to one that champions economic and social development, appeals to aspirations for upward mobility and crusades against corruption. The BJP realizes that it cannot win elections by relying exclusively on the banner of Hindu nationalism, and understands that its militant Hinduism only appeals to a narrow core constituency while scaring away other voters concerned about the consequences of such extremism on the delicate fabric of a pluralist society. The BJP also supports a muscular stance on national security and was the party in power when India exploded five nuclear devices in 1998. It now professes to be a voice of moderation on communalism, and in the 2014 campaign Modi managed to shrug off responsibility for the anti-Muslim pogrom in 2002 that erupted in Gujarat shortly after he was elected Chief Minister in that state. These Gujarat riots were prompted by a massacre by Muslims of Hindu pilgrims returning from Ayodhya on a train earlier in 2002. Although a judicial inquiry cleared Modi of legal responsibility for the bloodshed, he has never really been able to clear his name in the court of public opinion. Martha Nussbaum concludes:

> There is by now a broad consensus that the Gujarat violence was a form of ethnic cleansing, that in many ways it was premeditated, and that it was carried out with the complicity of the state government and officers of the law. (Nussbaum 2008, 50–51)

Modi presides over the most right-wing government ever in independent India and his election seemingly signals that Hindutva beliefs have a widespread appeal that transcends region, caste and class divides. Moreover, given his reputation, it is extraordinary that Muslims accounted for 9% of his aggregate votes. So what to make of the Modi moment? How can he reconcile the competing expectations of supporters—economic reformers, hardline Hindu ideologues, industrialists seeking red carpet treatment, small-scale retailers seeking protection, and the urban poor with upwardly mobile aspirations? This is an immense challenge and if reforms prove difficult to implement there will certainly be a temptation to "reveal himself as the champion of Hindutva that he has always been at heart" (Vajpeyi 2014).

The prospect of a more assertive Hindutva enjoying democratic legitimacy troubles Indian intellectuals who embrace a secular identity. Pankaj Mishra, one of India's most acclaimed writers, despairs about the state of contemporary India, still in thrall to the West, deracinated from indigenous traditions and suffering from widespread materialism, corruption and inequality (Mishra 2013). Mishra is critical of India's triumphal celebration of independence and robust secular democracy, focusing instead on the tragedy of failures, lost opportunities and nationalistic hubris. He laments that, "India displays even more garishly than China the odd discontinuities induced by economic globalization" (Mishra 2012, 308). In his damning assessment, the world's largest democracy is discredited by gross disparities and crass materialism, issues that a resurgent Hindu nationalism ignores. He also notes with wry irony that, "the biggest beneficiaries of globalization find shelter in such aggressive ideologies as Hindu nationalism" (Mishra 2012, 308).

South Korea

Independent Korea had inauspicious beginnings as it was divided between the US and the Soviets, provoking a domestic backlash against superpower intervention. This led to an insurrection on Jeju Island in South Korea between 1948 and 1949, which was brutally repressed by local police, paramilitary forces and the South Korean military, claiming the lives of as many as 30,000 and leading to the destruction of 70% of the island's villages. Interestingly, the conflict pitted Japanese collaborators who dominated the police and administration against leftist rebels who opposed the American military government and its efforts to install a handpicked leader, Syngman Rhee. For nearly half a century afterwards, the government tried to cover up the uprising, making it a crime to even mention it, and subjecting those who did to beatings, torture and imprisonment. Islanders waited until 2003 for a formal government apology and until 2009 for the findings of a Truth and Reconciliation Commission. Democracy has made it possible for Koreans to exhume such painful memories and expose wrongdoing, but without judicial accountability.

Paradoxically, the Korean War (1950–1953) made Korean democracy possible, but also postponed its realization. This war pitted US-led UN forces fighting for South Korea, against North Korea with substantial Soviet support and critically important Chinese armed intervention. It was a defining Cold War proxy battle between ideological rivals who vied for hegemony and influence around the world. It ended in stalemate and armistice rather than a peace settlement, establishing a de facto border at the 38th parallel, a Military Demarcation Line over which opposing troops still glower; in the demilitarized zone (DMZ) that separates South and North Korea tensions occasionally erupt into spasms of limited violence.

The division of the Korean Peninsula remains a festering wound in the Korean psyche, although public opinion polls indicate that older and younger generations have different views about the desirability of reunification. Younger Koreans seem more indifferent and worry about the potential costs and disruption that might ensue, mindful of Germany's experience in the 1990s. Moreover, the gaps between the Koreas—economic, social, political—are far wider than those that existed between East and West Germany, and the division has persisted longer.

The legacy of the peninsula's fratricidal civil war created conditions inimical to democracy because both Koreas became heavily militarized due to the potential for resumption of hostilities. South Korea was a US client state and its leader Syngman Rhee was chosen by Washington, not the people. During the Rhee regime there were rigged elections, and his regime was as corrupt as it was authoritarian, without any of the efficiencies. Rhee's downfall was caused by street protests against a rigged election in 1960, creating an opening for military strongman Park Chung-hee.

Park's government was authoritarian even if he observed certain democratic formalities such as naming a cabinet and rigging elections. But Park could never douse the Korean democracy movement and his undemocratic ways discredited him in the eyes of the nation even if many lauded his economic achievements. His security forces beat, arrested and tortured many young Koreans willing to sacrifice much in support of democracy. Kim Dae-jung, the democracy icon who became president in 1998 and was awarded the 2000 Nobel Peace Prize, was one of his most prominent critics and challengers. Kim blasted Park's dictatorial powers and for this, and doing unexpectedly well in the rigged elections in 1971, was banned from politics and sentenced to prison.

In 1979, Park was assassinated by his director of the KCIA (Korean Central Intelligence Agency), but rather than ushering in democracy, General Chun Doo-hwan seized power and subsequently held sham elections. He too had Kim Dae-jung arrested, and sentenced him to death for his alleged role in the pro-democracy uprising at Gwangju in 1980 that opposed Chun's dissolution of the National Assembly and declaration of martial law. Washington intervened and Kim went into exile in the US. Chun never enjoyed a shred of legitimacy and was forever tarnished by the bloody suppression in Gwangju, unleashing the paramilitary against unarmed students who valiantly withstood the assault and gained the respect of the nation. Gwangju became a symbol of people power, inspiring subsequent Asian uprisings against authoritarian rule across Asia in the 1980s. Chun is also remembered for jailing some 60,000 Korean citizens and abusing their human rights under the guise of re-education and social cleansing.

As we discuss in Chapter 6, Chun's government was awarded the 1988 Summer Olympics. This was considered a PR coup for the government at the time, but heightened international media scrutiny in the run-up to the Olympics helped the pro-democracy movement and increased pressure on Chun to make way for a successor. His handpicked successor Roh Tae-woo prevailed in the 1987 elections with 36% of the vote because the two candidates associated with the pro-democracy movement, Kim Dae-jung and Kim Young-sam, both ran for election and divided the opposition.

Eventually, Kim Dae-jung became president in 1998, helped by the political fallout from the Asian economic crisis that slammed the Korean economy. His election marked the first time in the history of Korean democracy that the ruling party peacefully transferred power to the opposition party by the ballot box. Although sentenced to death by Chun Doo-hwan, Kim rose above vindictive retribution by pardoning Chun. In the 2000s, South Korean democracy was perhaps the most robust in Asia, with a vigorous media and vigilant Netizens holding officials accountable. Alas, they also hounded Kim's successor Roh Moo-hyun (2003–2008) after he left office, leading to his suicide in 2009.

Roh was a liberal human rights activist representing the so-called 386 generation of "thirtysomethings" (3) who attended university in the 1980s (8) and were born in the 1960s (6). This generation is associated with the pro-democracy protests against authoritarian government, promoting conciliatory policies towards North Korea and cooler relations with the US. The conservative government of his successor, Lee Myung-bak (2008–2012), launched a politically motivated probe into bribery allegations involving his family. The same fate awaited Lee, limiting his effectiveness towards the end of his term in 2012. Such is the fractious, no-holds-barred nature of Korean democracy.

The election of Park Geun-hye in 2012 was a close fought battle, but the daughter of Park Chung-hee prevailed by a slim margin. She won the older and more conservative vote while her opponent won the younger, more liberal vote in a deeply divided polity. The legacy of her father is a mixed one for Ms. Park, as some recall the heady days of rapid economic growth, while others focus on his repressive policies and close ties with Japan; he served in the Japanese military prior to independence. This is a major political handicap in 21st-century South Korea because Japan is vilified over unresolved historical grievances and, owing to the vagaries of democracy, this history card is opportunistically and regularly played by politicians to garner support. Under these circumstances, her father's legacy renders Ms. Park vulnerable to accusations that she is soft on Japan, so she has taken a hardline on colonial history issues, which has sparked a significant worsening in bilateral ties.

While the impact of democracy on South Korean society has been profound in terms of civil rights and freedoms, it has also had a significant influence on foreign policy. Prior to democratization at the end of the 1980s, controversies over issues such as the Dokdo Islands (called Takeshima in Japan), forced labor and comfort women, which have seriously undermined relations with Japan in recent decades, had not been an issue. Now they are a key feature of East Asian geo-politics as two US allies remain divided by the shared past. Democracy has also promoted greater transparency and raised citizens' expectations about their right to know. Documents from the normalization negotiations with Japan that led to the 1965 Treaty on Basic Relations were disclosed to score political points and embarrass certain politicians, but the explosive revelations whetted the public's appetite for more, while making politicians less enthusiastic about transparency because of the unintended consequences. When these archives were opened to the public in 2005, people were outraged to discover that some of the $800 million in grants and loans provided by Japan to resolve all issues of compensation from the colonial era, 1910–1945, was designated for individual compensation. Hardly any of this money was distributed to victims and instead was allocated to heavy industrial and infrastructure projects at the behest of Park senior. This duplicity rankles and is another reason why the past resonates so loudly in contemporary South Korea and why the public's right to know remains controversial and constrained.

Indonesia

Indonesia has experienced four phases of democracy: (1) Parliamentary (1949–1957); (2) Guided Democracy (1959–1965); (3) New Order (1967–1998); and (4) Transition and consolidation (1999–). Democracy in Indonesia was discredited in the 1950s because it proved highly fractious and ineffective, and was supplanted by the undemocratic (and also ineffective) Guided Democracy under President Sukarno. He was nudged aside in 1966 by military intervention as the bloodletting unleashed in the autumn of 1965 began to abate. During President Suharto's New

Order (1967–1998), democracy was reduced to ritualized elections designed to ensure regime continuity, with a very thin veneer of democratic legitimacy. In between elections the New Order suspended democratic politics and stifled dissent. Since 1999, Indonesians have embraced a democracy that has become surprisingly robust and resilient despite the long shadows of prolonged military-dominated authoritarian government and the failures of democracy in the 1950s.

From the outset, Sukarno was ambivalent about the wisdom of adopting western-style parliamentary democracy, doubting that party competition and fractious debates would prove effective in a culture accustomed to the traditional consensual decision-making style (*musyawarah-mufakat*) practiced in villages. Given the enormous problems facing the new nation, it is not surprising that democracy did not prove to be a magic wand. Sukarno, with military backing, decided to end what he viewed as a failed experiment and declared martial law in 1957 to crack down on regional rebellions. In 1959 he established Guided Democracy and reinstituted the 1945 Constitution that granted broad powers to the executive. Sukarno called it democracy with leadership, but he proved to be an unreliable guide.

He tried to reconcile contradictions and assert a unity of purpose that defied evident realities. His concept of NASAKOM, first articulated in the late 1920s, asserted a blending of nationalism (in this context meaning the military), Islam and communism, reflecting the prevailing fault-lines of Indonesian politics. His syncretic instincts aimed at creating a space where advocates of competing ideologies and agendas might constructively work out differences. Suspending democracy was a strategic retreat, while NASAKOM was an attempt to overcome the bitter enmities between stakeholders that could not be sloganeered away. Each, however, had an Idea that could not accommodate the others. Guided Democracy was consistent with a stronger secular state and prevailed over Islamic rebellions, but undermined government institutions and lacked coherent policies. As a result, the economy nosedived and Sukarno alienated the military with his Konfrontasi campaign (1963–1966), provoking an undeclared, low-intensity border war with Malaysia on the island of Borneo (Kalimantan) that proved a costly distraction from Indonesia's considerable real problems. With gathering economic problems and political turmoil, Guided Democracy lost credibility.

Sukarno's working relations with communist political leaders may have seemed reasonable given the Partai Kommunis Indonesia's (PKI) considerable membership, the third largest in the world at the time, but resulted in his ouster in the murky events of September 1965 known as Gestapu (see Chapters 7, 8 and 9). The orthodox narrative presents the military as thwarting a communist coup against Sukarno, thereby saving the nation. This narrative is vigorously contested, but in the aftermath it is clear that the military cooperated with Islamic groups to eradicate communism in Indonesia, causing massive bloodshed and as many as one million deaths. Subsequently, the military ushered in New Order democracy under Suharto.

The New Order was so named to draw a distinction with the poor governance under Sukarno and to inaugurate a fresh new era of responsible government and political stability. On March 11, 1966 Sukarno ostensibly signed over power to

General Suharto who then moved to ban the PKI and depose Sukarno's cabinet ministers. It was essentially a dictatorship that prioritized stability and promoted a Green Revolution, population control, rural electrification and other measures aimed at raising living standards. It stage-managed six elections with successive victories by Golkar, the military's version of a party; membership was mandatory for civil servants. The real legitimacy of New Order democracy, however, rested on maintaining stability and sound management of the economy. Yet, this stability relied on repressive methods while crony capitalism concentrated the benefits among the favored few. Those questioning or challenging the New Order's dubious legitimacy could expect harsh consequences until the system ran out of credibility.

Suharto was forced out of power in 1998 owing to the collapse of the economy, and his vice president B.J. Habibie took over. He allowed largely free and fair elections in 1999 that were won by the party led by Sukarno's daughter, Megawati Sukarnoputri. Habibie came second, but due to his role in allowing East Timorese to vote their way out of Indonesian rule (see Chapter 10), his nationalist credentials were tarnished. At that time parliament elected the president and chose Abdurrahman Wahid, leader of a small moderate Islamic party that was part of an improvised coalition. Known as Gus Dur, this nearly blind cleric had the unenviable task of being the first post-New Order leader and had to contend with powerful status quo actors from that era and intensely partisan politics in a system that had not yet embraced democratic values and norms. And Indonesia was in crisis, racked by chaos and violence across the archipelago. The New Order stability was fast unraveling, and finally a corruption scandal led to Gus Dur's impeachment in 2001, and Megawati assumed power. In response to the infamous Bali bombing in 2002, her government passed a new anti-terrorism law that expanded the powers of the military and police, which sparked a nationalist backlash among Indonesians who viewed her as an American puppet and worried that her support for the US war on terror might undermine democratic consolidation. Megawati also proved a feckless leader and her administration lost legitimacy due to widespread corruption. In 2004 she lost the first direct presidential election to Susilo Bambang Yudhoyono, who was reelected in 2009. His decade in office was undistinguished, but not marred by major crisis or scandal, sustaining the democratic transition. Perhaps the greatest achievement was in managing the response to the 2004 tsunami that devastated coastal Aceh and seizing that opportunity to end the secessionist insurrection there (see Chapter 11).

Under the New Order, the doctrine of *dwifungsi* claimed a twin role for the military in the security and political realms, reflecting the leadership's perception that it must serve as guardian of the state. In practice this meant an end to civilian rule and a military presence in top posts at all levels of government throughout the archipelago, including unelected reserved seats in parliament, averaging about 15% of all seats until declining to 7% in the 1998 elections; in 2004 the military finally relinquished its reserved seats. The military's decision to retreat from politics owed much to an internal consensus on the need to reform the military, insulate the institution from political machinations and nurture professionalism. Its return to the barracks has bolstered democratic consolidation, but it retains extensive power and there is an implicit agreement that its officers will not be held accountable for past human rights abuses or shady ongoing business activities.

In national elections in Indonesia's post-New Order democracy, the Islamic vote has fluctuated between one-third and one-quarter of the vote. Since this is divided among several parties, Islam has not become a dominant or monolithic political force, but the popular appeal of religion pressures secular parties to adjust and accommodate. In the 2014 parliamentary elections, the combined tally of five Islamic parties amounted to nearly one-third of the total votes cast, with the National Awakening Party (PKB) gaining about 9% of the vote, making it the largest Islamic party. It is the political vehicle of the Nahdlatul Ulama (NU), Indonesia's largest Islamic social organization with 40 million members, centered in east and central Java. The National Mandate Party (PAN) gained almost 8% of the vote and represents Muhammadiyah, the second largest Islamic social organization with 29 million members. These Islamic organizations operate a network of branches at the local level addressing various unmet needs, including education, while expounding a moderate Islam. Their clerics and leaders condemn religious extremism and intolerance in terms of Islamic values that are more in tune with Indonesian norms. As such, Indonesia does not seem in danger of being hijacked by fundamentalist Islam, but its citizens are increasingly endangered by the unchecked rise of Islamic vigilante groups.

In the 2014 presidential election Joko Widodo, popularly known as Jokowi, prevailed in a closely fought contest against millionaire businessman Prabowo Subianto. Jokowi surged from being an obscure mayor of the ancient capital of Solo in central Java to the governorship of Jakarta and then the presidential palace, an unprecedented meteoric rise for a political establishment outsider of humble origins. His populist style and anti-corruption crusade resonated powerfully with people fed up with SBY's disengaged leadership. But Jokowi's massive lead in the polls was whittled down to single digits on the eve of the election as Prabowo engaged in attack politics, relying on US consultants, and played the Muslim card, currying favor with various Islamic parties that have backed the growing intolerance towards religious minorities that marred SBY's era. He also tried to use Jokowi's tolerance towards the nation's Shiite minority (most Indonesians are Sunni) to his political advantage.

Prabowo is most notorious for his role as commander of the special forces under his father-in-law President Suharto, and his alleged role in orchestrating riots and killing students in Jakarta in 1998. But most of Indonesia's young voters don't recall or care about those episodes, and indeed Prabowo's tough rhetoric and assertive grandstanding presented a stark contrast to the more low-key Jokowi, and help explain his better-than-expected showing. Jokowi in the end won because the less privileged see him as their advocate and Indonesians support his track record of anti-graft campaigns and efforts to protect indigenous producers from globalization. But the fragmented parliament—his party only holds one-third of the seats—raises doubts that he can become a transformational leader, and indeed he rules under the shadow of party leader Megawati who played a key role in his cabinet choices. Internally, there are high expectations that he will promote Indonesia's fundamental Idea—Unity in Diversity—and reassert tolerance for religious minorities. There are also hopes that he will provide needed leadership on dealing with the long-running problem of Papua that has festered because security forces have played too prominent a role in Jakarta's engagement with this far-flung province (see Chapter 11).

One-Party Rule

One of the striking features of all five countries is the prolonged period of what effectively was one-party/military rule in the latter half of the 20th century. The CCP has ruled China continuously since 1949 and has demonstrated a combination of ideological flexibility, opportunism and ruthlessness to retain power. In South Korea there was prolonged military rule from 1961 to 1987; while former General Suharto ruled Indonesia from 1966 to 1998. Both were authoritarian governments that staged elections in order to claim legitimacy without embracing democratic practices. In South Korea and Indonesia the military played a decisive political role in suppressing dissent and democratic aspirations. As mentioned above, in Indonesia the military had an official political role based on the concept of dwifungsi that enshrined the military's dual security and political roles.

Japan features a multi-party democracy, but the Liberal Democratic Party has dominated Japanese politics since it was established in 1955. It jousted with the once powerful Japan Socialist Party (JSP), but this party had faded into oblivion by the late 1990s. The LDP was ousted briefly in 1993 and again in 2009, but overall since 1955 Japan has been a one-party democracy. Congress, like the LDP, has dominated Indian politics for most of the post-independence era, although since the 1990s the BJP has become an effective rival for power, whereas Japan as of 2015 has no effective opposition.

In all of the countries, the prolonged monopoly on political power raises questions about the nature of democracy and has sparked criticism of stagnation, dysfunction and a democratic deficit. On the other hand, especially in Japan and South Korea, stable government has facilitated policy continuities that have promoted development and raised standards of living. This development state model involving extensive government intervention in markets, close coordination between the public and private sectors and industrial targeting has delivered remarkable results. The CCP's development model based on communist ideology had disastrous bouts of impractical policymaking and political turmoil. However, the CCP managed to initiate a transformation in economic policies in the late 1970s that overcame the calamitous convulsions and policies of its first two decades in power. Since then, emulating key aspects of Japan's model, the CCP has delivered impressive growth and improved living standards, catapulting some 300 million people out of poverty. Under Suharto, technocrats trained in the US and advised by the World Bank and IMF implemented policies with his backing and, as in China and South

Korea, were largely insulated from democratic pressures. While crony capitalism, corruption and repression were hallmarks of the Suharto era, the government did raise living standards and ensured political stability conducive to economic growth. Certainly the New Order democracy was deeply flawed, curtailed civil rights and involved extensive human rights violations, but its development record was relatively good by regional standards.

India too had prolonged one-party rule, and initially Nehru tried to insulate economic policymaking from parliamentary politics by entrusting technocrats. But increasingly politics shaped policymaking as pandering to constituencies for electoral advantage came at the expense of efficient allocation of resources and sustainable polices. Under Congress, India became known for the "Hindu rate of growth," meaning moderate steady growth based on extensive state intervention and unsustainable subsidies, which led to a meltdown in government finance by the end of the 1980s. In 1998, Suharto's New Order also ended in a financial meltdown, but this owed more to external developments—the Asian financial crisis—than poor policy choices.

Has India's democracy been reduced to the confines of campaigns and elections, but otherwise functioning, or mostly faltering, in suspended animation? Sunil Khilnani argues that the robust democratic vision of Nehru has not been realized and has mostly been frittered away. While Indians may well be the most highly politicized in the region, their enthusiasm for democracy confronts a shoddy level of governance that compares unfavorably with the other nations in our sample. Corruption, massive and petty, dominates political discourse and daily life, yet passing strict laws to curb it has been an epic struggle. The Aam Aadmi Party (AAM; Common Man Party) ran on an anti-corruption platform and surprised pundits in December 2012 when it won 28 out of 70 seats in the New Delhi state assembly and took power briefly in a coalition government. A brand new party improvising an organization and team of candidates managed to overcome entrenched insiders and capture the imagination of India's disenchanted voters. The animated campaign featured volunteers roving the streets wearing Gandhi caps and wielding straw brooms, sweeping the streets, and the political establishment away, with their gesture politics. They campaigned on the politics of the daily, promising water services to those in India's capital who had long gone without, and lower electricity prices, which had been fixed at high levels owing to collusive practices exposed by the party.

The AAM tapped into widespread exasperation with the ruling, hereditary mainstream political class that for long had been preoccupied with feathering its own nest rather than improving the lives of ordinary citizens. After forming a coalition government at the end of 2013, the AAM and its leader, Arvind Kejriwal, engaged in the theater of politics, taking to the streets and staging sit-ins to protest undemocratic practices such as the behind-the-scenes dominance of Indian politics by Mukesh Ambani, a billionaire businessman, and gas price fixing. Kejriwal refused to move into the palatial chief minister's residence and eschewed the official limousine, showing that he would not be coopted by the trappings of power. When its coalition partner, Congress, refused to back anti-corruption legislation, the AAM dramatically resigned from government in February 2014, after only 49 days in power. Fighting corruption was its signature policy and Kejriwal refused to compromise, setting him apart from mainstream politicians more intent on getting and keeping power than promoting good governance. In 2015, the AAM reprised its New Delhi victory, but it has been beset by internal feuding.

In China, President Xi Jinping has led a crackdown on academic freedom as a number of professors have been dismissed or detained. This purging of professors from leading academic institutions is part of a wider campaign against free-thinking intellectuals advocating various political reforms, defending the Chinese Constitution, calling for liberalization, discussing John Stuart Mill or urging equality for minorities. The Party is showing it has the power to repress, but in doing so appears to lack confidence that it can prevail in the contest of ideas vital to democracy. Ironically, while scholars find themselves removed from the classroom for trampling on sensitive topics, members of the blogosphere seem to enjoy greater intellectual freedom to discuss taboo topics. This virtual democracy in cyberspace provides an outlet and discussions can be carefully monitored and pruned back at the Party's discretion. A series of political directives banning liberal topics from the classroom since President Xi took power signal that the CCP is not contemplating significant political liberalization and indeed, by making an example of prominent intellectuals, is reverting to form where intimidation and coercion stifle democratic discourse and aspirations. The cyber pressure valve notwithstanding, the freedom of expression remains akin to the fine art of walking on thin ice.

The political sclerosis besetting China and the entrenched interest groups that have discredited the Party make invoking nationalism the path of least resistance. In these circumstances a nationalistic circling of the wagons is far too tempting even if it undermines China's smile diplomacy in the early 2000s of reassuring neighbors that its growing power and influence do not represent a threat. China's more assertive nationalism in the region finds a receptive domestic audience. The risks are not deemed as critical as a restive populace. Diverting attention to the disputes in surrounding seas to stoke a unifying nationalism helps the Party in many ways to buy time to deal with domestic problems while nurturing loyalty to the state.

In conclusion, it is clear that democracy has sunk deep roots in Asia and is a key element of national identity and Asian values. Democratic civil liberties, transparency and accountability, checks and balances on those in power, and peaceful transitions in power between political rivals are the good governance gold standard in four of our nations and are also desired by many Chinese. Democracy has become the stage on which nationalism is contested and asserted, shaping national identity and tempting politicians to embrace more extreme positions to win electoral advantage in ways that heighten regional tensions and reduce the scope for compromise. In our next chapter we turn to sport and how this also serves as a stage for nationalist posturing, identity politics, branding and war by other means.

6

Sports Nationalism

Is sport the new opium of the masses? This updating of Marx's dictum about religion resonates powerfully in a world of global sports superstars watched and marketed through the international media. People around the world are obsessed with sports, or at least watching them, reading and discussing about them, and otherwise consuming them through branded apparel, from hats down to sneakers and choice of colors, whether local teams or national sides. Even in the remote backwaters of Asia, in the most unlikely places—think Laotian monks in Luang Prabang, novices in Bhutanese monasteries and villagers in remote Myanmar and East Timor—sports fever is widespread, fed by satellite television that reaches almost everywhere; poor hamlets of dilapidated shacks are improbably festooned with giant satellite dishes that seem spectacularly out of place, suggesting priorities and the seemingly unlimited reach of television.

Sport spectacles like the FIFA football World Cup command worldwide audiences as nations battle for supremacy. Even in nations without a direct stake in the outcome, fans deliriously cheer goals scored by foreign "stars," while English Premier League football's Manchester United commands legions of fans throughout Asia. As Eric Hobsbawm observes, "The dialectics of the relations between globalization, national identity and xenophobia are dramatically illustrated in the public activity that combines all three: football" (Hobsbawm 2012, 89). The pandemonium is on display at a museum in Seoul that has a room shaped like a soccer ball where one can watch replays of the South Koreans' stellar performance in the 2002 FIFA World Cup on a massive wrap-around screen and feel the thumping sounds of their football-crazed fans cheering in deafening surround sound. There are also elements of homogenization as rivalries resemble each other regardless of the sport and international organizations and hierarchies are replicated. And, it

Nationalism in Asia: A History Since 1945, First Edition. Jeff Kingston.

doesn't really matter where the sport originates, as they become indigenized in identities and transformed into iconic symbols of nationalism

Cricket, another quintessential Asian sport, can seem much more like a religion during important test matches, while young Chinese men can't get enough of NBA basketball, similar to Japanese fans and US Major League baseball, especially since Japanese stars have made their mark in America's national pastime. When the Japanese national team won the World Baseball Classic twice, in 2006 and 2009, beating the Americans at their own game, the nation exulted in jubilation and pride. Nations also take pride in hosting major events like the Olympics or Commonwealth Games as they provide nation-branding opportunities to showcase progress and virtues. Indonesia has made its mark in world badminton, but this has not really translated into a nationalist obsession. And, while Indonesia has hosted regional sporting events, again the nationalistic repercussions have been muted; so in this chapter the focus is on the four other nations and their experience on the global sporting stage.

International sporting events are a chance to compete against teams, players and specialists from other nations and thus can serve as an outlet or pressure valve for national rivalries. Sports can thus serve as a relatively peaceful substitute for more violent and destructive expressions of nationalist passions; something like war without the shooting. The playing fields are the battlefields where nations sublimate martial inclinations, ideally in an atmosphere of comradely cooperation and sportsmanship. Yet it doesn't always work out that way and national sports rivalries may do nothing to dissipate nationalist rancor and can actually inflame passions. This was evident at the Asia Cup 2004, hosted by China, when local fans rioted after Japan defeated the home side in the final. In fact, throughout the football tournament Chinese fans booed the Japanese side and drowned out the Japanese anthem, conduct that was ascribed to anger over unresolved historical grievances projected onto the pitch.

Sports setbacks and scandals can also sting national pride, especially for sports that are embedded in national identity. Japanese media, for example, expressed national embarrassment about the poor performance of its judoists at the 2012 London Olympics, prompting public criticism and soul searching. From this disappointment a major scandal erupted over the extensive verbal abuse of judoists by the male coach of the women's team and the failure of the Judo Association to do anything about the women's complaints. This issue came to the fore at a time when the nation was reeling from the suicide of a high school boy who had been physically abused and berated by his coach. The media suddenly launched a moral panic about the widespread practice of corporal punishment in sports at all levels in Japan, with a cascade of cruel and heartrending revelations, and videos of grueling practice sessions shot by players with their cell phones. The reliance on corporal punishment (*taibatsu*) and verbal abuse is long established in the Japanese sports world and considered crucial to training and instilling mental toughness. Thus, there was a generalized awareness of such practices and they were tacitly condoned, but as gruesome cases came to the fore, tolerance shifted to outrage, challenging norms that had prevailed in Japan long after tolerance for such abuses had evaporated around the world. Clearly, the shame of being "outed" globally mattered. What Japanese had long considered a version of "tough love" suddenly became something society found objectionable, at least in public discourse. Polls indicated that many people, including players subject to the abuses, still thought such practices helpful, but social acceptance of such practices is fading and there is greater scrutiny of how coaches conduct themselves.

Sumo is considered the quintessential Japanese sport, one that has been around in its organized form since 1757. Very large men, some weighing more than 200 kilograms, grapple with each other in a sport that relies on size, strength and technique. Since the 1990s foreign *rikishi*, as grapplers are known, have come to dominate the sport. Between 2003–2015, Japanese born rikishi won only five out of seventy-eight tournaments and since 2006, none until January 2016, a prolonged drought that wounded national pride. Since 2003 there has not been a single Japanese *yokozuna* (grand champion), while in the 2000s there have been four Mongolians who have attained this rare and prestigious ranking, and in the 1990s two Hawaiian behemoths also became yokozuna. Despite foreign dominance of the top ranks, sumo popularity has bounced back from its own taibatsu scandal in 2007, in which a young rikishi was beaten to death, and revelations of gambling (2010) and match-fixing scandals (2011). The Mongolians have their own rich wrestling tradition and, unlike the Hawaiians who relied on size and strength, are admired for their consummate technique, although one was forced to retire due to his unseemly nightlife escapades. Rikishi, especially yokozuna, are expected to be dignified and models of decorum, or at the very least to stay out of the gossip magazine headlines and not have run-ins with police. In 2003 the sumo association imposed a limit of one foreign-born rikishi per sumo stable, reflecting concerns that skilled foreign rikishi might be too much of a good thing.

Overall, the Japanese public has accommodated foreign dominance of sumo, but expectations that judoists dominate in World Championships and Olympics have not been matched by results, prompting a collective shaking of heads in dismay familiar to sports fans around the world. The hopes of one billion rest on the shoulders of the 11-man Indian national cricket team, and when it is in poor form and not dominating there is much handwringing and disquiet. In much the same way South Korea thinks it "owns" tae kwon do and winning is taken for granted, while losing is a matter of shame.

China and Indonesia have long dominated badminton, a sport that has roots in an ancient Chinese game, and are intensely competitive, as the world found out at the 2012 London Olympics. It turned out that female players from both nations and also South Korea deliberately threw matches to improve their draws in the next round and thereby improve their chances of winning a medal. While it may have been sound strategy, it did not conform to Olympic norms of proper conduct and the World Badminton Federation expelled eight women players for a lack of sportsmanship and disgracing the game. In all three nations this was an unsettling development, with anticipated medals lost, aggravated by a humiliating moment on the world stage. By contrast, also at the 2012 Olympics, the Japanese women's football coach admitted to the media that against South Africa he played for a draw, and deliberately did not go for the win, also with an eye to a more desirable draw in the next round, but there was no disciplinary action taken.

The capacity of sports to ignite and amplify nationalist passions and prejudices is as extraordinary as is their power to console, unify, uplift and generate goodwill. In July 2011 the Japanese women's football team defeated the US and won the FIFA Women's World Cup. This was an extraordinary achievement, marking Japan's first victory ever over the Americans and its first championship. It happened in an awful year for the Japanese people, reeling as they were from the horrific March 11, 2011 tsunami that pulverized coastal towns in northeast Japan and caused three nuclear reactor meltdowns. The relentlessly depressing news put the nation into a collective mood of despair and so the stunning victory lifted spirits by providing a rare feel-good story amid all the misery and suffering, one that briefly took minds off the terrible tragedies. Similarly, the success of the Beijing Olympics raised Chinese spirits following the devastating 2008 Sichuan earthquake.

In this chapter we consider mega-events hosted in Asia, including the three Summer Olympic Games in Tokyo (1964), Seoul (1988) and Beijing (2008), the 2002 FIFA World Cup jointly hosted by Korea and Japan, and finally the 2010 Commonwealth Games hosted by India. These sporting spectacles were showcases for these nations and inspired nationalistic outpourings while also facilitating international diplomacy and embracing, to different degrees, the dictates of globalization. Beyond the economic impact of vast public works spending to prepare necessary infrastructure and sporting venues, to some extent the mega-events also had significant social and political repercussions. But first we examine two sports that many Asians are crazy about, featuring bats, and balls flung at batters at speed and with spin. The bats are made from wood, willow for cricket and ash for baseball, but the two games have little else in common except that both have served as repositories of national identity and exemplars of national character, and neither originated in Asia.

Cricket

> Since the 1990s cricket has been the strongest register of national consensus and of nationalist aspirations, often times acting as a soothing balm at a time when the nation has been in the throes of communal tension. (Nair 2011, 575)

India is the home of cricket, but all of South Asia is fanatical about the sport, as Pakistan, Sri Lanka and increasingly Bangladesh make their mark on the game.

Cricket is India's national sport and all-encompassing obsession. Triumph in the 2011 World Cup, co-hosted with Sri Lanka and Bangladesh, meant India's team did not disappoint national expectations for victory and reinforced feelings of national pride riding high on India's economic boom. Cricket is the stage on which India has often shined, but prior to its victory in the 1983 World Cup, India had won only one

World Cup match, back in 1975. Its 1983 championship shifted the center of cricket to India, where the mass audience dramatically transformed the commercial possibilities. This coincided with the spread of satellite television and the growth of a middle class, launching a dream scenario for marketing. It was also the first time that a developing nation seized a pivotal role in the international sporting world.

There is no doubt that Indians promoted significant innovations in 21st-century cricket, in the form of the speedy Twenty20 format and the Indian Premier League (IPL), which have had a far-reaching influence in globalizing the sport, boosting revenues and reaching vastly greater audiences. Introduced by the British during the colonial era, the Indians are writing new chapters in the annals of the game, punctuated by nationalistic enthusiasm for the national team, and considerable pride in India's pivotal role in transforming cricket with entrepreneurship and showmanship, generating spectacular revenues and rampant corruption (Astill 2013). Lalit Modi, the brains behind the IPL, adapted an English football model, the English Premier League, to local conditions and created a lucrative business model. Although implicated in scandals of systemic corruption and abuse of power, he managed to introduce a flavor of Bollywood to the staid cricket grounds, mutually reinforcing sources of popular national identity. The IPL is a mirror for India's new middle class—brash, materialistic and successful—and commands their attention because there is a sense of shared stardom and exuberant confidence; nationalism as a marketing strategy. India's demographic dividend, a relatively youthful growing population, is nowhere more evident than in the commercial success of cricket and the aspirational lifestyle it embodies. The IPL's audience—mostly young urban middle-class, and a significant percentage of women—is the Holy Grail for marketing and as such attracts massive sponsorship. The IPL promotes a tech-savvy, youthful and globalized image that appeals to and boosts national pride, promoting a Shining India, far from the lingering realities of poverty, sectarian violence and economic stagnation. The marketing savvy of cricket has spawned numerous offshoots; cell phone use rocketed from 234 million in 2007 to 770 million by 2011 and many apps were developed to ensure that cricket fans got their daily fix with constant updates, instant scoreboards and various other cricket-related services. The rise of contemporary India coincided with the runaway growth of cricket under Indian stewardship and thus sport fed into broader nationalistic expectations that India would play a greater role in global affairs and become a leading power.

Cricket is far more than a game in India and serves as a touchstone of national identity. It is a source of self-esteem even if only experienced vicariously as a fan. Other nations have their national sports, but none of these comes close to the all-encompassing, feverish passion for cricket that prevails in India. Whereas people in most nations spread their loyalties among various sports, in India cricket reigns supreme, the singular focus of a sport-crazed people. Match-fixing scandals and corruption have generated a profound sense of betrayal in a country accustomed to corruption as a way of life, precisely because cricket is a sacred way of life and hallowed ground. Cricket stars are much more than celebrities—they are iconic figures who inspire a level of devotion usually reserved for deities. The retirement of Sachin

Tendulkar in 2013, at the ripe age of 40 after playing at the highest levels of the sport for nearly a quarter of a century, notching a record 200 test matches, scoring 100 international centuries (100 runs scored in a game) and becoming the highest run-scorer in the history of the sport, prompted widespread grief. This was a watershed moment for many fans who grew up idolizing the nation's perennial premier batsman, watching him perform skillfully, efficiently and effortlessly. He has been called the most revered Indian since Mahatma Gandhi and the God of cricket. His departure was celebrated with great fanfare, but also deeply mourned because aside from his ethereal skills with the cricket bat he was a man of impeccable manners, virtue and humility despite all the adulation and accolades. He emerged as a national star and hero just as India's economy was revving up in the 1990s, and was a familiar figure amid profound socio-economic upheaval, and unsullied by match-fixing and other corruption scandals. He became a nominated member of parliament and philanthropist, in short someone to inspire Indians accustomed to uninspiring leaders. His memoirs, *Playing It My Way* (2014), became a runaway best-seller

In a country so colossally divided by region, ethnicity, language and religion, cricket is a fountainhead of common Indian identity, a language and passion that creates social cohesion and enables Indians to bond and feel united. Cricket embodies culture, society and the economy like nothing else and nurtures a reservoir of shared pride and collective identity. Previously, players hailed from mostly middle- and upper-class backgrounds, but contemporary cricket teams feature more socio-economic diversity and players come from all over India, reinforcing the idea of India based on inclusiveness and merit. In many respects, the sense of cricket as a principled way to conduct oneself is seen to exemplify the desired national character that is very rarely on display. Cricket pervades everyday life in India, a frenzied devotion that is immediately obvious, from the ubiquitous street games to the media's saturation coverage. For big matches, the television audience in India can reach over 400 million viewers.

Sporting competition is supposedly a healthy outlet for nationalistic or communal passions, diverting battlefield passions onto the playing field. The destruction of the Babri Mosque in 1992 by Hindu chauvinists plunged the nation into violent rioting and collective insanity. The splendid 183-run performance by Mohammad Azharuddin, the Indian captain, against England in 1993 proved a healing moment since he was a Muslim player. His performance drew widespread praise and much was made of a Muslim leading the national team to a pride-inspiring victory, helping to quell communal tensions. Cricket diplomacy has also helped build bridges with Pakistan over the years, although it has not prevented them from being torn down. For example, the IPL conducts annual auctions for players as a way to spread talent around the league, but in 2009, following the 2008 Mumbai terrorist attack, not one Pakistan player was selected by any team in the auction despite some excellent talent.

Supposedly, national teams represent their nations and manage to transcend differences through sportsmanship and professionalism, but often sports competitions intensify rivalries and the thirst for victory breeds a passion for revenge and retribution. Certainly the relationship between Pakistan and India is *sui generis*, nations sundered at birth, divided by religion and baptized in blood. The great commonalities of shared history and civilization are overshadowed by contemporary differences rooted in politics and religion. But the people of both nations have a cricket craze, and the national rivalry that has sparked four wars has also spilled onto the cricket grounds where matches are played with a special intensity because national pride is at stake. Cricket is India's secular religion, one that cuts across class, linguistic, regional and religious schisms, except when it doesn't.

The headline read: "Students suspended for cheering wrong team" (*New York Times*, March 7, 2014). Sports fans immediately understand the connotations of the wrong team, meaning that one has transgressed a boundary of loyalty that brings negative consequences, whether it is at British football matches where hooligans impose their preferences by often violent means, or anywhere one is rooting in the minority. It turns out that Kashmiri college students cheered for the Pakistani national cricket team in a televised match with India. The 67 offending students/fans were suspended and removed from their dorms, with the university explaining that it was unacceptable to root against the national team. There was also concern about repercussions and reprisals by Indian fans, and it did not help that India lost the match.

It is not clear to what extent the students were venting resentment about decades of Indian military repression in Kashmir where half a million Indian troops are stationed, but there are grounds for suspicion that this was an outpouring of Kashmiri nationalism. As discussed in Chapter 10, these security forces and paramilitary groups are often implicated in random killings, violence and disappearances, but have not been held accountable. The partition of India in 1947 gave birth to Pakistan, an explicitly Islamic republic, and Kashmir has remained a disputed territory ever since; India and Pakistan have fought three wars over Kashmir. Kashmir has a majority Muslim population, which has few outlets for accumulated grievances under New Delhi's martial rule, where curfews, checkpoints and violence are common and the civil liberties and tolerance enshrined in India's constitution are observed selectively and often ignored. Free speech is sacred to democracy and a constitutional right, but in India remains an ambiguous liberty. It is circumscribed by laws that prohibit free expression deemed hurtful to some groups, creating a pretext to ban books, bar speeches and, apparently, cheering for the wrong team. The logic of clamping down on free expression is the deadly reality that hurt feelings carry potential for violence in a nation where communal rioting has been frequent, widespread and destructive.

Supporting the wrong team in this case meant India's mortal enemy, and given the bad blood between the nations, fanned by war and repeated incidents of Pakistani-instigated terrorism, the students certainly knew they were being provocative. And yet, given India's proud democratic tradition and embrace of tolerance, this small incident speaks to larger problems. The emotions of Indian nationalism are explosive and dangerous for the large Muslim minority which serves as a handy target for a public frustrated by various issues, including the failure of the government to prevent or respond to terrorist incidents instigated by Pakistan's intelligence services. This episode evokes the expression of shame by one of India's preeminent historians, Ramachandra Guha, who recalled driving through a Muslim enclave in Mumbai during a Pakistan–India cricket match and seeing large Indian flags draped from windows and balconies (Guha 2012). He felt it was shameful for all Indians that these Muslim Indians had to go to such lengths to demonstrate their loyalty as a means of warding off attacks by Hindu militants ever eager to portray local Muslims as a fifth column of Pakistani intrigue. Cricket, the magisterial game that enthralls Indians and unites them in a singular passion, is embedded in Indian national identity. As such it is also an outlet for fractious nationalism and simmering grievances. Certainly the story of cricket in India is far larger than such small isolated incidents, but they reveal how complex domestic grievances such as Kashmir become expressed in national rivalries that are not easily defused by sports and can be inflamed by them.

World Baseball Classic

Japan is not only king of Asian baseball but also won the two inaugural World Baseball Classics (WBC), making them the real world champions despite American conceits about their own World Series of baseball. South Korea and Taiwan also have baseball leagues, and the South Korean team has done well against Japan, with both teams motivated by nationalist ardor and patriotic zeal. Losing to any team is hard to swallow, but losing to each other takes the pain to another level.

Japan won against South Korea in 2006 and again in 2009, pulling out an extra innings victory that added much to the thrill of winning and the agony of defeat. The US Major Leagues are the pinnacle of the sport and unlike in football there is no international parity in the form of the English Premier League, Spain's La Liga or Germany's Bundesliga. Yet the US has not done well in the WBC, not fielding strong teams with top players, and evincing little enthusiasm or interest in an event that was dreamed up by Major League Baseball (MLB) to make money and as part of a global promotion and marketing strategy. Unexpectedly, the WBC proved popular with fans, especially in Asia and Latin America, but even in the US, despite the team's poor performance. This success also serves as a riposte to the International Olympic Committee (IOC) decision to drop baseball from the Olympics after Beijing 2008. The nationalistic nature of national team competition appeals and fans enjoy watching players giving it their patriotic all, in contrast to pampered and ungracious superstars who couldn't be bothered to even participate.

Japanese are fanatical about baseball, practicing and playing the game like modern-day samurai, dedicated to the Way of baseball (Whiting 2009). Pitchers throw until their arms are sore and then throw some more; fielders have a 1,000-fungo drill; and total dedication is the name of the game. It is a game of blood, sweat and tears, one that showcases national character. The national high school baseball tournament features a regional elimination format that transfixes the nation twice a year during the spring and summer championships. These games are covered live on television and boast high viewership ratings, with packed stadiums of fans loudly urging their teams on, led by boisterous cheerleading teams down to the last out. This high school baseball tournament is a national ritual that is part of Japan's collective identity in ways that Americans find hard to fathom. The South Korean national high school tournament is played with the same intensity and devoted following.

Japanese are proud that some of their superstars have done well in the Major Leagues—Hideo Nomo, Ichiro Suzuki, Daisuke Matsuzaka, Hideki Matsui, Yu Darvish and Masahiro Tanaka—but they also have a chip on their collective shoulder about the preeminence of American baseball. The WBC is by invitation and MLB arranges everything, soliciting no input from other nations' baseball bodies, naturally generating resentment. There is a sense that Americans are arrogant and rely too much on natural talent, while Japanese are proud that they make the most of their potential by constant practice and all-out effort. In Japan, when the WBC rolled around, the best players came forward and the nation fielded its best team, one completely dedicated to winning. Beating the US team was special and winning the first two WBCs filled Japanese with nationalistic pride and not a little hubris. Forgotten were the humiliating routine thrashings by US Major League teams touring Japan.

It does not take much to stir up bad blood between the Koreans and Japanese and so the WBC clashes provided ample opportunities to extend the national feuding. Ichiro Suzuki, a superstar in Japan and the US, set a number of Major League batting records, and impressed his teammates and fans with his dedication and all-out effort, in addition to superb fielding. He stirred controversy with provocative remarks aimed at the Korean team, in 2006 saying he wanted to show the Korean and Taiwanese teams how much better Japanese baseball is and how long it would take them to catch up. After Japan lost two games to the Korean team in the 2009 WBC, on the eve of the third game, in what was the championship final, Ichiro stated it would be just too humiliating to lose a third time, a comment dripping with condescension and incendiary innuendo. The Koreans had not helped matters by planting their national flag in the pitcher's mound after their second win. In the final, Ichiro drove in the winning run in extra innings and Japan prevailed. What remains unclear is why the Koreans pitched to Ichiro, one of the game's all-time best hitters, with first base open. They could have walked him, and indeed this is fairly standard practice, so the decision to pitch to him was unusual and attracted considerable commentary in the post-game analysis. It seems that the Koreans challenged him because they wanted to show him up for his disrespectful comments; nationalist passions trumped good baseball strategy.

East Asian Olympics

The Olympic Games illustrate how sports can be a fruitful way of building understanding and creating a web of exchanges that bring nations together and give credence to supporters' claims that they promote mutual understanding and amity.

They are a safe venue for expressions of nationalistic enthusiasm as fans cheer on the athletes, who serve as state surrogates, engaging in "combat," with displays of national flags and playing of national anthems for the medal winners. Nations take the medal tallies seriously as a measure of national strength and physical prowess. The Olympics are also the ultimate branding event, a global platform where a nation can define itself to the rest of the world and assert a national narrative both at home and overseas.

Japan (1964), South Korea (1988) and China (2008) staged the Summer Olympics in what are often referred to as their "coming out parties," a celebration of achievements, a showcase of national cultures, strengths and virtues, and a fundamental rebranding of the nation. In East Asia the host nations outdid themselves with state of the art facilities, smooth logistics and snazzy architecture that wowed visitors and viewers around the world. The Olympics may indeed spring from the cradle of western civilization—and in modern times have been dominated by western athletes and significantly influenced and subsidized by the US media through its outlays on television rights and commercial sponsorship by global brands—but it is misleading to portray the East Asian Olympics through the subaltern's lens, because this overlooks agency by the hosting nations and how they exploited the Games in pursuit of their own agendas (Collins 2011). Naturally the hosting countries sought to impress and measure up, but they also wanted to promote internationalization of the Games for their own political purposes. Each hosting nation has been a beneficiary of the global trading regime, and their successes in joining the international system, overcoming adversity and raising citizens' living standards are a cause for celebration. Japan, South Korea and China each indigenized the Games in their own way while also showing the world what they wanted to be seen for, and stood for, and what they were contributing to the world. In a sense they were pioneering the path towards the 21st-century "Asian Century," an incremental and gradual process as the center of the world has shifted from West to East. Significantly, Japan and South Korea are US client states, as allies and leading economic partners, and thus it is important not to discount the prevailing Cold War politics of the modern Olympics; they showcased the capitalist camp's better development record *vis-à-vis* the Soviet bloc. China, as a former US Cold War adversary and growing regional rival, one shunned by western governments in the wake of the violent suppression of the Tiananmen Square pro-democracy movement in 1989, clearly saw a major opportunity in hosting the Games to reclaim political legitimacy and gain global affirmation.

Ever rising budgets (not adjusted for inflation), from Tokyo's modest \$2.7 billion, to Seoul's \$8 billion, to over \$42 billion in Beijing, witnessed the Olympics evolve to a much grander scale, putting this rite of passage out of reach for nations of lesser means. To put it in perspective, Japan's outlays were more than triple the \$800 million of reparations it paid South Korea in 1965 for four decades of repressive colonial rule; but Tokyo's staging was relatively spartan compared to what was to come, making do with more of the existing facilities for both sports and housing the athletes, while the opening ceremony was low-key by current standards. The Games were more modest in that era due to the IOC's commitment to amateurism under the stewardship of Chairman Avery Brundage (1952–1972) and his reluctance to embrace the commercialism that began with the 1984 Los Angeles Olympics. Beijing's price tag came in at just under Japan's annual defense budget, but was exceeded by the over $50 billion spent by Russia on the 2014 Sochi Winter Games.

There is much to debate about the intangible influences of the Games and their legacies, but the tangible impact can be seen in the transformed cityscapes as the governments bulldozed, displaced, modernized, renovated, redesigned, cleaned-up polluted waterways, and decorated their capitals. Staging the Games successfully and impressively and gaining the world's admiration inspired these expensive and extensive undertakings, imbued with national pride and staged to enhance national stature. The Olympics may indeed contribute to internationalization and generate a dynamic of sports diplomacy, but in East Asia, national pride and nationalist sentiments rendered the Games into national projects that spared no expense, brooked no failure and, once they commenced, aroused unalloyed public support and enthusiasm. Naturally preservationists see the urban makeovers rather differently, bemoaning what was lost to the wrecking ball, but the Olympics and nationalist imperatives took precedence over such concerns. The massive spending on trophy projects and the necessary infrastructure provided a huge public works stimulus for economies that were already doing well, and paved the way for further urbanization by expanding transport networks and redevelopment. The Olympics generated revenues, but, more importantly, contributed to the ongoing growth impetus and established the national brand, reaching a worldwide audience. Building up the tourist infrastructure and advertising the "product" also aimed to attract surges in tourism, but that has proven less successful.

Hosting is a barometer of economic progress, measured not only in terms of industrialization and exports, but also in terms of improved living standards and national capacity to handle the logistics and meet ambitious deadlines. In East Asia the Olympics focused on the themes of harmony and peace; Japan and China stressing their peaceful rise, while South Korea used the Olympics to promote political reforms at home while seeking peace on the peninsula and diplomatic relations with the eastern bloc of Soviet communist nations and China. The theme song for the Seoul Olympics—"Hand in Hand"—became a chart hit in 17 nations, perhaps the first sign of the hallyu wave of Korean pop culture that gained momentum and became a global phenomenon from the late 1990s. For China, the theme was "One World, One Dream," an assertion of shared aspirations and universal values that marked an effort to reinforce the nation's "smile diplomacy," reassuring other nations that its meteoric rise was a peaceful and unthreatening development; albeit with mixed results.

For Japan, the Olympics marked its return to the comity of nations and a chance to put to rest unpleasant wartime memories. The Games trumpeted that Japan was back with a surging high-tech industrialized economy and commitment to peace. For South Korea, the 1988 Olympics marked a political watershed as it coincided with the end of authoritarian government. In important ways the Olympics actually contributed to South Korea's democratization as heightened international media scrutiny pressured the government to deliver more meaningful political reforms than it intended. It was also a chance to showcase the economic prowess of one of the newly industrializing countries (NICs), nicknamed the Asian Tigers (including Taiwan, Hong Kong and Malaysia), that were following in the wake of Japan's ascent. Like Japan, South Korea's image, to the extent it had one, was indelibly associated with a bloody and devastating war (1950–1953). The ensuing poverty and military rule reinforced negative images of a country with a proud heritage. The conversation about South Korea when it won the Games in 1981 was about Gwangju, the southwestern city where troops slaughtered students in 1980. It was a risky choice for the IOC because it awarded the Games to a regime with blood on its hands on a divided peninsula where the belligerent nations were in a state of suspended war, an armistice that in the 1980s appeared very fragile. Moreover there was a high risk of a boycott as the Olympics had become embroiled in Cold War politics, with successive boycotts in 1980 (Moscow), over the Soviet invasion of Afghanistan, and 1984 (Los Angeles), in retaliation. Due to Seoul's anti-communist fervor and lack of relations with communist states, it took the deft diplomacy of IOC chairman Juan Samaranach to rescue the Games from the ideological battlefield. Ironically, the 1988 Games occurred just before the 1989 fall of the Berlin Wall and the ensuing collapse of the Soviet Union, making them the last of the Cold War Olympics where the capitalist and communist camps battled for supremacy in sports competitions. Overall, based on medal tallies, the Soviet camp won the sports battles even though it lost the ideological war and never dispelled doping allegations.

South Korea in the 1980s was not nearly as well known as Japan in the 1960s or China in the 2000s, so the Games were an unprecedented opportunity to introduce the nation to the world, and it succeeded in making a fairly good first impression despite a horrific opening ceremony where doves were consumed by the Olympic flames, boxing matches apparently rigged, and high-profile athletes were found guilty of doping.

Olympic Redemption and Nation Branding

Staging the ultimate global sports extravaganza was an opportunity to assert and shape new national identities. Tokyo was the first non-white, non-Western nation to host the Olympics, and the first in Asia to do so, and is now the only city to have won the right to host the Games three times—1940, 1964 and 2020. It is seldom remembered that Tokyo was supposed to host the Olympics in 1940, but was prevented from doing so by international condemnation of its bloody rampage in China. The Games were shifted to Helsinki in 1938, but canceled in 1939 following the Soviet invasion of Finland as Europe again descended into the abyss of war. Japan had pointedly not been invited to the 1948 London Olympics, the wounds of war too fresh, and its 1953 bid for the 1960 Games suffered from lingering wartime ill will and the fact that Melbourne, also in an inconvenient time zone for US television audiences, hosted the Olympics in 1956. The UN's acceptance of Japan as a member in 1956 signaled Japan's rehabilitation, creating favorable momentum for its 1959 bid for the 1964 Olympics.

In 1964 there was great significance in the symbolic return to the community of nations after the scarring isolation of World War II. Tokyo was in the midst of the so-called "economic miracle," the days of double-digit growth in GNP. Ironically, Tokyo won the bid to host the 1964 Olympics during Prime Minister Nobusuke Kishi's controversial tenure (1957–1960); Kishi was a former Class A war crimes suspect deeply implicated in wartime slave labor involving Chinese and Koreans. At the time of winning the bid in 1959 there were decidedly mixed feelings about hosting the Games among Tokyoites so soon after large swathes of the city had been incinerated in the March 1945 US firebombing. There were also worries about the high costs and diversion of resources, but by the time the Olympics rolled around, public enthusiasm rallied and over 70% of the viewership watched with rapt fascination what the nation had managed to pull off.

The 1964 Olympics represented a national rebirth, a way of overcoming past enmities and rebranding Japan as a successful high-tech economy and pacifist nation. That same year Japan was inducted into the Organization of Economic Cooperation and Development and, a month before the Games, hosted the annual meeting of the World Bank and IMF. Japan had rocketed into the top echelon of developed nations and was eager to show why. The government ensured that the *shinkansen* (bullet train) high-speed rail service linking Tokyo and Osaka was ready just in time for the Games, to show off this impressive technology when the whole world was watching. It was a proud moment for the nation, basking in the glory of the international media extolling its virtues and being accepted again as a responsible and upstanding nation, one that showed guests unparalleled warmth and hospitality (*omotenashi*).

To get ready for the Olympics, Tokyo's infrastructure was revamped, an elevated Metropolitan Expressway was built, sewers and flush toilets were installed, new hotels were built and architectural gems unveiled, while the city's infamous red light districts were toned down. The cacophony and disruption of construction, the human dislocation, the huge cost and everything else inconvenient and undesirable about the Games were swept aside in the national mania to do the nation proud. Taxi drivers and hotel clerks took English cramming lessons so they could enhance visitors' experiences, while the Games were shifted to October due to the stifling humidity and heat of Tokyo in summer-time. These were the first Games broadcast around the world in color, relying on satellite transmissions, and the first to use computer technology to keep scores, while introducing a new sports timing system and photo finish decisions. The acclaimed documentary, *Tokyo Olympiad*, captured the events for posterity, featuring not only the highlights, but also the personal stories of the athletes.

Japan was reborn on the world stage, a heady experience that boosted the national spirit emerging from the long shadows of war. The rich array of art and cultural exhibits staged for the Olympics skirted the issues of empire and war, instead drawing visitors' gaze to Japan's rich cultural heritage. The 1964 Olympics were also memorable for the opening ceremony when the Olympic torch at the top of the stadium was lit by Yoshinori Sakai, a student who was born in Hiroshima the day of the atomic bombing, August 6, 1945. Live on international television, members of Japan's Self-Defense Forces accompanied the torch into the stadium, and Emperor Hirohito, Japan's wartime leader, declared the Games open, placing in the foreground two institutions that carried a great onus of responsibility for the Pacific War (1931–1945). It was a turning of the page for Japan, putting the wartime rampage and defeat behind it as the new Japan raced to the future. There was huge symbolism in Emperor Hirohito attending the Games, where the national anthem (Kimigayo) was sung and the Japanese flag (Hinomaru) was proudly displayed while Japan's Self-Defense Forces marched into the stadium and also guarded the Olympic Village, all less than two decades after surrender. Talismans of what had been discredited, these wartime symbols were rehabilitated and subsumed within Japan's refurbished image as a peaceful nation. The Games represented an unthreatening way to boost nationalism and rekindle pride in the nation. Tourist arrivals from overseas were a disappointing 70,000, well short of the projected 130,000, but the investments in tourism capacity and the ample coverage of Japan's attractions carried long-term benefits. And this being Japan, the logistics went smoothly.

By all measures the Games were a stunning success, except perhaps for Dutchman Anthonius Geesink winning the gold medal in the judo open weight division. These days, as judo has spread around the world, Japan's judoists struggle to maintain dominance in a sport they once considered a birthright. But in 1964, losing in judo of all things was a shock to the nation, one that was cause for considerable national angst. The gold medal won by the women's volleyball team, nicknamed the Oriental Witches, against physically much more imposing teams, made up for that setback and stoked national pride in what Japanese believe to be national traits—perseverance and good teamwork. The Soviet media coined the outlandish nickname in trying to explain away the shocking defeat by Japan of their top-ranked women's volleyball team at the 1962 World Championships held in Moscow (Macnaughtan 2014). This heightened expectations and pressures for the 1964 Olympics and the Oriental Witches delivered what the nation had dared to hope for. It was also payback as relations with Russia and the Soviet Union had never recovered from Japan's surprise defeat of Russia back in 1905. Subsequently, in 1945 the Soviets unilaterally abrogated a non-aggression pact signed with Japan, capturing some 600,000 Japanese troops in the waning days of the war, and went on fighting even after Japan surrendered, seizing islands north of Hokkaido that remain disputed territory and are part of the reason the two nations have not yet signed a peace treaty ending World War II (see Chapter 10). Japanese also seethed at the poor treatment, harsh conditions and forced labor in the Soviet prisoner-of-war camps in Siberia where some 60,000 Japanese prisoners died, while the rest languished for a few years after 1945 before being repatriated. Olympic gold in the final against the Soviet women didn't settle the score, but was welcome and fanned patriotic sentiments.

Aside from settling scores, the women's gold medal in volleyball on the final day of the Games in 1964, with an unheard of national viewership of 85%, was a shot in the arm for national pride and a watershed in Japan's postwar sporting history, one that remains part of the 21st-century conversation of great moments in sports. It is hard to exaggerate the impact this victory had on the nation, leaving a legacy subsequent national volleyball teams have found burdensome, as they are always compared. The men's volleyball team also made it to the podium with a not too shabby bronze medal performance, adding to the nation's higher than expected medal haul of 16 gold medals and a total of 29 medals, placing it third in the overall medal rankings. Japan's Olympic athletes had done the nation proud.

The 1988 Seoul Olympics were also a coming out party for South Korea, showcasing how far it had come since its war devastation in the early 1950s and, significantly, how far it was outshining North Korea. But most of all it was a celebration of South Korea's democratization and the end of military rule. South Korea had experienced its own economic miracle under President Park Chung-hee during the 1960s and 1970s, but it was an authoritarian and repressive government. Park had taken over through a military coup in 1961 and presided over a period of rapid economic growth and modernization, but was assassinated by the head of his intelligence services in 1979. In the aftermath, as we discussed in the previous chapter, General Chun Doo-hwan led a military coup and seized power, prompting nationwide pro-democracy protests in 1980 demanding an end to martial law. The government cracked down on the protests, closed universities, and extended curbs on civil liberties, the free press and political activities. Chun mobilized troops and arrested student leaders. He subsequently became notorious for the slaughter of pro-democracy demonstrators, mostly students, in the city of Gwangju in May 1980. Anti-Americanism erupted due to Washington's complicity in Chun's coup and use of deadly force to quell pro-democracy demonstrations. This tragedy was South Korea's global scarlet letter and gave impetus to pro-democracy forces, subsequently leading to the 1987 direct presidential elections and the military's return to barracks, ceding political power to civilians. But back when the IOC awarded Seoul the Games in 1981, nobody anticipated these welcome developments as pro-democratic forces felt betrayed by the international community. It seemed that the IOC was rewarding and legitimizing a brutal government that was repressing popular yearning for freedom and representative government.

Hosting the Olympics, however, drew heightened international media scrutiny and criticism, pressuring Seoul to get on with democratization. The Chun government was delighted to win the right to host the Games in 1981, and basked in the legitimacy this conferred, but miscalculated that the prospect of losing the Games and national "face" would pressure pro-democracy activists to refrain from civil unrest. In fact, mounting international pressures to deliver democracy cornered the Chun administration, forcing it to make substantive concessions. This entailed lifting restrictions on political and civil liberties and an end to authoritarian rule, essentially asking Chun's authoritarian regime to preside over its own dissolution as the price of hosting the Olympics. Given pressures for accountability over the Gwangju Massacre and other abuses of power, the military sought a means to protect its institutional interests while also facilitating democratization, leading to Roh Tae-woo (1988–1993) becoming South Korea's first cleanly elected president in 1987. During the election campaign in June 1987, Roh promised significant political reforms and engineered President Chun's early departure from office as a concession to pro-democracy forces. Their potential for disrupting the Games carried the embarrassing possibility that the 1988 Olympics might be relocated (Munich was considered). Problematically, Roh was a former general and Chun crony implicated in the crackdown on pro-democracy forces, so his election seemed to perpetuate military political influence in the guise of civilian rule. Emboldened by the pre-Olympic limelight and international support, however, pro-democracy forces pushed for meaningful reforms and Roh had to deliver on his campaign promises. He won only because the two civilian pro-democracy candidates, Kim Dae-jung and Kim Young-sam, divided the pro-reform vote, so he ruled on sufferance rather than with a mandate.

Like Tokyo, Seoul had a massive facelift for the summer Games, sprucing up the city and making sure that the logistics would work smoothly. Canadian sprinter Ben Johnson set a record in the 100-meters dash but became the first world-famous athlete disqualified for failing a drug test, scathingly dismissed in the media as, "hero to zero in 9.79 seconds." This was the final Olympics for the Soviet Union and East Germany, although nobody knew that at the time. Overall South Korea put in an impressive performance, coming in fourth in the medal tally, although there was controversy over some dubious boxing decisions that favored South Korea.

The Seoul Olympics were a major success in rebranding and showing the world, as Tokyo had in 1964, that South Korea was an economic powerhouse. But the greatest significance was the role that hosting the Games had in promoting democratization, and how pro-democracy forces shrewdly used the power of international shame to compel the military to concede more than it wanted to, in line with the Olympic motto, "Faster, Higher, Stronger." While Cold War boycotts of the Olympics in 1980 and 1984 politicized the Games, the Seoul Olympics is the leading example of this extravaganza promoting meaningful political reform, reinforcing domestic pressures for democratization.

For China, the 2008 Games were a chance to dazzle the world and it delivered with efficiency and verve. The opening ceremony was an eye-catching multi-media extravaganza evoking the nation's rich cultural heritage and history, telling the stylized story of a nation to rapt audiences at home and around the globe, estimated at some 2 billion viewers worldwide. It told a story of what China has contributed to the world, including paper, the printing press, the mechanical clock, the magnetic compass, and gunpowder, the latter amply on display with one of the most amazing firework shows ever, anywhere. Amidst the pomp, glitter and spectacular fireworks there was a powerful display of Beijing's economic success, a vindication of the 1978 reforms championed by Deng Xiaoping. Beijing's facelift was impressive, with an array of arresting architectural gems, even if it lost some of its most charming neighborhoods to the Olympic wrecking ball. China's athletes also delivered, winning the overall medal tally with 100 and taking the most gold medals by far (51 vs. 36 for the USA), providing ample reason for citizens to rejoice in the nation's success on such a prominent global stage.

But the 2008 Games did not significantly burnish China's reputation on human rights and freedom of expression. Authorities did allow some additional latitude for foreign journalists, but at the same time tried to prevent them meeting with "troublemakers," sidelining stories about food safety, and limiting access to Tibet and Xinjiang, regions beset by widespread ethnic and religious tensions (see Chapter 11). Much has been written about the iconic Olympic venues designed by leading international architects, sparing no expense, especially the visually arresting "Bird's Nest" stadium that cost $450 million alone, and the blue and bubbly "Aqua Cube" that endowed Beijing with the cool factor—architecture as urban branding. The overhaul of the urban infrastructure with new subways, roads, rail links, an expanded and impressive airport, anti-pollution measures and computerization vastly upgraded and modernized the nation's venerable capital. But the wholesale razing of the alluring Old City, including centuries-old cultural and architectural gems, drew strong international criticism. The efficiency of China's authoritarian governance ensured that everything was built on time and worked, but at a massive cost to the city's charm and distinctive cityscape (Yu and Liu 2011). This architectural annihilation also drew domestic protests, but they proved no match for the urban redevelopment juggernaut in the name of the Olympics; reeducation camps awaited those who persisted in complaining.

The charming hutongs or small alleys, cramped housing and collective dwellings were largely for the old and the "have-nots," but they were occupying prime real estate in the city center. The Olympics provided a good opportunity to "modernize" these neighborhoods, but the benefits of this urban renewal were not equally enjoyed as it triggered a surge in property prices that priced many people out of the area and pushed them into Beijing's outlying districts. The new luxurious downtown spaces of exclusivity created with public funding catered to China's new elite, many of whom benefit from close Party connections and illicit payoffs. What was a dream for some became a nightmare for others, underscoring the disparities, nepotism and crony corruption that stir popular resentments. Paradoxically, of the three East Asian hosting nations, only China officially embraces egalitarianism, but the consequences of the Beijing Games were the most inequitable. The costs were paid from the public purse while a narrow elite reaped the rewards, a widely circulated media story that reinforced negative international perceptions of the new China (Aiyar 2008).

Yet the uneven distribution of the spoils did not dampen the upsurge of nationalist pride in the endeavor. Seven years of frantic preparations showed what the collective will and power of China could produce, and even if domestic critics bemoaned the costs and greed that animated the project there is no denying that the Chinese people basked in the reflected glory of the most extravagant Games ever, one that showed the world that China had arrived and did so in style. The Games boosted national pride, signifying China's global economic ascendancy, celebrating and cementing the nation's international status. They were, in the words of the IOC president Jacques Rogge, "truly exceptional Games" and drew a global audience of 4.7 billion.

Unlike in Seoul where the Olympics promoted democratization, the Beijing Games reinforced the legitimacy of the CCP by showcasing the efficiency of a one-party, authoritarian state eager at every turn to depoliticize the Games and deflect criticism about repression. The success of the Games was owned by the CCP and they were part of a larger ongoing process of manufacturing consent by appealing to national pride and stoking nationalistic emotions (Brady 2009). As noted above, the Games provided a good excuse to redevelop downtown Beijing, but they also gave authorities good reasons to upgrade internal security and surveillance. Authorities invoked the need to prevent terrorist incidents and any other disruptions by dissident groups, like the banned spiritual movement Falun Gong, to justify vast budgets and manpower devoted to this end. Ironically, to win the bid to host the Games, Beijing agreed to introduce limited political reforms, but in this respect there was no significant impact, while police state surveillance powers increased dramatically. Beijing, rather than embracing press freedom, actually used the Games as a pretext to exert more control over information while downplaying political issues, ethnic conflict and food safety problems (Reporters Without Borders 2009).

The Beijing Olympics were like a product launch, an unprecedented, sustained campaign of nation branding aimed at shoring up the Party's domestic credibility (Brady 2009). The Olympics constituted a campaign of mass distraction aimed at diverting attention away from corruption, inflation, unemployment, disparities, pollution and repression, a propaganda effort to depoliticize the Chinese people and bolster patriotism, especially targeting youth. The CCP seeks to manufacture consent by portraying the Party and the status quo as the best and only option, one that commands loyalty because it delivers despite any flaws. The crisis of credibility generated by the crackdown on the pro-democracy movement in 1989 led the CCP to recalibrate its propaganda campaigns and the Olympics provided a useful vehicle to do so. The Party instructed the public and media on how to behave during the Olympics, a sustained initiative of thought control that reflects changes in the way that the Party exerts political power.

The "welcoming the Olympics" campaign enjoyed state-orchestrated saturation coverage, leaving nothing to chance. Journalists had to undergo special training sessions on how to cover the extravaganza, what not to cover, and how to counter foreign criticisms. Drawing lessons from its failed 1993 bid for the 2000 Olympics, derailed by lingering human rights concerns triggered by the 1989 Tiananmen Square crackdown, Beijing relied on international PR firms to lobby for its bid. They adroitly appealed to the IOC, arguing that awarding Beijing the Games would promote human rights and lead to political reforms, tapping into the Seoul scenario. Beijing made commitments to bolster such expectations, aimed at an international audience, but apparently the Chinese people were not informed.

The Beijing Olympics propaganda campaign was part of a larger strategy for keeping the people politically disengaged, what Brady evocatively terms the "political mummification of the nation" (Brady 2009, 6). The Olympics and sports enthusiasm were used specifically to boost patriotism among youth, to build pride in the nation that would bolster the status quo and continuation of Party rule. The Olympics were a perfect opportunity for reshaping the national brand and burnishing the national image while consolidating domestic political control. It reinforced the "peaceful rise" campaign aimed at reassuring other nations that China's emergence was unthreatening and good for the world. It was a show of strength that impressed both domestic and global audiences. The 1989 iconic image of "tank man"—a lone pro-democracy demonstrator in Beijing facing down a tank—was "retired." The New China gleamed and impressed, showcasing innovation, efficiency, organization and unity, airbrushing out the flaws. The opening ceremony is a case in point as Mao Zedong, the founding father, was noticeable by his virtual absence in the festive presentation of China's history. The apparent disconnect between Maoism and the contemporary Party is of little concern to those who grew up in the post-1978 reform era in the New China.

The timing of the event—August 8, 2008 at 8 p.m. Beijing time—highlighted the fusion of tradition with the modern, rehabilitating the ancient practice of numerology and China's rich civilization, once derided as feudal and counter-revolutionary. The Party has unabashedly shrugged off its revolutionary origins, positioning itself as the bastion of the status quo and the stability and prosperity that confers, basking in the reflected glory of the Games. Now there are new frontiers in space to conquer and new dazzling displays to divert attention and orchestrate consent, the Party as magician relying on smoke-and-mirrors to perpetuate its grip on power. Those who predicted the evolutionary sidelining of the Party with the growing middle class clamoring for a greater political say, inspired by liberal western models of multi-party democracy and civil liberties, underestimated the capacity of the Party to reinvent itself and coopt younger generations by choreographing patriotism, sports being a powerful means of doing so.

The international torch relay preceding the Olympics generated controversy as pro-Tibet demonstrators seized the media spotlight to draw attention to their cause. In March 2008, protests in Tibet, and the inevitable crackdown, influenced perceptions about the March–May torch relay. The powerful nationalistic backlash among Chinese all over the world demonstrated the effectiveness of China's spin-masters in stoking Olympic patriotism. Drawing attention to human rights issues or political repression was summarily dismissed as anti-China bias, represented as symptomatic of how western nations could not accommodate or cope with Asia's new giant. Officials repudiated criticisms as envy tinged with racist prejudice, appealing to and amplifying patriotic pride. Protecting the national image thus became a shared concern binding the Party with the public. This concern was clearly evident in the tightly scripted Beijing Olympics, a mass mobilization campaign designed to both awe and mislead, a 21st-century Potemkin village (Brady 2009, 19).

As we discussed above, the East Asian Olympics contributed to nation-building in different ways, but the massive boost in international prestige that the Games conferred undeniably stirred nationalist pride in each host nation. Japan projected the image of a normalized, pacifist economic powerhouse, while South Korea celebrated development and democratization. China put to rest a century and a half of national humiliation and regained honor in the eyes of its own people and the world, announcing at the same time with great fanfare that the 21st century would be the Asian Century.

World Cup 2002

The co-hosting of the FIFA World Cup soccer championship in 2002 by South Korea and Japan was remarkable for a number of reasons. This was the first time the World Cup was staged in Asia and the first time that two nations were designated as joint hosts of the tournament. Given frequently prickly bilateral relations, it was a surprising choice foisted upon the two reluctant collaborators by the organizing committee. Two nations that have argued angrily and endlessly about a shared past, and have sullen and frosty relations as a consequence, were suddenly thrust into a situation demanding compromise and cooperation. It seemed as if the organizers had a wickedly twisted sense of humor.

The co-hosting surprise provided an unanticipated chance for the two countries to overcome their historical animosities and build a basis for warmer ties. The problem is that invoking slanted histories plays well on both sides of the Sea of Japan, known as the East Sea in the Korean Peninsula. Japanese leaders have grown exasperated with what they view as Korea's fierce clinging to old wrongs, while Korean ire is provoked by Japan's seeming rush to bury an unexamined history, to downplay if not deny crimes involving forced labor and the comfort women, and its willful neglect of Korean sensibilities involving prime ministers' visits to Yasukuni Shrine and new textbooks that gloss over the worst aspects of Japan's colonial rule on the peninsula (1910–1945).

Breaking out of this pattern of recrimination and distrust required a level of courage, statesmanship and vision that has proved elusive for too long. Interestingly, Emperor Akihito (1989–), the son of Emperor Showa (1926–1989), showed the way forward by unflinchingly looking at the past and emphasizing fraternal ties as the basis for building a more fruitful relationship. He did what he could to help ensure that the co-hosting would not descend into more bickering and recriminations. In his annual message in 2001, Emperor Akihito courted controversy by publicly acknowledging for the first time that the imperial line descended from Korean ancestors. By confirming to the Japanese public what scholars have long known, Akihito was obviously trying to set the tone for an improvement in bilateral relations and make a case against ethnic chauvinism: "they are we." Clearly, this gesture is in line with a series of his previous initiatives to express sincere contrition about the past and promote reconciliation between Japan and its regional victims. The lost decade of the 1990s was a time when the Imperial Household, despite constitutional constraints, demonstrated courageous leadership in tackling the unfinished business of World War II that has impeded improvement in Japan's regional relations. Akihito stepped forward as assertively as possible, and helpfully, to undo the accumulated harm of neglecting, denying and minimizing past wrongs committed during his father's reign. These efforts to put Japan's inglorious past behind it in a manner acceptable to past victims are offset by ongoing denials by opportunistic politicians who seek to valorize past misdeeds.

Partly as a result of the monarchy's efforts, the 2002 FIFA World Cup turned out to be far more than soccer at its best. It was also a showcase for a sustained and fruitful bilateral cooperation that suggests the potential and possibilities for overcoming the animosities that have built up between the countries. During 2002, prior to the tournament, both countries organized a series of cultural exchanges aimed at breaking down negative stereotypes, and the media coverage towards Korea in Japan was unusually favorable and sympathetic. The impasse in bilateral relations arising from disputes over textbooks and Prime Minister Koizumi's provocative visits to the Yasukuni Shrine, stood in stark contrast to warm grassroots exchanges and a determined effort by the Japanese media to portray Koreans in a more favorable light. Internet chat-rooms still featured some of the more familiar jingoism, but also demonstrated that young people in both countries are not necessarily prisoners of the past and locked into the animosities that have defined bilateral relations since Korea was liberated from Japanese colonial rule in 1945.

During the tournament, various polls suggested that Japanese perceptions of Koreans had improved. After Korea's controversial victories over Spain and Italy, many western commentators openly complained about questionable calls and match fixing, but Japanese viewed this as little more than sour grapes and obviously took a Pan Asian pride in Korea's surprisingly good showing, making it to the semi-finals and finishing fourth. Even though Korea's team advanced farther than the Japanese team, Japanese were good sports about their neighbor's success and supported them to the end. It appears that this goodwill was not reciprocated in Korea, as fans there were seen to be supporting Japan's opponents and cheering its setbacks. The stadiums in South Korea were a sea of red pandemonium as exuberant fans donned red T-shirts and took their role seriously as the 12th man on the pitch, with loud and non-stop cheering and drumming, with similar scenes in public squares around the nation where crowds gathered around massive video screens, with an estimated 10 million gathering in Seoul's streets over the course of the tournament. The blues of the late 1990s financial crisis were temporarily forgotten as the nation basked in the glory of the team's success, a rare moment of national harmony and shared happiness.

Perhaps most remarkable were the displays of feel-good nationalism that swept over the Japanese archipelago during the tournament. People spoke of little else, media coverage was obsessive, and Japan's better than expected performance, advancing to the quarter-finals, was enthusiastically appreciated. Even the prime minister acknowledged that he had played hooky from his duties to watch a match during work hours, joining millions of new fans caught up in soccer fever. The press loudly denounced Tokyo Governor Shintaro Ishihara, an ardent nationalist, for his comments on the eve of the tournament when he dismissed the French coach of

Japan's national team, Philippe Troussier, as a typical third-rate foreigner and lousy coach who was taking advantage of Japan. His excellent coaching was widely seen as crucial to Japan's vast improvement and solid performance in the tournament and thus Ishihara's jibes backfired, making him appear both churlish and clueless.

Wild street celebrations by young Japanese with the hinomaru (a red sun on a white background) painted on their cheeks, screaming with unabashed and unrestrained enthusiasm for the national team, were all part of an unanticipated moment of mass hysteria, a moment of feel-good nationalism when flag waving and loud banzais erupted from a people long reluctant to voice such sentiments. Newscasters bubbled with enthusiasm and television stations repeatedly ran the highlight reels, stoking pride in a team whose glory was eagerly embraced by a nation desperate for an escape from the relentlessly bleak economic news. June 2002 was a month of mania, a time when it appeared very few Japanese were not caught up in the hoopla. It was a moment of liberation from the burdensome past, from looking over the collective shoulder at the outside world, and a time to shed inhibitions, ambivalence and let it all hang out. A normally buttoned-down citizenry was basking in the reflected glory of the national team and savoring the precious moments.

These displays of nationalism are notable precisely because they would hardly merit a remark in most countries. When Japanese engage in the usual celebratory gestures and displays common in other nations, it is somehow different. It is different because such unguarded moments are rarely displayed. While the world watched and the global media carried images far and wide, Japanese put to rest more than a few stereotypes in laughing, yelling, high-fiving and having fun. The meek, self-deprecating, stoic and terminally reserved and conformist automatons imagined overseas suddenly came to life sporting various shades of dyed hair, diverse fashions and a bubbly zest. Such effusive displays of nationalism were reassuringly rooted in a decidedly internationalist context, and were thus unthreatening and shorn of their darker connotations. The tournament provided a healthy and cathartic release for a nation where nationalism and patriotism have been conflated with militarism and associated with past excesses and atrocities. This new "nationalism lite" seems light-years away from the 1930s "valley of darkness."

The thaw in relations between Korea and Japan peaked in the final game held in the Yokohama Stadium when President Kim Dae-jung sat beside Emperor Akihito, an important sideshow to the main event between Brazil and Germany. This was an image pregnant with meaning and ironies, one unimaginable only a decade before. The former leader of the Korean democracy movement, once abducted in Japan by KCIA agents intent on killing him, was now the honored guest of an Emperor committed to reconciliation and laying to rest the ghosts of the past. Ironically, those in Japan who most strongly support a revival of the imperial system, a motley collage of ultranationalists, mobsters and political extremists occupying the right-wing spectrum of conservative politics, are also those who are least willing to support this Emperor's agenda of healing. Their symbol of reawakened nationalism has inconveniently distanced himself from their agenda and promoted a more humanitarian and pacifist sense of nation predicated on assuming responsibility for the past, demonstrating contrition and reaching out to past enemies.

Commonwealth Games 2010

Inevitably, the 2008 Beijing Olympics serve as a benchmark to assess the Commonwealth Games (CWG) hosted by New Delhi in 2010, because China and India are often compared due to their billion-plus populations and economic trajectories. If indeed the 21st century turns out to be the Asian century, these two behemoths will play a pivotal role, and what they each delivered in terms of the Games experience and what they achieved in shaping and asserting a new and modern national image is a basis for comparing national branding. Certainly both Games gave a jolt to national pride and nationalistic sentiments, but the overall assessment not surprisingly favors China. The CWG are also a mega-event but on a smaller scale than the Olympics and do not command the same global attention. Moreover, Beijing spent about three times as much money on preparations and proved to be far better organized. New Delhi hoped to show the world that it too deserved recognition for its impressive economic growth and to demonstrate that it deserved a place among the leading global cities. The evident desire to impress, however, was not matched by a sense of urgency after winning the bid in 2003 as shambolic preparations proceeded fitfully and slowly. In many respects, the CWG appeared to be an accident waiting to happen, an anti-nationalist extravaganza of embarrassment and failure. In the event, the CWG came off with very few hitches despite dark warnings about missed deadlines, delays and inadequate facilities. These dire predictions persisted up until the last moment and only dissipated in the glow of an impressive opening ceremony in a packed stadium of 60,000 that showed India's incredible capacity to entertain and put on a riveting show, ending with the spectators giving a rousing rendition of the national anthem. Twelve state-of-the-art sports venues were all ready on time, the athletes' village pleased the guests despite some problems, the stadiums were packed and, perhaps most impressive of all, India had its best ever medal haul, coming in second overall. By the time that sexy starlets wrapped up the Games in exuberant Bollywood style at the closing ceremony, there was a collective sense of pride leavened with a sigh of relief, and more than a little disbelief, that New Delhi had miraculously produced a stunning spectacle against the odds. But did anyone outside India notice? Overall, there is a lingering and undeserved perception of a fiasco and serious damage to Brand India, what Ramesh Thakur (2014) called "a showpiece shambles."

It was never going to be easy as responsibility and authority were widely dispersed and coordination was limited. New Delhi was in many respects the antithesis of Beijing where unified resolve galloped relentlessly forward and preparations went like clockwork. Chronic backlogs and corruption are daily experiences for India's citizens so few were surprised at the chaos and malfeasance that plagued the CWG preparations. The initial cost estimate of just under \$500 million ballooned to \$15 billion, making these the most extravagant CWG ever. By contrast, four years earlier Melbourne staged the CWG for a modest \$2.9 billion, barely over the original estimate. The New Delhi cost overruns reflected poor management and an expressed desire to stage the best Games ever no matter the cost. This was a chance to show off and pull a mini-Beijing, buff the national reputation and show that the Indian miracle was not just hype, but the early scathing reviews in the Indian and international press suggested that the effort would backfire. Poor governance and transparency led to revelations of staggering corruption as well-connected businessmen bribed their way into contracts and then imposed extortionate cost overruns.

Given the CWG were meant to put New Delhi on the map and rebrand the nation as modern, hip and efficient, an attractive site for investment, finance and leisure, the CWG kept attracting all the wrong kind of attention. The national branding campaign of Incredible India seemed like a bad joke. If anything, as a branding exercise the CWG represented a PR nightmare, reinforcing perceptions about rampant corruption, endless delays, inefficiency and bureaucratic red tape. From a sporting perspective, however, the CWG were a success and India's performance was unexpectedly strong, winning 101 medals and besting Great Britain, generating a nationalist frenzy of gloating and giving a big boost to developing a national sports culture that has in the past focused entirely on cricket. Certainly China's brawny sporting machine remains a distant goal, but for a nation of a billion, the abiding shame of Olympic failure was partially alleviated by the CWG successes.

Overall, the legacy of the Games has been largely negative, highlighting India's problems rather than its strengths. India made a statement to a large global audience, but left a bad impression. While the nation pulled it off, the international media never really updated the premonitions of disaster. Credit was due, but the success went unheralded in the global conversation, and even among Indians, few doubted that it was only a miracle that prevented an epic debacle, hardly a vote of confidence. From a branding perspective the CWG proved an unmitigated disaster, failing to showcase New Delhi as a global city. But now, with a state-of-the-art airport and an impressive Metro system, tourists are enjoying the benefits in a city that has become far easier to navigate, even if it is more polluted than Beijing and also boasts epic traffic jams.

As in Beijing, the CWG provided a pretext for massive urban renewal. There were vast improvements in transportation facilities, while significant investments in new power plants ensured there would be no blackouts during the Games. Building new facilities and venues meant displacing large numbers of urban poor, including at least 100,000 families. Evictions were carried out in a ruthless manner and compensation mostly misappropriated as the sleek modern India swept aside unwanted slum dwellers (Menon-Sen 2010). Paradoxically, public discourse bemoaned the rampant corruption while overlooking the mass dislocation of New Delhi's downtrodden that were made homeless by the trophy CWG projects. This elimination of shantytowns and ghettos to make way for the CWG was not ignored entirely, but to the extent that the CWG attracted condemnation from civil society activists, the storyline was corruption. In a way this was a microcosm of the larger issues regarding caste and religion; evicting 35,000 marginal Muslim families from land they occupied on the banks of the Yamuna River to build a lustrous promenade might not be as sexy a story as billions in ill-begotten wealth, but is another important dent in the "best ever" Games narrative. The destitute and unwanted migrants were pushed off and out, part of a campaign to clean up the city and make it look more presentable while removing those who represented "old" India and threatened the presentation of a modern India. The media defined the nightmare in progress as the impending catastrophe of shamefully inadequate preparations and exorbitant graft, diverting attention from how the underclasses suffered extensively from the CWG's ambitions. Few of the displaced were consoled by the building of a new lawn bowls complex on top of what had been their community, or all the other impressive facilities that have become "white elephants," costly projects that now serve hardly anyone. New Delhi is not alone in building venues without a post-Games purpose—no tenants, few users, just like Beijing—but that is little solace for those who were shoved aside to make way for the grand projects.

The nation did gain something, however, from the massive funding scandals and scams. The CWG corruption allegations inadvertently launched a major political movement in New Delhi promoting anti-corruption legislation. The CWG's accidental legacy renders them a potential watershed in India's political history (Majumdar 2012). The intention of highlighting the new ultra-modern India was derailed by the stark reminders about the perils and hassles of doing business there. It also stirred long simmering resentments about the prevailing culture of venality and cocoon of impunity that enable the elite to fleece the public purse with hideous abandon. As discussed in Chapter 5, Arvind Kejriwal, the leader of the AAP (Aam Aadmi Party), took India's political establishment by surprise in the New Delhi state elections in 2012 by tapping into public anger about the shabby and dubious deals rampant at the CWG. The AAM was established to pressure the government to eradicate corruption and abuses of power, and the CWG played a useful role in highlighting the endemic problems and launching this powerful political movement. For decades Indians had put up with various shenanigans and cash and carry politics, but the CWG was a catalytic event that galvanized citizens into demanding accountability and honest governance, and an end to corruption. They rallied behind the AAM, a populist movement seeking a government that actually embraces the modern practices promoted in the CWG sloganeering. By exposing the pervasive rot, the CWG thus gave impetus to those who want to clean it up. The brooms wielded by AAM volunteers campaigning in the 2012 New Delhi state assembly elections were a visual representation of this yearning.

As in Beijing, the haves got richer and the have-nots were pushed aside, but more like Seoul, there were positive political repercussions. Perhaps the most unsung legacy of the 2010 CWG is the unintentional reinvigoration of a sclerotic democracy and organized political action by citizens against a rapacious elite, putting corruption at the top of the nation's political agenda—significant achievements that have eluded China and remain a source of gathering resentment.

In assessing the Olympics and CWG, each delivered infrastructural development that facilitated further economic growth and expansion. So too the Games also inspired efforts to tackle pollution problems and improve the environment, with decidedly mixed results in Beijing and New Delhi where air pollution remains a serious threat to health. In all these cities, the Games led to significant displacement, but less so in Tokyo due to the relatively modest scale of the Games. This urban dislocation had uneven benefits, accentuating disparities especially in Beijing and New Delhi. In each case the initial public enthusiasm was muted, but as preparations progressed the public rallied around the project. In all cases the Games stoked nationalistic pride—even skeptical Indians were won over in the end—and featured exuberant displays of feverish nationalism. In the case of Japan, with the shadows of war still lingering, the national rebranding featured an astounding makeover from vicious aggressor and plunderer of Asia to a pacifist economic powerhouse boasting cutting-edge technologies. South Korea also rebooted its image, or at least got on the global radar screen, showing off its democratization and launching its global pop culture wave. India and China achieved more mixed results as some negative perceptions endured or were reinforced.

In the next section we focus on historical controversies and how they animate nationalist passions, examining national traumas, museums and textbooks to gain a better understanding of how the past resonates in contemporary Asia and why it is important.

Part III

Shackles of the Past

Part III

Shackles of the Past

7

Chosen and Unchosen Traumas

National traumas play an important role in shaping national identity. Shared catastrophes and collective suffering constitute a powerful anvil on which to hammer out a useful national identity for those in power. Yet some traumas are chosen for this task of nation-building and promoting national unity while others are ignored or marginalized. In some respects, ignored traumas reveal more about a nation than the chosen traumas, representing a subversive and hidden narrative that is sidelined for various reasons. The chosen traumas are selectively drawn and presented in ways that favor those in power and tend to glide over aspects or experiences that don't conveniently fit the consolidating narrative of shared ordeal. Traumas are especially useful because they are the basis for compelling narratives of victimization and thus forge emotional bonds while advancing political agendas and eliding inconvenient problems. Those in power constantly pick at the scabs of past trauma because they are far more useful when festering and not meant to be healed. Repetition of the story, focusing on vivid and horrific details, helps keep the pain alive and passes it down to the next generation. Precisely because traumas are prepared for public consumption, they necessarily involve a certain degree of simplification, and an artful reimagining. There is good and evil, heroes and villains, perpetrators and victims, and a certain level of coherence implausibly attached to chaotic events where in reality there are gray zones, clarity where there is blurriness, firm conclusions where there is uncertainty. History draws on facts, but how they are connected and interpreted establishes a narrative, a mosaic that conveys a desired message. In contrast to the theme of sports discussed in the preceding chapter, trauma-driven nationalism encourages extreme demonization and violence while bestowing legacies of intolerance and animosity that are easily reignited. Below we discuss the chosen traumas of China, India, Indonesia, South Korea

Nationalism in Asia: A History Since 1945, First Edition. Jeff Kingston.

and Japan and what they help us understand about their national identities and how these are contested and instrumentalized.

China

China's chosen traumas have evolved since 1949, but a recurring theme is the century of humiliation that preceded the CCP's victory in the civil war against the Kuomintang. The Party has stoked the fires of angry patriotism by frequently invoking the "century of humiliation" (Callahan 2010; Wang 2012). The humiliation meme emphasizes foreign imperialist bullying and exploitation of China from the mid-19th century. China's weakness at that time left it vulnerable, a lesson that is relentlessly driven home in contemporary discourse. It is impossible to overstate the extent to which the century of humiliation is invoked to nurture patriotism, sacrifice and unity, a wound that is kept raw to motivate and inspire Chinese to serve the state and make China strong. Harping on the collective trauma of humiliation generates a resentful nationalism prone to sanctimonious views about what is rightfully China's due. The international status quo was established when China was weak, so it too represents humiliation, legitimizing Beijing's quest to modify that status quo. Thus other claimants' arguments based on international law confront China's sweeping historical claims and a deep sense of injustice about past wrongs that need to be righted. Now that the Party has made China more powerful, it is time for a settling of scores. The powerful grip of humiliation on the national psyche is also useful in distracting attention from a string of Mao-made traumas.

Between gaining power in 1949 and his death in 1976, Mao inflicted numerous traumas, but for obvious reasons these events did not serve the Party's purposes. National identity under Mao was recast in the Party's image, a struggle against a dark and feudal past and the forces of imperialism that had drained China of its wealth and nurtured a comprador class—a trajectory conflated with the vanquished Kuomintang—that left the Chinese at the mercy of foreign exploitation. National identity was centered on class conflict and the CCP's glorious road to power from the caves of Yenan to the seat of power in Beijing. It was a peasant-led struggle to regain control of the nation's destiny, a long battle to overcome the century of humiliation. The depredations of the western powers, and the subsequent ravages of the Japanese Imperial Armed Forces in the 1930s and 1940s, were an object lesson in the costs of weakness and lack of unity and vigilance. The CCP was intent on reinventing China and promoting a revolution that would overturn and erase the old order, one that had left China divided and poor, unable to respond to the threats of imperialism. The Party required everyone to exhibit revolutionary zeal, bear hardships without complaint, meet unrealistic quotas, and renounce Chinese traditions and civilization. Anyone failing to toe this line risked being denounced as a counter-revolutionary and the dire consequences that entailed.

National identity thus became whatever the Party said it was, and under Mao national identity was rooted in Maoism. Mao and the Party demanded unequivocal loyalty. The colossal upheavals unleashed by Mao—the Great Leap Forward and the Cultural Revolution—tested revolutionary ardor and patriotic loyalty as Party, Mao and nationalism became conflated. Any setbacks were attributed to counter-revolutionary forces, those who stood in the way of the revolution who must be swept aside. Failures then became signs of opposition rather than mistaken policies, proving the need to redouble loyalty to the Party and heed its warnings about rooting out counter-revolutionaries. Paradoxically, the Party's pervasive failures boosted its power and harsh methods. The New China was a revolutionary China committed to eradicating feudal legacies and their proponents, justifying extensive repression and centralization of power under Mao Zedong, the totalitarian icon.

Under Mao, factionalism divided the Party and intrigue was rife. He may have been paranoid, but he did have real enemies and there were numerous doubters. Mao was astute in keeping powerful enemies close and purging them as necessary. He also relied on close allies to assist in the inevitable power struggles. While the Party was not monolithic and the power struggles were real, the Party tried to cultivate and project a monolithic China and forge unity by reminding everyone that there was much unfinished business and the revolution was still underway. National identity was based on continuing revolution, allowing Mao and the Party to improvise along the way and to explain away their failures. Mao sought friendly ties with Japan due to the Cold War with the US and his split with the Soviet Union, and thus downplayed the Japanese rampage. Mao's villains were the Kuomintang pre-1949 and the USA post-1949, while the trauma of Japanese aggression in China from 1931 to 1945 was blamed solely on Tokyo's militarist clique. Mao actually thanked Prime Minister Kakuei Tanaka in Beijing in 1972 when they met to normalize relations, emphatically pointing out that Japan's help was crucial to Mao's victory in 1949 because the Imperial Armed Forces weakened the Kuomintang.

But new times require new traumas and post-Mao China chose to focus national identity on anti-Japanese sentiments and victimization by Japan. Since the early 1980s, the Chinese government has increasingly vilified Japan. This trend gained momentum after the brutal suppression of pro-democracy protests in 1989. Following the Tiananmen Square crackdown, the CCP began to promote "patriotic education," a campaign that emphasized the atrocities perpetrated by Japanese troops in China between 1931 and 1945. The CCP portrayed itself as the savior of the nation, thus shoring up its tattered legitimacy. But public opinion was aroused by this patriotic education, ensuring that the younger generation know more, and are angrier, about this shared history than their elders. This is reinforced by an endless series of television dramas vilifying the Japanese; in 2012 alone it is estimated that some 1 billion Japanese soldiers were killed on Chinese television and in Chinese films.

The economic reforms that started in 1978 have also created political space for commercial mass media. These newspapers, magazines and television stations are linked to established state-owned media, providing them with political cover. Compared to the relatively staid coverage in the state media, however, commercial media tend to sensationalize stories because they need to attract an audience. Thus, when disputes break out over issues involving Japan, the commercial mass media often take more extreme positions than the government. This market-driven sensationalism shapes popular discourse and national identity by harping on the traumas inflicted by the Japanese and caricaturing Japanese public opinion about the nations' shared history, inaccurately reinforcing perceptions that most Japanese support revisionist views of history that downplay or deny Japanese atrocities and contemporary responsibility for these acts. The spread of the Internet in the 21st century has also had a profound impact on public opinion (Shen and Breslin 2010). Internet activists can shape public opinion and mobilize demonstrations. These tend to be relatively younger people who have gone through the patriotic education, who portray compromise and diplomacy as weak and unprincipled, fanning public anger against the Japanese while constraining the government's room for maneuver.

Clearly, the state has extensively shaped public opinion through patriotic education, while its selective tolerance of media sensationalism, public protests and Internet activism, along with periodic crackdowns, is indicative about state control over public opinion (Reilly 2011, 2014). But, in contributing to an environment favorable to anti-Japanese xenophobia, and tolerating greater freedom in the media and Internet, public opinion has gained a certain degree of autonomy. The government is not above using the nationalist xenophobia to gain leverage in negotiations, but in doing so it has created political space for public opinion that it cannot always control. From the Party's perspective, the great danger is that anti-Japanese demonstrations might morph into anti-CCP protests focusing on widespread grievances about disparities, corruption, abuses of power and environmental problems. This occurred in 2010 when anti-Japanese protests became a cover for anti-government sentiments.

Ironically, since the government strictly limits public protests with the exception of anti-Japanese protests, Japan-bashing has its uses for those seeking to criticize the government, while the government sees such protests as a useful negotiating tool. Ai Weiwei, the celebrated artist, wryly jokes that the Chinese should thank the Japanese for giving them the right to protest in China. While public opinion in China is managed, the state cannot ignore grassroots opinions that tend to be more stridently nationalistic. To the extent that the CCP conducts a moderate diplomacy that reassures the world while attaining strategic objectives incrementally, it runs the risks of being seen as spineless and undermining national interests by being reasonable. The Chinese state has demonstrated on numerous occasions that it can suppress or derail public opinion, turning it off and on at will, although this is increasingly more difficult to accomplish.

I happened to be in Nanjing on the 75th anniversary of the Nanjing Massacre commemorated on December 13, 2012, and that same day Chinese airplanes buzzed over the airspace of the disputed Senkaku/Diaoyu islands, escalating Sino-Japanese tensions (see Chapter 10). The local newspaper the next morning showed a picture of the planes flying over the islands adjacent to a picture of the anniversary ceremony at the Nanjing Massacre Memorial Museum. The timing of these two events and how they were depicted may have been a coincidence, but an unlikely one. This linking of the contemporary territorial dispute with the traumatic past underscores

Figure 7.1 Nanjing Massacre Museum Provides Guidance to Visitors. Photo © Jeff Kingston.

the impact of unresolved historical grievances that are essential to understanding Chinese perceptions about the Senkaku/Diaoyu dispute. In such ways, traumas are used to orchestrate nationalist sentiments, while others are best forgotten.

Great Leap Forward (GLF), 1958–1961

This is perhaps the most misrepresented or overlooked trauma in China, a series of colossal policy errors implemented at Mao's behest with savage disregard for the human consequences. The GLF was aimed at transforming China by promoting rapid industrialization and collectivization of farming and thereby shifting it towards communism. It was an unmitigated disaster. Forty-five million deaths, almost as many people as the current population of Spain, is grim evidence of the Party's ruthless disregard for a people in whose name it ruled. Dikotter argues that the GLF left Mao discredited and vulnerable, driving him to initiate the horrors of the Cultural Revolution to retain power and exact revenge on his detractors, real and imagined (Dikotter 2011).

Mao's fingerprints were all over this man-made tragedy, but Party opportunists and those who feared Mao's wrath did nothing to stop the madness. Apologists for Mao's magnificent blunders argue that the GLF death toll is exaggerated, and insist it was a short-lived aberration, that rogue cadres were the ones wreaking havoc, and that the Soviets and US share blame because they refused to provide grain that could have averted widespread starvation. These excuses do not add up or bear scrutiny; the simultaneous breakneck industrialization and collectivization of the countryside, the essence of the Great Leap Forward, was Mao's brainchild, an epic blunder doomed to failure. Not only did he browbeat the CCP leadership into adopting this policy, he refused to acknowledge that it was causing sharp reductions in harvests while contributing nothing to industrialization. Voices of reason were sidelined or purged, replaced by cadres and leaders who understood that their careers depended on implementing disastrous policies and conjuring up rosy assessments.

Mao was not in the dark—he knew what was happening, but blamed "rightists" for sabotaging the project. Cadres who criticized the GLF were hunted down, stripped of power, often beaten and jailed, and replaced by opportunists who had few scruples about enforcing compliance by any means necessary. The death toll includes 2.5 million people who were beaten to death and another 3 million who died in the Chinese gulag. In the archives Dikotter found a curious GLF-era document, "Why and How Cadres Beat People," suggesting it was a matter of state concern.

The famine could have been averted, but only at the cost of Mao's pride. The GLF was his strategy to overtake and outshine the Soviet Union, and thus Soviet offers of grain were turned down because acceptance would entail an embarrassing admission of failure. Exports of grain from China were maintained throughout the famine in order to pay off loans, while grain purchased on international markets was used to fulfill pledges to Albania, Cuba and other countries in Asia and Africa.

The GLF was the maelstrom Mao inflicted. By instigating a climate of fear and frenzied witch-hunts, Mao ignited target-fever among local leaders, who made unrealistic reports to prove their value and loyalty, while the Party relied on arbitrary and ruthless violence to terrorize and impose its will. Since it had so few carrots, the CCP relied on the stick, literally its weapon of choice in the ubiquitous beating sessions.

The GLF remains a quasi-taboo subject, and although, like the Cultural Revolution, it is being exhumed in China, these twin traumas constitute a withering indictment of the Party and as such are handled carefully. Certainly Netizens know a great deal about what happened and books and blogs have lifted the veil of ignorance and silence. However, the Party of continual revolution is now the Party of stability, one eager to distance itself from the undeniable horrors and miscues of these "unchosen" traumas and the chaotic upheaval they inflicted on tens of millions of Chinese. Certainly one cannot gauge the impact of a trauma by numbers of deaths alone, but the Party's disastrous policies put it in uncomfortable company with the pre-1945 Japanese. Naturally the depredations of foreign forces are a more convenient and compelling target than the Party's self-inflicted traumas, and unlike Imperial Japan, the Party can also claim credit for vast improvements in public welfare. But this history can't be suppressed or justified and as it gains a wider audience it inevitably tarnishes the Party. In response, the modern Party has distanced itself from the sins of the old, repositioning itself as a responsible force for stability while keeping the public in the dark and simultaneously spreading blame.

India

India's chosen trauma is Partition, the 1947 division of the sub-continent into Islamic Pakistan and mostly Hindu India that came with independence from British rule. Jawaharlal Nehru celebrated Independence in his "Tryst with Destiny" speech, proclaiming that, "A moment comes, which comes but rarely in history, when we step out from the old to the new, when an age ends, and when the soul of a nation, long suppressed, finds utterance." His eloquence matched the exalted moment of ending 350 years of British influence in India, but it was a bittersweet celebration because on August 14, 1947 Great Britain partitioned India and established the Islamic Republic of Pakistan. The British moved towards Independence with determination and speed, hastily exiting before they could be drawn into the sectarian violence and what appeared to be an impending civil war between Muslims and Hindus. The precipitate decolonization embraced by London meant preparations for the handover of power were rushed and inadequate, making it appear that the British were eager to jump off before the looming train wreck. The British left behind a variety of problems for the locals to sort out, including unresolved border issues that have sparked wars between India and Pakistan. There are numerous reasons for Partition, but a leading factor was the British colonial policy of divide and rule, one that inevitably accentuated differences because Hindus and Muslims were administered separately. The British conducted censuses that categorized people by their religion and used that as a basis for administering them differently.

The two main local political actors in this drama were the Indian National Congress (founded in 1885) and the All India Muslim League (founded in 1906). While the processes undermining colonial rule and unifying Indians in their resolve to gain independence are complex and incremental, 1919 proved a pivotal year. This was the year of the Amritsar Massacre involving British troops firing on 20,000 unarmed Indians, an incident that highlighted the brutal nature of colonial rule. It was also when the British institutionalized communal representation with reserved seats for minorities in the legislature. In the following year, Gandhi began his non-violent, non-cooperation movement, *satyagraha*, aimed at achieving independence, which incrementally undermined British pretensions and led to the end of colonial rule.

In 1940, Muhammed Ali Jinnah, leader of the All India Muslim League from 1913 and eventual founder of Pakistan in 1947, called for the establishment of an independent Pakistan and partitioning of India. In 1943 the Muslim League passed a resolution demanding the British "Divide and Quit," meaning carve out a separate Muslim homeland in the sub-continent and end colonial rule. His policy contrasted with that of the Indian National Congress Party which launched the Quit India Movement in 1942, demanding that Great Britain simply leave. The British were more favorably disposed towards Muslim politicians because they offered welcome support for Great Britain in World War II, while Congress, at Gandhi's behest, opposed giving any support to the war effort and demanded immediate independence, launching a campaign of civil disobedience and withdrawing from politics. Jawaharlal Nehru, among other Congress leaders, was arrested for obstructing the war effort even though he personally wished to support the Allies.

There were a number of reasons why Muslim politicians felt anxious about life in Hindu-majority, independent India. Hindu chauvinists took stands that fanned fears and antagonism over various identity issues, ranging from language, favoring Hindi over Urdu, to calling for a total ban on the slaughter of cows, based on religious precepts, that sparked alarm in the Muslim community. In addition to outbreaks of communal violence, Congress and Muslim League leaders were unable to reach compromise on establishing a united India, making division look inevitable and less risky.

The process of Partition in August 1947 was a deeply scarring trauma, claiming as many as one million lives and leaving both nations devastated. Sprees of rioting, looting, rape and murder cast a long shadow over Independence and poisoned communal and bilateral relations. Irresponsibly, the British failed to clearly demarcate certain border areas, and some of the territorial allocations defied reason and history. For example, two frontier regions, Punjab in the west and Bengal in the east, were divided between India and Pakistan, resulting in violence and sowing the seeds of lingering irredentist unrest. In these two disparate regions, the British created an "impossible nation" of East and West Pakistan separated by language, ethnicity and thousands of kilometers of India's territory that lay in between.

The trauma of Partition cast a shadow beyond 1947. In 1971 Pakistani armed forces committed widespread atrocities in East Pakistan in reaction to the results of the national election that gave victory to the Bengali-dominated east. The violent mayhem unleashed by the Pakistani military, aimed at overturning the election result and preventing a power-shift, led to an exodus of Hindus from East Pakistan to India, creating a massive refugee crisis. It also sparked the third war between India and Pakistan in the post-Independence era, with India prevailing despite Pakistan receiving considerable support from the US (Bass 2013). Partition was also the genesis of the Kashmir problem that continues to haunt India and generate tensions with Pakistan (see Chapter 10).

The British are deeply implicated, but Congress and the Muslim League also bear responsibility for the bloodbath, a collective guilt that also extends to the large numbers of people acting as vigilantes or involved with religious-based paramilitary groups who carried out the carnage. Fifteen million refugees crossed the newly established borders because of their religious identities, uprooted from their ancestral homes and the communities where they had long coexisted peacefully with neighbors from various religions. The sad fact was that peaceful coexistence was the pre-Partition norm, but this reassuring reality was shattered when people became defined solely by their religion and became vulnerable to the machinations of political opportunists (Khan 2007).

Partition thus was the deadly opening act of Independence and has resonated powerfully ever since, a nightmare that has entered into the popular imagination. It is a gory narrative of victimization, one that sharpens the sectarian divide. The retelling of these painful stories fans communal antagonisms and animosity towards Pakistan among India's Hindu majority. The victims are the martyrs for Hindu chauvinists, the people whose blood sacrifice must be honored and revenged. The large Muslim community remaining in India, nearly 15% of the population, has paid the price over the years. In the aftermath, Nehru steered the nation away from the abyss and stifled sectarian interests that sought to establish a state based on Hinduism (see Chapter 1).

Indian national identity is strongly defined by the freedom movement and the battles to achieve independence. The leaders of that movement—Gandhi and Nehru—are national icons, the founding fathers of the nation. Their successful agitation against the British that led to the end of colonial rule is central to the heroic, feel-good narrative of nation. It was the struggle won, the culmination of the nationalist struggle for dignity and freedom. Yet, Partition baptized Independence and is another less gratifying source of identity that is rooted in and amplifies communalism. The BJP, and associated Hindutva organizations, tap into the emotions and identities associated with this touchstone of national identity, mobilizing the shared trauma to whip up support based on vilifying Muslims. Hindus, Muslims and Sikhs, along with Bengalis and Punjabis, committed atrocities, providing martyrs for various groups, and the basis for contemporary scaremongering and vilification essential to fuel communal hatreds and fears. This particularly gruesome trauma haunts the nation and remains a potent reminder of what can go wrong, and serves as an object lesson in the dangers of allowing such passions and intolerance to go unchecked. The legacies of nationalism unleashed also haunt contemporary Japan.

Figure 7.2 Golden Temple, Sikh Holy Site Attacked by Indian Security Forces in 1984. Photo © Jeff Kingston.

Japan

Japan's chosen trauma since 1945 has been the devastation of war caused by reckless military leaders who led Japan into a cataclysm, one that devastated Asia but also led to the deaths of nearly 3 million Japanese civilians and soldiers. The atomic bombings of Hiroshima and Nagasaki in August 1945 epitomize the folly of war, serving as powerful symbols of Japan's suffering and reinforcing its commitment to pacifism. Overall, Japanese have paid much more attention to their victimization rather than their role as victimizers, and the atomic bombings have been central to this narrative. This self-absorption overshadows and diverts attention away from Japan's ravaging of Asia—at least 15 million dead and 100 million displaced in China, 2 million dead from wartime famine in Indochina, the death of over 1 million Indonesian laborers and a million Filipinos, tens of thousands of comfort women subjected to sexual slavery in military brothels, and a swathe of plundering and destruction throughout the region. Mistreatment of tens of thousands of Allied prisoners of war figures prominently in postwar perceptions about Japan, as survivors have kept painful memories alive, but they are marginalized in Japan's mainstream narrative. Certainly many Japanese have not averted their eyes from the suffering their nation's aggression inflicted on Asia, but the consequences have been downplayed in textbooks (see Chapter 9) and by successive conservative governments since the US Occupation ended in 1952.

The national identity drawing on this trauma is one of pacifism as enshrined in the 1947 Constitution that was written by the US Occupation forces. This identity has been one that embraces the judgments of the International Military Tribunal for the Far East, Japan's equivalent to the Nuremberg Trials. In signing the 1951 Treaty of San Francisco, Japan acknowledged it was the aggressor and guilty as charged. This treaty brought an end to the war among signatories, and an end to the US Occupation, while providing the basis for continued basing of US military forces in Japan. The Treaty of San Francisco has been the foundation of the postwar order in Japan, although reactionaries have always contested what they view as "victor's justice," a reference to the one-sided and lopsided verdict at the IMTFE that places all blame and responsibility on the Japanese. But the pacifism based on war trauma has sunk deep roots in Japan that remain resilient in the face of various attempts to lift constitutional constraints on the military. Article 9 of the Constitution which relinquishes the right to wage war and maintain armed forces has become a powerful talisman of peace that Japanese value as intrinsic to their national identity even if Japan's military forces are large and advanced and it has the eighth largest defense budget in the world.

Prime Minister Shinzo Abe moved in 2014 to reinterpret Article 9 by cabinet decision, thus bypassing constitutional procedures required for revision, to allow for "collective self-defense," meaning that Japan's military forces could be deployed to defend an ally under attack. Prime Minister Abe understood that he lacked sufficient political or public support to revise the Constitution, going through the mandated political process of gaining two-thirds approval in both houses of the Diet and a majority in a national referendum. The public reaction was overwhelmingly negative, with over 60% opposing his decision and 80% complaining that it was done too hastily and without sufficient explanation. In 2015, Abe persuaded the Diet to approve legislation that allows Japan to exercise the right of collective self-defense and thus fulfill commitments he had agreed to in the new US-Japan Defense Guidelines adopted earlier in 2015. The Abe Doctrine significantly expands what Japan is prepared to do militarily in support of the US, but public support for this initiative is very low—only 23% in a 2015 Pew poll and 14% in a subsequent NHK poll in June 2015.

Militarism, like nationalism, remains a powerful taboo in Japan, but one that is incrementally receding. Conservatives complain that Japan's postwar national identity is based on a renunciation of nationalism, but they are contesting this unusual state of affairs in the 21st century. Their trauma is the masochistic history Japan has been obliged to accept, asking why Japan alone has been asked to shoulder responsibility for the outbreak of war and its dreadful consequences.

Central to this line of reasoning is the insistence that Japan fought a defensive war, one motivated by Pan Asian solidarity and aimed at liberating fellow Asian nations from western colonialism. Revisionists argue Japan was isolated and threatened by the international system in the 1930s and that the war that ensued featured atrocities by all sides, not just Japan. These revisionists also point to the post-World War II decolonization of Asia as vindication of Japan's struggle. This self-vindicating and exonerating interpretation is the basis of the revisionists' chosen trauma—victor's justice. The judgments of the IMTFE dispensed this victor's justice, promoting a narrative of war that lays all blame on Japan and, by only prosecuting Japanese war criminals, asserts that only Japanese committed war crimes and atrocities. Reactionaries feel that this is a humiliating narrative that is unfair and biased. There is considerable resentment that China and South Korea continually invoke the horrors of the past for diplomatic advantage. Younger Japanese also wonder why they are being asked to take responsibility for incidents that date back to their grandfathers' generation. Revisionists have nurtured support for their valorizing narrative and in the 21st century find a receptive audience suffering from perpetrator's fatigue.

Japan is beginning to exhume some of the painful wartime traumas that had long been marginalized in public discourse and commemoration. On the night of March 9–10, 1945 the US dropped incendiary bombs on eastern Tokyo, incinerating an estimated 100,000 civilians, injuring a million more and leaving a million homeless. Setting aside Hiroshima and Nagasaki, it is the single most destructive bombing raid in history, far surpassing Dresden and Hamburg in the nightmarish annals of urban infernos, leaving behind a 41-square-kilometer swathe of smoldering ruins and grimly panoramic vistas where vibrant communities were suddenly obliterated. Since the millennium there has been increasing media coverage of this traumatic incident, detailing for example the high percentage of women and children killed in the fires.

The commander of the firebombing campaign that systematically razed dozens of Japanese cities was General Curtis LeMay. He promoted the switch from conventional bombs to incendiaries and timed the Tokyo raid to coincide with windy weather, knowing the fires would spread more rapidly in the kindling of Tokyo's wooden housing. The firebombing was not solely a matter of damaging Japan's factories and infrastructure. This aerial terror was also vengeance, payback for Pearl Harbor and mistreatment of prisoners of war, and was intended to inflict maximum suffering on the civilian populace and lower their morale. The line between military and civilian targets had been crossed well before this by both sides, but never on such a monstrous scale.

Despite this "terror bombing," Japan's military leaders were undaunted as they persisted in waging a war they knew they could not win. They were gambling on a decisive final battle in the hope that inflicting heavy casualties on invading American troops would improve the terms of surrender. The US insistence on unconditional surrender raised worries about what would befall Emperor Hirohito, and military leaders were also mindful that they risked being held accountable for the horrors they had inflicted throughout Asia unless they could secure a negotiated peace.

Prolonging the war meant there was a price to be paid and, as in most modern conflicts, civilians paid the highest price. The firebombing campaign left some 5 million homeless throughout Japan, and killed perhaps 500,000 civilians, with a further 400,000 wounded (excluding Hiroshima and Nagasaki). LeMay also oversaw Operation Starvation, an aerial mining operation in Japan's coastal waters and ports designed to disrupt shipping and distribution of food. This supplemented a very effective submarine blockade.

So why are so few Americans aware of this grisly chapter of what historian John Dower (1987) has characterized as a race war, one waged without mercy? Perhaps because the comforting narrative of the Good War (World War II) fought by the Greatest Generation persisted long after it was discredited, burying Allied war crimes. And which country, aside from Germany, has taken the full measure of its darkest chapters? Here, Japan and the US share some common ground.

In the 21st century, more Japanese are reconsidering the national wartime trauma in ways that undercut the postwar consensus. Prime Minister Abe is only the most prominent advocate of overturning this consensus. This revisionist view asserts that the real trauma was not Japan's wartime conduct or suffering, but rather defeat and the negative verdict on Japan's actions. Thus, Japan's chosen trauma of wartime aggression and suffering that bolsters pacifism is being contested with increasing vigor by those who seek to instill pride in nation and stoke the embers of nationalism. Moving forward for these revisionists means revisiting and rehabilitating a discredited past when Japan ran amok in Asia. For them, the goal is finding redemption in the ashes of war while ending Japan's postwar pacifism.

South Korea

South Korea's chosen trauma is the era of Japanese colonial subjugation and humiliation between 1905 and 1945. Colonial rule began in 1910, but was preceded by five years of increasing Japanese encroachment following the Russo-Japanese war

(1904–1905) that ended in Tokyo's victory. Scholars distinguish between different phases of this colonial rule, but in the popular mind it was an unending nightmare of ruthless suppression and exploitation. Unlike in our other nations, this narrative of victimization and suffering prevails unchallenged and there is a consensus that there were no redeeming aspects or benefits of Japanese rule.

There is no doubt that Japanese rule involved sustained repression of Koreans' political aspirations for independence. From the assassination of Queen Min in 1895 and the relentless repression of the independence movement, until the last of the comfort women and forced laborers were recruited in the waning days of World War II, Japanese rule throughout the peninsula was cruel, disdainful and insistently humiliating. It is thus not surprising that this is Korea's chosen trauma.

Anti-Japanese sentiments are intrinsic to Korean national identity and the angry nationalism that feeds on and inflames antipathy toward Japan. Similar to China's long standing anti-Japanese nationalism, Korea's anti-Japanese nationalism developed from the onset of Japanese aggression in 1905 and propelled the independence struggle until 1945. This painful history is one of the few things Koreans can reliably agree on and thus politicians often play the history card, invoking Japanese perfidy to boost their sagging popularity.

The biggest controversy over this trauma involves those who collaborated with the Japanese, many of whom have gone on to play prominent roles in post-1945 South Korea in business, politics and the military. Nationalist verdicts on the colonial era made collaboration a taboo subject, one that did not fit into the prevailing narrative of victimization by Japanese. This collaboration angle haunted the nation in the recesses of collective memory, but did not emerge until the late 1990s, principally because those who had the most to lose from public scrutiny of their colonial-era resumes remained influential. President Park Chung-hee (1961–1979) was in the Japanese colonial armed forces, embodying the trans-war continuities in the Korean elite. Awkwardly, his postwar trajectory resembled Japan's own historical experience, coming to power in a military *coup d'état* in 1961 and then promoting state-led industrialization with significant assistance from Japan whose goodwill he assiduously cultivated (see Chapter 5).

During South Korea's authoritarian era until 1987, all sorts of sensitive issues were kept under wraps and silence prevailed over the collaboration issue because too many of the powerful were tainted. Democracy flowered in the 1990s under Kim Young-sam (1993–1998) and Kim Dae-jung (1998–2003), but it was not until the 21st century that the collaboration issue became politicized, a way of discrediting opponents rather than an attempt to fundamentally reconsider the colonial era. Excavating this sensitive, murky and layered history has been fraught with trauma because it is morally explosive and so many are implicated for actions that have a different meaning and significance now than during the colonial era, when options were limited. The moral condemnation has overshadowed critical analysis of the collaborator's role in postwar Korea and the triangular relationship with the US and Japan. Contemporary perceptions map uncomfortably on the colonial tableau where coercion, intimidation, power and cooperation were deeply intertwined. Judging survival strategies then by contemporary standards is polarizing and in some respects misleading, but again shows how the scarring of traumas does not fade in collective memory.

The politics of collaboration continue to resonate in contemporary South Korea. In 2005 Prime Minister Roh Moo-hyun launched an investigation into the family backgrounds of politicians to determine whether there were collaborationist skeletons in their closets. The intention was to embarrass the party led by rival Park Geun-hye, Park Chung-hee's daughter, as a way to challenge the patriotism of her conservative party members. Problematically, the plan backfired as it became apparent that many members of Roh's party were also implicated. The inconvenient truth is that many professionals, elite civil servants and politicians hail from families that collaborated with the Japanese, so vindictively outing them is an attack on Seoul's influential upper crust. In 2013, Park Geun-hye's Education Ministry approved a new textbook that downplays collaboration and asserts that those who worked with the Japanese colonial authorities did so under coercion. This high-profile intervention drew criticism from scholars and teachers who worry about the distortion of history, suggesting how important the issue of colonial collaboration remains in postcolonial South Korea's catalogue of traumas made in Japan. No issue is more sensitive or controversial than Korean brokers' involvement in the coercive and deceptive recruitment of tens of thousands of comfort women (Soh 2008).

There is no risk of exaggerating the influence of the colonial past in contemporary South Korea. As we discuss in other chapters dealing with textbooks (Chapter 9) and museums (Chapter 8), Korea's shared history with Japan resonates powerfully seven decades on, perhaps excessively so. Certainly Japan has not helped matters by not taking the full measure of this history, and adds to the trauma when prominent politicians question apologies offered and quibble about details of horrific acts, as Prime Minister Abe did in 2007 when he disputed the level of coercion used in recruiting comfort women. Some Japanese politicians have frequently apologized for this past, but their reactionary colleagues have repeatedly undermined these apologies by justifying or minimizing misdeeds. Their repudiation of apologies has raised legitimate doubts among Koreans about the extent of Japanese contrition and remorse, while Japanese complain that their apologies fall on deaf ears. This is frustrating for Washington because it undermines its efforts to promote more effective trilateral relations with its two Asian allies. With some prodding by the US, on December 28, 2015 President Park and Prime Minister Abe struck a deal aimed at ending the controversy over the comfort women, but this vague agreement sidesteps thorny issues and resolves very little of this traumatic history and is thus unlikely to represent what Foreign Minister Fumio Kishida termed a "final and irreversible resolution" (Japan and Republic of Korea Foreign Ministers' Meeting, December 28, 2015).

What about the trauma of the Korean War (1950–1953), a war that claimed the lives of 3 million people and laid waste to vast stretches of the peninsula? Certainly this is not a forgotten or buried trauma because the two nations remain divided and in a state of war. The armistice has been threatened by saber rattling and violent incidents involving the military forces, a confrontation that has persisted for so long that it has become almost fossilized and efforts to overcome this impasse have abated. Ardent desires to roll back the "temporary" division of the peninsula at the 38th parallel gave way to building improved ties during President Kim Dae-jung's "Sunshine Policy" in the 1990s, and to a 21st-century emphasis on managing the nuclear threat and the Kim dynasty transitions in the North. The stalemate on the peninsula is complicated by North Korea's nuclear weapons capability, first demonstrated in 2006, one that gives credence to the threats of annihilation periodically issued by Pyongyang. There have been efforts since the mid-1990s to convince Pyongyang to abandon its nuclear weapons program, but it has conferred so much leverage that it has become a lifeline for the regime, one that it has little incentive to concede. Certainly the costly nuclear program has come at the expense of public welfare and led to international sanctions that leave North Korea diplomatically and economically isolated. But it has been an effective regime survival strategy and it has enabled Pyongyang to maximize concessions and food and energy aid. In this respect, it has diminished expectations for a peaceful reunification of the peninsula, perpetuating the trauma of separation. The nuclear weapons program has also been more affordable than modernizing North Korea's outdated conventional forces, making denuclearization undesirable.

North Korea is an uncomfortably close enemy, as South Korea's capital, Seoul, is only 31 miles from the border and within easy range of North Korea's formidable

Figure 7.3 Wartime Soldiers from South and North Korea Embrace Above the Gap That Still Separates the Peninsula. Photo © Jeff Kingston.

arsenal. All males are required to undergo military service and there is extensive indoctrination about the enemy. The older generation favors reunification of the peninsula, although there are differences about how to achieve this, while the younger generation is much less keen on this agenda and more worried about the costs it would entail given how backward North Korea is economically. Comparisons are often drawn with the reunification of Germany which cost some US$1.9 trillion between 1989 and 2009, the equivalent of one-half of Germany's economic output in 2008. In that period East Germany's output rose from 33% of that of West Germany to about 70%. South Koreans are aware that the gap between North and South Korea is far wider now than that between West and East Germany in 1989, and many see no compelling point to reunification given the colossal financial sacrifices they would have to bear. The population of South Korea is about 50 million while that of North Korea is about 25 million. South Korea's gross national income was estimated to be 38 times larger than North Korea's in 2013, or about 19 times as large on a per capita basis.

Finances aside, the division of the Korean Peninsula is a festering wound in the national psyche in ways that the 1980 Gwangju uprising clearly is not (see Chapter 5). The struggle for democracy is embedded in Korean national identity and a source of pride for those who risked so much to overthrow authoritarian government. While their sacrifices are not exactly ignored, they do not figure prominently in contemporary discourse. Aung San Suu Kyi, Myanmar's democracy icon, planted a tree at the memorial cemetery for the victims, acknowledging the inspiration that they gave her countrymen during the 1988 uprising against military misrule in what was then known as Burma. Yet the student movement protesting martial law and demanding democracy is a largely overlooked trauma among Koreans outside the southwest region where Gwangju is located. Perhaps what they fought for has been achieved and is now taken for granted and there is a mainstream bias both against this region and the leftist activism the students symbolize.

Indonesia

Under Sukarno, Indonesia's chosen trauma drew on colonial Dutch rule and anti-western, anti-neo-imperialist sentiments. As with Nehru and Mao, Sukarno was suspicious of capitalist domination of the world system and resented this. Dutch efforts to prolong their colonial rule and subsequently carve off Papua reinforced his perceptions and resentments, ones that he widely publicized in Indonesia (see Chapter 11). This trauma created a general sense of ongoing exploitation and domination despite political independence. Given how impoverished and weak Indonesia was when he took the helm in 1949, and the very real prospects for disintegration, it is a tribute to Sukarno's charisma and powerful oratory that Indonesia survived as a national entity. He railed against the imperial powers and sought common cause with the other "have not" nations, cooperating with Nehru to launch the non-aligned movement by hosting the Asia-Africa Bandung Conference in 1955. It was a symbolic rejection of the superpower-centered politics of the Cold War, an ongoing trauma for nations that did not want to become embroiled in the Soviet-American competition to dominate global politics. Sukarno's chosen trauma—the predatory nature of imperialism and capitalism—helped to explain widespread poverty, even if it did not justify Sukarno's poor economic policymaking that contributed to the gathering economic crisis. Railing against the US, he declared that Indonesia did not need its aid and that his countrymen would sooner eat pebbles than kowtow to arrogant imperialists. Shortages of food and fuel and high inflation eroded already low living standards and demoralized the nation. Sukarno's support for land reform also generated discontent in the countryside. From 1962, PKI-linked groups carried out campaigns at the village level mobilizing the poor against landlords, officials and moneylenders, who responded by arming themselves and forming paramilitary groups.

Sukarno's anti-western grandstanding that drew on the colonial trauma alarmed military leaders who believed that he was soft on communism and too impetuous to govern well. Sukarno was also closing the door to assistance from western countries and as a result relying more on the Soviet Union. Indonesian Islamic leaders shared the military's concerns about Sukarno's leftward tendencies and mercurial rule. The mass celebrations of the fiftieth anniversary of the PKI in 1965 contributed to the feverish pitch, and it appeared that the PKI was getting the upper hand as Sukarno's health deteriorated. Despite trying to reconcile the various powerful forces in Indonesia with his doctrine of NASAKOM (nationalism, Islam and communism),

Figure 7.4 Bas Relief Depicting Indonesian Horrors of 1965 Pancasila Sakti Monument. Photo © Jeff Kingston.

tensions were gathering under Sukarno's Guided Democracy and there seemed little hope for improvement (see Chapter 5). Sukarno also provoked anti-communist forces inside Indonesia and in the West by declaring the Jakarta–Pyongyang–Beijing–Hanoi axis. His polarizing politics were a significant factor leading to the bloody events of 1965–1966 and his ouster from power. Suharto, his deeply implicated successor, made this Indonesia's selectively chosen trauma, a humanitarian disaster on an epic scale.

Gestapu

Indonesia's greatest post-independence wound, one that still festers, is relatively unknown in the world even though it is one of the most murderous convulsions in the 20th century. The slaughter began in 1965 and continued into 1966, when as many as one million people were hacked, shot, bludgeoned and garotted to death, mostly in Central and East Java, Bali and North Sumatra, but throughout the archipelago, mostly at the instigation of military units and various right-wing paramilitary groups. It is clear that the military did nothing to intervene to stop the slaughter and did much to facilitate it. The killings were sparked by an aborted coup on September 30, 1965 (Gestapu, the acronym in Indonesian), allegedly orchestrated by the PKI, that led to the death of six top generals and a lieutenant. The subsequent bloodbath fed on gathering grievances and resentments during an unprecedented period of mass politicization.

Whether or not one believes that the PKI orchestrated the kidnapping and killing of the generals, and there is considerable disagreement over this, right-wing generals stepped in and mounted a counter coup (Roosa 2006). Military forces in Jakarta under the command of General Suharto seized power and imposed martial law while hunting down suspected communists. The PKI was the third largest communist party in the world at the time so there were many targets, but the killings went beyond a red purge and also claimed the lives of tens of thousands of ethnic Chinese. The armed forces, paramilitary vigilante groups and Islamic youth organizations all participated in the savagery. Village feuds were also dredged up while the killings also settled old debts. The paroxysms of auto-genocide lasted several months all over the archipelago. Tens of thousands of leftists, including Prameodya Ananta Toer (1925–2006), Indonesia's most famous novelist, were sent to live in prison exile on remote islands. The military presided over and actively participated in this horrific tragedy, carrying out killings, arrests and torture while also supplying weapons and transport to paramilitary organizations and Islamic youth groups.

Amid this carnage, General Suharto assumed power, sidelining Sukarno under what amounted to house arrest, and getting him to sign over power in March 1966. In 1967 the New Order was proclaimed under President Suharto, who remained in power until 1998 (see Chapter 5). He invoked and perpetuated the fears of 1965 to strengthen and consolidate the New Order's power. This meant engineering a useful history, depicting the PKI as the mastermind of the bungled coup by leftist colonels and Suharto mobilizing the military to heroically save the day. In school textbooks Sukarno was also implicated in Gestapu, but here the New Order had to tread carefully as he was a nationalist icon deeply revered by the public (see Chapter 9). The highly selective official narrative of the chosen trauma focused on the deaths of seven officers while shifting blame for, and marginalizing the massacre of, several hundred thousand people, an organized forgetting of an "unchosen" trauma that always lurked behind the sanitized version (see Chapter 8).

Indonesians are now reconsidering this buried trauma, especially the role of the military, but this dark and precarious past remains shrouded in mystery, fear and denial. The legacy of 1965 still haunts Indonesia because so many families suffered not only from the killings but also the ostracism that ensued, inflicting deep psychological scars on people who had to suffer in silence and alone. Political prisoners have been released from their remote island detention centers, but still face administrative harassment because of their links, however tenuous and exaggerated, to the still banned PKI; even people who only danced at PKI anniversary celebrations were arrested and exiled. The lingering stigma haunts families even half a century later. In 2012 the National Human Rights Commission concluded that crimes against humanity had occurred in 1965–1966, and that the military command and certain individual officers bear responsibility, but there have been no prosecutions. The institutionalized cover-up of military crimes persists and also extends to those committed in East Timor (1975–1999), in Lampung and Tanjung Priok in the 1980s, and during the insurgencies in Aceh and Papua. These other traumas remain marginalized in national discourse, but are part of the New Order continuum and the abuses of power that catapulted the military to power and sustained its rule.

The powerful perpetrators of Gestapu have mostly died, but subjecting this exhumed history to a new postmortem remains fraught with political ramifications and difficulties. The veil of secrecy remains heavy, and lifting it would cross red lines as Indonesia's 21st-century democracy is based on a tacit agreement that the military will not be held accountable for its 20th-century crimes and is also not subject to contemporary corruption inquiries. This cocoon of impunity has been the price of the military returning to barracks and withdrawing from formal political power, a price that many Indonesians probably feel is worth paying. But not everyone agrees with reconciliation without justice or retribution, and some argue that ending immunity for the military is essential to consolidate democracy and civilian rule.

Coming to terms with this nightmarish past, and confronting the terrible price paid by victims and their surviving families, was never going to be easy, but is especially fraught because the trail of blood leads to the military. During the New Order, the communists were blamed and the military valorized, a triumph of good over evil, but the story of the mass killings was silenced. The government glossed over the horrific events in textbooks, focusing on the military-as-savior narrative. It also produced a movie that was televised annually during the New Order to popularize its version of events. Of course this does not mean everyone believed the military's self-exonerating account, and there were doubts from the outset that Beijing was involved and that the PKI had orchestrated a coup, but inside Indonesia such skepticism was not openly expressed. Doubters could easily be portrayed as communist sympathizers and risked losing jobs, or imprisonment, exile and extra-judicial violence. The paramilitary gangs such as Pacasila Pemuda killed with impunity during and after Gestapu, and subsequently remained engaged in organized crime with powerful backing from the military. So during the New Order, doubters and dissidents were discreet, but here and there people would pour out their hearts, talk of the terrible things they had seen or heard about, and subvert the official story. It is hard now to imagine that the tropical paradise of Bali was convulsed by the killings and that some of the beaches favored by sunbathers and surfers were once blood-soaked; one informant told me in 1985 about his childhood memories from two decades before of military trucks disgorging their tied-up human cargoes, battered but alive, and the prisoners being hacked to death with sickles and machetes in front of his eyes.

During the New Order, responsibility for the mass killings was fudged and blame shifted to communists, a storyline that let the military and its collaborators off the hook. There was an orchestrated silence about the military's role in the carnage and about the vigilantes it unleashed on the nation at a time when those murdered were all "suspected communists." This version of the trauma served various purposes. It conferred legitimacy on the military by crediting it with saving the nation from communism, while their role as perpetrators was pushed to the side and the victims vilified as communists. This satisfied conservative pillars of the New Order—especially the military and Islamic groups. The shared trauma established a basis for a common identity based on anti-communism and justified the government and security forces remaining powerful and vigilant, placing strict limits on political and civil liberties in the name of preserving public order and security. This legitimized the military's concept of dwifungsi, establishing its twin security and political roles. Beyond traditional security threats, the military's political role in preserving stability justified maintaining an extensive presence throughout the archipelago. This political role facilitated repression, rooting out subversion and dissidence, curbing civil society, and limiting democracy to periodic elections that were not free or fair. Thus the institution that had "saved" the nation invoked the chaos of 1965–1966 to justify its authoritarian policies and acted in support of President Suharto, consolidating his power and eliminating any opposition.

The new national identity based on anti-communism also positioned New Order Indonesia to draw closer to western nations and the benefits this conferred in terms of foreign investment, debt rollovers, access to fresh funding and support from international financial institutions such as the World Bank and IMF. Amid Cold War intrigues, the CIA is implicated in the military coup and the ousting of the anti-American President Sukarno in favor of the pro-western government of President Suharto. It was a significant boost for American influence in the region, bringing a strategically located, resource-rich, anti-communist nation into its camp.

Indonesia's national identity drawing on this trauma was constructed on false premises, but it is only since Suharto's ouster that the nation has begun reassessing this experience and reallocating blame. In the immediate aftermath of Suharto's ouster, violence broke out around the archipelago as long-simmering tensions suddenly erupted, especially in Kalimantan between locals and migrants over land and resource issues (Lloyd Parry 2005). The military had long maintained that only its firm control stood between the people and chaos. The sudden spate of communal violence, beheadings, reports of cannibalism, ninja killings and targeting of ethnic Chinese in 1998 and 1999 seemed to vouchsafe the need for authoritarian government. It seemed like the traumas of the past had returned with a vengeance, signifying the fragility of political stability. There were eerie and unsettling echoes of the events from the mid-1960s when society careened out of control and descended into a maelstrom. In the intervening three decades there had been no attempt to come to terms with this gory history as the perpetrators buried it and imposed an exonerating narrative, intimidating victims into silence.

Since 1998 and Suharto's ouster, the mass killings have been discussed and new information has been disseminated, but the massacre remains shrouded in mystery and the reckoning remains incomplete. There is much more to the saga than the people running amok and conducting a series of violent reprisals against the vilified communists, but this story remains largely untold. The taboo was broken in 2000 when President Abdurahim Wahid made a public apology to the victims, acknowledging that groups affiliated with the Islamic organization he headed, Nahdlatul Ulama, were involved in the massacres. This was not a revelation to the victims' relatives and friends, and it was broadly known among the better-informed circles, but it was the first public declaration of responsibility and expression of remorse by a national leader. It is not surprising that a reckoning could not begin until Suharto was out of the way because such a process inevitably exposes the lies embedded in the official version of the trauma and could only implicate Suharto and other powerful perpetrators and instigators in the military. Peeling back the layers of deliberate obfuscation discredits the New Order and its authoritarian rule, spattering the military's reputation and credibility. Exaggerating the threat of communist subversion was used to justify political repression and prevent inquiries into abuses of power and extensive violations of human rights. The victims' families stayed silent, living in fear because they knew what could happen. They and the families of political detainees became "untouchable," their traumas unmentioned and unaddressed. In villages and urban communities, the murderers remained, coexisting with those who knew what they had done to their relatives and friends, but who were powerless to exact revenge or do anything about it since these men were part of paramilitary gangs or Islamic groups with powerful connections.

In 2004, for the first time school textbooks mentioned the military involvement in the large-scale massacres, but under pressure from the military and Islamic groups the attorney general ordered them burned and restored the old version praising the patriotic campaign that led to fewer than 80,000 deaths, well below the prevailing consensus of at least 500,000 and probably considerably more (see Chapter 9). Probing this dark chapter of Indonesia's past strikes an unwelcome discordant note as the nation glories in its democratic transition and nations around the world laud the country for its remarkable transformation to stable democratic rule in a multiparty system with changes of power between parties, all accomplished in the brief period since Suharto stepped down in 1998. Nobody then imagined that the transition would be this smooth and fast, as the military has withdrawn, at least formally, from politics. But history may be catching up.

The parliament set up a Truth and Reconciliation Commission, but it never got off the ground after President Yudhoyono failed to appoint members and the Constitutional Court ruled the body unlawful. In 2012, the overdue reckoning gained momentum when the Human Rights Commission published its investigation into the New Order abuses, indicting the military for the 1965–1966 killings and implicating the security forces in extra-judicial killings during the 1980s. The commission urged that the perpetrators be prosecuted and that the president offer an apology and compensation to victims' relatives. Civil society organizations have advocated the same remedies, but none of this has happened. Even though the top-level officers involved have all died, the powerful military opposes such initiatives because they inevitably would tarnish the institution and undermine its credibility and self-appointed role as guardian of the nation. This is the unfinished business of the New Order.

The 2014 Oscar-nominated documentary, *The Act of Killing* (2013), captures the mood of that bloody era and the unworried attitude of the killers and their absolute lack of remorse for the horrors inflicted. The director, Joshua Oppenheimer, managed to convince some of the killers to reenact their crimes and they appear very unselfconscious about doing so. Apparently, they don't worry that they will be held accountable—not a misplaced confidence in light of current conditions. One elderly man showed exactly how he garroted victims and advised that it is better not to wear white when bludgeoning people. It seems that the perpetrators lived a "party animal" lifestyle, drinking, taking drugs and womanizing amidst the carnage. It is a riveting depiction of the banality of evil. The murderers in the documentary joyously recall the atrocities they committed, explaining that as the winners they had nothing to apologize for, or worry about. Oppenheimer followed up with another documentary, *The Look of Silence* (2014), focusing on a traumatized family finally confronting a man responsible for a relative's death during the maelstrom.

Repudiating the myths that have surrounded and obscured the chosen trauma carries potentially powerful repercussions. The past is horrific, reason enough to avert collective eyes, but the problem is that the accusations implicate the fathers of the still powerful. For example, President Yudhoyono (2004–2014) is married to the daughter of Sarwo Edhie Wibowo, who was head of the special forces in 1965–1966 and as such heavily implicated in the massacres. There is no incentive to face up to past crimes, and those who seek accountability are weak in the face of the institutions that stand to lose from a forthright reckoning. As one of the vigilantes puts it in *The Act of Killing*, "War crimes are defined by the winners. And I am a winner." The exhumation of this past continues as media investigations, books and novels about this trauma prove popular among Indonesians too young to have been eyewitnesses, but still interested in finding out what happened and why. It is a sign of the times as Indonesia struggles with this reckoning and continues its democratic transition, the new touchstone for national identity and pride in the post-Suharto era.

The above discussion elucidates some of the ways that chosen traumas and their reverberations have become central to national identity in our five countries. In East Asia these traumas continue to divide Japan from its neighbors as memories of suffering feed antipathies and make for convenient scapegoating of Japan while diverting attention from homegrown problems. As we noted, along the margins of those chosen traumas are ancillary or downplayed traumas that don't fit nationalist narratives, but won't stay buried. In the next chapter we examine how some of this troubling past and traumatic legacies are represented in Asia's museums and memorials.

8

Museums and Memorials

Museums and memorials often serve as repositories of selected memories that provide a window onto defining experiences of a nation. As such they reveal a nation's soul, its anguish, its dreams and painful legacies. The nationalist narratives on display present a past for contemporary consumption, one that serves a political purpose. The ghosts of the past that haunt these sites linger in the collective imagination, wraiths and apparitions that kindle shared remembrance and invoke powerful and primordial sentiments. These talismanic shrines to painful experiences and reminders of loss evoke nationalistic passions and promote unifying storylines. They are often sites of collective remembering of traumas endured, portals into the past that impart lessons and promote nationalism. Like textbooks (see Chapter 9), museums are influential in constructing national identity.

In this chapter we examine some representative museums and memorial sites to illustrate how they serve to promote nationalist narratives and sustain grievances and tensions. The focus is on East Asia because the national sagas and traumas depicted in the museums of Japan, South Korea and China resonate more controversially in the present. Chinese and Koreans deploy history to promote national unity based on shared trauma inflicted by Japan, and also to divert attention from contemporary domestic problems and to gain diplomatic advantage. This mobilization of the past in contemporary Asia accentuates divisions and amplifies tensions. It also makes Koreans and Chinese acutely sensitive to how Japan depicts their shared history from 1895 to 1945. The Yushukan Museum adjacent to Yasukuni Shrine in Tokyo embraces a vindicating, exonerating and glorifying version of this narrative that minimizes or ignores the traumas while shifting responsibility and portraying Japanese as the principal victims in this era of clashing imperialisms. As such the Yushukan burnishes Yasukuni Shrine's talismanic role as ground zero for an

Nationalism in Asia: A History Since 1945, First Edition. Jeff Kingston.

unrepentant view of Japan's rampage through Asia from 1931 to 1945 and discredits reactionary politicians' glib assertions that in going there they merely wish to honor the souls of those who died for their country and pray for peace. Naturally, this revisionist narrative is anathema to Chinese and Koreans and provokes an angry nationalist backlash where the battle lines are extended to museum spaces. In contrast, the Hiroshima Peace Memorial Museum features an anti-war narrative reminding visitors about the horrors Japanese suffered as a result of the 1945 atomic bombing of the city, one of contemporary Japan's central traumas underlying pacifist sentiments. In Hiroshima, inevitably, there is more about what happened to Japan than the devastation it perpetrated.

India's and Indonesia's museums that focus on the perfidious colonial power, and the nationalist struggle for independence, are relatively uncontroversial. In both cases, the official national genesis story is broadly accepted. Good examples are the Red Fort complex in New Delhi and the Monas Museum in Jakarta which present fairly standard and unchallenged narratives. Their focus is mostly on what happened before achieving independence and it does not excite contemporary domestic or international controversy.

India

The Red Fort War Memorial Museum features military themes and the role of Indian soldiers who fought on behalf of the British. In this complex there is also the Swantrata Senani Museum housed in British barracks that tells the story of the Quit India movement, aimed at ending colonial rule, and honors the heroes of the Indian National Army (INA), including Netaji Subhash Chandra Bose, who fought with the Japanese during World War II and were arrested for sedition following Japan's surrender in 1945. (Bose, however, died in a plane crash and his grave is in Tokyo.) In honoring the INA there is curiously no comment on Japanese Pan Asianism or the aims of its Holy War, a powerful silence that indicts Japanese claims. These "mutineers" were never prosecuted, as the British were rushing for the exit and Indian nationalists viewed them as patriots and freedom fighters. Overall, the unsparing depiction of the British Raj on display at the Red Fort is unchallenged inside India or indeed in Great Britain. In 2013 when Prime Minister David Cameron visited the memorial site of a notorious British massacre in Amritsar, he fell short of an apology, but expressed remorse. In no way did he deny, downplay or shift responsibility for the tragedy, as Japan has done, although it is worth pointing out that Japan has offered numerous apologies and expressions of regret for its war crimes that reactionaries swiftly repudiate. Similarly, there is no museum in Great Britain that disputes the Red Fort's account of events (as there is in China and South Korea disputing the Yushukan's version of events) and no mainstream British political constituency promoting a revisionist history about colonial rule in India that seeks to whitewash the past, as there is in Japan.

There may be concerns, ones shared in Tokyo, that the demands of British colonial victims could escalate, as happened in Kenya when Mau Mau victims sought compensation in 2013. This redress of about £3,000 for each of the 5,228 living survivors represents a settlement for the brutal repression of the Mau Mau Rebellion (1952–1960) which also includes funding for a memorial site in Nairobi, without any admission of legal responsibility. Compensation for past misdeeds took a novel turn in 2014 when Caribbean nations issued demands for debt forgiveness for past colonial-era transgressions from the UK, Netherlands and France, marking the first time that historical grievances have been invoked for writing off loans. So anxieties regarding redress aside, the Indian narrative of the shared colonial past is not resolutely challenged in the UK as is Japanese imperialism in East Asia. It is curious that there is no Partition museum in India (there is one in Jamaica, New York), given that this tragedy is perhaps the nation's deepest wound, an absence that suggests the collective agony remains too controversial and dangerously divisive.

Indonesia

The Monas dioramas that encircle the basement space of central Jakarta's nationalist monument present details on Dutch colonial rule and the nationalist awakening, key moments in the pre-World War II struggle for independence, the Japanese interregnum (1942–1945), and the final struggles with the Dutch before gaining independence in 1949. Again, much of this narrative is not a subject of dispute in Indonesia and not a source of rancor in relations with the Netherlands or challenged there. Beneath the towering spire of Monas the most controversial aspect relates to Papua as the official history on display is deployed to buttress Indonesia's claim, and to legitimize annexation of the territory in 1969 (see Chapter 11). The Monas dioramas depict the unjust prolongation of Dutch colonial rule in Papua after national independence in 1949 and Indonesia's heroic struggle to regain its territory. Monas presents the controversial Act of Free Choice in 1969, by which Jakarta annexed Papua, as a straightforward display of unanimous public approval by assembled tribal elders wearing their traditional vestments. Papuans and various international organizations dispute this official story regarding the incorporation of Papua (or Irian Jaya as it was then named by Indonesia), stressing instead Indonesian duplicity and coercion in the process that discredits the Act of Free Choice and thus Jakarta's annexation. US Embassy cables at that time also cast doubt on the legitimacy of this dubious referendum and how free and fair it actually was. Washington, based on Cold War logic, supported the annexation because it was more interested in wooing anti-communist Indonesia and President Suharto (1967–1998) while protecting a vast mining concession in Papua recently awarded to an American firm. Currently, these controversies about how the Papua story became an Indonesian story are not causing serious rifts between Jakarta and other governments (except when foreign journalists are arrested), but do sustain Papuan identity and their ongoing struggle for independence. Indonesian security forces try to quell these aspirations, with tragic consequences, instigating violent clashes that attract international media coverage and rock bilateral relations with Australia, the one nation in the world that has done most to expose the plight of Papuans.

Monas, opened in 1965, was also subject to some deft ideological re-engineering. Sukarno designed the original dioramas in 1964, but the New Order that ousted him needed to reinforce its legitimacy so added some additional scenes. These included a scene that showed Suharto receiving notification of the transfer of power to him from Sukarno so that he could restore order, a document known as Supersemar. This particular diorama was not completed until 1976 and was carefully considered, with input from Suharto. He had always claimed that he had not attended the cabinet meeting where the March 11, 1966 transfer of power order was confirmed because he was ill. Thus, undignified as it may seem, Suharto is shown in pajamas lying in bed surrounded by officers showing him the power transfer document they had persuaded Sukarno to sign. This diorama was intended to reinforce the notion that Suharto reluctantly took on the burden of power rather than orchestrated events in order to do so, as is now widely believed (McGregor 2007).

The Armed Forces Museum (Satriamandala—Sanskrit for Sacred Place for the Knights) in Jakarta, initially opened in 1972, is more controversial because it continues to present a discredited version of the gory events of 1965 that was propagated and imposed in New Order Indonesia (1967–1998). This narrative is reinforced at the Lubang Buaya Memorial Park and Museum where seven kidnapped officers were killed by the communists and discovered at the bottom of a well. The Lubang Buaya (pit of crocodiles), as the well is known, has a luminous crimson aperture evoking the ominous event that led to Suharto taking over the government and presiding over a bloody rampage that claimed several hundred thousand lives all over the archipelago. One can sit on the marble ledge and lean over the low-slung chains to peer into the dayglo vermilion abyss, backed by a commemorative plaque and fronted by a sign warning not to enter; the surrounding sand has been showered with coins tossed by visitors as if it was just any wishing well. Oddly, couples lounge on the cool marble under the pavilion erected above the crocodile pit, taking refuge from the sun in what would seem to be not the most romantic spot in Jakarta. The New Order narrative asserted that at this site cadres of Gerwani, the PKI women's corps, mutilated the generals' genitals and then engaged in a wild sex orgy, events that are not depicted at the memorial site and almost certainly never happened.

This sacred space of martyrdom is just in front of the Pancasila Sakti memorial with seven statues of the six murdered generals and a lieutenant standing in uniform beneath a giant bronze eagle, fiercely vigilant and bedecked with the military's coat of arms hanging on its chest, its talons gripping a banner proclaiming Unity in Diversity, the national motto. Beneath this dais is a massive wrap-around bas-relief in bronze, perhaps 40 meters from end to end, depicting the scenes of carnage and chaos, that leaves no doubt that this was a communist-instigated inferno. There are scenes of sickle- and machete-wielding peasants and a beheading in progress. Visitors recognize Sukarno, wearing his familiar peci cap and holding a book entitled NASAKOM

Figure 8.1 Memorial to Military Officers Whose Murder in 1965 Sparked Widespread Massacres. Photo © Jeff Kingston.

(his syncretic doctrine combining nationalism, Islam and communism), flanked on his left by an angry-looking farmer ominously gripping a sickle (a communist symbol), next to several soldiers, one holding up his right hand as if trying to stop something and gripping a weapon in his left. In the background, directly over Sukarno's right shoulder, we see a man with wrists bound sitting on the ground and scenes of pitched battles between armed soldiers and peasants wielding staves, sickles and knives. Scenes of mayhem and carnage are richly portrayed, faces frozen in pain and murderous intent, women and children looking on in horror at the violence that envelops them, while in front of the ravaged bodies there is a helmeted military officer, calmly pointing his finger at the killing fields.

Amid lurid scenes of chaotic butchery there is a banner emblazoned with PKI Madiun, a reference to the communist uprising in 1948 in eastern Java that was quickly and brutally repressed, severely weakening the PKI. Leaders of this movement had accused Sukarno of collaboration with the enemies of the Indonesian people and being a slave to the Japanese and Americans. After this uprising was quelled, the Americans began to intervene more assertively in Indonesia's negotiations with the Dutch, hoping to improve relations with what they hoped to be an anti-communist government. That perception did not last long as Sukarno's vehement anti-imperialism came to target America, which helps explain subsequent US support for regional rebellions in Sumatra and Sulawesi in the 1950s. The CIA was implicated in these uprisings as well as the events of 1965 that brought the ouster of Sukarno, a vocal critic of the US, and the rise of Suharto, a more amenable leader.

Returning to the bas-relief, the scenes of slaughter are eerily lifelike, bound bodies being dumped in a hole, scythes raised to strike, arms raised in beseeching surrender, a glaring farmer, left fist clenched, shouting out angrily while raising a sickle in his right hand, ready to kill. Just below the Lubang Buaya where the bodies were dumped, there is a beady-eyed crocodile, mouth agape showing rows of sharp teeth. And next to the crocodile is a dancing woman, evoking the gruesome story of the communist women's brigade (Gerwani).

Below the exuberantly detailed bas-relief is a sign expressing hope and determination that such scenes will never again be experienced in Indonesia. There are also orderly scenes of troop carriers with armed soldiers standing guard along the thoroughfare, with another portrayal of Sukarno, holding a document, the so-called Supersemar, dated March 11, 1966, signifying the orderly transfer of power to Lieutenant General Suharto by Sukarno, empowering him to use whatever means necessary to restore order. As discussed above, this document is pictured at Monas, and also cited in school textbooks to legitimize Suharto's New Order government and seizure of power. The next day Suharto banned the PKI, and the following week he arrested 15 of Sukarno's ministers, as he moved to consolidate his grip on power. In March 1967 Suharto became acting president, and he remained in power for the next three decades. There is also a courtroom scene of the communist instigators being prosecuted and held accountable, next to a short-sleeved President Suharto standing at a microphone-laden podium, the picture of a calm leader restoring law and order, the basis of his legitimacy.

On the same site as the Lubung Buaya Memorial and the Pancasila Sakti is the self-explanatory Museum of PKI Treachery. Inside there are numerous displays that detail the perfidious actions of the PKI that threatened independent Indonesia. The museum was opened in 1990 at Suharto's behest to remind visitors that the eradicated threat of communism, a threat always invoked by the New Order to buttress its legitimacy, had been real and urgent. It remains a historical curiosity, cavernous and no longer much visited, revealing the ideological mindset of the New Order, a regime that embraced and promoted a national identity inspired by anti-communist sentiments. From there one can pass into a Hall of Heroes, military leaders who fought for independence, saved the nation from the PKI and played prominent roles in the New Order. Nowhere else in Indonesia do they still retain the iconic status conferred on them here.

China

In China one is spoiled for choice among various museums promoting an anti-Japanese narrative aimed at bolstering support for the CCP and nationalism. On the outskirts of Beijing near the Marco Polo Bridge where hostilities between Japanese and Chinese troops erupted in July 1937 and escalated into full-scale war, there is the Museum of the War of Chinese People's Resistance Against Japanese Aggression. In 2008, just after the Beijing Olympics, the building was festooned with the ubiquitous event banner, "One World, One Dream," an expression of harmony, one that unintentionally recalls the Japanese wartime goal of Hakko Ichiu (eight corners of the world under one roof), in stark juxtaposition with the museum's focus on Japanese depredations. Then there is the September 18th Museum in Shenyang that commemorates the Japanese initiation of hostilities in Manchuria in 1931. Japanese officers in the Kwantung Army staged an attack on a Japanese train, blaming Chinese terrorists, and used this as a pretext to launch a full-scale attack to subjugate this province in northeast China and establish the quasi-autonomous state of Manchukuo. The museum is sited where the bombing took place and is designed to look like a massive open book emblazoned with the infamous date. The displays and photographs attest to the horrors endured during the Japanese military campaigns and subsequent occupation. There are many more possibilities, but here I focus on two museums in Nanjing and Chengdu that embody the role of museums and memorials in shaping Chinese identity and stoking nationalism.

Nanjing Massacre Memorial

On July 7, 2008, officers of the Japanese Ground Self-Defense Force visited Nanjing, the ancient capital of China, for an artillery demonstration—a visit barely mentioned in the Chinese media, even though it was the first time Japanese soldiers had returned to the scene of the crime—the Nanjing massacre—since Japan surrendered in World War II in 1945. Unlike in recent years, there were no special commemoration rites on the anniversary of the so-called Marco Polo Bridge Incident of July 7, 1937 that Japan used as a pretext to launch a large-scale invasion of China. Later that year, on December 13, 1937, Japanese troops entered Nanjing and unleashed a reign of terror, executing prisoners of war and civilians, raping women by the thousands, and burning and looting the city. The savagery persisted for six weeks, leaving the once-grand capital of China a shattered and smoldering husk. Tokyo and Nanjing are only three hours distant by plane, but in terms of war memory they are poles apart, and prospects for reconciliation over the shared history of China and Japan appear remote. Although the political leadership in both nations has episodically agreed that contemporary relations should not be held hostage to history, such efforts have not been sustained. As one Nanjing-based scholar told me, reconciliation must be based on recognition of what happened—and there are too many troubling signs that such recognition is absent among Japanese conservatives who dominate the political establishment.

Unveiled at the end of 2007, Nanjing's newly renovated and expanded Massacre Memorial resembles a tomb; a somber structure fronted by a moat and several bronze statues depicting the agonies endured by those caught up in the maelstrom. Passing through the turnstile—admission is free after local protesters complained the museum was profiting from others' suffering—eyes are drawn across an

Figure 8.2 Nanjing Massacre Victim. Photo © Jeff Kingston.

Figure 8.3 China Asserts That the Japanese Massacred 300,000 Chinese. Photo © Jeff Kingston.

expanse of gravel to a bell tower and black marble wall where the iconic number 300,000 is emblazoned and incised in several languages. This is a recurrent image throughout the exhibit, one that reiterates the official estimate of the number of victims. Inside there is a chamber where visitors can hear the amplified sound of a drop of water every 12 seconds, said to be the frequency of death during Nanjing's six-week ordeal.

Yang Xiamen, a professor of international relations at the Jiangsu School of Administration and the translator of Iris Chang's book, *The Rape of Nanking* (1997), explains: "Ironically, thanks to the revisionists (in Japan), the government spent lots of money and time to collect all of this evidence and build this museum to display it." In his view, one widely shared in China, efforts in Japan to minimize, downplay or obfuscate the extent of wartime atrocities and Japan's responsibility since the early 1980s have provoked a Chinese official response and public anger about Japan's lack of contrition. Yang suggests that the controversy over Nanjing also reflects the globalization of human rights discourse since the 1990s.

Did the Chinese government whip up a unifying anti-Japanese nationalism in the early 1980s to shore up Deng Xiaoping's legitimacy and deflect attention away from his adoption of controversial market-oriented reforms? On the contrary, Chinese specialists on the massacre assert that the government was not so savvy or prescient to manipulate history in this manner. In their view, Japanese whitewashing of the two nations' shared history forced the Chinese government to abandon its emphasis on building a future-oriented relationship, which had been evident in Beijing's agreement—following normalization of relations in 1972—to renounce compensation. They blame Japanese revisionists for impeding reconciliation by igniting an ongoing bilateral battle over history with their attempts to whitewash war memory and shirk Japanese responsibility.

The revisionists cast a disproportionately long shadow in China. The Japanese people do not monolithically embrace the valorizing and exonerating view of the war cherished and endlessly promoted by Japan's revisionist conservative elite (Saaler 2005). Chinese, however, uncritically accept Iris Chang's monochromatic and misleading view of war memory in Japan suggesting that most Japanese are in denial about the wretched past and eager to embrace a vindicating narrative (Chang 1997). In China, there seems little recognition of the vibrant scholarship on Nanjing by Japanese researchers who have toiled for decades to present an accurate and damning view of what happened. This guilty verdict by Japanese historians, denied by Japan's resolute revisionists, is vouchsafed in a survey conducted by a veterans' organization of those who served in Nanjing at the time. Ironically, those who perpetrated the atrocities acknowledge their crimes—crimes that those born after the events are now trying to deny.

The Massacre Memorial emphasizes that the Japanese invasion is typical of what happens to weak and backward nations, conveying a message that is explicitly supportive of Deng's modernization reforms. The lesson of Nanjing is thus one insisting that China must overcome past humiliations and control its destiny by becoming a wealthy and powerful nation.

Visitors descend into the museum, first confronting a replica of the city walls assailed by the sounds of bombardment, air-raid sirens, anti-aircraft guns blazing, and a video of the bombers. From this auditory assault, the deafened visitor proceeds to a tranquil room with a reflecting pond shimmering with electric candles, over which projected images of victims' faces float toward them. Above, a ceiling glows with the number 300,000 as a bell solemnly tolls. A sign explains: "A Human Holocaust: An Exhibit of the Nanking Massacre Perpetrated by the Japanese Invaders."

The displays of photographs, newspaper articles, diary excerpts and artifacts trace the trail of sorrow and pillage from Shanghai to Nanjing, with a video of the aerial bombing projected overhead. The horrors of what happened are richly featured, leaving visitors in no doubt about the scale of the destruction as the Imperial Japanese Army raped, looted and burned their way from the coast all the way to Nanjing. What happened there is understood as a culmination and concentration of the malevolence witnessed all along the invasion route. There is an excavation of a mass burial site with several skeletons piled one upon another, grisly evidence that was exhumed from beneath the museum during renovations. In this gallery of horrors, there is a room that graphically portrays in photographs, confessions, testimony and soldiers' diaries the means of massacre: shooting, bayoneting, beheading, burning and drowning. We also learn that thousands of women who were raped were also murdered as a standard procedure to eliminate witnesses, and we can see some of the victims humiliated as they were forced to pose for pornographic photographs by their rapists.

Toward the end of a numbing array of multi-media displays there is a room with a battery of 18 video monitors that show films and documentaries about the massacre. Alongside, there is a 20-by-20-meter archival wall with folders containing what information is known about the documented deaths in Nanjing. The wall insists that there is much to answer for and overwhelming evidence that Japanese forces perpetrated extensive crimes against humanity, much of it drawing on the testimony and eyewitness reports of Japanese soldiers and journalists. It is an imposing edifice that Japanese revisionists have tried, unsuccessfully, to undermine by pointing to small flaws, mistaken attributions and exaggerations. They try to discredit the victims' forest of evidence by grasping at small branches.

Sadly, the discourse over Nanjing has been bogged down in endless debates over exactly how many civilians, combatants and prisoners of war were killed by Japanese soldiers. For Japanese revisionists, holding Nanjing hostage to a sterile numbers debate is the best possible outcome. Since there is no way to verify exactly how many were killed, and under what circumstances, then—in their view—nothing can be asserted, diverting inquiry away from more important questions such as why the soldiers were allowed to run amok for so long and why the cover-up has been so extensive and persistent. Unfortunately, by making the number 300,000 such a prominent part of the memorial, inadvertently the Chinese facilitate Japanese revisionists' efforts to deflect attention away from how much is known about the sacking of Nanjing. What is clear is that an inordinate number of civilians and unarmed prisoners of war were executed in cold blood, not in the heat of battle as apologists assert. Moreover, Japanese officers and officials at the time systematically sought to cover up the very crimes that perpetrators, surviving victims, officials and observers have all acknowledged.

Given that there is so much credible evidence, it is lamentable that the curator has included some displays that have been discredited. For example, the "100-man beheading contest" attributed to two Japanese officers was invented by the Japanese media to stoke patriotism and public support for the troops while boosting sales. Allowing revisionists to cast doubt on a few exhibits helps them sow seeds of doubt about the entire enterprise, at least for Japanese seeking a less sullied history. Still, even if the contest never happened, there was no glory in the casual beheading and machine-gunning of many captured Chinese soldiers with their hands tied behind their backs, the standard practice for dealing with surrendered enemies, from which the "contest" was concocted.

The final image as one emerges from the memorial is a towering obelisk inscribed with "Peace," which flickers in a reflecting pool. It is a jarring juxtaposition to the violence and mayhem featured inside, an unconvincing accessory that fails to persuade. One young Chinese man bluntly confided that the museum left him angry, reinforcing his already hostile views toward the Japanese. He said: "Yes, we like Japanese technology, gadgets and machines, but not the people. At that time, they always referred to us Chinese as pigs, but here we see who was really an animal and inhumane." As a repository of war memory, this is a museum that stirs animosity and righteousness in ways that seem unrelated to peace and reconciliation. One can't begrudge the Chinese their insistence that this nightmare be remembered, and lessons heeded, but the nationalist rancor it arouses is not just about the past.

On December 13, 2012, the Nanjing Massacre Museum held a ceremony to mark the 75th anniversary of the city's nightmare. Among some 9,000 who gathered for the ceremony, most were school students, but there were also a few survivors participating in this ritualistic remembering of Japanese war crimes. And thus a new generation of Chinese was baptized in contemporary battles over war memory that seep into and shape overall bilateral relations. At the entrance of the Nanjing Massacre Museum, there is a sign reminding visitors that it is a site for "civilized visiting and rational patriotism"—suggesting this may not always pertain.

Air-raid sirens sounded all over the city at 10 a.m., piercing the din of traffic and construction as they reminded everyone about the Japanese nightmare. That day, too—underscoring just how relevant the past is to the present—a Chinese maritime surveillance plane for the first time entered the airspace over a disputed group of uninhabited islets in the East China Sea, known as the Senkaku Islands in Japan and Diaoyu in China (see Chapters 7 and 10). Coincidence perhaps, but the next morning's front pages in China were dominated by headlines and photos of both events side-by-side—so ensuring an indelible connection of past wrongs and contemporary tensions.

In 2012, I walked through the Nanjing Massacre Museum with Tian Z., 28, who had spent about half his life in Japan, where he graduated from university. As for the Nanjing Massacre Museum, he told me:

> I didn't like it as I felt it was conveying the Communist Party's intentions. The museum is one of the so-called Patriotism Education Bases in China … [it's] supposed to remind and warn the Chinese how backward the country was and how the Communist Party changed the fate of the nation. And it featured many political slogans; for example, I noticed President Hu Jintao's "Harmonious Society" concept was quoted in the panels.

Tian noted, however, that society is not very harmonious in China, for very good reasons, as

> the youth here are frustrated with the inequalities, the wealth gap, environment, public manners and lack of freedom and freedom of expression. Such people may simply think Japan is the 100-percent bad guy and China was the victim and China's backwardness may be partly due to Japan's invasion … On the other hand, China's youth are also eager for everything material-wise and information-wise—and most still watch Japanese animation, while many fancy sushi and Japanese fashion brands.

He added:

> China suffers from no rule of law and no democracy. It's not a country where anyone can succeed based only on merit. There is widespread discontent but no options. It is like a hall of mirrors where everything is distorted, and what you think you see and know is not what it seems. History doesn't really matter; China's real problems are corruption, pollution and lack of freedom. Japan at least has order and safety.

A local scholar confided:

> Ordinary people believe the propaganda that Japan doesn't have enough regret over the past. Those who are more informed understand that this is not the case. Beijing is trying to marginalize events in the past to focus on the future. Unless some Japanese say something outrageous to provoke the Chinese, people are pragmatic.

He adds:

> Of course we would welcome some gesture by Japan. Making a clear statement about what happened and apologizing would help. But it is important that Japan does not do or say anything negative.

But this is a temptation that Japanese reactionaries find hard to resist, as Prime Minister Abe visited Yasukuni Shrine on December 26, 2013, derailing bilateral relations. And in 2015, Japanese textbooks no longer refer to what happened in Nanjing as a "massacre," adopting instead the more innocuous designation of "incident" (see Chapter 9).

Jianchuan Museum

Chengdu, the capital of Sichuan Province, is about 1,400 km northwest of Nanjing and is home to the spectacular panda breeding center. Less well-known is the Jianchuan museum, more than an hour's drive outside the city. It is an unusual, sprawling museum complex of 13 buildings, privately owned and operated. It displays various Chinese traumas ranging from the foot-binding exhibits that occupy an entire building, to the anti-Japanese war of resistance, the Cultural Revolution, and most recently the 2008 Sichuan Earthquake.

A powerful earthquake devastated Sichuan Province in 2008, killing nearly 90,000 people and leaving 4.5 million homeless. Given that many devastating earthquakes have struck the region over the past century, museum visitors could not help but wonder why the government's emergency disaster preparations were so woefully inadequate. Officials remain sensitive about the collapse of so many public school buildings while adjacent structures were able to withstand the seismic jolts. This led to widespread speculation that corrupt officials turned a blind eye to building-standard violations, leading to the death of many school children. During my 2010 visit the controversial exhibit was "temporarily closed," but not entirely inaccessible.

Japan's wartime excesses are the main feature of the museum, but my Party cadre guide complained, "There was not enough about Japanese atrocities." It depends on your taste for such things, but the Jianchuan Museum cluster doesn't exactly deny the Japanese their due. As the museum pamphlet explains, "The Anti-Japanese War Museum series is composed of the Hall of the Core of the Resistance, the Hall of the Conventional Battlefront, the Hall of the Sichuan Army in the War of Resistance, the Hall of the Heroes of the Flying Tigers, the Hall of Unyielding Chinese Prisoners of War, the Chinese Heroes Statue's Plaza, and the Anti-Japanese Veterans' Handprints Plaza." To my mind, five buildings seemed sufficient to get the message across, especially when you throw in the two plazas.

The Handprints Plaza near the entrance is visually captivating—a series of large opaque glass panels emblazoned with vermilion handprints of aging veterans from the 1937–1945 conflict. The prisoners-of-war hall is also a powerful exhibit as you enter a structure designed to replicate a prison and soon discover just how horrible being a prisoner of the Japanese must have been. One of the quirkiest galleries features the practice of foot-binding. It is a fascinating peek at the hard-to-fathom practice of breaking young women's feet and binding them tightly with cloth to ensure they would remain dainty. One can only wince when looking at the tiny shoes on display.

This prosperous and fertile region in southwest China suffered a series of Mao-made disasters. Apparently there are plans to commemorate an even greater trauma, the Great Leap Forward—another brave effort to broach a touchy subject that explores the Party's checkered legacy. During the Great Leap Forward (1958–1961), when as many as 45 million Chinese died due to Mao Zedong's colossal policy blunders, Sichuan was one of the regions hit hardest by the famine. The region also suffered more than its share during the Cultural Revolution

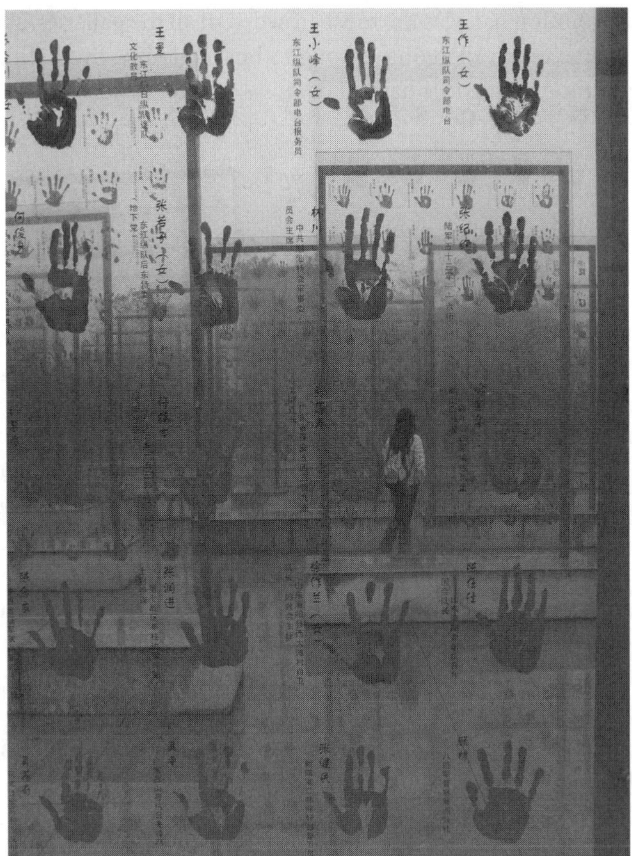

Figure 8.4 The Handprint Plaza Is Emblazoned with Vermilion Handprints of Chinese Veterans from the 1937–1945 Sino-Japanese Conflict. Photo © Jeff Kingston.

(1966–1976) because many local people had wartime links with the nationalists (Kuomintang). Commemorating these traumas is a touchy political subject, but Jianchuan brims with controversy.

The building devoted to the Cultural Revolution has an intriguing entrance through a curtain that thrusts the unsuspecting visitor into a long, dark, narrow hall reverberating with the clamorous sounds of a large crowd chanting and screaming as you walk toward a large video projection showing Mao waving his Little Red Book of quotations in front of a rapturous and reverential audience. It is very unnerving—like being thrown back into that time of mass hysteria and random viciousness. Mao-mania is the subject of the exhibits and there are all sorts of mementos. One of the interesting inclusions is a series of the annual New Year covers of the *People's Daily* from 1966 to 1976. It always shows a portrait of Mao, but it's an image that grows in size until 1971 and then shrinks steadily thereafter—perhaps a useful political barometer as the gruesome toll mounted and Mao distanced himself from the paroxysms of violence and destruction. Interestingly, during my 2010 visit the Cultural Revolution hall was the most crowded of all the galleries, as middle-aged visitors of an age to recall living through those terrible times find something compelling about revisiting this painful past.

Japan

Yasukuni, Yushukan and War Memory

If a single monument can be considered to encapsulate militant nationalism and Japan's failure to offer a convincing repentance for its war record, it is Yasukuni Shrine. The shrine is controversial not because it is a memorial to 2.47 million subjects of the Japanese empire who gave up their lives for the Emperor in past wars, but rather because it is a potent symbol of militarism and veneration of the Emperor. Most of those honored at this privately operated Shinto shrine died during Japan's invasions and campaigns in Asia and the Pacific from 1931 to 1945. About 1,000 Class B and C war criminals have been enshrined there without controversy. In 1978, however, 14 Class A war criminals were enshrined there as "gods" and Yasukuni Shrine is now inextricably linked with the men held responsible at the Tokyo Trials for Japan's bloody rampage through Asia. For the victims of Japanese aggression this enshrinement constitutes a sacrilegious act that honors the wartime leaders deemed most responsible for Japanese war crimes. One could not imagine that any post-World War II German leader would visit a site honoring Nazi leaders and promoting a revisionist history justifying their wartime actions and goals. That is precisely what makes Yasukuni Shrine so controversial because it is not just a sacred site or merely a place to honor the war dead. It is a prominent stage for an exculpatory narrative of Japan's wartime actions, one that is richly displayed at the adjacent Yushukan Museum operated by the shrine authorities.

Commemorating the war dead at Yasukuni Shrine in central Tokyo resonates with political purpose. While Japanese attitudes to Yasukuni are complex, it has undeniably become a focus for a vindicating version of the nation's wartime history. One of the reasons Japanese leaders give for visiting the shrine is simply to honor all those who died during the war. Prime Minister Junichiro Koizumi (2001–2006) justified his six visits on the grounds that it was unseemly to discriminate among the dead and thus he was honoring all equally, including the war criminals. This perhaps reflects a widespread perception among Japanese that the IMTFE was a kangaroo court that served up a biased "victor's justice."

Conservatives have long chafed under the victor's war narrative that denigrates Japan's Pan-Asian aspirations as empty rhetoric justifying its own imperial ambitions in the region. For some Japanese, the Class A war criminals put on trial were remote from the acts of which they stood accused: they were not convicted of actually committing the atrocities, but rather were held responsible for crimes against humanity, for leading Japan into war and failing to prevent atrocities that the military committed on distant battlefields. Thus some Japanese consider that their convictions were unjust and that the tribunal failed to recognize Japan's legitimate reasons for going to war, including a variety of western provocations, racism, and colonial subjugation of Asia.

Yasukuni is also a touchstone for domestic controversy because it is a Shinto religious facility and official visits encroach on the division between the state and religion enshrined in Article 20 of the Constitution. This is a sensitive issue because during the war, state-sponsored Shinto was linked with Emperor worship and was used as a vehicle to inculcate loyalty to the government and mobilize popular support for the war. Shinto is thus tainted, in the eyes of some Japanese, by its dubious links with imperialism; and Yasukuni, as the focal point of wartime Shinto, is considered the temple of ultra-conservative nationalism where the most regrettable aspects of Japan's military past continue to be venerated. Yasukuni is thus laden with symbolism that reverberates loudly and divisively both within and outside Japan.

It is telling that since 1978 neither Emperor Showa (Hirohito, 1926–1989) nor his son Akihito (1990–) has visited Yasukuni Shrine, because the enshrinement of 14 Class A war criminals in that year indelibly politicized this sacred site. By honoring the war criminals as "gods" the shrine has embraced an unrepentant stance on Japan's wartime conduct. The imperial boycott constitutes a silent but powerful repudiation of this historical view and rebuke of contemporary Japanese reactionaries who are resolutely trying to rehabilitate Japan's wartime past.

As we discussed in Chapter 2, this war memory emphasizes that Japan's war in Asia (1931–1945) was justified and fought to liberate Asians from western colonialism. In this valorizing narrative featured at the Yushukan Museum, there is no mention of Japanese atrocities or the victims. This sanitized remembrance venerates the 14 Class A war criminals, the architects of the war under whose authority the excesses were committed, and recasts them as martyrs. The war is depicted as a legitimate act of self-defense, and the judgments of the International Military Tribunal for the Far East, accepted in Article 11 of the Treaty of San Francisco signed by Japan in 1951, are challenged. When Prime Minister Abe (2006–2007; 2012–) calls for overturning the postwar order, he means the one-sided condemnation of Japan's wartime actions that Tokyo agreed to in the Treaty of San Francisco that brought an end to the US Occupation, and the pacifist constitution that the US drafted and imposed. Abe has long supported lifting constitutional curbs on Japan's military, and in July 2014 announced a controversial reinterpretation of Article 9 that allows Japan to engage in collective self-defense, a major departure from postwar pacifism.

Since its renovation in 2002, the Yushukan has promoted a narrowly nationalistic narrative concerning divisive issues of war memory. Japan's invasion of China became a campaign to quell Chinese "terrorism"—a post-9/11 narrative that demonstrates just how much the present impinges on the past. The old and musty exhibits of the old Yushukan I first visited in the 1980s had more the look of a rarely visited, dusty antique shop. The new gleaming version is bursting with slick propaganda, asserting a glorifying and exonerating narrative of Japan's shared history with Asia. Visitors learn that Japan was fighting against Chinese "terrorists" and are encouraged to believe that this was a "war on terror" provoked by Chinese terrorism. Japanese intentions were noble, but misunderstood, leading eventually to the US imposing embargoes with the intention of provoking resource-poor Japan into war. In response to a backlash in the US, curators withdrew this accusation.

The narrative of what happened in Nanjing on display at the Yushukan Museum is a lesson in the politics of war memory. The video clip on the capture of Nanjing shown there is especially disingenuous. Viewers see Japanese troops raising their hands in a banzai salute atop the walls of the city and then the film cuts to a Japanese soldier distributing food to hungry-looking Chinese children and elderly Chinese. In a triumph of chutzpah over history, visitors are told that the Japanese victory in Nanjing meant that, "residents were able to live their lives in peace." The main film shown at the Yushukan puts a spin on Japan's advance into Asia, with a female narrator emotionally insisting: "None of the officers and soldiers went to the battlefields for the purpose of cruelly invading and looting. They fought purely for the sake of their families and the state they loved." The contrast with the Nanjing Massacre Memorial could not be greater.

At the Yushukan, there is no mention of invasion, aggression, massacres or atrocities committed by Japanese troops in China. Improbably, the suffering of Japanese is the only suffering on display. On exiting the Yushukan one wonders about the voices of the millions of Asians who died as a result of Japan's "war on terror," the collateral damage of Pan-Asian liberation. In this memorial, Japan is the victim, provoked by Chinese "terrorists" and scheming Americans. The Yushukan is an invaluable time machine, allowing visitors to understand what it must have been like to live in Japan in that era of heavy-handed censorship. It is also an object lesson in how the present is imposed on the past.

The last image visitors see upon leaving the museum is a memorial to Justice Radhabinod Pal who sat on the Tokyo Tribunal. He issued a dissenting opinion in which he questioned the legal standing of the tribunal in terms of international law, the retroactive application of laws and the failure to hold the Allied forces accountable for their war crimes, concluding that the guilty verdicts were unjustified. Since then rightists have invoked Pal, misleadingly alleging that he found the war criminals innocent. Pal did not deny their war guilt, but rather indicted the deeply flawed judicial process that railroaded them, the so-called "victor's justice."

The Yushukan has reinforced Yasukuni Shrine's image as a powerful symbol of Japan's lack of contrition regarding its wartime actions and efforts to assert a one-sided, exculpatory narrative. The Yasukuni spin on history is deeply flawed; depicting Chinese resisting Japan's invasion as "terrorists" is gratuitously insulting to the Chinese people and all those who gave their lives to defend their homeland against Japanese imperialism.

Paying Tribute

Powerful right-wing nationalist groups ensure that Yasukuni will never be forgotten. The War Bereaved Veteran's Family Association (Nihon Izokukai), the Association of Shinto Shrines (Jinja Honcho) and Nippon Kaigi (Japan Conference) are large conservative groups that pressure politicians to pay respect to the nation's war dead in exchange for well-organized electoral support and generous funding. Both have longstanding ties with the ruling LDP, and party leaders regularly serve as the president of Nihon Izokukai. Paying obeisance at Yasukuni is, for such associations, a political litmus test.

When Prime Minister Nakasone broke the taboo on official visits in 1985, the subsequent uproar led to an 11-year hiatus in prime ministerial visits. Prime Minister Junichiro Koizumi (2001–2006) conducted his six visits amid a media circus and provoked the expected rebukes from Beijing and Seoul. Ongoing efforts to promote reconciliation with the two nations that suffered most from Japanese imperialism were derailed by Koizumi's apparent nonchalance toward historical sensitivities. While his homage to the war dead inflamed international opinion, many Japanese shrugged their shoulders about the visits and wondered what all the fuss was about. Some argue that such homage is *atarimae* (natural), because all nations commemorate the sacrifices of their soldiers who have died in past wars.

It would be misleading, however, to assume that there is a national consensus on Yasukuni visits, and that those who support, or at least accept, the visits by top politicians knowingly assume all of the attendant historical baggage. It is important to bear in mind that there is considerable domestic opposition to Yasukuni visits. Predictably, pundits suggest that such visits reflect a resurgent nationalism, but what is interesting is that Koizumi was rather isolated on Yasukuni. In 2005, five former prime ministers from his conservative party and various business leaders and media outlets urged him not to visit Yasukuni. Leading political parties like New Komeito, a coalition partner in the Koizumi and Abe cabinets, publicly oppose the visits, as does the Japan Communist Party and the Socialist Party of Japan. New Komeito's support base is the Soka Gakkai, a large Buddhist lay organization that has also called for an end to shrine visits. State-sponsored Shinto has been associated with systematic discrimination against Buddhism since the Meiji era, and there is a lingering wariness about government ties to Shinto among the vast Soka Gakkai membership of several million. The mainstream press also carries critical commentary about Yasukuni visits that belies simplistic notions of the Japanese nation monolithically defending the visits and embracing a bellicose nationalism. Unlike in Europe where fringe parties tend to be the standard-bearers for controversial nationalistic sentiments, visits to Yasukuni Shrine are favored by the mainstream, dominant party. In Japan, the ultranationalistic fringe is a core constituency of the LDP. High-profile visits to Yasukuni are thus aimed at rallying core supporters and ensuring their continuing largesse in funding election campaigns and mobilizing the vote.

But Yasukini visits are also a political statement by Japan's conservative leadership that it is time to turn the page on history and look forward rather than dwell on events in the early 20th century. There is considerable resentment that China and South Korea play the history card for diplomatic advantage, and a feeling that other nations are intruding on a right all nations exercise: honoring the nation's war dead. The endless controversy generated by such visits underscores, however, a singular failure in postwar Japan: how to honor soldiers without alienating former foes and current allies.

Japanese prime ministers need not visit Yasukuni Shrine in order to commemorate the war dead. A viable alternative is the nearby Chidorigafuchi "tomb for unknown soldiers" that draws relatively few visitors. Each year on August 15, the government holds a ceremony at Chidorigafuchi expressly to honor the war dead, and it is thus an ideal venue for a prime minister to pay his respects without courting controversy. On August 15, 2013, Prime Minister Shinzo Abe went there, laid flowers and prayed, a conciliatory gesture undone by his December 26, 2013 pilgrimage to Yasukuni Shrine. He had always regretted not visiting Yasukuni Shrine while premier in 2006–2007, but sought redemption of a sort in doing so on the one-year anniversary of becoming prime minister for a second time. Washington issued a swift and sharp rebuke, as it had repeatedly urged Abe not to go and saw his visit as a reckless gesture derailing attempts to promote better relations in Northeast Asia and reinvigorate the alliance with South Korea. By visiting the war shrine, Abe invited criticism and managed to make Japan look like the regional troublemaker, in the same year that China militarized its territorial disputes in both the East and South China Seas.

The politics of Yasukuni ensure that it will remain an important symbol of Japan's militaristic past. Nationalists bridle at suggestions of alternative sites to pay respect to the war dead precisely because what is at stake is not just the souls of fallen soldiers. The critical issue of the shrine is about national pride and sustaining a more glorious, unapologetic narrative of Japan's past. In contrast, Ienaga Saburo, a noted historian who led the fight against reactionary distortions of the nation's history in textbooks for more than four decades until his death in 2002 (see Chapter 9), argued that while the souls of the fallen soldiers must be honored, it should not be by deifying them. In his view, Japan must ensure that the mistakes of the past are not repeated by exposing the crimes of leaders who sacrificed these soldiers as cheap cannon fodder for unworthy reasons; only then will the war dead be truly honored. In his view, by conflating the issues of nationalism, patriotism and filial piety, those who support retaining Yasukuni as the de facto national war cemetery are defending an outmoded and reactionary ideology.

Conservative politicians are invoking atavistic symbols of nationalism aimed at reawakening pride in nation to offset growing insecurity, and a loss of faith in the government. They are also seeking to rally the public and cultivate a sense of shared purpose. In such an atmosphere it is not surprising that some people and politicians seek refuge in reassuring symbols and gestures of nationalism. However, these siren songs from the past don't resonate, as regional opinion polls show that Japanese are the least nationalistic in Asia.

Yasukuni is an awkward talisman, but it remains useful to stimulate a vibrant public discourse about Japan's shared history with Asia and prevent it from receding into the past. Stirring controversy forces the media, academia, politicians, businessmen and the public to confront this tragic era over and over. Yasukuni places Japan's failed efforts to come to terms with this history in the limelight at home and abroad, and in that sense serves as a powerful reminder about the costs of unbridled nationalism and the nation's unfinished business on reconciliation.

It would be misleading to assume that the revisionist views on display at the Yushukan are widely propagated in Japanese museums. The small Kyoto Peace Museum at Ritsumeikan University depicts atrocities carried out by wartime Japanese forces in Asia. It also examines earlier Japanese expansion and colonization and shows the domestic hardships suffered as a result of economic shortages and bombing raids, while also drawing attention to wartime repression of thought and expression. There is also the Women's Active Museum on War and Peace at Waseda University, featuring information and displays regarding the wartime comfort women system of sexual slavery. The more conservatively oriented Showakan Museum across the street from the Yasukuni Shrine drew controversy when it was being built in the 1990s because the curator claimed there was no space for an "apology corner," meaning exhibits that acknowledged Japan's war responsibility, but exhibits related to the war and firebombing of Tokyo convey the hardships endured and folly of war. For example, visitors can see that residents of Tokyo were instructed to dig foxholes and take refuge there covered with a wet tatami mat as preparation for firebombing raids; essentially they were being asked to bury themselves.

A recrudescent nationalism in Japan under Abe, however, is affecting how war memory is displayed in public spaces. For example, in 2015 the Osaka Peace Museum, under pressure from Osaka mayor Toru Hashimoto, removed exhibits about Japanese wartime aggression, and the museum now focuses exclusively on the wartime suffering of Osaka's civilian population.

Atomic Bombing

The Hiroshima Peace Museum presents the horrors of the atomic bombing on August 6, 1945, confronting visitors with the nightmarish consequences—70,000 people instantly incinerated, thousands of others fatally radiated with terrible burns that made their flesh fall off, and the city center flattened; the cumulative death toll through the end of 1945 is estimated at 140,000, including some 20,000 Koreans brought over to work in factories. Displays explain that Japanese imperialism inflicted significant suffering on Asia, beginning with the 1895 Sino-Japanese War. Japanese expansionism from the 1930s in Asia is depicted as a "war of aggression" that brought grievous harm to the region, leading to war with the US. It is also noted that Hiroshima was an important military headquarters and that a significant number of the victims of the atomic bombing were soldiers. It was not always so. When I first visited the Hiroshima museum in 1981, it was a much simpler space that focused exclusively on depicting and documenting the consequences of the atomic bombing. There was no attempt to explain why the atomic bomb was dropped there or to provide any historical context for visitors to contemplate. The message was: the nuclear conflagration happened and this is what ensued.

By 1995, the museum had expanded and by then included dioramas that helped visitors understand the historical context. There is an interesting contrast with the

Smithsonian Air and Space Museum's failed attempt to mount an exhibit in 1995 on the fiftieth anniversary of the atomic bombing that questioned the orthodoxy that President Truman made the right decision to drop the bombs, hastening the end of the war and thereby saving a million American soldiers' lives. Many scholars, in the US and elsewhere, have contested this narrative and criticized Truman. The curator wanted to present a more balanced perspective and thought that the fiftieth anniversary would be an ideal time to do so. The Veterans of Foreign Wars and various other conservative groups disagreed, lobbying the US Congress to block the exhibit since the museum depends on public funding. Thus, the more comprehensive exhibit originally planned was scaled back, and critical views and items that were designed to depict the human suffering inflicted were excluded because they did not fit into the official narrative of the "Good War" that has persisted in the US.

Hiroshima has also courted controversy by long denying recognition to the Korean victims of the atomic bombing and refusing to allow a monument

Figure 8.5 Commemorating the 20,000 Koreans Who Died in the Atomic Bombing of Hiroshima. Photo © Jeff Kingston.

commemorating their deaths in the Peace Park, claiming disingenuously that this vast area had no room. A cenotaph engraved with names of Korean victims of the atomic bombing, with a turtle-shaped base, was completed in 1970 by the Korean Residents Union of Japan, but it was not relocated to the park until 1999, where it is festooned with garlands of origami cranes. This memorial epitomizes the complicated memories of Hiroshima, a military garrison city that embraces the sorrows and tragedies of militarism and yet took overly long to recognize the shared fate of resident Koreans, many of them brought to Hiroshima as forced labor.

Local Memory

State-led memory as the source of nationalism and identity politics often confronts local dissonance as memories diverge. Differences in what is emphasized, neglected or marginalized are instructive. For example, there is considerable controversy in Japan about the fierce battle waged in Okinawa in the waning months of World War II. These differences center on the Battle of Okinawa (April–June 1945) in which some 100,000 Japanese soldiers died along with 14,000 Allied troops. Dispute focuses on the deaths of well over 100,000 Okinawan civilians, perhaps one-third of the population, and who is to blame. The national narrative focuses on the brave defense mounted by Japanese soldiers who died protecting their homeland from enemy invaders. In this version, indiscriminate attacks by the invading Allied troops took a high toll in civilian casualties. In the Prefectural Peace Memorial Museum, however, Okinawa is positioned as being caught in between the Japanese troops and the US forces. The defense of Okinawa at a time when the outcome of the war was no longer in doubt bought some time for the home islands, but the islanders are depicted here as sacrificial pawns who died for a lost cause not of their making. Okinawans even today feel culturally distinct and distant from Japan's "inner islands" and have long resented Japanese discrimination. The issues of identity and prejudice date back to Okinawa's official incorporation into Japan in 1879; before that the islands were the Ryuku Kingdom, inhabiting the interstices of Chinese and Japanese assertions of sovereignty.

The Prefectural Peace Memorial Museum portrays Japanese troops as acting harshly towards islanders during the Battle of Okinawa, summarily executing some for speaking in the Okinawan language (not intelligible to Japanese) because they were not trusted and suspected of being spies. Based on eyewitness reports by survivors, the Japanese soldiers are also accused of instigating group suicides by Okinawans, distributing grenades among them for this purpose. Japanese wartime propaganda vilified the Americans and convinced many Okinawans that suicide was an honorable way to die given what atrocities the barbaric Americans were likely to commit. Others were simply ordered to commit suicide. Okinawan survivors also testify that Japanese soldiers confiscated their food, raped many women, used them as human shields, and in some cases pushed them out of shelters into the field of fire.

This inglorious depiction of the Imperial Armed Forces has long riled Japanese reactionaries and in 2007, during Shinzo Abe's first stint as premier, the Education Ministry moved to revise textbook content regarding the Battle of Okinawa. It did so by instructing publishers to reword descriptions of the civilian deaths so as not to directly implicate Japanese soldiers in the civilian suicides. For Okinawans, this betrayal is part of their identity, based on eyewitness testimony and displayed at the Prefectural Peace Memorial Museum. Thus, central government efforts to whitewash the issue of instigated suicides in public schools nationwide in 2007 enraged Okinawans, sparking a massive rally of 110,000 islanders in the capital Naha. This was the largest political rally ever on the islands, expressing local outrage and calling on the government to retract its efforts to blur responsibility for the suicides. Subsequently, in 2008 an Osaka court ruled that indeed there had been military involvement in the mass suicides, but in 2015 the newly approved textbooks again elide Japanese responsibility for instigating group suicides of Okinawans.

South Korea

In South Korea's history museums, the shared past with Japan features an angry remembering with graphic depictions of suffered endured and atrocities inflicted, thus highlighting unresolved grievances that stoke the embers of resentment and hatred while nurturing a sense of shared degradation mixed with defiant patriotism. There is an unremitting indictment that permits no room for a spirit of "forgive and forget," a message that seems to doom reconciliation initiatives. Museums and memorials about Japanese colonial rule explicitly nurture a national identity rooted in anti-Japanese nationalism, not only ensuring the odious past is not forgotten, but also mobilizing it in the present to forge an unassailable common identity of stoic and heroic resistance, extolling a collective sacrifice for the nation and unity.

The red-brick buildings of the Seodaemun Prison History Hall in Seoul look more like an old factory than an infamous colonial-era prison where the Japanese government in Chosen (colonial name for Korea) incarcerated and tortured anti-colonial activists and political agitators. The facility now serves as a museum of Korea's colonial nightmare under the Japanese, featuring numerous dioramas, cramped cells, scenes of torture and screams of pain. It is an unnerving space of cruelty, a crypt for the hidden horrors of the past. There is a table where one can sit hooded wearing a wicker basket, arms extended and manacled at the wrists, reenacting how the fingernail torture was administered. Some prisoners were put in small solitary cells, subjected to physical and psychological torture designed to break their spirit; one was named the ink cell because it was perpetually dark.

Seodaemun was the largest of 16 prisons built throughout the peninsula in 1908, "with the aim of suppressing the Korean patriots who were fighting to regain national

Figure 8.6 Seodaemun Prison Museum Attests to Horrors of Japanese Colonial Rule. Photo © Jeff Kingston.

sovereignty." Renovated in 2010 for the centennial marking the onset of Japan's colonial rule, the Seodaemun exhibits now convey more about the colonial-era history, explaining for example that the space of the facility was expanded 30-fold in the 1930s to accommodate the increased number of Korean independence activists. Established with a capacity for 500 prisoners, by the end of the colonial era Seodaemun housed 23,532. At that time there were 261 warders—Korean employees referred to as "faithful first-line puppets"; before the 2010 renovation the delicate topic of colonial collaborators was not raised. The museum explains that on average there were "30 or so prisons in each city, making the country like a huge prison." Ironically, very few were located in what is today North Korea, often portrayed in contemporary media as a massive gulag.

Unlike in China, there is no dwelling on national humiliation. In the National Resistance Hall of the museum, visitors learn that "the Korean people were never frustrated about the annexation but actively launched independence movements." It is a story of brave and unrelenting resistance by staunch patriots, despite Japan's "harsh colonial rule, making Koreans fall into a state of slavery and frantically trying to liquidate Korean culture and language." It was an "incessant struggle" in which "the whole of Korea" participated, an assertion that elides the reality of extensive collaboration. Torture devices, shackles, and a separate execution building where prisoners were hung, convey the grim nature of colonial subjugation. So too a sign that says that in the "heroic struggle" activists targeted Japanese and pro-Japanese Koreans, again complicating the narrative with collaboration. On the second floor, there is a bright, spacious room where the walls are decorated with mugshots of some 5,000 prisoners, mostly young women and men, who died in detention. There is also a mock-up of the dead body pick-up room that was located in the basement of the execution facility where relatives could retrieve the bodies of their loved ones.

One sign proclaims: "Torture—A Tool for Ruling the Colony." We learn that water and fingernail torture, and savage beatings, were common practice in the underground torture chamber where prisoners were interrogated. To intimidate them, they were kept waiting their turn in an adjacent "temporary detention room" so they could hear the sounds of torture and moans of pain, and anticipate what lay in store.

Near the entrance to the execution house—a separate structure with a room and stage replete with gallows and trap door where prisoners were hanged—is the "wailing poplar," planted in 1923, while near the exit to this lugubrious temple of death is the secret "corpse removal exit," a hidden underground passage. Finally, one wanders to a reconstruction of the women's wing built in 1918 that was demolished in 1979, a space where visitors seem to linger, drawn perhaps by the cell of illuminations—glowing pictures of women inmates on screens reflected in mirrors. In addition, one can look down through the glass ceiling of a typical cramped cell and ponder what it must have been like.

Although unacknowledged in the museum's pamphlet, the museum has tackled the controversial use of the jail to incarcerate a new generation of dissidents by South Korea's military regimes from the 1960s to the 1980s, thereby linking the pro-independence and pro-democracy struggles as well as the Japanese colonial and South Korean military regimes. There are several cells on one corridor with displays featuring the stories of these political prisoners, although after the 2010 renovations one can no longer see the messages these prisoners scratched onto the walls. One plaque explains that the prison was operated until 1987, and in it, "many democratization activists during the despotic regime after liberation were imprisoned, tortured and died."

So the post-2010 version of Seodaemun embraces a more controversial history, complicating what had been a straightforward prosecution of the Japanese by implicating Koreans in collaborating with the colonial regime as warders and therefore part of the colonial system of subjugation. Moreover, the museum now tells the previously untold story of the prison's role in the suppression of the pro-democracy movement, a place where political prisoners opposing a succession of Korean authoritarian regimes were jailed, tortured and killed. In that sense Seodaemun has become a powerful symbol of resistance against the 20th-century arc of tyranny that besieged the peninsula, connecting colonial and independent Korea, underscoring the painful evolution from an oppressed nation to its democratic flowering since the end of military rule in the late 1980s. It reminds us of the cycle of abuse that extended from generation to generation, under different repressive regimes, but leaving similar scars. The indictment of the South Korean military, forced now into the dock alongside the nefarious Japanese, is a bold statement signaling just how far democracy has come. This story took time for the telling and is part of the broader search for truth and reconciliation that has proven elusive. But, the pain persists because, like the Japanese, South Korea's military henchmen have not been held accountable, and won't be.

In the next chapter we turn to textbooks and how they also are battlegrounds, featuring competing narratives that seek to influence the next generation's views on these issues of truth, reconciliation and accountability.

9

Textbook Nationalism and Memory Wars

On March 1, 2013, President Park Geun-hye urged Japan to take responsibility for past wrongs and demonstrate contrition for the suffering it inflicted, stating, "The dynamic of [Japan] being the aggressor and [Korea] being the victim will never change, even after the passage of 1,000 years." She added,

> We can open up a future of common prosperity with Japan only when Japan honestly reflects on the past. Japan should have a correct view of history and assume a responsible attitude to open an era of Northeast Asia in the 21st century as a partner.

The speech was made on the 94th anniversary of a Korean uprising against Japanese colonial rule in 1919 at the opening of a second museum focusing on the disputed territory of Dokdo that Japan claims as Takeshima. Interestingly, by referring to all of Northeast Asia, President Park upped the ante, underscoring that the shared past is harming Japan's contemporary relations with China as well. Can Japan afford to maintain what neighbors view as an inadequate historical perspective? What does President Park mean by a correct history, and where can one find examples of this?

In this chapter we focus on textbooks in East Asia, because this is where Chinese, Japanese and Koreans learn about the past and where the "memory wars" have been fiercely contested. Textbooks are a critical resource for understanding how governments seek to shape national identity and foster common perspectives in their citizens. Since they were invented in the early 19th century, textbooks have served as important tools for governments to nurture the idea of nation and promote national unity. They impart values and knowledge intrinsic to national identity and cultivating nationalist sentiments. The central governments in Tokyo, Beijing and Seoul all exert control over textbook content and as such textbooks represent

Nationalism in Asia: A History Since 1945, First Edition. Jeff Kingston.

what authorities want students to know and believe about the past. Thus, textbooks influence popular perceptions of the past while also providing insights on what lessons of history are officially condoned and ignored. Textbooks have been a source of transnational controversy in East Asia since the 1980s because the manner in which the past is represented stirs memories and enmities, but also because transformations in these societies have caused a reconsideration and reexamination of the traumatic past they share. Before delving into East Asian textbook wars, however, we briefly consider the domestic battles in India and Indonesia.

Hindu Nationalism and Textbooks

The politics of textbooks in India illuminate nationalist efforts to control the narrative. The standard storyline about the British Raj and the national independence struggle is not disputed, but that leaves several centuries and other controversies up for grabs. The Hindutva movement of religious fundamentalists seeks to significantly revise selected aspects of Indian history, especially regarding the sub-continent's Muslim heritage and the glories of the Mughal dynasty between the 16th and 18th centuries. The Mughal rulers were Muslims, but did not impose a theocracy or Islamic identity, instead forging bonds through a Persianized culture. Historians regard the Mughal era as one of religious tolerance and a time of peace, economic growth and cultural flowering. There was a centralized administration and at its height the Mughals ruled over one-quarter of the world's estimated population. So there are good reasons why this is considered a golden age in Indian history, and that is precisely why Hindu zealots seek to downplay it. Their first opportunity came under the BJP-led coalition government (1999–2004) when the party that represents Hindutva and is supported by various militant Hindu organizations commissioned a rewriting of national textbooks. Saffron is the movement's symbolic color, so critics targeted the so-called "saffronization" of history texts written by experts tapped by the Hindu nationalist government. This Hindu revisionism disingenuously depicted India's Muslim rulers as barbarous invaders and the Mughal era as a dark period of medieval colonial rule under Islamic subjugation that extinguished the glories of preceding Hindu empires. One revisionist textbook claimed that it was actually Hindus who commissioned and designed the Taj Mahal, the Red Fort and the Qu'tb Minar, all widely recognized as stunning examples of Islamic architecture. The texts also challenged the prevailing mainstream consensus among Indian historians that India developed through mass migrations and trading links with neighboring empires, and is a hybrid civilization based on multicultural borrowings. Hindu zealots prefer to portray the uniqueness of Hindu civilization and resilience to foreign intrusions, and marginalize Muslim and other foreign influences. The texts also left out the crucial detail that it was a Hindu chauvinist who assassinated the national icon Mahatma Gandhi in 1948, and for obvious reasons preferred not to delve into the European fascist influences on those who first propagated Hindutva's ostensibly nativist ideology.

With a change of government in 2004, a panel of expert historians commissioned by the Congress Party examined the revisionist texts and recommended discontinuing their use in the nation's classrooms. Congress espouses religious tolerance and sees the Islamic minority as an important constituency, so it backed restoring the mainstream consensus evident in previous textbooks. In 2014, however, the BJP regained power and sought to reinstate its revisionist history glorifying Hindu influences, justifying Hindutva grievances, and marginalizing Islamic contributions to Indian culture and civilization. Hindu activists have formed groups to advocate changes in schoolbooks and syllabuses in educational institutions all over the country and enjoy the backing of Prime Minister Modi. This politicization of history textbooks and attendant culture wars is familiar to anyone following similar battles around the globe.

Indonesia's Discordant Continuities

When President Suharto was ousted from power in 1998, his New Order (1967–1998) regime was unpopular and ripe for reconsideration. Until then, textbook appraisals of his policies were hagiographic, extolling all he had accomplished as the self-proclaimed "Father of Development" while overlooking authoritarian policies, corruption and state-sponsored violence and repression. As we noted in Chapter 7, the events of 1965 remain one of the lingering controversies in modern Indonesian history, but with the passing of time and the ouster of the main actor and his death in 2008, it seemed time to rewrite the old narrative that pinned all the blame on the PKI (Indonesian Communist Party) for instigating the coup and praising the military for saving the nation from these machinations. In looking at recent textbooks, however, there are considerable continuities in the New Order narrative that can be better understood in the context of the burning of secondary school history textbooks by 14 publishers on the orders of the Attorney General in 2007. He objected that these textbooks failed to mention the 1948 communist rebellion in Madiun during the anti-Dutch campaign for independence by the fragile Indonesian republic. This rebellion has long drawn the ire of Indonesian nationalists who have condemned it as an act of treachery threatening the independence struggle. More importantly, the torched textbooks didn't clearly establish that the PKI was responsible for initiating a coup that precipitated military intervention in 1965. By law, textbooks remain required to refer to Gestapu, the September 30th Movement, as a communist plot, usually by the acronym "G30S/PKI" (Gerakan 30 September/ Indonesian Communist Party). The Attorney General justified his action because the textbooks threatened the "unity of the nation" by challenging "accepted truths" and lacking sufficient vigilance about the lingering dangers of communism.

Textbooks that escaped the conflagration don't completely parrot the New Order narrative, but do show signs of a "cut and paste" continuity of anti-communist narratives about the events of 1948 and 1965 and depictions of Sukarno's chaotic rule (Tan 2008). The newer textbooks tend to be more critical of Suharto and the

New Order and offer different explanations for his downfall in 1998, but remain curiously vague about the grisly mass killings that ensued after the 1965 military coup sidelined Sukarno and placed Suharto in power. The perpetrators are very briefly identified as Islamic religious groups and the armed forces, engaged in what are euphemistically referred to as acts of revenge and sweeping-up operations, but the vast scale of the massacres is not mentioned and the killings are not condemned as criminal acts.

Although more recent scholarship implicates the military in plotting a takeover and purge (Roosa 2006), the New Order narrative remains resilient: the army thwarted the communist coup, disbanded the PKI, and focused the government's resources on improving living conditions. Textbook authors do add some new critical analysis to existing interpretations in revised editions, leading to sometimes incoherent and inconsistent narratives that don't evaluate competing versions or present a systematic assessment of the New Order. There are risks in getting too far ahead of the government on this reckoning so instead the textbooks feature a sprinkling of the new on the old. Many of the New Order assumptions and myths are important to those who came of age in that era and who remain in power with much at stake. These old guard, contemporary actors see and justify what they did then in terms of New Order narratives and thus oppose extensive revisions, but with the passage of time these appear inevitable. If Japan's experience is any indicator, however, time does not always prove to be a great healer.

Japan's Textbook Battles

The battles over textbooks have been fought within Japan since the 1950s as liberal educators and the left-wing teachers' union (Nikkyoso) have resisted conservative governments' efforts to whitewash the past. In 1958, the conservative Liberal Democratic Party enhanced the Ministry of Education's textbook screening authority in order to influence the content of textbooks and purge them of an ostensible left-wing bias. Left-wing in this context meant critical of Japan's wartime conduct and promotion of pacifism. So despite US efforts during the Occupation (1945–1952) to decentralize education and curb government authority over textbook content, the central government bureaucrats reasserted control over what was taught in Japan's schools by rigorously enforcing teaching guidelines and censoring textbook content.

Perhaps the most famous actor in this prolonged battle between the state and progressive historians was Saburo Ienaga, a Tokyo University professor who wrote textbooks. He challenged the textbook screening process in the courts for four decades, losing many cases but winning some important decisions that did, by the end of the 1990s, curtail government powers to censor textbooks. Ienaga drew attention to how the government presided over a whitewashing of Japan's wartime history, including controversial topics such as the Nanjing Massacre in 1937–1938, the biological, chemical and vivisection experiments of Unit 731 in Manchuria during the 1930s and 1940s, forced labor, and the comfort women system of sexual slavery. He argued that it was essential that young people learn the realities of what Japan had done so that the lessons of the war could be passed on. In his view, only by forthrightly and critically examining Japan's war record could the sacrifices of soldiers and citizens be honored. He fought against glorifying or justifying the war, and denying or minimizing the atrocities, because he thought that would dishonor the 3 million Japanese who lost their lives. He also thought it crucial that young Japanese understand that militarists hijacked the nation into a devastating rampage through Asia and not only focus on Japan's victimization. Ienaga, like many Japanese who lived through the war, sought to bolster pacifism as a foundation of postwar Japanese national identity.

Overall, close scrutiny of Japan's textbooks reveals that the narrative of Japan's history presented in textbooks did not change very much between 1950 and 2005 (Dierkes 2010). Education officials promoted a fact-based, chronological history rather than an analytical, interpretive or thematic approach that might inflame domestic opinion and invite criticism. Japanese students are not exposed to graphic accounts and consume a history devoid of explicit moral judgments. Of course there were choices in what facts to include, emphasize, marginalize or ignore, but this was the least controversial approach because it avoided critical analysis or assigning responsibility that might be inconvenient or polarizing in a nation that has been deeply divided over its colonial and wartime past and where consensus remains elusive about what happened, let alone why and at whose behest. In this context, the detached, fact-focused approach is preferable because there is not much Japan can get passionate about without trampling on the dignity and sensitivities of neighbors who have become progressively more prickly and embittered about the past. Turning down the heat on history may make sense to the Japanese government, but this bland narrative provokes Chinese and Koreans because it suggests to them that Japan is still ducking responsibility.

Thus students in Japan are taught, and take university entrance exams, based on a chronological, information-focused approach to history. This emphasis on names, dates and facts, in which causal connections are largely unexplored, allows the Ministry of Education to appear to embrace a neutral stance on the national narrative, even though it intervened extensively to fend off inclusion of critical analysis like Ienaga's. While history textbooks were subject to the Ministry of Education's conservative interventions, with information corrected and added, in general schoolbooks were insulated from wider political battles until the 1980s. The bureaucrats saw their role as defending the nation from the "subversive" Japan Teachers Union and its preference for Marxist historiography. Teachers were required to use designated texts but could also introduce other materials that were not government-approved, giving them some leeway in the classroom.

For Japan's neighbors, and many Japanese too, the non-analytical approach to history adopted in Japan is problematic in that students do not examine the causes of militarism or atrocities committed by the Imperial Armed Forces. Coverage of the war emphasizes the suffering of the Japanese during air raids, and highlights the atomic bombing of Hiroshima and Nagasaki. In general, students learn that war has dreadful consequences, but don't explore the causes, or study in any detail the consequences, of Japanese aggression. The Nanjing Massacre, for example, was not mentioned in textbooks until 1977, and was referred to as an "incident" (*jiken*) without presenting the gory details, analyzing why it happened or assigning responsibility for the outrage. There is no broader analysis of Japanese militarism, wartime ideology or reasons for popular support of the war and militarist leaders. Nor is there any critical analysis of why those wartime leaders were subjugating China and attacking Pearl Harbor even though they knew that doing so would almost certainly lead to catastrophe (Hotta 2013).

In the 1980s Japan was becoming a more expansive regional power due to its economic success. As Japan's influence spread, there were growing concerns about whether Japan had learned the lessons of the past and what its plans were for the future in a region it dominated. The enshrinement of 14 Class A war criminals at Yasukuni Shrine in 1978 suggested that remorse about the wartime excesses might be receding at a time when Japan was becoming more assertive and powerful in Asia. In this context, the international furor over the 1982 textbook screening represented lingering regional doubts about the degree of contrition in postwar Japan.

A major diplomatic row in 1982 was sparked by Japanese media reports, later proven inaccurate, that the government was mandating substitution of the word "advance" for "aggression" with respect to Japan's invasion of China (Shin and Sneider 2011, 249). Even though the Japanese media report was misleading and there was nothing new about the Ministry's word preference, this incident fueled a sharp rise in anti-Japanese sentiments among Chinese, only four years after the two nations had signed a Treaty of Peace and Friendship in 1978, normalizing relations. Textbooks became a litmus test of trust, especially after the government embraced the "neighboring nations clause" in 1982 to defuse the diplomatic crisis, specifying that textbooks should "promote international friendship and cooperation" by not antagonizing neighboring nations with insensitive representations of their shared past. This textbook diplomacy sought to quell anger in China and South Korea about how Japanese textbooks downplayed or misrepresented traumatic events, marginalized sensitive topics or sought refuge in euphemisms. Having agreed that textbooks must take into consideration historical sensitivities in the region, the Japanese government gave them a basis for intervention, one that it came to regret and effectively disavowed in 2013 under Prime Minister Abe.

Abe regards the neighboring nations clause as a misguided concession based on a misunderstanding prompted by misleading Japanese media reports. In his view the resulting crisis was therefore unjustified, and the neighboring nations clause undesirable, because Japan ceded control over its master narrative, one that all nations claim as a sovereign right. Abe and like-minded Japanese conservatives believe that Japan should become a "normal nation," one that is not subject to constraints on its military, not unilaterally pacifist, and does not allow other governments a say in how it teaches history to students, or indeed where politicians can pay respects to the war dead. This aspiration for normalization is divisive domestically, and puts Japan on a collision course with its neighbors who feel that Japan's past actions, and their victimization, should give them a voice in how this history is represented.

Should the victimizer have the right to unilaterally decide how to portray a shared history without consulting its victims? That is a question that haunts East Asia and is a factor in regional tensions because China and South Korea have invested much in this past as a source of identity and feel they occupy the moral high ground in this memory war. Some Japanese, however, believe that their neighbors are playing the history card to gain diplomatic advantage. Although many Japanese acknowledge that wartime misdeeds are a burden that can't be shrugged off, East Asians are surely right that Japan has not taken the full measure of their shared and painful past. Yet, by relentlessly hammering Japan on the anvil of history they do seem to be exploiting the issue and have sparked a backlash among Japanese who feel the unending shrill denunciations are cynically manipulated and overlook Japan's significant post-1945 contributions to regional peace and prosperity.

From the early 1990s, mounting evidence about Japan's wartime misconduct, and pressure from China and South Korea, led to revisions of Japan's textbooks in 1994. While the textbooks did not go into great detail, they did feature coverage of wartime atrocities including the Nanjing Massacre and the comfort women. This "textbook diplomacy" provoked a hostile backlash from Japanese rightists who complained of bias and accused the government of promoting masochistic history. So just as Japan was adopting a more forthright stance, in 1996 conservatives launched the "Tsukurukai," a right-wing group of academics, pundits and politicians aimed at promoting a revisionist history and rewriting Japan's textbooks. This revisionist history rejects the more self-critical history presented in the 1994 textbooks and seeks to rehabilitate Japan's wartime and colonial history, asserting that Japan was acting on behalf of fellow Asians by trying to liberate them from the yoke of western imperialism. This Pan-Asian liberation myth is often invoked by rightists to justify Japan's actions, and indeed it was a powerful ideology at the time, but it is subject to extensive criticism by Japanese historians who point out that the reality was quite different. Pan-Asian liberation was essentially a fig-leaf for Japan's aggressive imperial expansion to secure its own interests, seeking access to natural resources to fuel a war of subjugation in China. Asian leaders at the time quickly soured on the leadership role Japan asserted under the aegis of Pan-Asianism as they confronted the yawning gap between the enticing rhetoric and the brutal reality.

Tsukurukai authored and published many books that proved popular with the general public, promoting a history that portrayed Japan in a positive light, necessarily downplaying or ignoring the atrocities. The right wing has also been effective in popularizing their narrative of history through manga (comic books) which are very popular in Japan. The Research Association of Liberal Historical Perspectives (Jiyushugi Shikan Kenkyukai) published the best-selling three-volume *Manga History of Japan: What the School Textbooks Do Not Teach* (*Manga: Kyokasho ga Oshienai Rekishi*), while Yoshinori Kobayashi is a prolific and incredibly popular manga author, rewriting history from a nationalist, right-wing perspective. He also participated in the Tsukurukai textbook-writing project.

In 2001 the Ministry of Education approved Tsukurukai's textbook for use in classrooms, provoking outrage in China and South Korea and harsh criticism within Japan as well. This textbook puts a positive gloss on Japan's modern history, focusing on favorable developments and only lightly touching on war-related controversies. So the step forward in 1994 in using textbooks to promote reconciliation generated a domestic backlash leading to publication of a textbook that presented a vindicating and valorizing narrative. The Japan Teachers Union denounced the textbook and nationwide only 18 out of 11,102 junior high schools adopted it, giving it a paltry market share of 0.4%. In 2005, the Tsukurukai textbook was again approved by the Ministry of Education and again did not gain a significant market share. However, other textbooks also retreated from the more forthright depiction of Japan's shared past with Asia that began in 1994. The comfort women became part of this narrative in the mid-1990s, but their story has largely been excised from recent textbooks, perhaps reflecting publishers' inclination toward self-censorship in response to perceived preferences of Japan's right-wing leaders, especially Junichiro Koizumi (2001–2006), Taro Aso (2008–2009) and Shinzo Abe (2006–2007, 2012–), and the explicit politicization of textbook screening and teaching guidelines in the 21st century.

South Korean President Roh Moo-hyun (2003–2008) denounced Japan's new history textbooks in 2005 and briefly recalled the South Korean ambassador to Japan over the incident. The South Korean government lodged a formal complaint against the revised Japanese textbooks with UNESCO and demanded a number of specific revisions. Chinese leaders did not directly raise the issue, but harsh media criticism and online agitation sparked large-scale popular protests targeting the Japanese presence in China. These textbook controversies also prompted an Internet petition campaign in China that collected 10 million signatures, opposing Japan's bid for a seat on the United Nations Security Council.

The revision of the Fundamental Law on Education under Prime Minister Shinzo Abe (2006–2007), aimed at promoting patriotism, signals more extensive political meddling in the teaching of history. Rewriting history, however, is contentious even when the battle lines are at home, as Abe learned in 2007 when the Ministry of Education issued new guidelines about teaching the Battle of Okinawa that watered down existing texts' assertions that Japanese soldiers instigated group suicides by Okinawans. As mentioned in the previous chapter, this sparked mass demonstrations in Okinawa because this fratricidal treachery is part of islanders' identity.

Textbook selection is decentralized in Japan and is the responsibility of 500 textbook screening committees established by local school boards, typically made up of local educators, experts and ordinary citizens who examine the various textbooks on offer and make a recommendation. In 2013, however, the central government under Prime Minister Abe began intervening in local textbook decisions, trying to prevent adoption of more critical texts—even on the tiny island of Taketomi in Okinawa Prefecture, without success as it confronts the backlash of the islanders' "little nationalism." In early 2014 the Ministry of Education issued new guidelines encouraging textbook publishers to adhere to government views and court rulings on history, leading to revisions that omit discussion of the comfort women.

The government also asked McGraw-Hill, a New York-based publisher, to alter its textbook description of the comfort women, asserting factual errors, as part of a global campaign to counter negative assessments of Japan's wartime system of sexual slavery. The textbook authors and publisher rejected the request, citing evidence and scholarly consensus backing their depiction of events while raising questions about why the Japanese government is meddling.

Textbooks and Reconciliation?

How might reconciliation on history issues begin? Europe provides a model of reconciliation as Germany has managed to overcome its horrific record and gain the trust of its neighbors who suffered so much from the two world wars it initiated. Systematically and slowly, Germany pursued reconciliation, beginning in the 1950s, by cooperating with its former victims in creating a mutually acceptable narrative of their shared history and thereby gaining their trust and enabling Germany to rejoin Western Europe. It was not easy or quick, but with sufficient political will and determination German authorities succeeded in this mission. In the context of the Cold War, and the threat of the Soviet Union, West Germany faced more than the moral imperative of coming to terms with its past; it was also seen as essential to Germany's future. West Germany could not survive isolation, and the price of reconciliation was a full reckoning without quibble and maximum contrition. Reconciliation without apology was impossible and atonement meant, aside from war redress, an undiluted acceptance of war responsibility. Textbooks proved to be a path towards reconciliation, but that path seems less promising in Asia.

The European model is based on transnational collaborative efforts to discuss shared histories, identify and narrow differences and work towards producing a common narrative. This does not require fully eliminating differences, but the process itself is a confidence-building measure that is designed over time to nurture trust and a spirit of compromise. Germany was able to do this despite its fraught history in Europe, indicating that it is an undertaking worth exploring. In these efforts UNESCO played a catalytic role in sponsoring cooperative textbook projects, helping to insulate them from political influences. The shared past, and simmering grievances, generate tensions and opportunism, and thus undertaking these projects under UNESCO auspices helped create a sense of impartiality and reduce nationalistic posturing.

In East Asia the onus is on Japan to take the initiative and propel the process because it was the perpetrator and the Chinese and Koreans are the aggrieved parties. There have been a number of bilateral history textbook writing projects since the 1990s, but the results have been meager in terms of influencing public discourse and classroom teaching. It is worth recalling that the successful German-Polish School Textbook Commission project launched in 1972 under the auspices of UNESCO took nearly three decades to issue common guidelines for teaching history. Similarly, the German-French textbook reconciliation efforts took almost four decades to bear fruit, so it is not surprising that East Asian efforts have made limited progress.

A trilateral joint research project that began in 2002, involving Japan, China and South Korea, was not state-sanctioned, meaning governments are not obliged to adopt the results. This project, involving scholars, educators and civil society actors, resulted in the 2005 publication of a textbook on East Asian modern history, published simultaneously in all three countries. The book, titled *History to Open the Future*, enjoyed brisk sales, totaling 80,000 copies in Japan, 70,000 in South Korea and 130,000 in China by the end of 2007 (Shin and Sneider 2011, 238). Although the book was not adopted by the respective school systems and got a cool reception by education officials and scholars in Japan, it has been used in youth exchange programs, and a revised edition has been published. In South Korea, a manga version of the book was also produced in 2007. For the Japanese government the composition of the trilateral textbook committee was problematic since middle school teachers and activists were involved. There are also doubts about Chinese scholars' independence and objectivity since they do not have freedom to disavow or stray from government positions on history. In such an atmosphere of distrust it is hard to seek common ground over the divisive issues of history, especially since it involves educating the young and shaping their sense of national identity. Conservatives in Japan decry liberals' penchant for what they view as a masochistic history and want to assert a history that imbues young Japanese with pride. But the whitewashed narrative they prefer is unacceptable to China and South Korea because it offends their pride and doesn't address the need to restore their trampled dignities. Given chilly relations between Japan and its neighbors, and an escalation of tensions in recent years, the context for textbook diplomacy appears unfavorable.

Memory Wars

It is also important to acknowledge the limits of textbook diplomacy given the intensity of hostility directed toward Japan. If Japan accommodated neighboring nations' perspectives and incorporated them into its textbooks, would such a gesture defuse the antagonism? Or would such a gesture only fuel further demands, creating an educational version of "whack-a-mole" where textbook writers and screeners would be constantly responding to new demands?

Given that contemporary national identity in China and South Korea is rooted in anti-Japanese struggles, and the humiliation and suffering endured at the hands of Japanese, depictions of this period are not detached or dispassionate. Victims have a tendency to probe their wounds and to find a dignity in detailing what was endured, while the government of Japan, as victimizer, has a corresponding tendency to downsize and marginalize shameful acts of the past. Chinese and Koreans believe that history teaching in Japan justifies or glorifies Japan's militaristic past, but that perception is inaccurate. Japanese textbooks are not promoting a collective amnesia, but equally they are not presenting a damning indictment that critically examines

Japanese imperial aggression in Asia. This history remains politically divisive in Japan as conservatives seek to minimize, rationalize, justify, glorify and valorize what most Japanese agree is a sordid chapter in their history. It may come as some surprise to readers that opinion polls in the 1990s and into the 21st century indicate that most Japanese are not in denial about wartime or colonial excesses and support the government doing more to acknowledge and atone for this past. But the conservative political elite has used its influence over textbooks to prevent a wholesale repudiation of what most Japanese would regard as an unredeemable history (Saaler 2005). For Chinese and Koreans accustomed to seeing Japanese in more black and white terms, monolithically villainous and collectively in denial, Japan's conservatives provide a perfect foil and irresistible target. Ironically, their bitter recriminations targeting Japan's incorrect views on history actually help Japan's conservatives, allowing them to argue that their neighbors are impossible and their demands incessant, thereby justifying an obdurate stance on history issues.

Japan is the easy target in this contentious debate, but Chinese and Korean textbooks offer little inspiration about how to teach history. Chinese texts are propagandistic and overwrought, brimming with outrage and victim's consciousness. Until recently they also exaggerated the role of the CCP in winning the war against Japan since it was the Nationalists that did most of the fighting; newer narratives accord them their due. Since the 1990s Chinese textbooks have promoted patriotic education to shore up the CCP's legitimacy, focusing much more on the malevolence of the Japanese than in Mao's era when the emphasis was on victory and recriminations focused on Japan's militarist elite.

South Korean textbooks also rigidly reflect official views and are infused with nationalistic passions that are virulently anti-Japanese. Interestingly, it was not until the 1990s that the comfort women appeared in Korean textbooks. This is an awkward subject given Korean collaboration in recruiting women and managing the comfort women system. In addition, there are conflicted patriarchal views about this era of national humiliation and deep divisions between conservatives and liberals about the path to democratization.

In 2015, Seoul decided to ditch privately published school textbooks and replace them in 2017 with a state-produced textbook titled *The Correct Textbook of History*. So Prime Minister Abe, constantly admonished by President Park Geun-hye to embrace a "correct history," will now know where to look for a "reliable" source. Most Koreans, however, oppose the government's efforts to impose a conservative narrative that downplays widespread political repression and human rights abuses inflicted by a series of military dictators in the post-World War II era, including President Park's father, Park Chung-hee. Private publishers have only been allowed to publish high school textbooks since 2003, a democratization initiative that infuriated conservatives because only one of the eight government-approved textbooks reflects their views and almost no schools use it. The contentious nexus of democracy and history sparked mass demonstrations in 2015 denouncing the government's plan to re-impose a state monopoly on textbook publication aimed at whitewashing the praetorian past.

Missed Opportunity?

The situation in Asia is complicated by the Cold War and the US role in absolving Emperor Hirohito of war responsibility, keeping Japan and China apart and pressuring South Korea to normalize relations with Japan in 1965 before there had been any efforts to realize a common view on the colonial past. By not holding Hirohito responsible for a war that was waged in his name the US avoided making him into a martyr for ultra-rightists and enlisted him in their efforts to demilitarize and democratize occupied Japan. But in doing so, the US ensured that many Japanese would also shrink from the burdens of history since if their leader was not held responsible, and he never himself explicitly assumed responsibility, why should anyone else feel responsible? Letting Hirohito off the hook also allowed everyone else off the hook except for a few thousand men prosecuted at various war crimes tribunals. They took the fall for the nation, and when the Americans left in 1952 they too were absolved and de-purged by the government. Part of the cost of the US departure was signing the Treaty of San Francisco, in which Japan accepted the verdict of the IMTFE regarding war criminals—a verdict that many conservatives now repudiate—and agreed to allow the US to maintain bases in Japan, mostly in Okinawa. This too is controversial, especially among Okinawans, most of whom oppose hosting the US bases on their islands.

Due to the Cold War, Japan did not normalize relations with China until 1978, postponing any initiatives to forge a common perspective about the past. Germany also balked initially at a full and forthright reckoning, but this gained momentum in the 1960s, benefiting from relatively fresh memories of war's devastating consequences that underscored why reconciliation was necessary. In contrast, Sino-Japanese history issues festered and suffered from prolonged neglect and a hardening of attitudes. As historian John Dower has argued, America's embrace of Japan's wartime conservative elite during the Occupation era was an expedient policy designed to quicken Japan's economic recovery and promote political stability, showcasing the superiority of the American system *vis-à-vis* the Soviet Union (Dower 1999). In doing so, however, the US put into power the very people who had most to lose from a candid evaluation of what they had wrought in wartime, with powerful implications for Japan's master narrative. Moreover, the US sponsored Japan, opening its markets and giving access to technology, meaning that reconciliation with victims of Japanese aggression was not imperative in the way it was for Germany—Germany needed to reintegrate in Western Europe while Japan had no such urgency regarding Asia. In this respect, the US insulated Japan from its history, and helped it regain a foothold in Southeast Asia through reparations agreements. These agreements provided export credits that countries invaded and occupied by Japan could use to buy Japanese products, thus facilitating Japanese firms' market penetration. But until Nixon's surprise normalization of ties with China in 1971, Japan was kept apart from the principal victim of Japanese aggression (1931–1945) and had no incentive to face a troubling past. This postponement of Japan's reckoning represents an important difference, with the European context favoring textbook reconciliation initiatives. One might think that the passage of time might present certain advantages in that wartime passions would soften and recede, but in Asia the opposite has happened; the past has become the subject of more heated and divisive confrontations even as the generation with direct experience dies out. The volatile mix of identity politics, state-orchestrated nationalism and history has undermined the prospects of textbook diplomacy in East Asia.

The Cold War also worked to divide Japan from South Korea. In 1950 the Korean War jumpstarted Japan's recovery as the US military placed large orders with Japanese factories, but the US-sponsored government in South Korea was focused on internal problems and under considerable pressure not to complicate relations with Japan over historical grievances that might embarrass a key ally in the Cold War battle to win global support. It was not until two decades after the end of Japan's colonial rule that the US brokered normalization between South Korea and Japan, in 1965 (Packard 2010). Given Seoul's precarious position facing a hostile North Korea and its dependence on the US for military support, it was unable to resist US pressures to strike a deal. Problematically, the Treaty on Basic Relations between Japan and South Korea pretended to "resolve" unresolved historical grievances by requiring Tokyo to provide $800 million in grants and soft loans as reparations, and Seoul agreeing to waive all further claims to compensation. But, this financial settlement was not accompanied by any *mea culpa* by the Japanese—no apology, no acknowledgement of wrongdoing or the pain inflicted, and no reconciliation initiatives, textbooks or otherwise. So the compensation did not solve any of the issues that divided the two nations, and indeed planted a time bomb that exploded in 2005 when the South Korean government released 1,200 pages of detailed reports on the negotiations. It emerged that Japan had offered to directly compensate 1.03 million Koreans conscripted for labor and the military during the colonial era, but Seoul had demanded that it be paid the redress and had taken responsibility for distributing the compensation. The newly released reports infuriated Koreans because their government had distributed very little money to the victims or their surviving families, diverting it mostly to infrastructure and heavy industrial projects. This led to demands that the government provide compensation as agreed to in the negotiations. It was in this context that the South Korean government's angry denunciations of Japanese textbooks in 2005 seemed like a diversionary tactic. Then in 2010 South Korea's constitutional court ruled that the government was violating the rights of the former comfort women by not doing enough on their behalf to secure compensation from Japan, a ruling that heightened acrimony and distrust over the shared past. Subsequently, South Korean courts have ruled in favor of former forced laborers demanding compensation from Japanese firms, again raising the heat over history.

The increasingly acrimonious contemporary disputes over the past generate pessimism over prospects for writing a mutually acceptable narrative of this shared history. Maybe the window of opportunity was missed, if ever there was a possibility. Post-Mao China was rapidly transforming in the 1980s due to Deng Xiaoping's revolutionary economic reforms, sparking an upheaval that spilled over into textbooks and war memory. In periods of liberalization and transition, authoritarian governments and elites tend to embrace and boost nationalism to consolidate their power. Thus, the 1982 textbook row mentioned above helped to boost anti-Japanese nationalism, as did the building of the Nanjing Massacre Memorial in 1985 (see Chapter 7). Oddly enough, until the 1980s the Nanjing Massacre was a suppressed trauma in Chinese history that did not fit with the triumphalist narrative of victory cultivated under Mao and expressed in textbooks. Moreover, Nanjing was the capital of Chiang Kai Shek's Kuomintang government so its trauma did not jibe with the communist wartime narrative. Only from the 1980s and with greater momentum in the 1990s did the CCP use textbooks to bolster patriotic education by focusing more on Japanese atrocities and China's victimization, a mobilization of the "century of humiliation" narrative that highlighted the CCP's vital role in victory and bringing that chapter to an end.

Politicizing the Past, Imperiling the Future

In the 1990s it became more difficult for Japan to meet neighbors' expectations on textbooks because history issues became more politicized. A confluence of events at the end of the 1980s caused an upheaval in regional history that still reverberates powerfully in the 21st century: (1) the end of military rule and the establishment of democracy in South Korea in 1988; (2) the death of Emperor Showa (Hirohito) in 1989; (3) China's post-Tiananmen decision to promote patriotic education from the early 1990s; and (4) the end of the Cold War. These developments generated tectonic changes in the landscape of memory wars. At the end of the 20th century, East Asia disinterred a hastily buried past and politicized history in ways that upended the staid world of educational pedagogy and textbooks. The historical stakes were rapidly and irreversibly increased, and respecting neighboring nations' sensitivities became far more difficult because Chinese and Koreans became much more sensitive about a greater range of issues.

In South Korea, military rule and authoritarian government gave way to robust democracy at the end of the 1980s. This sudden political opening unleashed civil society, memories, and the media, bringing long suppressed anguish to the fore as Koreans took the measure of their history under Japanese colonial rule. The story of the comfort women was taken up by civil society organizations, forcing the nation to confront this humiliating chapter and leading the government to press the Japanese government about its longstanding denials. Ironically, the comfort women issue does not figure prominently in South Korean textbooks, and in 2013 one draft textbook suggested that the issue was largely resolved, much to the surprise of Koreans and Japanese; this idiosyncratic assessment was subsequently revised.

While the Showa Emperor was alive (this is how Emperor Hirohito is referred to because emperors are posthumously known by their reign name), there was a collective reluctance to acknowledge many of the horrors committed in his name during Japan's rampage in Asia from 1931 to 1945. Certainly many Japanese historians tried to promote a fuller and more honest assessment, but the Ministry of

Education screened textbooks and compelled authors to revise their narratives. Emperor Showa's death in 1989 liberated Japan's wartime history from the constraints and taboos that had been respected while he was alive. The "forgotten" past was exhumed as the archives yielded their secrets, diaries and sensitive reports were found, and Japanese historians challenged prevailing narratives and published extensively about cruel events and ghastly abuses. Suddenly in the early 1990s the Japanese public confronted a cascade of grisly revelations well beyond what most imagined because their education had left them in the dark and unprepared.

Confronted with compelling archival evidence of government complicity in recruiting comfort women and operating comfort stations, in 1993 Yohei Kono, the chief cabinet secretary in Prime Minister Kiichi Miyazawa's cabinet, issued the Kono Statement, declaring that Japan accepted responsibility for the comfort women system, apologized, and would teach students about this as a gesture of atonement. The Kono Statement was issued in the year Abe was elected to the Diet and he has worked to discredit and overturn it ever since.

Just as history was being reexamined and reconsidered in South Korea and Japan, the Chinese Communist Party began promoting patriotic education in order to regain legitimacy following the violent suppression of the pro-democracy movement that had burst out in Tiananmen Square in 1989. The protesters also criticized corruption among party cadres and nepotism, striking at the Party's sense of moral superiority and signifying that the public's faith in the Party was flagging. In order to restore a semblance of legitimacy for the CCP, the government promoted patriotic education and focused on the wartime feats of Mao and the CCP guerillas in defeating the Japanese. Until this time, Chinese textbooks had emphasized a triumphalist narrative of twin victories over Japan in 1945 and then the Nationalists in 1949. The horrific incidents and experiences that have since come to the fore were downplayed. The march of history under the banner of communist revolution had been forward-looking, not dwelling on China's victimization or the goriest details of Japanese aggression. That suddenly changed in the 1990s when it became necessary to remind younger Chinese what the CCP had sacrificed to protect the motherland. Suddenly, vilifying Japan became a strategy for bolstering the CCP's legitimacy while inculcating patriotism and loyalty to the state among younger Chinese. Textbooks were revised to denounce the Japanese invasion and atrocities and highlight the CCP's heroic struggle against them. This complicates the task of textbook reconciliation efforts since education in China is enlisted to inculcate anti-Japanese resentment. The end of the Cold War also precipitated reconsideration of Japan's wartime record as barriers fell and the conspiracy of silence abated.

Japanese are beginning to show signs of perpetrator's fatigue, while the aggrieved parties seem disinclined to recalibrate their sense of victimhood. Japan in the 21st century is clearly not the Japan of the 1930s and 1940s, but inordinate doubts are raised about this in China and South Korea. In both countries the Japanese are demonized in textbooks as the young are indoctrinated with horrific images that nurture a national identity rooted in anti-Japanese sentiments that make little room for the prevailing reality in contemporary Japan.

Japanese feel that their post-1945 history is not given due recognition and think that Japan's contributions to Asian peace and prosperity over the past seven decades should earn it far more kudos than its neighbors are willing to concede. Instead they cling to an angry remembering and don't appear inclined to accept anything but sustained, abject kowtowing, making prospects for reconciliation seem remote, if not impossible. Reconciliation can succeed only where the victim and victimizer can both regain dignity, but Japanese have good reason to believe that their neighbors insist on humiliating Japan and are not interested in reconciliation or softening differences in perspective. Indeed, keeping Japan squirming on the hook of history is far more politically useful than reconciliation, so the mutual vilification industry in textbook wars commands the high ground.

But Japan also has itself to blame because it has yet to take the full measure of its shared history in East Asia and appears overly hasty in wanting to turn the page of history before it has been read or absorbed. Moreover, the political elite sends mixed messages, with some apologizing and demonstrating contrition while others repudiate such gestures. Who speaks for Japan about the past? Official statements of remorse always seem undermined by discordant and unapologetic voices. Visits to Yasukuni Shrine by Japanese leaders convey an unrepentant view about Japanese imperial aggression and raise questions about the sincerity of Japanese apologies. Outspoken conservatives assert repeatedly that the Asia-Pacific War was an anti-colonial crusade, a war of liberation rather than a war of aggression. It is understandable that Japan's aggrieved neighbors don't appreciate that most Japanese are contrite about this past because elected leaders present a different image.

Prime Minister Shinzo Abe is an unabashed revisionist who thinks that Japan's textbooks have been too masochistic in representing Japan's history and advocates they be substantially revised to help nurture pride in nation. Conservatives believe that Japan's sense of identity has been distorted because textbooks present a one-sided view critical of wartime Japan and the devastation the Imperial Armed Forces inflicted on Asia during the war. Restoring pride in nation, therefore, must start with sweeping changes in what children learn in school. Abe believes that Japan has been unfairly singled out and vilified and is unapologetic about Japanese colonialism in Korea or aggression in China. This is not a majority view among Japanese, but it is a common view among Japan's conservative elite. They seek to spread their perspective by revising textbooks to remove what they term "masochistic" history.

Words matter and so does media coverage of sensitive historical issues. Media sensationalism and distortions tend to incite and escalate spats over history textbooks. One prominent example is the Tsukurukai Japanese history textbook mentioned above that was adopted by less than 1% of schools in Japan, but attracted at least 99% of international media coverage on textbook issues. This spotlight on the most extreme textbook, favored by reactionaries, conveyed the impression to Chinese and Koreans that this is how Japan teaches its history, when in fact it was the least popular textbook and was scarcely used at all in the classroom. But the media needs attention-grabbing headlines and thus Chinese and Koreans have the misleading impression that Japanese educators harbor such reactionary views.

And this is what they want to believe because intrinsic to the angry and resentful history narrative nurtured in these countries is Japan's refusal to face up to its wrongdoing.

There is probably no textbook Japanese could write or teach that would satisfy Chinese or Koreans because their national identity is firmly rooted in anti-Japanese sentiments, and the sense of victimization has increased over the decades since 1945, fervently embraced by those who have no direct experience of that time. If we recall that textbooks are about shaping national identity, there is little inspiration for Japan in the events of the 1930s and 1940s, or colonial rule in Korea from 1910 to 1945. To the extent that Japan seeks to redeem this awkward history in textbook accounts it faces the wrath of those it victimized. It is also unlikely to unequivocally accept all that it is denounced for because some of its neighbors' allegations are questionable and exaggerated. In China and South Korea, textbooks assert a victim's narrative, one that nurtures anti-Japanese patriotism that has political purpose. As a unifying target, invoking Japanese perfidy is convenient for political leaders in both nations. This is not to downplay what Japan inflicted on these countries, but merely to acknowledge that the temptation of playing the history card has not been resisted.

Abe and other nationalists have long argued that textbook revisions are crucial to restoring national pride and overcoming decades of masochistic history. In 2014, the Ministry of Education in Japan revised its curriculum guidelines regarding how to teach about territorial disputes with neighboring countries. These guidelines pressure teachers, publishers and textbook authors to toe the government line. Revised textbooks for middle schools (2016) and high schools (2017) are subject to the new guidelines. By calling on teachers and textbook writers to clarify that Japan's claims to the disputed islets of Takeshima and Senkaku are consistent with international law, the new guidelines threw down the gauntlet and attracted the expected ire from South Korea and China who also claim the disputed islands, which they call Dokdo and Diaoyu respectively. The textbook guidelines assert that there is no territorial dispute with China over Senkaku/Diaoyu because Japan's position under international law is unassailable, echoing official diplomatic rhetoric while ignoring the actual state of affairs. There clearly is a dispute whether or not the Japanese government wants to recognize it, and China vigorously contests Japanese claims, especially since 2012 when Japan nationalized some of the islets. As discussed at greater length in Chapter 10, this move was seen in Beijing to violate an understanding that neither side would attempt to assert sovereignty, while China would not challenge Japan's administrative control.

Japan's new textbook guidelines do not reference efforts by the three nations to manage the disputes and are designed at inculcating an uncompromising nationalistic perception of the dispute among students, one similar to textbooks in China and South Korea. In this regard, the new guidelines represent a step towards hardening attitudes among Japanese and also highlight the government's efforts under Prime Minister Abe to ensure that textbooks follow the government's positions and instill a narrow-minded nationalism on issues that divide Asian neighbors. Given the widespread perception among Japanese that education is not adequately developing students' critical thinking skills, the shift towards a uniform and uncritically examined position on the key historical disputes that spark regional tensions appears counterproductive. This initiative also dims the prospects for textbooks contributing to reconciliation.

Japan is moving towards the more assertive and confrontational histories embraced in China and South Korea. Are there special burdens of history that the aggressor cannot shirk, requiring that it assume responsibility for reconciliation even if neighbors act with little regard for nurturing a sense of compromise and common ground? Increasingly Japan's conservative leaders seem to think no, that being responsible and reasonable on textbooks has backfired, encouraging ever greater demands and bolder assertions, and so are now promoting equally unilateralist views that reduce the already limited prospects for managing history. As much as it is convenient for China and South Korea to shift blame onto Japan, and indeed Tokyo's inadequate record of acknowledging and atoning for past misdeeds gives them ammunition, they have been too ready to escalate and vilify in ways that impede reconciliation for domestic political benefit. In this context, Prime Minister Abe's dismantling of the neighboring nations clause is understandable since it remained an unreciprocated gesture, an offered olive branch that was spurned. By taking a more assertively nationalistic stance in the classroom, Abe appeases his hardcore supporters, but is sowing seeds of rancor among contemporary youth.

In 2015 the Japanese government budgeted $425 million partly to promote its views on wartime history and territorial disputes, evidence of how high the stakes have become. This globalization of the history wars in a bid to influence world opinion, especially in the US, is a PR effort designed to offset similar efforts by Seoul and Beijing. Japan as the perpetrator is in no position to pitch an exonerating or mitigating narrative because any efforts along these lines to "set the record straight" make Japan look unrepentant and in denial. The Germans understood that caviling was never an option and as a result have made far greater headway on reconciliation.

Vanishing Comfort Women

New textbooks approved by the Ministry of Education in 2015 (for use from 2016) show that there is reason to be concerned that "correct" history is being sacrificed on the altar of Abe's patriotic education reforms. Nanjing is no longer a "massacre" after being downgraded to an "incident," the military's role in instigating group suicides by Okinawans is obscured, and the comfort women are absent.

The Kono Statement promises to teach the lessons of this sordid saga, but due to Abe's 2007 patriotic education law, and the 2014 teaching guidelines, the comfort women have virtually vanished from all of the government-approved textbooks used in middle schools. In the one new textbook that does touch on the issue, the Ministry of Education insisted that this minor publisher delete a comfort woman's testimony because her account contradicted government views, and the publisher was also required to include a disclaimer that states there is no proof of Japan's direct involvement in forcible recruitment. "By insisting on this statement in textbooks, the Japanese government is directly and blatantly violating the Kono declaration, which Abe repeatedly says his government 'inherits,'" says Tessa Morris-Suzuki, a professor of history at Australian National University (personal communication).

The 1993 Kono Statement says:

> We shall face squarely the historical facts as described above instead of evading them, and take them to heart as lessons of history. We hereby reiterate our firm determination never to repeat the same mistake by forever engraving such issues in our memories through the study and teaching of history.

The new textbooks are part of a wholesale retreat from the more penitent views towards history that prevailed in the 1990s. In 1997, six out of seven texts mentioned the comfort women, while in 2002 only three out of eight did. Education Minister Hakubun Shimomura gave a glimpse into the Abe administration's thinking on the matter of textbooks during a 2012 interview with right-wing businessman Motoya Toshio. "People have come to think that they, and their country, are bad through a masochistic view of history," Shimomura said. "I think the Japan of today is exactly the emotionally defeated country that the U.S. hoped for right after the war" (*Big Talk*, 257, December 28, 2012, 4).

Conclusion

Reconciliation between Japan and its neighbors remains in limbo because issues of war memory and apology have not been resolved. Stereotypical images of Japanese collectively in denial about the atrocities committed by the Imperial Armed Forces, however, are grossly misleading and overlook the more prevalent view accepting wartime guilt and favoring atonement. In his excellent study featuring media and cultural analysis, Hokkaido University's Philip Seaton persuasively argues that, "Japanese war memories are not nearly as nationalistic as they are frequently made out to be" (2007, 130). Seaton points out that war memory is fiercely contested among Japanese, and collective amnesia is impossible given this robust discourse. He asserts that the English-language media consistently misrepresents the true state of war memory among Japanese by focusing too much on attempts by conservatives and the ruling elite to impose a glorifying narrative of the war that emphasizes Japan's victimization. This "orthodoxy" of a nation shirking war responsibility overlooks the significance of memory rifts in Japan. In examining textbooks, other educational materials, television documentaries, films and printed media, Seaton finds that progressive views critical of Japan's wartime aggression and accepting responsibility are more representative of Japanese opinion. In the 2000s, however, there has been a noticeable rightward shift in public discourse and in textbooks as publishers respond to new guidelines and gloss over or drop controversial topics such as the comfort women.

Although memory rifts in Japan remain vigorously contested, perhaps more than in any other World War II combatant nation, this goes unrecognized in China and South Korea where the "orthodoxy" of an unrepentant Japan in denial goes unchallenged. In assessing the future of war memory, it appears that a hardening of irreconcilable positions on shared history will remain an impediment to improved relations in East Asia. As mentioned above, textbooks have also been drafted into the battles over disputed territories, which we discuss in the next chapter.

Part IV

Flashpoints and Fringes

10

Nationalism and Territorial Disputes

Tensions in Asia are escalating over numerous territorial disputes and overlapping claims that arouse bristling nationalism. Competing claims between nations are flashpoints that can potentially spiral out of control, with disastrous consequences. Typically there is a managed brinksmanship that aims to avert war, but posturing, saber rattling, clashes and skirmishing can spark miscalculations with terrible consequences, leading to three wars between India and Pakistan in Kashmir alone. The tensions also fan mutual suspicions and undermine prospects for confidence-building measures, while there is also risk that the political and diplomatic strains will impede development of economic relations. What appear as lines or dots on a map can assume exaggerated importance, becoming a touchstone of national identity precluding compromise on what are posited as inherent and inviolable rights. In some cases in Asia these are longstanding zones of animosity; in others they are newly salient, but precisely because they are suddenly endowed with political importance they are no less risky and indeed potentially more so.

In this chapter we examine flashpoints in Asia and assess the geo-political implications.

East Asia

Japan has territorial disputes with Russia, South Korea and China over disputed islands that do not appear important enough in terms of economic value or strategic imperatives to justify the probable costs of conflict. But nationalistic impulses in all of the relevant nations make these islands hotly disputed zones of contention where room for concessions and compromise is very limited and calculations are not

Nationalism in Asia: A History Since 1945, First Edition. Jeff Kingston.

always based on a cost-benefit assessment. Japan, being at the nexus of all these regional disputes, is keenly aware of linkage and thus concerned not to make concessions in any of the cases out of concern that rival claimants will demand the same. Yet, this diplomatic posture makes progress difficult, complicated by nationalist political pressures that raise the stakes for any leader seeking an accommodation. Problematically, the festering disputes serve nationalist agendas on all sides to the extent they remain unresolved and thus any breakthrough initiatives face strong domestic opposition. Sometimes having an enemy and a target for nationalist political energies is quite useful, especially if overlapping claims can be managed to avoid a clash. This shadow boxing and posturing for domestic constituencies is important to bear in mind when analyzing East Asian territorial disputes.

It is also striking that Japan's territorial disputes have all escalated since the turn of the century. Russia, China and South Korea are all more assertive diplomatically as a result of strong leaders, growing clout and nationalistic fervor, and all have longstanding grievances with Japan that have festered and grown more intense. Perceptions that Japan is stagnant and in decline may have emboldened its neighbors, as have periodic strains in the US–Japan bilateral alliance. Clearly the immense power shift associated with the rapid emergence of China as a global economic powerhouse aspiring to regional hegemony has also altered the strategic calculus in numerous ways; for example, it has become the leading trading partner of South Korea and Japan. In addition, nationalistic gestures by politicians in Japan have been counterproductive, inciting anti-Japanese nationalism in China and South Korea that impedes dialogue over territorial disputes.

Prime Minister Abe's nationalistic grandstanding at the Yasukuni Shrine at the end of 2013 was directed at his political supporters, and earned him a bounce in the opinion polls, but jingoistic posturing incites a regional backlash, amplifying nationalistic sentiments in ways that complicate territorial disputes. Abe's agenda of seeking public support for lifting constitutional constraints on the military, and boosting the defense budget and military capabilities so Japan can expand security cooperation with the US, has been an uphill battle. The Japanese are attached to the Peace Constitution and mindful of the dangers of military adventurism that Article 9 guards against. Abe's security agenda therefore benefits from Beijing's belligerent blustering and muscle flexing over territorial rows with Japan in the East China Sea and Southeast Asian nations in the South China Sea. Beijing has made extravagant maritime territorial claims based on its nine-dash line, or "cow's tongue," producing maps that assert what are purported to be historical rights. It is now backing up these claims through intimidation and expansion of its maritime military capabilities. China as regional bogeyman is thus helpful for Abe to push through his security agenda despite a reluctant Japanese public. Again, this is a reminder that provocative rhetoric and gestures are geared towards getting political mileage from nationalistic rows. Problematically for East Asia, all the leaders find nationalism a useful distraction from domestic problems and a reliable way to boost their support, meaning that territorial issues are in some respects far too useful to resolve. Incidentally, between 2012 and 2014 new leaders came to power in each of our focus nations, all eager to appear resolute, meaning unyielding stances that impede territorial compromise.

Russo-Japanese Dissensus

The four islands—Kunashiri, Etorofu, Habomai and Shikotan—that Japan calls the "Northern Territories" and Russia the Kurils are located between the northern Japanese island of Hokkaido and Russia's Kamchatka Peninsula. The Soviet Union invaded and seized the four islands at the end of World War II, after Japan announced its surrender on August 15, 1945. From the Japanese perspective, Soviet and now Russian claims to, and occupation of, the islands are therefore illegal. It is not forgotten that the Soviet attack violated the neutrality pact signed with Tokyo in 1941. Moscow naturally sees things differently, viewing its reassertion of sovereignty as justified because Japan seized the islands pursuant to the 1905 Treaty of Portsmouth that concluded the Russo-Japanese War. From Moscow's perspective, the islands were "war booty" and thus subject to the 1943 Cairo Declaration requiring Japan to retrocede territories gained by force of arms. In addition, in February 1945 Soviet leader Joseph Stalin met with US President Franklin Delano Roosevelt and British Prime Minister Winston Churchill at Yalta, making various agreements to secure Soviet entry into the war in the Far East. Germany's defeat was imminent, but Japan seemed far from capitulating and so Roosevelt was eager to get Stalin to attack Japanese positions in Manchuria and Korea. The Cold War between the US and Soviet Union had not yet commenced so such cooperation was deemed desirable. As agreed at Yalta, Stalin launched his attack on August 9, 1945, three months after Germany's surrender, mounting a successful blitzkrieg through Japan's depleted defenses in Manchuria and Korea. The Soviet forces continued fighting even after Japanese soldiers surrendered, seizing the disputed islands by September 1945. Whether taking them as payback or spoils of war seemed less important to Stalin than asserting Soviet interests in the Far East and making a claim for participating in the occupation of Japan. Washington was not prepared to allow this, as bilateral relations had deteriorated sharply in the summer of 1945 over the collective occupation of Berlin. But equally it had no compelling reason to challenge the Soviet presence in the Kurils.

Since 1945, the Soviets (and now Russians) have maintained that the Yalta Agreement with the Allied powers specifically granted them sovereignty over the Kurils in exchange for going to war with Japan. Moreover, in the 1951 Treaty of San Francisco, Japan specifically,

> renounces all right, title and claim to the Kurile Islands, and to that portion of Sakhalin and the islands adjacent to it over which Japan acquired sovereignty as a consequence of the Treaty of Portsmouth of 5 September 1905.

Moscow never signed the Treaty of San Francisco, but takes it as affirmation of the Yalta Agreement; both documents were signed by the US. Japan insists that the four islands are not actually part of the Kurils and thus they were not renounced. In 1956, Tokyo and Moscow were on the verge of resolving the impasse by splitting the islands, but the US pressured Japan not to agree, invoking the Cold War logic that its ally should not be striking a deal with the enemy. Since then, Japan has insisted on return of all four islands and diplomatic relations have never been normalized.

As a result, bilateral relations have been chilly, although there have been several Japanese overtures and initiatives. During the final years of the Soviet Union at the end of the 1980s under General Secretary Mikhail Gorbachev, Japanese hopes for a breakthrough rested on Moscow's need for economic assistance. Gorbachev's political weakness, however, and secessionist demands by various republics in the USSR, precluded any territorial concessions. The 1991 collapse of the Soviet Union intensified Russian nationalism, limiting prospects for concessions despite a faltering economy and need for capital and technology. The political vacuum that opened in the wake of the USSR's disintegration threatened and thus intensified Russian identity and under the circumstances no leader was prepared to risk inciting a domestic backlash by giving up territory.

Russia entered the 21st century with renewed swagger, buoyed by a spike in world energy prices that improved government finances and a new leader, Vladimir Putin, who is assertively patriotic and appeals to nationalistic voters. His political strength and indisputable credentials as a fervent nationalist put him in a unique position to reach a deal with Japan, but a succession of Japanese leaders have been insisting on the return of all four islands, a non-starter for Moscow. In Japan, agreeing to anything less than the return of all four islands is politically difficult because the nationalist rhetoric on this issue has been so strident and Japan's leading mainstream parties support this hardline position. The ongoing dispute has actually escalated in recent years, illustrated by President Dmitry Medvedev's tour of the islands in November 2010, the first by a serving Soviet or Russian head of state. This elicited harsh criticism from Japanese Prime Minister Naoto Kan, and prospects for reaching a compromise on settling the dispute seemed more remote than ever.

The island issue is framed in both countries in highly nationalistic terms that depict the disputed territory as indivisible from the nation and intrinsic to national identity. Citizens in Japan view the islands as an example of Russian/Soviet perfidy, a reminder about Moscow's unilateral abrogation of the 1941 Neutrality Pact and seizure of the islands after Japan's surrender in August 1945. This is not obscure or forgotten history in Japan as nationalist soundtrucks are heard frequently in Tokyo, especially near the Russian Embassy, demanding that Moscow return the islands; and Northern Territories Day is celebrated every February 7th in Japan, a nationalist festival of gatherings where right-wing activists, prominent politicians and relatives of islanders voice their unswerving commitment to regaining all four islands. Amidst this nationalistic political theater, in 2013 two Russian jets apparently violated Japan's air space in Hokkaido on February 7, a blunt reminder perhaps of Russia's equally adamant stance that sovereignty over the four islands is not in dispute.

The lack of a peace treaty—the two nations have been in a state of war since 1945—and failure to resolve the territorial dispute have not impeded growing trade and investment since the mid-2000s, so there is less incentive for Moscow to make territorial concessions. The Kurils have limited economic value aside from fisheries, and there is no confirmed oil or gas potential, while mineral deposits are not easily mined. Strategically, the surrounding waters are considered useful, but not crucially so, especially as the Russian Far Eastern Fleet is a shadow of what it was during the

Soviet era. Indeed, Japan is not viewed as a threat to Russia in the Far East and certainly security concerns focus more on China. The economic costs of chilly relations are more tangible. Given the proximity of Russian gas fields to Japan, it is surprising that energy trade and investment are not far larger, but the territorial issue and competition complicate economic relations. China is a rival customer along with South Korea, a situation that plays to Russian advantage. Clearly bilateral energy ties are developing, especially in the wake of the March 11, 2011 earthquake, tsunami and nuclear meltdowns. The consequent shutdown of Japan's nuclear reactors boosted Russian exports of liquefied natural gas and oil, while Japanese investment in developing energy resources in Russia's Far East has gained some momentum.

Russia is intensely aware of Japan's other territorial disputes with China and South Korea, all flaring in the early 21st century. Curiously, not long after Japan and China faced off over the arrest of the crew of a Chinese fishing vessel in September 2010, Medvedev visited Kunashiri, underscoring Japan's multiple fronts on territorial disputes. He was also perhaps reminding Japan that it should soften its negotiating position—insisting on all four islands—if it wants to conclude a peace treaty and make a deal. Clearly any deal will be on Moscow's terms as Russia understands that Japan has more to gain even if it has to settle for only two islands.

Prime Minister Shinzo Abe resorted to Olympic diplomacy in 2014, meeting President Putin in Sochi after attending the opening ceremony; this was his fifth meeting with Putin since taking office at the end of 2012, more than any other national leader. Despite Russian actions in Crimea and Ukraine, Abe pressed ahead with a peace deal as a means to end Japan's diplomatic isolation in East Asia, boost bilateral relations and move forward on negotiations over the islands. Abe, like Putin, is uniquely positioned to do so because of his impeccable nationalist credentials. Putin seeks to extract maximum investment commitments to help develop Siberia's vast natural resources, leveraging the competing energy needs of Tokyo, Seoul and Beijing.

Russia's difficult relations with the US, Japan's ally, complicate the situation, as does Putin's coordination with China on many global issues in contesting US initiatives. The Russian seizure of Crimea from Ukraine in 2014, and involvement in the subsequent conflict centered in eastern Ukraine, make it even more difficult for Abe to reach an accommodation with Putin because it would antagonize Washington. US inaction in defending Ukraine from Russian intervention reinforces concerns among some Japanese analysts that the US might not prove a reliable ally if China takes similar action over their disputed islands in the East China Sea. These anxieties seem unwarranted as the situations are quite different and there is no security treaty commitment with the Ukraine remotely equivalent to the US–Japan alliance. China is also unlikely to draw inspiration from Russia's adventurism given the vast differences in situations—i.e. Crimea was once part of Russia so there are extensive ties in terms of history and language; Russia has unmatched military assets on the immediate scene; and this is an inhabited land area providing relatively easy access. Even so, among some Japanese, Russia's actions cast a long shadow over the situation in the East China Sea.

Sino-Japanese Brinksmanship: The Senkaku/Diaoyu Dispute

The Sino-Japanese dispute over a handful of uninhabited rocky islets in the East China Sea has escalated ominously over the past decade. Located between Taiwan and Okinawa, the islands known in China as the Diaoyu and in Japan as the Senkaku (and also claimed by Taiwan) have been under Japanese administrative control since 1895. The Chinese government wants to change this status quo and has taken a series of steps to do so such as dispatching vessels and planes to the area and declaring an Air Defense Identification Zone that encompasses the disputed islands. Such actions, which are condemned by Japan and Washington as provocations, are Beijing's way of normalizing its claims.

Brinksmanship involves pursuing a dangerous, confrontational policy up to, but not reaching, the point of no return, a gray zone where provocative posturing falls short of conflict and violent clashes. Developing this synchronized art of not crossing the line is risky given the tit-for-tat actions incited by the provocations and the potential for miscalculation and escalating retribution. It involves a diplomatic dance of finely attuned anticipation, knowing your enemy and striking a balance between sensible caution and applying pressure, discerning the calculus behind the nationalistic taunting and prodding and figuring out how far to respond. With much at stake as nations balance precariously on the edge of the abyss, it also means signaling intentions. Of course, all of this fine-tuning and careful calibrating is complicated by what can be deafening nationalistic "noise" that makes it hard to discern the precise meaning of gestures and what is being signaled.

Relations deteriorated sharply from 2010 when a Chinese fishing boat rammed a Japanese Coast Guard vessel, and the crew were arrested. This sparked a major diplomatic crisis and widespread anti-Japanese demonstrations in China. Large crowds attacked Japanese stores, smashed Japanese brand vehicles and even targeted Japanese patrons at restaurants. Beijing maintained that it had an informal agreement with Tokyo to deport rather than arrest anyone over intrusions into the disputed zone, an understanding that LDP politicians later confirmed, but had apparently not conveyed to the DPJ after it took power in 2009. Moreover, ramming a Japanese Coast Guard vessel is not just an intrusion into disputed waters. In the tense aftermath, the US affirmed with hairsplitting precision that the islets are covered by the US-Japan Mutual Security Treaty because they are under Japanese administrative control, but clarified that this has no bearing on rival sovereignty claims.

In April 2012, the then Governor of Tokyo Shintaro Ishihara provoked a diplomatic crisis with China by signaling his intention to purchase three of the Diaoyu/Senkaku islets from their private Japanese owner. The public quickly donated nearly $20 million to do so. Beijing was furious and Japan's central government feared that Ishihara would use the islands to cause mischief in bilateral relations. Ishihara is well known for his contemptuous views towards China and his ardent nationalist views. He succeeded in forcing the government into preemptively buying the islands in order to sideline him. He also infuriated China and managed to shift Japanese political discourse to the right. In an unusual moment of candor, the Japanese

Ambassador to China publicly criticized Ishihara's plans to purchase the disputed islands, warning that doing so would cause a serious rift in relations. This sensible advice was ignored and he was sacked for his troubles. In September 2012 the central government finalized the purchase, effectively nationalizing the islands. This precipitated angry denunciations from Beijing and anti-Japanese demonstrations around the nation. In one notorious incident, a Chinese driver blocked the Japanese Ambassador's car in order to seize the Japanese flag and desecrate it. Diplomatic relations remain chilly even as economic relations have remained strong, and sales of Japanese consumer products recovered from an initial sharp drop. This situation is described as "cold politics, hot economy," as the mutual economic interdependence has been insulated from territorial disputes and recriminations over history. But there are concerns that the Asian paradox—deepening economic, human and cultural exchanges amidst frosty diplomatic relations—is unsustainable. Indeed, since 2014 there has been a sharp drop in Japanese investment in China, partly due to the perceived risks and the slowing Chinese economy.

Given the high degree of mutual economic interdependence between China and Japan in the 21st century, there is a consensus that war would be so damaging to the entire global economy that it is highly unlikely. Not unimaginable, but a scenario few care to contemplate given all that is at stake. At the World Economic Forum at Davos in 2014, Japanese Prime Minister Shinzo Abe stirred controversy when he likened the current situation in Asia to Europe a century earlier when everyone assumed that war between Germany and Great Britain was unthinkable right up until World War I erupted. His message was that everyone should not be complacent about tensions in Asia and end up sleepwalking to war, as European leaders had done in the early 20th century. Abe was accused of warmongering, perhaps because he had recently paid respects at Yasukuni Shrine, the spiritual center of Japanese militarism, but his blunt message was a useful reminder that economic relations and rational calculus don't always prevail and that a small incident can spiral out of control.

It is worth recalling that nobody imagined that a Serbian nationalist's assassination of Archduke Ferdinand of the Austro-Hungarian Empire in 1914 would spark a conflagration engulfing the entire region. In these early years of the 21st century, such a spark could come from uninhabited rocky islets claimed by Japan, China and Taiwan. The US military alliance with Japan, and repeated declarations that the disputed Senkaku/Diaoyu islands are covered by the bilateral alliance, may well lessen the likelihood of an isolated clash escalating into a wider conflict, but such also was the calculus of the balance of power in Europe in 1914. Again, Asia's peace and prosperity rest on the assumption of rationality prevailing; however local commanders and national leaders can make small missteps that appear measured but can have inexorable and undesired consequences, taking nations over the brink, especially in the current climate of competitive nationalism.

As noted in previous chapters, there is a temptation to amplify nationalistic issues to shore up legitimacy and deflect attention away from difficult problems, so territorial spats can be useful. The Chinese Communist Party is trying to maintain one-party rule in the face of pluralist pressures, a slowing economy and a growing crisis of legitimacy due to corruption, environmental degradation, and income inequalities, among other problems. The Senkaku/Diaoyu dispute thus serves as a useful diversion of popular discontent away from embarrassing issues to a controversy that nurtures anti-Japanese unity and highlights the government's stalwart efforts to restore the nation's dignity.

The overlapping islet claims have become highly contentious based on differing historical and legal interpretations. At the risk of overly simplifying a complex legal tangle (leaving Taiwan's claim to the side), China asserts that the Diaoyu were war booty seized by Japan in 1895 and thus, by virtue of the 1943 Cairo Declaration involving the US, UK and Nationalist China, should be retroceded to China by Japan, which was stripped of other territories it gained through imperial aggression. In 1943, Japan's colonial Taiwanese government administered the Diaoyu; after 1945 the Japanese empire was dismantled and Taiwan was no longer subject to Japanese sovereignty or administrative control. The Potsdam Declaration issued by the Allied powers in July 1945 was an ultimatum that Japan surrender unconditionally. In signing the instrument of surrender with the US in September 1945, Japan formally accepted the declaration's terms that embrace the Cairo Declaration; this was the basis for stripping Japan of its control over Taiwan, Korea and other territories seized by aggression from 1895.

The Potsdam Declaration states,

> The terms of the Cairo Declaration shall be carried out and Japanese sovereignty shall be limited to the islands of Honshu, Hokkaido, Kyushu, Shikoku and such minor islands as we determine.

In the Sino-Japanese Joint Communiqué issued with the normalization of relations in 1972, Japan agreed that, "it firmly maintains its stand under Article 8 of the Potsdam Declaration." So Beijing maintains that Japan, in maintaining administrative control over the islands, is not heeding what it has agreed to. Tokyo's decision to assert its sovereignty by nationalizing the disputed islets in September 2012 is thus seen as a gross provocation and also a betrayal of commitments undertaken in the 1970s to shelve the issue of sovereignty for future resolution.

Japan sees things a bit differently. Tokyo asserts that the islets were terra nullius when they were seized in January 1895, before the end of the Sino-Japanese War (1894–1895) and the signing of the Treaty of Shimonoseki that ended hostilities. The treaty, while granting Japan a substantial financial award, Taiwan and other adjacent small islands, does not specifically mention the Senkaku/Diaoyu and thus Tokyo asserts that they are not subject to the Cairo Declaration and therefore remain Japanese territory. China counters that the seizure of the islets amid ongoing hostilities renders them war booty.

Beijing also maintains that in 1972, when Japanese Prime Minister Kakuei Tanaka and Chinese Premier Zhou Enlai met in Beijing to normalize diplomatic relations, and again in 1978 when Japanese Foreign Minister Sunao Sunoda met with Vice Premier Deng Xiaoping, the question of the Senkaku/Diaoyu was discussed. China claims that the leaders agreed to shelve the question of sovereignty for future resolution, while leaving the islands under Japanese administration. The Japanese government maintains that there was no such agreement, although a prominent confidant of Tanaka, retired LDP politician Hirofumi Nonaka, caused a stir in mid-2012 when he acknowledged that Tanaka had told him there was. The British archives also confirm that in 1982 Prime Minister Zenko Suzuki told Margaret Thatcher about the Japanese government's policy of shelving the territorial dispute.

At any rate, the status of the disputed islands was left ambiguous in the 1951 Treaty of San Francisco, a festering Cold War legacy also evident in Japan's long-standing territorial disagreements over islands with Seoul and Moscow (Selden 2013). After World War II, the US occupied the Okinawan islands, under which the Senkaku were administered, and used them for bombing practice. In 1972, with the reversion of Okinawa to Japanese sovereignty, the Senkaku were also placed under Japanese administration. But the US State Department made clear that this move did not prejudice underlying claims to sovereignty. China asserted sovereignty over the islands for the first time in 1971. The pending 1982 United Nations Convention on the Law of the Sea increased the potential value of the islets as a basis for resource claims in territorial waters, and a survey indicated there might be significant hydrocarbon resources in that area.

Aside from a 2008 agreement for joint development of natural gas in the East China Sea outside the contested zone, a project that has not yet materialized, Beijing and Tokyo remain at loggerheads. In early 2013 *The Economist* opined that the countries seemed to be slipping towards war, and soon after a Chinese naval vessel pointed its missile-firing radar at a Japanese frigate, the step taken immediately before firing. It was a reckless act in a series of upping-the-ante decisions that raise concerns about the Chinese agenda and the prospects for regional peace and stability. As the incidents and scars accumulate, and mutual trust evaporates, this high-stakes game of chicken, and winner-takes-all approach to the islands, seems at best a dead end and at worst an avoidable nightmare.

Looking at these desolate rocks, inhabited only by goats, one wonders what all the fuss is about. They seem so inconsequential and the risks taken all out of proportion. Japan and China have presented legal arguments about their respective claims of sovereignty, but it is highly unlikely that this argument will be settled in the International Court of Justice or by any other arbitration panel. The territorial issue has become so politicized that any *modus vivendi* will require a political agreement and some form of compromise that at the moment seems a remote possibility.

To summarize, there are four main factors driving this territorial dispute: (1) unresolved historical grievances; (2) Chinese sense of injustice and bias in the international system; (3) natural resources; and (4) strategic ambitions.

Starting with the grievances, Japan initiated two wars in China, in 1894–1895 and 1931–1945, and inflicted enormous damage, including an estimated 15–20 million deaths in the latter conflict. The Chinese feel, with good reason, that the Japanese government has not adequately acknowledged or atoned for the nature and extent of the atrocities committed by the Imperial Armed Forces during this 15-year rampage. While it is true that the Japanese government has broadly apologized on numerous occasions, these apologies are undone by denials, minimization and shirking war responsibility on the part of prominent Japanese politicians and pundits. The apologies seem more perfunctory than sincere, with no grand gestures such as in 1970 when German Chancellor Willy Brandt dropped to his knees in front of the memorial honoring the victims, mostly Jewish, of the Warsaw Ghetto Uprising in Nazi-occupied Poland. Instead, Japanese and Chinese historians and their governments continue their battles over the past, while in Japan there is a growing sentiment that no apology would ever suffice because Beijing is using the past to keep Japan diplomatically disadvantaged in the present.

These unresolved historical grievances are closely tied to the sense of injustice and bias among Chinese towards the global status quo. The 20th-century international system was created when China was weak and isolated, and it had no say in shaping the institutions, agreements or frameworks that are the foundation of the status quo. This international system is indelibly connected with China's century of humiliation as the powers that be subjected China to humiliating unequal treaties favorable to the imperial powers, including Japan. The contours of the contemporary international system, especially international law, were shaped by an international order that facilitated foreign domination and exploitation of China, and this helps explain resentment against it today. As a rising power with regional hegemonic ambitions, China seeks to modify the status quo in its favor, but this challenges the US-Japan regional hegemony. So when China invokes history and Japan counters by invoking international law in arguing their cases for sovereignty over the Senkaku/Diaoyu, Beijing believes that there is a considerable gap between what it considers justice and the established system of international law.

The Japanese position is clear. There is no territorial dispute. Clearly, there is a dispute, but Tokyo believes that if it officially agrees that there is, it would undermine its legal position and encourage China to make further demands. Japan has exercised effective administrative control for more than a century, and under international law this is the gold standard of sovereignty. The Japanese have presented evidence from Chinese archives that suggests that in 1950 Beijing acknowledged Japanese sovereignty and actually referred to the islets by their Japanese name. Further, the Japanese contend that it was only after oil exploration surveys in 1968 suggested vast hydrocarbon reserves that Beijing suddenly asserted its claims in 1971.

Competition over the presumed natural resources in the adjacent seabed and China's strategic ambitions are driving escalation of the dispute. The Chinese have issued a nine-dash map that delineates China's sprawling maritime claims in the East and South China Seas, a unilateral assertion that has also sparked territorial rows with Southeast Asian nations, notably over the Spratly Islands with Vietnam and the Scarborough Reef with the Philippines. This map of China's claims is as much about resources as it is about strategic naval aspirations. Above all, the nine dashes are a projection of national power and regional ambitions to reclaim China's centrality in Asian affairs that it enjoyed until the 19th-century arrival of imperialist powers. In this sense, the nine-dash map represents a "back to the future" nationalism, invoking past glory and overcoming the century of humiliation. Securing the grandiose claims of the nine dashes has thus become a touchstone of national identity, a symbol of the pride that Chinese feel in their nation's reemergence as a power to be reckoned with. In this contest, Beijing has confidence that time is on its side. This assessment rests on the expectation that eventually displacing the US as the leading economy in the world will bring about a regional power shift favorable to China. In the meantime, the Diaoyu/Senkaku are seen to bottle-up the Chinese navy and constitute an impediment to its plans for "blue ocean" access and capabilities.

Tensions over the disputed islands are a microcosm of the larger geo-strategic contest between China and the US/Japan in Asia. US Secretary of State Hillary Clinton addressed the brewing impasse at the 2010 ASEAN Regional Forum conference in Hanoi, Vietnam when she spoke of the need to maintain freedom of navigation and suggested China pursue multilateral dialogue and diplomacy with other claimants to disputed territories. It was then that she first mentioned that the US-Japan Security Treaty applies to the Diaoyu/Senkaku. Under the Obama Administration, China policy shifted from engage and cooperate where possible, to one leaning more frequently towards a strategy of isolate and contain. China sees the US meddling in regional disputes as part of this strategy and counters that the US is fostering instability and instigating confrontations.

For Chinese, thus, the ongoing disputes with Japan and ASEAN are a proxy for strategic competition with the US for supremacy in the Asia-Pacific region. The gains from China's "smile diplomacy" in the early 2000s, reassuring neighbors that a rising China is unthreatening, have evaporated as its new more muscular diplomacy has set off alarms and left China increasingly isolated and quietly criticized in the region. Its nationalistic assertions have generated considerable concern within the region about Chinese hegemonic ambitions and what that might mean for surrounding nations. Clearly, China's territorial disputes with Japan, Vietnam, the Philippines, Indonesia and India have heightened anxieties and nurtured an arc of wariness about prospects for a Pax Sinica. Simon Tay points out that some Asian leaders have reservations about the American regional security presence and pattern of unilateralism, but are far more afraid of an American exit leaving the region prey to Chinese ambitions (Tay 2010). Growing security cooperation in the region between the US, Japan, India and ASEAN may look like a containment policy in Beijing, but seems like a sensible hedging strategy and insurance policy to the rest of Asia. Paradoxically, increasingly assertive Chinese nationalism over disputed territories has undermined its national interests in Asia, where it is valued for trade and investment, and admired for its economic prowess, but feared and resented for its desire to call the shots unilaterally.

In Japan, China's rise is undermining confidence that Washington will protect Japan. Would America risk a confrontation with China over the Senkaku at the expense of US interests, or accommodate China and sacrifice Japan's interests? Washington is hoping that it does not have to make such a choice, but in Tokyo there are gnawing doubts about whether the alliance remains reliable. Tokyo surely understands China's growing frustration over the Senkaku as it has experienced exactly the same exasperation with Russia's refusal to acknowledge that there is a territorial dispute with Japan regarding the Kurils/Northern Territories and South Korea's stance over the Dokdo/Takeshima islands. Clearly the disputes, recognized or not, serve to stoke nationalism in ways that map onto other agendas.

Distractions and Agendas

As noted earlier, while large crowds were demonstrating in 2012 against Japan over the territorial dispute, Ai Weiwei, the internationally famous dissident artist, sarcastically remarked that Chinese should be thanking the Japanese because the government only allows demonstrations if they target Japan. His remarks echo widespread views that the demonstrations are state-orchestrated, dialed up and down when useful. Indeed, the demonstrations are a useful pressure valve in a society smoldering with popular discontent.

Playing the Japan card is also a way of changing the channel. In 2012 in the run-up to the Party Congress and leadership transition, the news was awful for the CCP. There were endless reports and popular blogs about corruption, and about how high-level Party officials were abusing their powers and how their families were accumulating vast wealth. But it was the purge of Bo Xi Lai from the Party, and the murder case involving his wife, that drew back the veil on the seamy ways and means of the government. It is a tawdry tale and few Chinese buy the official version, assuming that it was more about purging rivals than securing accountability and the rule of law. Bo's financial irregularities and abuses of power, reported extensively in the media, are assumed to be the norm among the Party elite. In 2012, for example, the *New York Times* reported that the family of Premier Wen Jiabao, perhaps the most revered and loved leader in 21st-century China, had socked away billions in assets based on dubious dealings. This became big news in China as the stench of corruption and sleaze reached from local cadres right to the very top of the Party hierarchy. Seldom is the Party's dirty laundry so prominently on display and thus, in this context, shifting attention to Japanese perfidy was expedient and effective. If there is one thing that Chinese can agree on it is a shared passion for vilifying Japan that feeds a penchant for embracing sanctimonious outrage and self-righteous nationalism. The lessons of national humiliation have been driven home and the Party reaps the windfall, but in doing so it has unleashed the genie of nationalism. In this context, advocating reasonable compromise runs the risk of denunciation, and emotions trump detached and pragmatic policy analysis. Emotions also run high in Japan's ongoing dispute with South Korea over a different set of rocky islets.

Dokdo/Takeshima: Islands of Eternal Dispute

Japan and South Korea are "frenemies," sharing much in common and enjoying close commercial ties, but remain hostage to a divisive history. Since 1953, Seoul has controlled these two rocky outcrops, a total landmass of 46 acres, but they were not a prominent source of bilateral tensions until 2005 when Japan became more assertive about its counter claim (Selden 2014). Tokyo claims that they are unlawfully occupied, while Seoul (like Japan with the Senkaku and Russia with the Kurils) does not even acknowledge that there is a territorial dispute. In South Korea, sovereignty over Dokdo is emotionally important to national identity and overcoming the indignities of colonial rule. As such, Japan's claims are dismissed as reminiscent of colonial-era injustices, while both sides make elaborate legal cases defending their positions. The competing historical claims provide no conclusive basis for settling the dispute (Dudden 2008). Suggestions to bring the case for arbitration to the International Court of Justice have not been pursued. South Korean officials oppose arbitration because it would be tantamount to admission that there is a dispute over something that is indisputable, and would add to the indignities that Korea suffered under Japanese rule. Koreans point out that Japan's claim dates back to 1905, precisely when Japan moved to assert control over Korea following its victory over Russia. The disposition of Dokdo is thus intertwined with the trauma of colonial subjugation and humiliation that lasted until 1945, a legacy that still agitates Korean national identity (Cumings 2005). There seems to be little prospect of a meeting of minds over these divisive rocks because the current dispute is rooted in a wider tableau of longstanding unresolved historical grievances.

The 1951 Treaty of San Francisco was drafted during the Korean War and there were concerns that acknowledging South Korean sovereignty over Dokdo might inadvertently award the islets to North Korea in the event it prevailed. The US was also keen not to alienate Japan by awarding the islets to Seoul. The deliberate vagueness and lack of clarity over sovereignty, not only over Dokdo, but also the Senkaku, might have seemed sensible then, but has proven a wellspring of regional tensions that have intensified in the 21st century (Hara 2007; Lee and Van Dyke 2010). In the 1965 treaty normalizing relations between Japan and South Korea, orchestrated by the US, Dokdo was also not mentioned, and thus Seoul's de facto control continued.

The 1982 United Nations Convention on the Law of the Sea (UNCLOS) suddenly increased the importance of both sets of islets (Dokdo/Takeshima and Senkaku/Diaoyu) because they provide the basis for establishing the right to claim territorial waters extending 12 nautical miles from the coastline and a 200-nautical-mile Exclusive Economic Zone (EEZ) (Drifte 2009, 2014). These legal developments suddenly ratcheted up the significance of the outcrops because of fishery rights and potential discovery of natural resources in the seabed. When UNCLOS went into effect in 1994, both Japan and South Korea claimed the 200-mile EEZ, creating yet another source of bilateral discord.

In 2005, Shimane Prefecture in Japan designated February 22nd as Takeshima Day; while in 2008 some Japanese secondary school textbooks for the first time asserted Japan's claims to the islands. As of 2011 all 12 Japanese middle school textbooks asserted these claims and four referred to South Korea's illegal occupation. Of course bilateral relations are not only about territorial claims, and at the grassroots level there is considerably more warmth and interaction than one would anticipate if focusing exclusively on diplomatic relations. Opinion polls suggest there is still a high degree of mutual disregard, but in the aftermath of Japan's massive earthquake and tsunami in March 2011, South Korea raised more charitable donations in the subsequent month than any other nation. In April 2011, however, Japan's Ministry of Foreign Affairs issued a bluebook asserting Japan's Takeshima claims, and donations dried up, a poignant reminder of how relations remain hostage to nationalism. This festering sore in bilateral relations is a symptom of the broader problems of these nations' shared and troubled past.

In August 2012, South Korean President Lee Myung Bak crossed a diplomatic red line by making an unprecedented landing on the disputed Dokdo/Takeshima islands, sparking harsh invective from Japan, ranging from government spokesmen and blaring soundtrucks to Netizens venting their spleen on the Internet. No previous Korean leader had set foot on the disputed territory, precisely because doing so would be considered recklessly provocative. Throwing fuel on the fire, Lee also demanded that Emperor Akihito apologize for Japanese colonial oppression (1910–1945) as a precondition for him visiting the peninsula. While Lee derailed bilateral diplomatic relations, his actions and words drew effusive reactions at home, and even inspired some Olympic drama.

At the 2012 London Olympics fans around the world got a taste of just how fiercely felt the territorial dispute can be. The day after Lee's visit, a South Korean soccer player celebrated a 2-0 victory over Japan in the bronze medal match by displaying a sign declaring, "Dokdo is our territory." He was banned from the medal podium, but lionized at home and exempted from compulsory military service. All over Seoul's subway system there are Dokdo posters, and there are scale models of Dokdo at the central station and the Korean War Memorial Museum, with much more at the popular Dokdo Museum in Seoul; while travel agencies promote Dokdo tours. The feud also has more macabre moments such as when Koreans severed their own fingers in front of the Japanese Embassy protesting Japan's claims, or when they flung rocks at the ambassador. Clearly, Dokdo has become an outsized flashpoint for South Korean nationalism and anti-Japanese sentiments. Such is the power of nationalism to endow what may seem inconsequential with powerful symbolism.

Oddly enough, Lee is probably the most pro-Japanese leader of South Korea since President Park Chung-hee (1961–1979). So why did he purposely provoke Japan in such a public manner? Dwelling on past misdeeds plays well with the public. Nationalism among Koreans is rooted in fiery anti-Japanese sentiments and Japan has long been a trump card for Korea's political leaders at times of declining popularity. Koreans are deeply divided—regionally, politically and generationally—but flaying the Japanese is reliably unifying and usually leads to a boost in the polls. Lee, whose approval rating sank to 17% before his visit, was ensnared in a corruption scandal involving his family, a common problem for Korean leaders. His party was also in trouble, with presidential elections looming, and he wanted to rally grassroots support. In addition, his gesture signaled frustration with Japan's repeated refusals to revisit the comfort women issue.

Nationalist posturing over the islands is nothing new, as in 2006 South Korea's president Roh Moo-hyun threatened force to prevent Japanese Coast Guard vessels

Figure 10.1 Museum Visitors Can Have Their Photo Taken with Dokdo as Backdrop. Photo © Jeff Kingston.

from mapping the adjacent seabed. Washington intervened with its allies to prevent the feud from escalating. In some respects, the US presence may actually be contributing to the brinksmanship as Tokyo and Seoul believe that Washington would not permit a violent clash to erupt, allowing both governments to act more provocatively than they might otherwise. The US is weary of the constant squabbling over history and wants both governments to get over the past, and get on with becoming reliable US allies that can cooperate more productively. US Secretary of Defense Chuck Hagel visited the Blue House in October 2013 to persuade President Park to ease up on criticizing Japan over unresolved historical grievances, and was apparently unprepared for the resulting nationalistic tirade. Park reminded Hagel that Germany's reentry into the community of Europe would have been impossible if its leaders had acted as irresponsibly as Japanese leaders towards its wartime history. She pointed out that Germany's unqualified acknowledgement of its war responsibility and significant gestures of contrition and atonement for Nazi war crimes were the foundation of its rehabilitation, reintegration and redemption, while Japanese still deny and minimize the havoc they wrought in Asia during Japan's imperial era from 1895 to 1945. Hagel came to understand that unresolved historical grievances drive and amplify the territorial standoff and limit prospects for any resolution, a situation with troubling parallels elsewhere in Asia.

Kashmir

Kashmir is a land of sweeping valleys and pristine lakes in the Himalayan region of northwestern India that is claimed in full by India and Pakistan and ruled in part by both. They have fought three wars over the region, in 1947, 1965 and 1999. China also asserts claims there and controls a much smaller portion of Kashmir in the northeastern area of Ladakh called Aksai Chin, a mostly uninhabited high-altitude desert area. The Sino-Indian war in 1962 was related to rival border claims partly in this region.

Kashmir is where Indian and Pakistani nationalisms clash, sidelining Kashmiri aspirations. Given its location and history, Kashmir serves as a lightning rod for India's Hindu chauvinists and their nationalist agenda. The territory embodies some familiar characteristics of nationalism—historical injustice, threat, border disputes, and fanaticism stoked by religious zealotry. A UN Line of Control, ostensibly a temporary boundary awaiting a plebiscite to gauge the popular will, separates Pakistan and India in what has become a heavily militarized zone of occupation. It is the unfinished business of the 1947 Partition, the disastrous British policy that sparked communal violence and led to the death of some 1 million amidst the uprooting and relocation of Muslim and Hindu communities. India has long accused Pakistan of arming, infiltrating and funding militant Islamic groups that periodically clash with Indian forces in Kashmir, and also backing terrorist attacks in New Delhi and Mumbai. India stands accused of a heavy-handed occupation in Kashmir where it has some half a million troops stationed; the population in the Kashmir valley is about 4 million and 95% are Muslim.

In 1947 Hari Singh was the reigning maharaja of Kashmir when the British hastened their departure and Partition took its toll in lives and political chaos. At the time some three-quarters of the population were Islamic. Fearing Pakistani designs on Kashmir, New Delhi convinced the maharaja to accede to Indian rule and dispatched troops to drive out Pakistani paramilitary forces. This precipitated the 1947 war that ended with a UN-negotiated ceasefire in 1948, with the promise of a plebiscite to allow self-determination by Kashmiris. This promise has never been implemented, and since then Kashmir has served as a major source of tension and contestation between the neighbors, again erupting into war in 1965 and 1999. Owing to periodic skirmishing and the possession of nuclear weapons by both claimants, Kashmir is considered one of the most dangerous and volatile flashpoints in Asia.

Kashmiri nationalism is viewed as a threat to Indian national unity and a secessionist movement that needs to be squashed. Ramachandra Guha (2012, 19) asserts that there are four main factors driving Kashmiri separatism: (1) distance from the

Indian cultural and administrative heartland; (2) the appeal of nationalism to young men; (3) legal impunity for Indian security forces committing human rights abuses; and (4) New Delhi's support for corrupt politicians in Kashmir. The excessive use of force to impose central control fans the flames of separatism, creating new martyrs to be avenged by successive generations of Kashmiris because the Armed Forces Special Powers Act shields soldiers from accountability. The escalating secession–repression dynamic creates a basis for ceaseless conflict.

Guha warns against romanticizing "little nationalisms" because they can be as ugly as the large Indian nationalism they confront. He also raises the issue of viability, questioning whether the tiny landlocked territory of Kashmir could become a sustainable state, economically and politically, or whether it might become "a receptacle for Al-Qaeda" (Guha 2012, 20). He suggests reconciling the little nationalism with the inclusiveness of India, providing meaningful autonomy within the Union. India is, after all, one of the most plural nations in the world, accommodating a large number of religions and ethnicities because of its capacity for diversity. But crafting a resolution that accommodates the agendas of both little and large nationalisms seems unlikely since they are antithetical in aims. Certainly Guha is correct to point out that the leaders of Hurriyat, the Kashmiri secessionist movement, do not seem inspiring candidates to lead Kashmir into a 21st-century land of the free, but they are a product of India's praetorian presence. Prolongation of the status quo of heavily armed occupation does not seem to offer hope for a more promising scenario or the emergence of better local leaders.

Othering the Muslim Menace

In February 2013, India executed a Kashmiri, Afzal Guru, for allegedly conspiring with militants who carried out an attack on parliament in 2001, triggering clashes in the strife-torn region. India holds Pakistan responsible for orchestrating the terrorist attack and the incident almost sparked the fourth war between the nuclear-armed rivals as 1 million soldiers were mobilized along the border. Security forces killed the five Muslim militants linked to Pakistan-based Jaish-e-Mohammed who conducted the attack. Guru was convicted of conspiring with them and offering shelter, but flaws in the prosecution's evidence and inadequacies of legal representation cast a cloud over the decision. His abrupt execution before his family was informed, and denial of a family funeral, aroused further ire in Kashmir and a degree of guilt among Indian liberals. Critics assert that the conviction was based on circumstantial evidence and the execution timed to electoral maneuvering as the Congress Party sought to deflect BJP criticism that it is "soft" on Islamic militancy. This politicization of justice is a dangerous menace given the volatility of nationalist and communal passions.

While India shifts blame to Pakistan and Islamic fundamentalists, it is not easy for it to deny the desire of Kashmiris to see the end of Indian occupation (*Economist* 2010). The 2014 film *Haidar*, based on *Hamlet* and a screenplay by Basharat Peer, a prominent Kashmiri journalist, shows why few of his fellow Kashmiris see any future under Indian rule. Kashimiris are subject to state-sponsored terrorism as security forces and their accomplices resort systematically to extra-judicial means to combat those who have become radicalized by the occupation (Peer 2010). While the specter of Islamic radicalism is invoked to justify repression, this diverts attention from local desire for freedom and overlooks that there is very little support among Kashmiris for a more fundamentalist Islam. Arundhati Roy, activist and Booker Prize-winning novelist, draws attention to the propaganda machine of Hindu fundamentalists that manipulates the media in India and vilifies Kashmiris to stoke popular nationalism among Indians (Ali 2011). In her view, Bollywood abets these efforts to caricature Kashmiris as bloodthirsty Islamic terrorists. Mishra also questions whether fundamentalism has much appeal in Kashmir, where a more tolerant Sufi Islam prevails, but in the post-9/11 world, Islam has become the enemy of convenience, one that justifies extreme actions (Ali 2011). Kashmiris are portrayed as the terrorist Other, agents of Pakistan, that must be suppressed by whatever means and who deserve what they get.

Successive generations of Kashmiris know India for its violence and curbing of civil liberties. Roy asserts that the excesses in Kashmir are part of a larger Islamophobia played out all over India:

> The Indian military occupation of Kashmir makes monsters of us all. It allows Hindu chauvinists to target and victimize Muslims in India by holding them hostage to the freedom struggle waged by Muslims in Kashmir. (Ali 2011, 71)

The notion that a predominantly Muslim Kashmir would become a hotbed of anti-Indian Islamic extremism if ceded to Pakistan or given freedom serves to justify the continued occupation. Viewed through the prism of Hindu nationalism, many Indians know Kashmir as a hotbed of Pakistani treachery, Islamic fundamentalism, and terrorism.

There is a curious silence about the Kashmir problem among India's reliably vocal punditry. It is an embarrassing situation because the military occupation and extensive human rights abuses are a black mark on India's reputation and draw attention to the yawning gap between professed democratic ideals and grim realities. It is, like the longstanding Naxalite uprising in large stretches of central India, a case where a near total reliance on security forces impinges on civil liberties and makes a mockery of democratic norms and values. The rule of law is ignored as the central government seeks to impose its writ by force of arms, generating a predictable backlash.

It is hard to measure the toll of Indian nationalism in Kashmir; over 80,000 civilians have been killed there during India's occupation and yet, except in times of acute crisis, it slips under the global media radar. Indians remain largely unaware of the brutal realities and are quick to rationalize the excesses as a necessary evil. Generations of Kashmiris have been traumatized by the faceoff and by the massive Indian security presence. It is an undesired occupation and one that most Kashmiris feel is the real threat to peace and prosperity.

Basharat Peer believes that Kashmir represents a stain on Indian democracy. Noting the massive Indian security presence, Peer dubs Kashmir a "siege democracy," insisting that in a referendum the people would vote overwhelmingly for independence. For Peer, "Kashmir exposes a blind spot in the self-deluding mainstream liberal consensus about the Idea of India, a monstrous conceit that ignores many realities on the ground" (personal communication, December 2013).

India's Tibet?

Does Kashmir represent India's Tibet? Perhaps, according to some Indian specialists at a seminar hosted by the Institute for Chinese Studies in New Delhi towards the end of 2013. Both have been subject to extensive violence and both are blind spots in public perceptions and mainstream discourse. Tibet's incorporation into modern China and Kashmir's into India were baptized by coercion and violence. Tibet was invaded and subdued while Kashmir succumbed to Indian threats and then became a battlefield where India and Pakistan vied for control. As with India in Kashmir, China maintains that its presence has had a positive influence and asserts that the feudal theocracy that previously ruled Tibet was exploitative and condemned Tibetans to servitude and poverty. While Chinese sovereignty over Tibet appears secure, China, like India in Kashmir, is subject to persistent and widespread criticism of its human rights record there. Nationalists in both nations are especially prickly about foreign recriminations and respond with dubious justifications laced with invective.

Certainly, the plight of Kashmiris does not arouse the global sympathy and support enjoyed by Tibetans. There are no internationally renowned Hollywood actors campaigning for a free Kashmir, and there are far fewer international human rights campaigners focused on Kashmir. While Chinese leaders face global hostility over Tibet, Indian leaders can travel overseas without worrying about being dogged by hostile demonstrations over abuses in Kashmir. This doesn't mean there is no international recognition of the human rights abuses in Kashmir, but it is not a black mark for India in the way Tibet is for China. Perhaps this is because there is no Kashmiri Dalai Lama—one of the most masterful spokesmen for any oppressed people anywhere.

Kashmir resembles Tibet in the unyielding central government insistence that independence is not an option. Both nations rely heavily on security forces to consolidate control and in both cases confront a religious-based opposition. But there the parallels end. Beijing actively encourages Hanification of Tibet by encouraging migration to promote assimilation. As a result, Tibetans have become marginalized in their own society and the Han control the local economy, another potent source of grievance (see Chapter 11). The spate of Tibetan self-immolations in recent years serves as a symbol of Beijing's dead-end policies and the depth of Tibetans' anguish over the accelerating erosion of their cultural identity and marginalization in their homeland.

There is concern that the presence of the Dalai Lama and the Tibetan government in exile in northern India negatively influences Sino-Indian relations. There seems to be a correlation between Tibetan unrest and rough patches in bilateral relations as Beijing seethes over Indian support for reviled "secessionists." Indeed, coinciding with Prime Minister Manmohan Singh's visit to China in October 2013, Beijing issued a white paper blaming the Dalai Lama and his supporters for instigating border problems. China occupies part of what Kashmiris consider their territory, but otherwise doesn't interfere

"Chindia," a concept based on civilizational ties and enormous but largely unrealized potential for robust economic ties, faces some tough realities beyond Tibetan issues. The 1962 border war with China may not remotely approach the 1947 Partition in India's closet of traumas, but it remains a powerful reminder that the two nations share a long border with vast un-demarcated stretches that remain a source of rancor and tensions. Indian troops were routed and since then the disparity in conventional military strength has widened considerably. In April 2013, just prior to Premier Li Keqiang's visit, intruding Chinese troops bivouacked in disputed territory, a novel way to announce the pending arrival of a dignitary. The platoon withdrew only after India acquiesced to Beijing's demands to destroy some bunkers. Since then, in keeping with his more assertive nationalism, Prime Minister Modi has ordered the building of more fortifications and infrastructure along the border, and avoided diplomatic niceties in explicitly referring to the dispute on his visit to Beijing in May 2015.

Returning to our discussion of Kashmir as India's Tibet, under Article 370 of the Indian Constitution, the state of Jammu and Kashmir enjoys a guaranteed special status granting autonomy and certain privileges and protections that serve as the basis of integration. One of the main differences with Tibet is that non-Kashmiris are prohibited from owning land in Kashmir. This protects Kashmir from being inundated by Hindu Indians and therefore allows them greater control over their economy. While most Kashmiris would prefer independence to autonomy, they have been able to better protect their cultural identity and avoid the fate of Tibet and Xinjiang where Han cultural imperialism spreads relentlessly and destructively (see Chapter 11). To some degree Kashmiri autonomy has been eroded over the years as it has been forced to adopt national laws and accept the Supreme Court's writ, but Article 370 has been an effective barrier and thus is targeted by nationalists.

The BJP and associated organizations have long campaigned to abrogate Article 370 because it is an affront to Hindutva and their vision of national integration on Hindu terms. Exclusion of Hindus from owning property in Kashmir and special status provide an opportunity for ethno-religious nationalist mobilization, again pitting the Muslim Other against the Hindu majority. Moreover, there are unresolved Hindu grievances in Kashmir. Chiefly these involve the Kashmiri Pandits, a Hindu Brahmin minority community that has mostly fled the state due to threats to life and property; many were landlords and suffered considerable losses. On the eve of independence in 1947, Pandits constituted nearly 15% of the Kashmiri population. Communal riots in 1948 and land reform in 1950 led to the departure of about 20%

of Pandits and by the 1980s they represented just 5% of the valley's total population. Subsequently, in the 1990s there was a mass exodus of Pandits as they were targeted by Islamic militants with Pakistani backing and subjected to violence and intimidation. By 2010 the number of Pandits living in the valley had declined to 3,445 people, down from approximately 140,000 in 1980. Many of the displaced Pandits languish in refugee camps in Hindu-majority Jammu, awaiting an improvement in the security situation that does not seem likely to develop anytime soon. Their plight is largely forgotten and neither the BJP nor Congress has done much to alleviate their difficult circumstances.

At the end of 2013, BJP leader Narendra Modi stirred controversy over Kashmir by calling for debate about whether or not Article 370 benefits Kashmiris and suggesting that rather than providing protection, this constitutional dispensation actually hinders development and undermines living standards. This shift in strategy from relying on arguments drawing on an emotional Hindu chauvinism to ostensibly focusing on rational development criteria and sound economic policies is similar to the BJP's overall makeover and the reinvention of Modi himself. Raking up Kashmir's special status was criticized as an electoral ploy to portray the BJP as the best party to promote economic development while also slyly appealing to chauvinistic elements in its Hindutva base that want to bring this frontier area under their sway. Critics have also asserted that removing that status appeals to Indian businesses seeking access to the commercial property and real estate market and tapping into Kashmir's tourism potential. Clearly, Modi touched a national nerve, stirring controversy and debate, as he surely intended.

East Timor

Indonesia invaded East Timor in 1975 and occupied this territory until 1999 when it held a referendum and the people overwhelmingly voted for independence. East Timor had been colonized by Portugal since the 16th century, while the Dutch half of the island, West Timor, was part of the Netherlands East Indies. When Indonesia won independence in 1949, it gained control over West Timor, while East Timor remained a Portuguese colony until 1974 when a military coup by left-wing officers toppled the government in Lisbon. Suddenly, with no preparation, all of Portugal's empire was given independence, including East Timor. At the time it was one of the poorest, least developed places on earth owing to Portugal's neglect and minimal investment in health, education and infrastructure. A civil war broke out between rival parties in East Timor, with Fretelin, a left-wing party, emerging victorious and declaring independence in November 1975. With Washington's blessing, Indonesia launched an invasion in December 1975 and incorporated East Timor as a province in 1976. The threadbare Cold War justification likened East Timor to Cuba, a potential threat to Jakarta that required resolute action to halt the spread of communism. In 1975 a defeated and war-weary US withdrew from Vietnam, raising concerns in Washington about losing regional influence to communist expansion. This anxiety drew on the 1950s domino theory embodying fears that Asian nations would be taken over by communist forces and topple in succession like dominoes, leaving all Asia under communism. In this context, US President Ford was happy to give a green light to President Suharto's invasion. The UN Security Council, however, did not recognize this change of status by force of arms, creating a major diplomatic problem for Indonesia through the end of the century.

The international community spotlighted extensive human rights abuses in East Timor by the Indonesian military. The long Indonesian occupation was brutal, causing over 100,000 deaths from military encounters and deprivation of food and medicine. Fretelin's guerilla forces enjoyed widespread public support and made the most of the island's mountainous terrain and jungle cover to sustain a fierce resistance against the larger and better-equipped Indonesian military. Over the years, Indonesia fought a losing battle in the global court of public opinion as news trickled out about various atrocities. In 1991 Indonesian security forces killed over 250 pro-independence demonstrators who had gathered at Santa Cruz cemetery in Dili following a church memorial service for a recently executed activist. Foreign journalists who witnessed the massacre mobilized international condemnation of Jakarta's brutality.

As a result, diplomatic isolation and pressure over East Timor mounted in the 1990s, tarnishing the reputation of President Suharto and Indonesia while highlighting the dark side of the New Order regime. In that sense, the occupation of East Timor was seen to be symptomatic of the violent nature of an authoritarian regime that staked its claim to legitimacy on maintaining stability, raising living standards, delivering growth and maintaining good relations with western governments. In many respects, Indonesia was viewed as a success story—a secular government in the world's most populous Islamic nation that followed the Washington Consensus on development and financial policymaking. As a resource-rich nation sitting astride the main waterways linking Asia with the Middle East, Indonesia was viewed as a strategic linchpin. It is thus not surprising that for many years western leaders averted their eyes from widespread abuses of power as *realpolitik* trumped political principles and humanitarian concerns.

The strategic calculus didn't change in the 1990s, but the media drew sustained attention to sordid realities in Indonesia and East Timor that redefined the global image of Suharto, known as the smiling general overseas and the father of development at home. Experts on Indonesia knew the score, but the spread of critical media coverage in the 1990s sparked an international furor about what few had cared to know about. The Indonesian government felt aggrieved by the sudden turn of events, with Foreign Minister Ali Alatas famously likening East Timor to "a pebble in the shoe," an irritant more than a major issue that undermined Indonesia's hard-earned international goodwill and support. The intensified scrutiny, however, snowballed into a major public relations disaster that Indonesia was unable to counter. What had previously been acceptable under Cold War rules no longer measured up to evolving international norms and values in the post-Cold War 1990s. The western media played a key role in Indonesia's fall from grace, making it awkward for western leaders to openly support Jakarta. For example, in 1994, the US suspended military aid to Indonesia due to human rights violations in East Timor.

East Timor was a critical flashpoint for Indonesia not because of the low-intensity guerilla campaign, but because it became its diplomatic scarlet letter. Indonesians knew little about the situation in East Timor and what they did know was largely influenced by government propaganda efforts that emphasized positive developments, and conspiratorial assertions about an international defamation campaign. After President Suharto stepped down in May 1998, his successor, Vice President B.J. Habibie, announced in a BBC interview his agreement to a referendum in East Timor that would include the option of self-determination. It does not appear that he had deliberated extensively within the government or with the armed forces over this rather significant initiative. But once he announced it and the international community and media praised the bold move, the casual remark took on a life of its own and led to a UN-supervised popular referendum in August 1999.

International criticism in the run-up to the referendum in 1999 sparked a powerful nationalist backlash in the Indonesian media and angry denunciations by various groups, including the military. There was an intertwined sense of embarrassment, defensiveness and anger that the UN was stepping in, suggesting that Jakarta was not to be trusted in facilitating a free and fair plebiscite. There were also strong feelings of betrayal on the part of Indonesian security and paramilitary forces in East Timor who suddenly faced the prospect of losing control to the guerilla forces that they had been trying to vanquish. What had they been fighting for? The paramilitaries were more vulnerable since they were often Timorese, who faced reprisals since they had collaborated with the Indonesian military and were implicated in human rights abuses. This was the explosive context in the summer of 1999 as the UN carried out its mandate amidst hostility and simmering violence. Knowing that Timorese preferred independence, security forces engaged in a blatant campaign of intimidation to keep voters away from the polls and remind them that there would be dire consequences if they voted for freedom. In the event, the turnout was high and 78.5% of the Timorese, expressing their nationalism, opted for independence under the watchful eyes of UN officials and international delegations of observers.

The scorched earth campaign by paramilitaries that ensued, with ample support from Indonesian security forces, was widely anticipated and proved to be a horrific reign of terror. Indonesia had invested far more than Portugal in raising living standards, promoting health and education, but the vindictive anti-independence forces were determined to erase all improvements and exact revenge on a people who refused to be cowed or to acquiesce to Indonesia's aggrieved nationalism and intimidation. This punitive campaign involved arson, targeting schools and clinics, ensuring that the newly independent East Timor would have a deep hole to climb out of. There were also random and targeted killings and disappearances as the newest nation appeared on the brink of chaos, and internecine violence threatened its very existence. Indeed that was precisely the intention of the instigators, for whom a free East Timor was a nightmare of lost privileges, frustrated ambitions and betrayal of Indonesian nationalism. They sought to create a pretext for the Indonesian military to intervene and hit the reset button on independence. But the Australian military answered the UN's call and dispatched troops to quell the violence and restore law and order. They did so, but not until after considerable damage had been done.

In 2002, East Timor became the first new state of the 21st century, and it has since tried to heal the scars inflicted during Indonesia's prolonged occupation. The two nations made an effort towards reconciliation with the bilateral Committee on Truth and Friendship (2005–2009). President Susilo Bambang Yudhoyono accepted the findings of gross violations of human rights, but it is fair to say that the prolonged deliberations did not promote much reconciliation because the Committee raised expectations among Timorese for justice and accountability that were not met. The Timorese leadership chose not to pursue justice, and accepted an incomplete reckoning, because they believed it was more important to develop a future-oriented relationship with their giant neighbor and saw more benefit from establishing trust and nurturing cooperation than from prosecuting perpetrators. For most Indonesians, East Timor is a matter of little consequence, a problem on the fringes of the sprawling archipelago, but it is precisely in the fringes where the dangers of nationalism are often in evidence, as we discuss in the next chapter.

11

Nationalism and the Fringes

Nationalism arouses solidarity and generates identity politics that carry onerous consequences for ethnic and religious minorities. Defining the "we" also defines who "they" are. Those that do not fit the mainstream mold, or in some way challenge that imagined community of insiders, can serve as convenient targets that bolster the mainstream identity. A useful "other," they are marginalized and harassed, as discussed in the preceding chapter in the case of Kashmir and Tibet, where inhabitants of a frontier area embrace distinctive identities. The project of defining the mainstream community depends significantly on those outside the imagined boundaries because "they" are not "us," generating a useful tension in forging a national identity that carries political consequences. Those who perceive they are at the fringes of mainstream society, either due to minority status or geographical location, and feel disadvantaged by exclusion from what is embraced by the prevailing mainstream national identity, may try to fully assimilate, find a niche within the mainstream, or seek an autonomous identity on the fringes—or a combination of all three coping strategies, depending on circumstances.

What Guha refers to as the "little nationalisms" of minorities and outlying regions are perceived as a threat by those advocating a unified and homogenous Hindu-centered national identity which is the antithesis of the original idea of India rooted in an all-encompassing unity that accommodates and honors the sub-continent's incredible diversity (Guha 2012). In responding to these perceived threats, the state tends to rely on soldiers and police for pacification, while intensifying processes of assimilation. Such efforts are intrinsic to the state's nationalism project, one aimed at strengthening a sense of "we" and establishing the figurative and literal boundaries of nation. Guha points out, however, that these little nationalisms can also be ugly,

Nationalism in Asia: A History Since 1945, First Edition. Jeff Kingston.

cautioning against romanticizing what can become localized thuggery, tyranny and random violence.

The competing identity politics in the mainstream and fringes of society carry a high risk of sectarian or communal violence, involving periodic outbursts of score settling or reprisals for what are deemed provocations. As we examine below, repression is a key consequence of nationalism at the fringes, one that entails political consequences threatening to security. State abuses of authority and impunity transform grievances into a collective identity, generating defiance, militancy and a cycle of violence. South Korea's volatile fringe is North Korea, but the divided peninsula is a rather unique situation beyond the scope of this chapter.

China's Fringes

Towards the end of 2014 Beijing confronted the angry little nationalism of pro-democracy protesters in Hong Kong, the so-called umbrella revolution. Locals were asserting a democratic identity that the Party deemed unacceptable since the protests targeted its reforms aimed at curtailing Hong Kong's democratic freedoms. Of course Beijing and its local representatives prevailed, but for the Party it was an embarrassing outburst because it was an assertion of an identity on the people's terms not dictated by the Party. Taiwan's robust democracy is another awkward issue for Beijing because it has also become intrinsic to that island's identity, reinforcing its image as a renegade province. Given the special status of these two territories, and intensive international scrutiny, the central government is careful in managing this southern fringe. Elsewhere it is a different story.

China is home to numerous small ethnic minorities, but multicultural rhetoric notwithstanding, ethnic Han culture dominates in a pervasive and often discriminatory manner. Balancing the dictates of national integration, China's overriding priority, with the need for managing ethno-cultural diversity has been an ongoing struggle, and in Tibet and Xinjiang an abject failure. Current policies of ethnic autonomy and minority preferences tend to accentuate ethnic segregation and limit interethnic interactions. Restrictions on ethnic mobility are also problematic, creating a "ghettoized" effect. Beijing has in effect locked in ethnic differences and disparities that undermine its goal of strengthening national unity. Reformers in China believe that substantial changes are inevitable, but implementing the integrationist policy adjustments they support will be subtle and incremental at best, a long-term process ensuring that tensions will persist, fanned by draconian security measures.

In strategically sensitive frontier border areas like Tibet and Xinjiang, adjacent to India, Russia and Central Asian nations, Beijing emphasizes security and consolidation of control. There are signs of greater security cooperation on curtailing cross-border support for Uighur separatists in Xinjiang, a priority for Beijing. China has moved diplomatically to secure its "near abroad" in Central Asia through the Shanghai Cooperation Organization, and has also invested vast amounts—$100 billion in 2013 alone—in various energy projects, spawning a web of connections in these nations with a vested interest in maintaining good ties. China's rapid economic modernization has also increased the importance of the vast natural resources of Xinjiang and Tibet; tapping Xinjiang's huge oil and gas potential proceeds apace, while the mineral and water resources of Tibet are attracting a massive influx of investments.

Minority policies have done little to nurture interethnic trust or improve interethnic disparities in income, education and employment. Officially, the regions enjoy some autonomy and there is a system of preferences for local minorities, but in practice Beijing and its representatives decide on policy issues, with relatively few local minorities benefiting amid institutionalized discrimination. Denigrating and condescending Han stereotypes about minorities are suffused with fear and a sense of threat. The Muslim Uighurs from Xinjiang, numbering about 8.5 million, and 6.5 million Buddhist Tibetans have resisted assimilation despite sustained efforts at "Hanification." Both groups harbor strong resentments against Beijing that sometimes erupt into violence, quickly and often brutally suppressed by security officials, ensuring a cycle of violence persists.

The fundamental problem is that the dictates of Han-centric nationalism don't leave much space for anything resembling multiculturalism beyond a Disneyfied celebration of colorful costumes and quaint or curious customs. The expanding economic and political brawn of Han Chinese weighs heavily on ethnic minorities and the rising China story has brought mixed benefits at best as they confront a Han triumphalism. It is worth emphasizing here that Chinese nationalism is all about Han nationalism. In a country that has lost its moorings while experiencing tremendous socio-economic convulsions, nationalism is a reassuring and expedient ideology that creates a sense of unity among a people experiencing yawning disparities, environmental devastation, corruption and other abuses of power. The Party has discovered a lifeline in nationalism, appealing to Han chauvinism to assert a dubious legitimacy. In such a context, non-Han Chinese face an accelerating threat to their way of life and identity. The Han have stoked antagonism through acts of cultural arrogance, ignorance and harsh oppression that reinforce local identities and resistance to assimilation.

The expansion of transport and communication networks has brought the fringes of China under ever-increasing Han sway, generating frictions and uncomfortable cultural clashes that have become the new norm. Once isolated, minority groups have increasingly lost the protection of distance and have become targets of ambitious development projects. In Xinjiang, colorful Uighur markets and communities have been razed and replaced with ugly concrete structures, while the glittery signs of progress Han-style are evident in enclaves separated from the bleaker conditions that prevail. The boom towns in the oil and gas regions of Xinjiang offer glaring contrasts to local lifestyles and living standards, a divide that is replicated in Tibet. In both regions, locals take a back seat to Han in commerce and government.

Uighurs and Tibetans resent this Han domination of the local economies, while government officials tick off the statistical advances that have been achieved in improving living standards and modernizing these "backward" regions. Understandably these minorities are not grateful for the claimed improvements that leave them feeling disempowered and downtrodden. The Tibetans and Uighurs, with good reason, attribute evident disparities to pervasive discrimination. Han get the best jobs, best salaries and live the relatively good life. As Han enclaves expand and disparities grow more visible and acute, there is a natural sense of relative deprivation. And the security forces are a praetorian presence that stirs tensions. Chinese explain their dominating presence in terms of skills and financial resources lacking in these remote frontiers in western China. They point out that by any measure—health, education, nutrition, living standards—both regions are far better off now than 20 years ago and can't quite understand why the people are so angry and ungrateful. Xinjiang's urban annual income doubled between 2000 and 2009, while rural incomes have tripled in the same time, growth is roaring and infrastructure is rapidly expanding. But as the Beijing-based author Wang Lixiong points out, unemployment is high and the influx of 8 million Han over the past five decades, now 40% of Xinjiang's population, is a major grievance (Wang 2014). Chinese officials blame the local people for not having the right qualities and explain their poverty in terms of their own failings, but locals feel that they are systematically excluded from sharing in the fruits of growth. It is this growth that has attracted an influx of Han, entailing greater encroachment on daily life which heightens political tensions.

Tibet

Tibet is an elevated plateau region to the northeast of the Himalayas. The dominant religion is Tibetan Buddhism and the people have their own language and culture and once ruled over an empire. Tibet was first brought into the Sinic orbit under the Mongolian Yuan dynasty in the 13th century, but continued to enjoy a degree of political autonomy, which increased dramatically in the 19th century as the Qing dynasty weakened and could no longer assert its influence. Following the collapse of the Qing dynasty, from 1912 to 1949 Tibet enjoyed de facto independence, but was isolated diplomatically and Lhasa was closed to the outside world. At the time, China's government was weak and increasingly menaced by Japan. Growing tensions driven by Japan's imperial designs and anti-Japanese nationalism erupted into war from 1931 to 1945.

In 1949, Tibet expelled all Chinese, a provocation that led to Mao's troops invading and establishing control in 1950. During the 1950s, China abolished slavery and serfdom while promoting land reform. It maintained a large troop presence and encountered sporadic rebellions and guerilla attacks. The Dalai Lama's siblings cooperated with the CIA, providing intelligence and contacts. In 1959 there was an uprising throughout Tibet challenging Chinese rule, but the People's Liberation Army (PLA) suppressed this and the Dalai Lama fled to India where he established a government in exile with the support of the Indian government. The 1962 Sino-Indian border war involved overlapping claims in Kashmir's Aksai Chin region and Southern Tibet, the latter area ceded to British India by Lhasa in 1914. The Republic of China at that time denounced this agreement as illegal and did not recognize the border. After winning the 1962 war, however, having made their point, Chinese troops withdrew north of the McMahon line that served as the de facto border between Chinese Tibet and Indian Southern Tibet, established in 1914.

In 1965 the region was renamed the Tibetan Autonomous Region (TAR), but half a century later the role of Tibetans in the upper echelons of the TAR government remains very limited and there is not much autonomy. Ethnic Han are assigned to state jobs in Tibet and various development projects in the region require expertise only available among ethnic Han. Beijing is also investing heavily in infrastructure to help tap the resources of Tibet and has constructed the world's highest railway to link Lhasa with Beijing, a symbolic connection demonstrating that Tibet is integrated into the mainland. This has led to a surge of tourism and inward investments to accommodate and service the tourists, but again the Han benefit disproportionately. The government has invested heavily in refurbishing Tibetan monasteries and cultural attractions so that the tourist can encounter the "real" Tibet and also to counter accusations that it is stifling Tibetan culture and Buddhism, but this PR campaign has had limited success.

In Tibet, the seeds of resistance were sowed in the 1950s and 1960s when China asserted sovereignty, suppressed rebellions and insurgency and dismantled the existing feudal social order. Following the 1959 uprising and the Dalai Lama's departure, an estimated 6,000 monasteries were destroyed and monastic estates were abolished. During the Cultural Revolution (1966–1971), Red Guards vandalized important heritage sites all over China, including Tibet. The widespread desecration of sacred Buddhist temples by Red Guards and abiding communist antipathy to the theocracy and religious practices that are the heart of Tibetan culture, community and way of life have created a clash of civilizations in the Tibetan plateau. The Chinese government has abandoned communism, but the brash nouveau riche materialism that has emerged equally threatens to overwhelm Tibet as Beijing expands tourism and extracts its natural resources to bolster economic growth, with scant concern for the environmental or social consequences. The ongoing "gold rush" involves massive mining operations for gold, copper, lithium, silver and chromium, while civil engineers divert watersheds and threaten regional river systems in South and Southeast Asia (Lafitte 2013). Along with spiritual desecration, this resource plundering and consequent environmental despoilment represents a further affront to Tibetans. They shoulder the attendant costs while Han reap the rewards. Similarly, China seeks to hollow out Tibetan culture and render it into a commodity for mass tourism, but this Han conceit of transforming Tibet into a theme park also rankles.

The bloody riots in Lhasa that erupted in 2008 and spread throughout the plateau belie Beijing's claims of "harmonious ethnic relations." Local Tibetans targeted ethnic Han businesses, venting their frustrations about the social, cultural and economic consequences of the increasing presence of strangers in their homeland. There was a harsh security crackdown and widespread human rights violations that sparked a wave of self-immolations, a "weapon of the weak" against the powerful state. Tibetan resentments have not abated and Beijing seems to have run out of ideas about how to lower tensions and make integration attractive to Tibetans, relying more on the stick than carrots.

Between February 2009 and May 2015 an estimated 141 Tibetans committed self-immolation to protest Chinese rule. The immolations embarrass the Chinese government because they make a tragic counterpoint to government claims about the benefits of Chinese development while underscoring the failures of Chinese attempts at multiculturalism. Authorities have suppressed media coverage of the immolations and arrested monks and supporters for inciting and coercing people to torch themselves. The Dalai Lama in exile is cautious about provoking China and refrains from commenting about the suicides because he doesn't want to hurt the feelings of relatives of those who have made the ultimate sacrifice. It is unlikely that Tibetans will achieve freedom or secure the Dalai Lama's return, but that does not keep them from hoping. Tibetan leaders seek common ground with the over 300 million Han Chinese Buddhists who also strive for greater cultural and religious freedom, but there are no signs yet of much solidarity.

Beijing has nixed greater autonomy and only pays lip service to respect for minority rights, relying instead on redoubled efforts to preserve China's national unity (Leibold 2013). A policy that combines a "melting pot" model of intensified assimilation and blaming external interference for ethnic tensions has proven a dead end. The Party has to cope with the legacy of marginalization and repression that has created huge impediments to enticing Tibetans to buy into what China is offering. Paradoxically, the Party's prioritization of maintaining stability militates against bold reforms, but continuing present policies is generating instability. Problematically, ethnic policies are a relatively low-level priority for China's leadership and ethnic issues only crop up when there is violence. Threats to public order are dealt with by intensified security measures that exacerbate grievances and perpetuate the cycle of violence.

The Dalai Lama has long been a nettlesome presence for Beijing because he has been an articulate spokesman for his people and has nurtured global sympathy for their plight. Based in northern India, where about 100,000 Tibetans live in exile, he is lionized around the world. He has been an influential ambassador for his people, meeting many heads of state while attracting considerable international media attention. When the Olympic torch toured Europe prior to the 2008 Beijing Olympics, at several points along the route Free Tibet protesters disrupted the procession, a tangible sign of the Dalai Lama's effective diplomacy in shaping global perceptions that leaves Beijing seething and prone to shrill denunciations.

China has had considerable success in intimidating governments into barring visits by the Dalai Lama to avoid giving offense, illustrating how Beijing's increasing economic clout has translated into powerful political influence. While human rights groups and the global media highlight Beijing's repressive security forces, curtailment of education in Tibetan language, and arbitrary arrests and disappearances of monks and nuns, governments are wary of doing so because it is bad for business. Beijing has let nations around the world know that there are consequences of official welcomes for the Dalai Lama—canceling contracts and otherwise economically penalizing nations that host such visits (Reilly 2012). Trade has trumped principle because China's threats are backed up by persuasive actions; nations that host the Dalai Lama can expect a 12.5% reduction of exports to China for the two years following the visit. Leaders around the world, including the US, have thus become reluctant to receive the Dalai Lama, at least officially, a disinclination that has expanded with China's economic growth.

The use of such unilateral economic penalties is not unique to China, but the more open muscle flexing is a relatively new development, one backed up by nationalist sentiments aimed at securing strategic objectives that include exercising sovereignty over what Beijing views as inherent territory. China relies on carrot-and-stick diplomacy to isolate the Dalai Lama, neutralize criticism over its human rights record, and influence other nations' policy towards Taiwan and maritime disputes. These are diplomatic red lines that nations cross at their peril, and thus they do so less and less frequently.

The Chinese version of sanctions is informal and relies heavily on not so thinly veiled threats involving large contracts that can be signed or concluded with competitors depending on a particular government's choices. This "purchasing diplomacy" targeting specific companies helps governments think about whether their principles are worth the adverse economic and political consequences. It has the virtue of flexibility because there are many opportunities to assign contracts and imposing or withdrawing such sanctions carries little cost for China. WTO rules prohibit trade restrictions for political purposes, but there is a national security loophole that provides China legal grounds for its purchasing diplomacy. These tactics also confer plausible deniability, as the non-award of a contract or cessation of export or import of an item can be explained away by other reasons, even if they may not be convincing. For example, amid a row with Japan in 2010 involving a Chinese fishing trawler ramming a Japanese Coast Guard vessel, China's rare earth exports suddenly slowed to a trickle. At that time, China controlled about 95% of the world's rare earth mineral supply, a critical input for a wide variety of high-tech products. Two months later, after securing release of the trawler crew, which amounted to a Japanese kowtow, exports resumed, undermining official explanations insisting that the stoppage of exports was entirely an administrative issue, not a sanction. China has also used sanctions to block fruit exports from the Philippines to put pressure on Manila over yet another maritime territorial dispute, further illustrating the ways that trade is wielded in the service of nationalism.

Beijing bridles at external meddling in what it considers internal disputes. The incorporation of Xinjiang in 1949 and Tibet in 1950 are Mao's legacy, expanding Chinese territory by one-third, and challenges to China's sovereignty in any form provoke a visceral nationalist response. Local unrest and international criticism have spurred a strong Han nationalistic backlash precisely because what is unquestioned in Beijing is being questioned. Beijing seems confident that time and development initiatives are on its side in this clash of civilizations, but it has a long record of underestimating the resilience of local nationalism as Tibetans struggle to retain their identity and cultural integrity. This Han myopia is also evident in China's far west province of Xinjiang.

Uighurs

The Islamic Turkic group called Uighurs once paid tribute to imperial China, but from 1912, following the collapse of the Qing dynasty, they enjoyed de facto independence, and in the 1940s their territory became the East Turkestan Republic. Subsequently, their homeland was incorporated into the People's Republic of China in 1949 and is known as Xinjiang.

There are an estimated 10 million ethnic Uighurs, about 80% living in China, with small communities in Kazakhstan, Kyrgyzstan, Uzbekistan, Turkey and Russia. As Turkic-speaking Sunni Muslims, they are one of the 56 ethnic groups recognized by the Chinese government. Uighur literally means "united" and refers to urban, oasis-dwelling and settled agriculturalists in contrast to the nomadic tribes in the region.

The Uighur image in China is associated with terrorist attacks, sporadic unrest, shady dealings and challenging Chinese rule. The collapse of the Soviet Union and the emergence of independent Central Asian states in the 1990s inspired similar aspirations among China's Uighurs. China's rapid industrialization since the 1990s has boosted demand for Xinjiang's natural resources, attracting large-scale investments and an influx of Han migrants who are torchbearers of a Han-dominated national identity that threatens Uighur identity with Sinification. Although Beijing ascribes violent incidents to terrorist groups such as the East Turkestan Islamic Movement, it appears that pent-up grievances over government repression, unequal access to jobs and government services, and curbs on religious practices are a major factor leading to growing discontent and radicalization of Uighurs. Under the circumstances, integrationist initiatives face deep levels of distrust and hostility. An upsurge of violence and terrorist incidents in recent years reduces prospects for reforms and increases reliance on repressive measures that perpetuate instability.

It is no longer just about history and territory, but rather a way of life, as Beijing infringes increasingly on the Uighurs' cultural and religious practices and frustrations rise over their lower status. Since the crux of the problem is political, the way forward depends on a political accommodation consistent with constitutional provisions for meaningful autonomy. But the signs are not encouraging, as Ilham Tohti, an economics professor and prominent advocate of moderate policy reform, was arrested in 2014 for inciting separatism and sentenced to life in prison. He has been dubbed the "Uighur's Nelson Mandela."

With moderates like Tohti ending up behind bars it is no wonder that militancy is on the rise, creating a dynamic of escalating violence as state security clamps down even further and more Uighurs give up hope for meaningful reforms. In 2014 alone, more than 200 people died in violent incidents that Uighurs say are a consequence of religious oppression and economic marginalization. Beijing identifies the problem as the extremism of a small group of separatists rather than acknowledging the broader desire for self-rule and religious freedom. The reliance on harsh methods only radicalizes the situation and makes it a more extensive security problem as militants seek support and find inspiration in the near abroad of Central Asia. In this febrile situation both sides are cutting off options as they retreat into a cycle of escalating state and terrorist violence.

In today's "Wild West" energy boom, the seeds of political tension in Xinjiang are not hard to find. The incoming Han and the local Uighurs—divided by class and ethnicity—do not seem to have found much common ground. While living in close proximity, they are worlds apart, putting the Uighurs on the wrong side of the tracks in their own home. Many relatively affluent Han reside in protected compounds because they fear the Uighurs.

China's problems in Xinjiang result from the absence of a strategy for wooing Uighurs. Uighurs have no stake in their governance, and under such circumstances, improvement in their status or their relations with the authorities seems unlikely. But while they may be poor and marginalized in contemporary China, the Uighurs' proud identity draws on the rich and colorful history of Silk Road trade, sagas of empire and Islam. Beijing has steamrollered over local sensitivities and worked to eradicate Uighur identity by suppressing religious practices, provoking a backlash.

The marginalization of Uighurs in their homeland has strengthened their identity and sense of persecution. Chinese is the language of upward mobility, but even this is a limited option for locals, as Han-managed companies entice Han workers to relocate to Xinjiang with higher wages and better benefits. Whether it is at the oil complexes or in the shopping malls, locals remain on the outside looking in. The natural resource bonanza in Xinjiang is only for the Hans, sowing a sense of relative deprivation. Ethnic polarization in Xinjiang has risen in recent years due to expanding restrictions on religion and cultural expression aimed at curtailing the ostensible menace of "separatism." This has sparked attacks by Uighur militants targeting the security presence, and reprisals by state security.

As noted above, Ilham Tohti, a prominent Uighur academic based in Beijing, was sentenced in 2014 to life imprisonment for inciting and organizing Uighur separatism. Apparently he erred in telling the international media that the root cause of problems in Xinjiang is not separatism, arguing that suppression of everyday religious practice is spreading discontent and an upsurge in religious militancy. Islam is a touchstone of Uighur identity so banning students from fasting during Ramadan, wearing Muslim garb or growing beards, in addition to restrictions on religious teaching of children, antagonizes Uighurs, who also resent limited Uighur language education. These policies are seen to represent China's efforts to extinguish Uighur culture and identity, sentiments shared by Tibetans. Beijing's crackdown on Uighur "terrorism" has thus been a self-fulfilling prophecy, pushing people to embrace a more radical Islamic identity. Contemporary Xinjiang thus presents a volatile mix of ethno-nationalism and heightened religious mobilization.

In the post-9/11 world, Beijing has cracked down on what it terms "Islamic extremism." National security and the "war on terror" are trumping concerns about religious freedom and human rights. This heavy-handed approach tramples on religious sensitivities and, as in Tibet, generates a deadly clash of civilizations. In 2009, for example, violent clashes in Urumchi, the capital of Xinjiang, left at least 200 and possibly 800 dead, and 1,600 injured, mostly ethnic Han. The security forces incited the interethnic violence, the worst episode in decades, by targeting a peaceful Uighur student demonstration. The ensuing rioting spread like wildfire in the kindling of deeply felt grievances. In response, the security forces stepped up draconian measures that feed these grievances and anti-Han sentiments.

March 1, 2014 became China's 9/11, the day that Islamic Uighur terrorists slashed their way into the collective consciousness of ethnic Han. That fateful day, a group of militant Uighurs attacked Chinese citizens in Kunming in Yunnan province with machetes, killing 29 and wounding 143 people. This savage attack was attributed to Uighur secessionist groups supporting the establishment of an East Turkestan. The desire for state revenge, China's "war on terror," reemphasizes the same repressive policies that have not been working. The Kunming attack followed an October 2013 incident in which a car driven by a Uighur family careened into a crowded sidewalk adjacent to Tiananmen Square in Beijing before crashing and bursting into flames. This "attack" was blamed on the East Turkestan Islamic Movement. East Turkestan is a name many Uighurs prefer for Xinjiang—it refers to a short-lived state in the 1940s before incorporation by China in 1949. State authorities believe these attacks signal that Uighur extremists are taking their fight outside the region and organizing terrorist attacks in the Han heartland. These brazen challenges to state authority, and the prospect of further such incidents, escalate repression and thus radicalize more Uighurs.

Chinese nationalist pique was evident in the criticism leveled at the US State Department for not initially condemning the Kunming incident as a terrorist attack. Since the early 2000s China has conducted what amounts to its Uighur counter-insurgency strategy under the pretext of the war on terror launched by the Bush Administration after 9/11. But Washington has not gone along with this ruse, and Beijing has been forthright in expressing its displeasure about what it views as US double standards. Subsequently, the US State Department did condemn the Kunming attack as an act of terrorism, somewhat mollifying Beijing.

China's Little Nationalisms

Prospects for ethnic policy reform are limited because longstanding repression has widened the gulf separating the aroused ethnic minorities of Tibetans and Uighurs from Beijing. There is little trust. Beijing's explicit Han ethno-nationalism has increased the stakes of identity politics, a politicization that feeds mutual antagonisms. Terrorist incidents targeting ethnic Han further limit the government's room for maneuver. While the Tibetans and Uighurs feel victimized, ethnic Han also feel victimized and have long complained that the state has coddled the minorities and given them unfair advantages and benefits. There is a strong emotional aspect of contemporary Han nationalism that is hyper-sensitive to criticism, international and domestic, and considerable cyber-nationalist anger is directed at the minorities for their ingratitude for all that has been bestowed on them. Even if Beijing could introduce more integrationist policies and move towards more genuine political autonomy for these restive regions, the legacy of violence and distrust imperils such efforts.

Beijing often invokes the ethnic problems of the former Soviet Union and Yugoslavia as object lessons for China to avoid. Although there is scant prospect of China being engulfed by ethnic turmoil, Tibet and Xinjiang are strategically important regions. Moreover, intensified economic exploitation is upping the ante, and thus loosening the state's grip is seen to be too risky. Even if Beijing is able to raise minority living standards significantly, and it claims it has done so already, there is little reason to believe that this would extinguish ethno-nationalist aspirations among the minority communities. Fundamentally, Tibetans and Uighurs feel that they have little input on decisions that affect their daily lives, while Beijing believes that their demands for autonomy go too far.

There is virtually no chance that Xinjiang or Tibet will separate from China, but preventing this phantom scenario drives China's security-first approach to managing ethno-nationalism. This invented menace stokes ethnic polarization, reinforced by Chinese racism and repression. If draconian security measures are the answer, both regions should already be pacified. Beijing has tried repression to manage its minority problems over several decades, with disappointing results, and more recently has emphasized improving living standards, but without efforts to more fully involve minorities in crafting policies and without granting them more autonomy in internal affairs, the unstable impasse and cycles of unrest will persist. It is increasingly clear that China's policy for integrating Xinjiang and Tibet—a mix of repression, development and Han migration—is not persuading non-Han communities about the benefits of Chinese administration. There is recognition among some Chinese experts that lifting restrictions on cultural and religious expression and consulting locals on building a roadmap towards peaceful and prosperous coexistence are necessary, but roadblocks in the form of public attitudes and government inertia remain. China, however, is certainly not alone in having volatile and sometimes violent minority problems. We next examine the situation in India.

Indian Muslims

The living standards of India's 177 million Muslims, about 15% of the nation's total population, lag those of the Hindu majority (80%), with lower levels of education and employment. Poverty is declining overall in India across all groups due to economic growth, but at a relatively slower pace in the Muslim community. A 2013 World Bank study estimated that 34% of Muslims in urban India (a higher percentage of Muslims are city dwellers) lived below the poverty line, compared to 19% of Hindus (Panagariya and Mukim 2013). Prime Minister Narendra Modi campaigned on his economic success in managing the state of Gujarat, but the World Bank study shows that the incidence of poverty there is relatively high for both Hindus and Muslims. Moreover poverty reduction has been much slower there for Muslims, declining by 11% since 1993 compared to a 74% decline among Hindus. Certainly higher fertility among Muslims contributes to the persistence of poverty, but the 2006 Sachar Report commissioned by the government revealed that Muslims were marginalized, with a low share of public sector jobs, formal employment, school and university places, and seats in politics. They earn less, have limited access to banks and finance, are less literate, and are a minuscule presence in the police and military forces. Congress long relied on Muslims at elections, not needing to point out the risks of a BJP-led government, but this practice of sectional pandering could not save the party from a humiliating defeat in 2014 and the rise of the BJP, the party that embraces an assertive Hindu-centric agenda.

As in China, Muslims are a target for discrimination and sporadic large-scale violence, often involving the complicity of politicians and government security forces. The 1992 razing of the Babri Mosque in Ayodhya by Hindu militants associated with the BJP was a watershed in communal relations, sparking periodic rioting and tit-for-tat violence ever since. In consequence, there has been a pronounced ghettoization of Muslims in urban areas as they seek protection within their own communities. These segregated areas typically are less well served by social services and lead to less interaction between Hindus and Muslims, accentuating the polarization. These ghettos also prove to be handy targets for Hindu militants, as occurred in Gujarat in 2002 when marauding rioters went on a rampage terrorizing Muslim enclaves.

In 2002, the state of Gujarat witnessed sectarian violence carried out by frenzied crowds, while police looked on. These Hindu militants were seeking revenge for the burning of a train carrying pilgrims from the disputed Babri Mosque site, claiming the lives of 58 Hindus. This religious dispute has sparked large-scale riots across the nation and challenges even today the nation's secular identity rooted in tolerance. The anti-Muslim rioting and looting was reminiscent of similar anti-Sikh incidents in New Delhi in 1984. Various government investigations into the Gujarat pogrom have come to different conclusions about culpability, but international human rights organizations assert there is considerable evidence that state authorities were involved with the sectarian violence and failed to intervene in a timely manner.

The slaughter of some 2,000 people in Gujarat, mostly Muslims, and displacement of 10,000 more over a period of four weeks occurred on Prime Minister Modi's watch as chief minister of the state. Some critics accuse him and the BJP of inciting the riots, while others wonder why security forces did not intervene sooner to stop the bloodshed. These allegations have not hampered Mr. Modi's political career and rise to leader of the Bharatiya Janata Party. Modi has a knack for turning the tables on his critics, managing to portray himself as unfairly persecuted and claiming that he has been found not guilty by a judicial inquiry. Until he became premier, however, he was barred from entry to the US over the allegations.

Ayodhya is a talismanic site of religious tensions and the ground zero of Muslim grievance in modern India, one targeted by chauvinistic Hindu fundamentalists who embrace an excluding and assertive Hindutva (Hindu nationalism). It is a sacred site that is claimed by both Muslims and Hindus and has sparked the worst sectarian violence in India since Partition in 1947. In 1992, Hindu fanatics demolished the Babri Mosque situated on the disputed site and erected a temple, enraging Muslims and sparking large-scale riots across the country. Rival claimants have taken the case to the courts, but the litigation has not resolved the dispute and the scars of antagonism and distrust linger.

The battle is over a 2.7-acre piece of land in Uttar Pradesh in northern India. The now demolished Babri Mosque had stood on the site since the 16th century. Hindus claim that it was built over the birthplace of Ram, a Hindu god, and a temple dedicated to him that had stood there previously, although there is no archaeological evidence for this assertion. In a curious 2010 ruling, the High Court divided the site into three parcels, awarding the most sacred and bitterly contested portion where the mosque once stood to a Hindu group.

The BJP were catapulted into power in 1998 on the back of the Ayodhya dispute, demonstrating the popular appeal of Hindutva. Voters were energized by the communal violence and the religious identity politics of the BJP. An investigation concluded that senior leaders of the BJP were involved in the demolition of the mosque, but nobody has been held accountable. In 2014 the BJP regained power and its election manifesto pledged to build a Hindu temple at the disputed site, a core commitment that it terms non-negotiable. The BJP-appointed governor of Uttar Pradesh, where the temple site is located, reiterated this inflammatory promise at the end of 2014.

Insurgent India

The rising India narrative remains unconvincing precisely because it overlooks the impoverished, lawless and desperate India that prevails, perhaps nowhere more than at the fringes to the northwest (Kashmir) and northeast. In addition, there are the Naxalites, members of a longstanding Maoist guerilla insurgency concentrated in central and eastern states, sparked by increased interest in exploiting mineral wealth that encroaches on the rights and habitat of tribal groups and contributes little to local development. The Naxalites have over 10,000 armed combatants and have survived significant government counter-insurgency campaigns since being identified as the nation's most serious internal threat in 2006. While Indians boast a thriving democracy and many hail its inclusiveness, local backlashes against the central state and its mainstream imperatives and prejudices provide a stark counterpoint. New land legislation has poured fuel on the fires of long simmering resentments, opening up resource-rich backward areas to mining businesses that have a poor track record in respecting local communities or improving their welfare. Here we turn to the situation in the remote northeastern region of Arunchal Pradesh, Assam, Manipur, Meghalaya, Mizoram, Nagaland, Sikkim and Tripura. This region is home to 220 ethnic groups and about 42 million people, mostly living in rural agrarian communities. Most of Arunchal Pradesh is regarded by China as South

Tibet, and irredentist tensions remain high as both countries issue passports with maps asserting sovereignty over the area. In 1962 Chinese troops overran Indian defenses here, and then withdrew.

The northeastern states, isolated from the sub-continent and connected by a narrow land bridge called the "chicken's neck" extending between Nepal and Bangladesh, confront the social problems of endemic poverty. In addition, the region is plagued by insurgencies, banditry and security forces run amok. In Assam alone, famous for its tea estates, since the late 1970s some 30,000 people have been killed in an insurgency led by the United Liberation Front of Asom.

As in Kashmir, the northeasterners' main grievances are associated with the Indian security presence and the lack of accountability when military and police commit abuses such as arbitrary arrests, torture and extra-judicial killings. This impunity means that security forces can operate above and beyond the reach of the law. The Armed Forces Special Powers Act (AFPSA), the 1958 emergency law that grants broad powers of search, arrest and authorization to kill, shields soldiers committing abuses from prosecution. The government claims it needs such powers to combat local militants and dacoits, while locals complain that serious human rights violations go unpunished. This abrogation of civil liberties and the unpunished excesses stir public discontent and generate support for militant groups.

In the summer of 2012 there was a sudden mass exodus from southern Indian cities by tens of thousands of Indians from the northeastern states. This flight was prompted by violence targeting them and the spread of threats and hate messages on social media. Fears that such attacks might spread led hordes to flee to their homelands, jamming transport networks and leading the government to block SMS text messaging in an effort to curb rumors and scaremongering.

The people from the eight northeastern states are regarded by the Indian mainstream as backward, impoverished and uncivilized. This "othering" of them is longstanding, as is their migration for jobs outside their region. In mainland cities, however, they are a visible and vulnerable population that routinely encounters the prejudice against minorities that is common in India. They tend to cluster in poorly paid service sector jobs and face discrimination due to their distinctive physical features. Many are Christian—another cause for discrimination. The violence and panicky flight home were prompted by sectarian clashes in Assam state between Muslims and the minority Bodo tribe. The Bodo resent the influx of Muslims into their tribal areas and there is growing tension over land, jobs and political power. Such sectarian violence is not new to Assam or elsewhere in the northeast and various groups are fighting for autonomy and secession, accusing the government of plundering their resources and ignoring development. About 75 people were killed in attacks and reprisals in 2012, while some 300,000 were displaced by the violence and shifted to refugee camps. Muslims staged sympathy demonstrations in Mumbai and elsewhere in the "mainland" and northeasterners were attacked and beaten by enraged mobs of Muslims. Despite promises by the Modi government to accelerate infrastructure development, the situation remains volatile. At the end of 2014, militants of the National Democratic Front of Bodoland (NDFB) retaliated against a government military offensive by killing 76 civilians. While there is local sympathy for the stated goals, and considerable frustration with the influx of outsiders competing for limited land and resources, the NDFB appears to be isolating itself from the local population through such reprisals and random acts of violence.

Assam exhibits what Guha terms the ugliness of the little nationalisms, but the main problem is the lack of accountability and exemption from the rule of law for security forces operating in the region. There is a crisis of governance and climate of impunity that leaves locals at the mercy of the militant gangs and hostage to thuggish security forces. The AFPSA has been in force in the state of Manipur, along the border with Myanmar, longer than in Jammu-Kashmir, resulting in widespread abuses that have discredited New Delhi and its armed forces' heavy-handed tactics. Promises to repeal the law have gone unfulfilled. There is a strong desire for law and order among local people, and for an end to rampant abuses. Elderly Manipuri women gathered in front of a military compound and stripped, inviting the soldiers to rape them as they have countless others. One local woman there has carried out India's longest hunger strike, repeatedly refusing food to protest the law that allows the security forces to act above the law (Peer 2014). Local frustrations and chaos are also evident in blockades, strikes, demonstrations and violence. For "mainland" Indians, the security problems and allegations of human rights abuses and impunity of security forces are not a significant issue. Overall, blinkered nationalism means that the central government and mainstream public opinion marginalize these people and their problems and at the first opportunity disingenuously accuse Pakistan of fomenting the unrest.

Indonesia

In 1998, the end of President Suharto's New Order regime sparked euphoric hopes and explosions of brutal violence around the archipelago. Under his authoritarian government, conflicts were suppressed through a reign of terror, creating a fragile and volatile situation. The tinderbox of grievances didn't need much of a spark, one that the collapse of the New Order provided.

Long-suppressed memories of the 1965 bloodletting generated apprehensions as Indonesia coped with the insecure legacy Suharto left behind. The end of the 1990s was a time of shadowy organizations, provocateurs, settling of scores and mysterious masterminds. Hopes focused on the return of the military to the barracks, asserting civilian control over government and security, and establishing democracy and the rule of law. But all around the periphery of the archipelago these hopes confronted a cycle of violence that spun out of control in Aceh, Irian Jaya, Papua, Sulawesi and Ambon. Armed separatist rebels and sectarian clashes threatened Indonesia's re-democratization and territorial integrity. The nightmare of an unraveling state beset with spiraling violence, often invoked to justify repressive measures under Suharto, had metamorphosed into reality. To varying degrees these insurrections and sectarian clashes have been contained, but below the surface the scars remain. In the post-Suharto era much has been revealed about state violence and widespread human rights abuses, but it is an incomplete reckoning and there has been no judicial accountability. This dubious bargain has kept the military in the barracks, but perpetuated distrust of the government and undermined civil society. Memories of past conflicts are aroused by human rights groups but marginalized in public discourse by the institutional interests of the security forces that prefer keeping a lid on an unsavory and discrediting past.

Since the end of the New Order authoritarian regime in 1998, the highly centralized administrative structure has given way to greater regional autonomy. This shift was a pragmatic adjustment to simmering anti-Jakarta resentments, the realities of diversity in the Indonesian archipelago, and the difficulties of micro-managing affairs remote from the center. This element of democratization has created opportunities for local vested interests and a decentralization of graft and corruption. Greater autonomy has also heightened identity politics in the regions. Political parties assert ethnic-based claims to political power and seek to reinvigorate local ethnicity, customs and practices to that end. In some regions this means elevating one local identity over others. Regionalism thus has had countervailing consequences, enabling assertion of identities that highlight autonomy and separateness from the mainstream while suppressing local diversity by crafting a regional mainstream. In some respects this process has turned the national motto upside down, emphasizing "diversity within unity." Identity politics has thus allowed freer expression of Indonesia's pluralism, while regionalism has imposed new orthodoxies that threaten local minorities.

Islamic Militancy

Human rights problems affecting minorities remain serious in Indonesia. Religious minorities are subject to violence and discrimination while the government and police have been tolerant of such abuses. Public opinion does not support Islamic religious extremism and the concomitant targeting of religious minority groups, but the government has encouraged and accommodated religious intolerance through discriminatory laws and decrees at the national and local level that deny freedom of expression to minority groups. Security officials do not adequately protect those who are threatened or attacked by militant Islamic groups, allowing these fundamentalists to play an influential role in Indonesia's 21st-century identity politics. They represent a small percentage of Indonesians, who overall tend to be religiously moderate, but the militants' penchant for violence endows them with disproportionate influence.

Indonesia has the world's largest Muslim population with 203 million adherents as of 2009, about 88% of the total population. Almost all are Sunni, and more tolerant Sufi traditions prevail, but about 1 million are Shia and 500,000 belong to Ahmadiyya. In general, Indonesia is known for a moderate form of Islam, but stricter observance has long been the norm in western Sumatra and in Aceh.

In Aceh, since 2001 the government has authorized shariah (Islamic law) courts and ordinances on proper dress and proper gender relations as part of its "special autonomy" agreement to end the separatist war waged in the province. These laws are enforced by a shariah police force known for harassment and arbitrary arrests and detention for transgressions such as dating and wearing tight clothing. Vice vigilantes try to promote religious virtue by enforcing bans on drinking, gambling and what is termed "seclusion"—couples of the opposite sex being alone together, even if in public places. There have been public canings in Aceh since 2005 to punish transgressors, while the fashion police ensure that women don't wear revealing or clinging clothing. It is the only province where such courts are authorized, although in Java some communities have passed ordinances requiring residents' behavior conform to conservative principles, i.e. women should dress modestly, not meet men alone, remain at home at night, etc. In 2014 the Aceh government moved to apply shariah law to everyone whether Islamic or not, although dropping demands for death by stoning for adulterers. Non-Muslims who are charged with offenses not criminalized by national laws are now subject to the shariah courts.

In Java there has been a longstanding dichotomy between *santri*, more orthodox adherents, and *abangan*, those who blend observance of Islam with local traditions and practices. Perceptions changed considerably after the Bali bombings in 2001 and 2004. Jemaah Islamiyah (JI), a terrorist organization in Southeast Asia, was implicated in these bombings, prompting strong anti-terrorist countermeasures by Jakarta that largely succeeded in rolling up JI networks. Many of the recruits were traced to *pesantren*, Islamic schools, near the ancient capital of Solo in central Java where observance of Islamic tenets previously had been more casual and syncretic. The teachers at these pesantren were santri and sought to spread more devout religious observance and a "purer" form of Islam shorn of indigenous influences. From the 1990s, a more fundamentalist Islam gained momentum in Indonesia, partly due to government meddling and social grievances, but also because of global developments in the Islamic world embodied in Samuel Huntington's concept of "clash of civilizations." Intensified globalization in the 1990s, fueled by the Internet and global media, produced a backlash and many found in Islam a comfortable redoubt for asserting collective interests and preserving local identities.

Incidents of violence by Islamic militants targeting religious minorities have become frequent in contemporary Indonesia. Often they act with impunity and when prosecuted they get light sentences, signaling an official tolerance if not complicity that emboldens such extremists. Restrictions on building churches and other non-Muslim houses of worship have become more arbitrary and draconian and infringe on freedom of religion. There have been prosecutions for blasphemy on the basis of "improper" teaching of the Quran and also atheistic postings on Facebook. In 2012 the Religious Affairs Minister declared that the minority Shia and Ahmadiyya Islamic sects were heretical and suggested they convert to the dominant Sunni faith, thereby subjecting them to dangerous attacks. Security forces have stood by while mobs attacked and killed sect followers, representing a scandalous tolerance for extremist intolerance.

Such extreme cases are not representative of mainstream Indonesia, but indicate that Islamic militants are influencing national identity politics in ways that are threatening to minorities. While freedom of religion is a basic right in Indonesia, security forces and government officials have decided otherwise, fanning the flames of sectarian violence. In 2006 Indonesia signed the International Covenant on Civil and Political Rights, but protection of minorities and religious freedom has not been observed. There are expectations that, compared to his predecessor Susilo Bambang Yudhoyono (2004–2014), President Jokowi Widodo will act more resolutely to promote public tolerance and extend government protection to minorities, who face problems that Indonesia's ethnic Chinese community know all too well.

Ethnic Chinese

Ethnic Chinese in Indonesia have suffered periodic violence since Dutch colonial rule began in the 17th century. Chinese merchants played a key role in the colonial economy, many serving as compradors assisting the Dutch in exploiting the rich resources of Indonesia. The numbers of Chinese increased dramatically in the late 19th century as the Dutch brought coolies from China to work in mining and the plantation economy. They came to play a dominant commercial role in the colonial economy, involving a visible role as merchants, shop owners, rice millers, tax collectors and moneylenders. During the anti-Dutch resistance that began after World War II ended in 1945, Chinese businessmen provided key assistance to the Indonesian forces. The Dutch failed in their attempt to reassert colonial rule and subsequently some Chinese businessmen enjoyed privileges and access because of the contacts they had made and the services they had rendered to the military during the struggle for independence. Nonetheless ethnic Chinese have been subject to various forms of legal discrimination since then.

Although the Chinese community is not uniformly wealthy, it is generally a target of popular suspicion and resentment. Chinese represent almost 2% of the entire population spread across the archipelago, but they tend to live in urban areas and about one-half live in Java. Many of Indonesia's richest tycoons are Chinese and they have enjoyed strong ties to the military and political elite. They are envied their wealth, and given their strong sense of community, clannishness and distinctive features, they stick out in society. In addition, Chinese are often landlords, moneylenders or small-scale shop owners who come into close contact with local people all over the archipelago, sometimes serving as a convenient lightning rod for social discontent.

As discussed in Chapter 7, in 1965–1966, Indonesia experienced tremendous political upheaval and violence, with ethnic Chinese suffering disproportionately. Many Chinese were killed as suspected communists, and because Beijing was alleged to have orchestrated the coup they were seen as potential fifth columnists. In addition, in the general mayhem, there was a settling of scores and in such circumstances Chinese merchants suffered the wrath of relative deprivation and anger of penury.

Under President Suharto's New Order government, relations with China were severed. There was a ban on Chinese language periodicals and use of ideograms out of fear that they might convey coded messages. Discriminatory laws and official practices were crafted to complicate ethnic Chinese claims to citizenship despite several generations of residence in Indonesia, assimilation into Indonesian society and lack of Chinese language skills. Like the *zainichi* (ethnic Koreans) in Japan, all ethnic Chinese were disadvantaged except for the business elite. Throughout the Suharto era there were widespread allegations of cronyism and corruption involving this elite, perhaps best depicted in graphic leaflets distributed during the Tanjung Priok riots in 1982 showing President Suharto, head tilted backwards, and Lim Sioe Liong, a prominent ethnic Chinese crony tycoon, pouring US dollars down his throat.

Unlike Indonesians of Indian or Arab descent, ethnic Chinese were required to have a document that proved their citizenship. This document was compulsory for all Chinese Indonesians 21 years and older and required for all dealings with the bureaucracy, from getting a passport to enrolling in university. No other citizens of Indonesia were required to have such a document. This discriminatory practice reinforced the gap between Chinese and other Indonesians and required them to prove their "Indonesianness" in ways others were not. In the post-New Order era this requirement has been scrapped, but Chinese Indonesians maintain that informal and institutionalized discrimination persists.

Like other minorities in Indonesia, the Chinese are free to express their ethnic identity in line with the national motto, "Unity in Diversity," a talismanic touchstone of Indonesian nationalism. Yet, like other minority groups, the Chinese don't feel their rights are protected by the state and they remain a target of discontent. During the 1997–1998 economic crisis, local Chinese traders and shop owners were a convenient scapegoat for widespread frustrations. Security forces actually orchestrated mob violence targeting Chinese in May 1998, to justify a general clampdown to preserve the New Order that appears to have been related to rivalry among top officers jockeying to succeed Suharto. In the staged riots, shops were looted and torched, and more than 1,000 ethnic Chinese were killed and hundreds of women raped. Prabowo Subianto, one of the top military officers implicated in organizing this rampage and kidnappings of pro-democracy activists, was Suharto's son-in-law. He subsequently became a wealthy businessman and, despite this notoriety, ran for president in 2014. This lack of accountability and absence of justice for victims of the riots creates a sense of vulnerability and distrust towards government authorities and skepticism about the realities of democratization. It is this impunity that makes minorities feel unsafe in Indonesia and beyond the protection of the rule of law.

Yet in some respects there has been remarkable progress in the legal and political situation of the ethnic Chinese, who had been resigned to being outsiders and scapegoats. The government in the early 21st century has repealed a range of discriminatory laws banning expressions of Chinese language and culture, and Chinese New Year has become a national holiday. Eliminating such taboos has gone a long way to encourage ethnic Chinese to feel more welcomed as citizens in a multi-ethnic Indonesia. Attendance of senior government officials and high-ranking military officers at Chinese cultural events is a dramatic symbol of change, one unimaginable during the New Order. Confucianism has been recognized as a religion (all Indonesians carry identity cards that identify their faith) and the legal bar on "non-indigenous" Indonesians becoming president has been eliminated. Indonesia's parliament has also passed legislation outlawing racial and ethnic discrimination. In making Chinese feel less like outsiders, the state has encouraged younger Chinese to explore their ethnic identity, and develop language skills, in ways their parents never felt secure in doing.

Significantly, since 1998 there have been no major anti-Chinese incidents, at a time when Indonesia has experienced episodic communal and radical Islamist religious violence. The absence of anti-Chinese violence shows the benefits of the shift in state-led attitudes towards this minority and greater support for a tolerant pluralism and multiculturalism, but because many are Christians they are still subject to persecution. But, ethnic Chinese remain wary of political participation, knowing from experience the perils of becoming an obvious target. In the 2012 Jakarta gubernatorial elections, some pundits made an issue of the Chinese ethnicity of the running mate of Joko Widodo, the eventual winner. A few public figures insinuated that this made him unacceptable to the Islamic mainstream, but with little success. The victory of Jokowi, as he is popularly known, is yet another sign that voters have not supported candidates representing extremism or appeals to ethnic chauvinism. When Jokowi was subsequently elected president in 2014, his deputy became governor of Jakarta, the highest post ever held by an ethnic Chinese in Indonesia.

While anti-Chinese sentiments remain in Indonesia, the government has taken steps to give Chinese political and cultural space within the multi-ethnic mainstream in ways that have accorded them new freedoms. The benefits of this shift in state-led attitudes are evident in the absence of overtly anti-Chinese violence. Yet, the emergence of regionalism has encouraged identity politics and ignited competition for domination in local arenas. Challenges to religious freedom have increased with the mainstreaming of a more intolerant Islamic identity with the complicity of the government. Politicians are now more wary of alienating mainstream constituencies and taking unpopular stands on behalf of minorities. As a result, ethnic Chinese remain in limbo, but others have it worse.

Papua

In this far-flung province in eastern Indonesia, occupying the western half of the large island shared with the nation of Papua New Guinea, violence and unrest are common. Locals' sense of identity and aspirations for independence clash with the consolidating dictates of Indonesian nationalism. The OPM (Free Papua Movement) seeks independence from Indonesia. It is a low-level insurgency enjoying widespread Papuan support, marked by public protests and flag-raising ceremonies calling for independence. Papuans feel ethnically, culturally and linguistically distinct from the Malay/Javanese mainstream, and 85% are Christian, accentuating a sense of being apart. Their discontent is reinforced by neglect, discrimination and disempowerment by a distant government in Jakarta. About half of the province's 3.5 million inhabitants are non-Papuans who have resettled there under the government-sponsored transmigration program (relocating families from densely populated areas), aimed at promoting integration and assimilation, an influx that generates tensions. Jakarta fears that Papua will secede, and finds this unacceptable. After all, Sukarno made Papua into a touchstone of national identity and grandeur, in his speeches often referring to the magnificent span of the archipelago "from Sabang to Merauke," a phrase that has become embedded in national discourse. Sabang is located at the tip of Aceh in northern Sumatra, the westernmost extent of Indonesia's boundaries, while Merauke is in Papua at the easternmost point; ironically these geographical bookends are both restive and chafe under Jakarta's rule. The idea of losing Papua is therefore not only about the vast value of its mineral resources, but certainly that is an additional key consideration.

The roots of confrontation stretch back to 1949 when the Netherlands acquiesced to Indonesians' desire for independence. As part of the agreement, the Dutch recognized Indonesian sovereignty over all of what had been the colony of the Netherlands East Indies except for western New Guinea. The Dutch promised eventual self-determination for the Papuans, arguing that they were ethnically distinct, while Indonesia claimed the former colony in its entirety and insisted that the Dutch not cling to a presence in the liberated archipelago.

Papua has been called many things since 1945, but independent isn't one of them. Under Dutch colonial rule it was Netherlands New Guinea. After Indonesia won independence in 1949 the Dutch tried to retain control over Papua, but Indonesian threats of armed intervention and international pressure forced them to relinquish control in 1962. The US Kennedy Administration sponsored negotiations between the Indonesians and Dutch, fearing that opposition to Sukarno's demands might push Indonesia towards Moscow's orbit. Under the shadow of Indonesian military incursions, the New York Agreement was reached in 1962 that awarded Indonesia control over West New Guinea (West Papua) after a brief UN-administered transitional period. The Dutch withdrew in 1963. The agreement obligated Jakarta to conduct an act of self-determination with UN assistance no later than 1969. After seizing control, Indonesia consolidated its grip and repressed local dissent and calls for independence. The US was resigned to Indonesia retaining control and was more influenced by Cold War fears of spreading communism than concerns about Papuan self-determination. In the run-up to the 1969 referendum, Sukarno was ousted from power in what amounted to a military coup. President Suharto, his successor, emphasized nurturing improved ties with western governments and worked with them to negotiate a large bailout and debt restructuring. He also signed a new more welcoming foreign investment law in 1967, in his first year of officially taking office. Freeport Sulphur (now Freeport McMoran), an American mining firm, was the first company to take advantage of the new law, gaining vast concessions in West Irian with considerable gold and copper deposits. Suharto's New Order regime, unlike Sukarno, was a government that Washington could do business with.

In 1969, UN officials conducted an Act of Free Choice which contravened the New York Agreement (Article 18) that gave all adult Papuans the right to participate in an act of self-determination consistent with international practice. But Indonesia, according to US Embassy cables at that time, would probably have lost a referendum and was determined to retain control at all costs. Overall, Papua was a marginal issue in Washington and did not matter enough to the international community to challenge a foregone conclusion and imperil relations with a strategically important country with bountiful natural resources. Suharto was seen to be pro-Washington and that was good enough. In the end, Indonesian authorities selected 1,022 Papuans to publicly vote with a show of hands, with a discrediting unanimity as it turned out, for integration with Indonesia. Apparently some of the delegates had no idea beforehand about the momentous import of the meeting, and in any event it was conducted under coercive circumstances with close monitoring by Indonesian security forces. Despite such irregularities, the UN "took note" of the results, thus supporting Jakarta's dubious act of annexation.

The Cold War bargain worked out well for Washington and Jakarta, but not so well for Papuans. Human rights organizations and other NGOs lobby for West Papuan independence, and publicize human rights violations, but with little effect. Within Indonesia, there is little discussion of Papuan matters. Successive administrative reorganizations have not helped improve the situation, and the independence movement persists despite prolonged repression. Jakarta passed a special autonomy law in 2001 to grant Papuans a greater say over local affairs, renaming the province Papua (it had been Irian Jaya since 1973). In 2003 President Megawati Sukarnoputri, daughter of Sukarno, moved to divide the province into three entities, sparking widespread protests over what was seen to be a divide-and-rule strategy. This decision, however, was overturned in the courts and now there are two provinces: West Papua and Papua.

Papuans have a range of grievances against the government, especially regarding the violence and rent-seeking behavior of security forces stationed on the island. Papua's vast resource wealth attracts foreign investment in mining that makes it valuable to Jakarta. The concessions to mining companies have become a source of tension as locals complain that their land rights are ignored and that they are not adequately compensated. The security forces are supposed to be there to keep the peace, but are accused of stirring up trouble through heavy-handed tactics. In the climate of unrest, these security forces sell protection to the companies. Security crackdowns provoke reprisals in a vicious circle of violence that requires political intervention, and greater oversight, by Jakarta, which has not been forthcoming.

In 2002 there was an attack on a group of American educators, killing 3 and wounding 12, souring bilateral relations with Washington. This was one of a number of attacks targeting the large mining operations of foreign multinational corporations operating in West Papua. The US investigation into the incident found that the Indonesian military carried out the attack and scapegoated the OPM. It appears that the Indonesian National Armed Forces (TNI) mounted the attack to get leverage with Freeport McMoran in negotiations over providing security for the company and its employees, a familiar tactic in Aceh. In addition, the TNI was hoping that the US would place the OPM on its list of terrorist organizations to elicit increased counter-terrorism assistance from Washington.

In Papua's multidimensional conflict, there are no winners. Pro-independence militants enjoy widespread support due to the security forces' excesses, a lack of economic development initiatives, and no tangible benefits from the 2001 special autonomy measures. As a result, locals are skeptical of Jakarta's professed desire to build trust. Local political institutions are dysfunctional and beset by partisan politics and score settling that stymie democracy and legislative action. In this political limbo, Jakarta lacks credible local partners to engage with, compounding the sense of neglect. Efforts to jumpstart development projects targeting locals have not delivered, and thus dialogue remains stalled. In this polarized situation it is difficult for the government and local opponents to find common ground on addressing local grievances. There are few signs of sustainable progress on social, economic and political concerns, and this lies at the heart of discontent and outbursts of frustration. Above all, the lack of police and military accountability for extensive human rights abuses and extra-judicial killings stirs bitter resentment that feeds the conflict.

In 2012, over 300 Indonesian soldiers ran amok, torching houses, beating and stabbing local residents, and killing a Papuan government official, while in another incident they committed yet another in a long line of extra-judicial killings of prominent independence activists. Such excesses have become routine, as has impunity for those who commit the abuses. These violent incidents conducted by security forces are another face of intolerance, making a mockery of the national motto, "Unity in Diversity." The crux of the challenge for Jakarta is to rein in such excesses because they have come to symbolize in the minds of Papuans everything wrong about the central government's presence in their homeland.

There are numerous recommendations about how the government could turn the situation around, but not enough action and oversight. Jakarta has promoted decentralization, shifting power and resources to local governments, but the consequent fragmentation of governance and endemic corruption have discredited this initiative and fueled strife and distrust. In the absence of more concrete benefits of Indonesian rule in terms of jobs, social services, education, and improved training and accountability for security personnel, separatism will continue to appeal to most Papuans.

Impunity for human rights abuses is a common thread in the fringes and usually rationalized in terms of shoring up political stability and ensuring that security forces' hands are not tied. Arbitrary punishment, detention, beatings, torture and extortion have become the face of Jakarta in the restive province. The killing of terror suspects in shoot-first encounters and in detention discredits government initiatives and sows distrust. This requires a major overhaul of security policy, which is not likely because the plight of Papuans is off the national radar screen and not part of a larger discourse on human and civil rights. The absence of a coherent government strategy to manage and mitigate evident problems demonstrates a lack of political will and is a recipe for continued separatism. President Jokowi has his work cut out for him if he wants to respond to local grievances because that means taking on the military establishment. There is a more encouraging example in Aceh, where the government cut a deal on autonomy that brought an end to a prolonged and violent campaign for independence.

Aceh

Aceh is the province at the northern end of the island of Sumatra, known for devout observance of Islam and a tradition of resistance to external control. The Dutch spent the better part of three decades pacifying the region in the late 19th and early 20th centuries. More recently, three decades of violent conflict ended in 2005 when the Free Aceh Movement (GAM) and the Indonesian government signed the Helsinki Memorandum of Understanding. Following the 2004 tsunami, which killed over 170,000 people in Aceh, the hardest-hit area, reconstruction efforts in the devastated province created a favorable context for ending the conflict.

Aceh had long chafed under Jakarta's rule due to resentment that the province did not get a fair share of oil and gas revenues, and because of the military's draconian presence. GAM and the military terrorized the local population, gaining from the presence of each other. For the military, Aceh was lucrative for selling protection to oil and gas businesses and thus GAM played an essential role in this racket because it represented a credible threat. In addition, the insurgency justified budgets and special territorial commands where there were opportunities for career advancement. In some respects the military's activities bordered on organized crime, involving arms and drug smuggling operations. GAM benefited from the military's counter-insurgency operations and the lack of accountability regarding such excesses, making it easy to recruit militants and extract tribute from local communities. While the military and GAM waged battle, there was also a degree of cooperation and collusion.

The 2004 tsunami created a window of opportunity to loosen the grip of the military and separatist militants as the government and international agencies and non-government organizations mounted relief and reconstruction activities. The relief and reconstruction needs in Aceh were overwhelming and GAM could not be seen to be standing in the way of aid and holding the people's interests hostage to their political agenda. The key to the Helsinki deal was greater autonomy for the province. GAM agreed to participate in the democratic process and secure its power at the ballot box, helped along by government agreement that local parties could participate; elsewhere in Indonesia only candidates from national parties can compete in elections.

This was a typical center–periphery conflict with locals seeking greater autonomy and a higher share of the hydrocarbon wealth. It is a case study of how unexpected events like the tsunami can have unforeseen consequences. Nobody anticipated that the 9.1 magnitude earthquake under the Indian Ocean that unleashed such a devastating tsunami would also produce an opportunity for resolving longstanding political differences. The peace transition is ongoing, but the fault-lines of conflict are now local as GAM's political successor Partai Aceh dominates the political scene, even as its support has ebbed. The peace dividend has delivered significant progress on reconstruction and greater regional autonomy on decisions—about the shariah law for example—but the political situation remains hostage to a continuing climate of fear, violence and impunity. Yet, overall this marks a remarkable if flawed transition from the prevailing pre-tsunami situation.

Japan

Compared to China, India and Indonesia, Japan has a relatively homogenous population, but appearances can be deceiving. The polished veneer of uniformity obscures a growing diversity. Between 1990 and 2010, Japan's foreign-born population doubled, and non-Japanese constitute about 2% of all residents. This figure is also misleading in that many ethnic Koreans born in Japan have naturalized in recent years, while one in 30 babies born as Japanese has one non-Japanese parent, further blurring the lines of an imagined racial purity.

To some degree there is a cosmetic multiculturalism that celebrates diversity, but this does not translate into a basis for asserting rights, promoting reforms or gaining access to power and services (Morris-Suzuki 1998). Ethnic Koreans, Chinese and *nikkeijin* (Japanese born overseas) constitute significant minority communities that all face discrimination and suffer from entrenched intolerance. The upsurge in Japanese nationalism in 21st-century Japan is fueled by the rise of China and the threat this poses to Japan. This reactive nationalism has increased intolerance, and Japan's Korean minority, the zainichi, have suffered the most. On the fringe, geographically and economically, Okinawans also have a cultural identity that is distinctive from "mainland" Japan and resent that the burdens of hosting US bases are disproportionately foisted on them. The indigenous Ainu of Hokkaido, ethnically and linguistically distinct from Japanese, have also been relegated to the fringes of Japanese national identity. The story of their marginalization and suppression of their cultural identity began in the 19th century, a sustained process that has taken away or weakened most of what gave meaning to the Ainu community. It survives, but only as a shadow of itself. Belatedly the government recognized the Ainu's indigenous status in 2008, but by that time their cultural heritage had become mostly a curiosity packaged for tourism.

In crafting the myth of mono-ethnicity, the collective gaze is averted from the Ainu, Okinawans, Koreans and Chinese, constituting some 4–6 million people out of a population of 126 million. But how can claims of homogeneity be sustained in the face of the evident diversity and growing assertiveness of previously silenced minorities? What drives a powerful ethno-nationalism that seeks to suppress ethnic heterogeneity and cultural hybridity? These important questions lie at the heart of Japanese national identity and its sustaining ideology.

Japanese imperialism bequeathed a legacy of diversity that haunts contemporary Japan. In 1945 alone, 2.3 million Koreans migrated to Japan to work in the war industries. During the Japanese colonial era, stretching from 1895 to 1945, an empire of diverse peoples was forged in Asia. At this time the Japanese empire was conceived by Japan as an extended family based on the concept of "gozoku kyowa" (the cooperation of five ethnic groups), and Manchuria was where Han Chinese, Manchurians, Mongolians, Japanese and Koreans lived together, although not often in harmony.

The nexus of race and empire formed a Japanese identity imbued with Pan-Asian paternalism and social Darwinist condescension. In important ways, Japanese national identity crystallized within the confines of these imperial encounters, establishing and amplifying a sense of superiority over other Asians. The collapse of Japan's empire in 1945 fundamentally altered racial discourse in Japan. The basis for multi-ethnicity had been the empire and without it a new social context emerged that proved fertile ground for nurturing a mono-ethnic identity, one that was shaped by the convulsions of rapid postwar modernization (Lie 2001). A reassuring monolithic "we" became the foundation for a postwar identity that broke with the eclectic and accommodating Pan-Asianism embraced in the first four decades of the 20th century. Japan became a more homogeneous nation based on mass migration to the cities and the media's promotion of uniformity in speech, manners, tastes and lifestyles.

Mono-ethnic Japan is, thus, a post-World War II construct that feeds nationalist aspirations and nurtures a sense of unity. This recalibrated national identity weighs heavily on Japan's minorities, but perhaps most egregiously on the ethnic Korean community.

Zainichi

The zainichi community of long-term ethnic Korean permanent residents in Japan constitutes the nation's second largest minority, one that has not fared that well. Most Koreans came to Japan during the wartime years, 1931–1945, looking for work or on a coerced basis. With the dissolution of the Japanese empire in 1945 they were stripped of Japanese nationality, but allowed to stay in Japan. In 1965 South Korea and Japan normalized relations and Tokyo agreed to grant the right of permanent residence to those Koreans in Japan who opted for South Korean nationality. As a result, about 350,000 Koreans (some 60% of all Koreans then residing in Japan) gained the right of permanent residence. Some 250,000 Koreans, supporters of North Korea, refused to apply for this status and remained "stateless." Following the 1981 revision of the Immigration Control Act they were also granted the right of permanent residence in Japan. Finally in 1991, Japan granted the legal status of "special permanent residents" to all Koreans (and their descendants) who had permanent resident status.

Younger generations of zainichi have attended Korean schools in Japan (many don't), but they are all fluent in Japanese, culturally socialized, and virtually indistinguishable from Japanese. However, even such assimilated Japan-born "foreigners" face discrimination and tend to have lower levels of educational attainment and income. Facing discrimination in Japanese firms, many zainichi have established their own businesses. Others have become celebrities, although often hiding their ethnic background. In addition, many *yakuza* (gangsters) are recruited from the zainichi community, reflecting the limited opportunities open to them.

As of 2010, the Immigration Bureau reported that there were 565,989 registered Korean residents in Japan, down from a peak of 688,144 in 1992. This figure does not include the 284,840 Koreans who had opted to become naturalized Japanese citizens as of 2005. There are over 60 Korean schools across Japan, but reduced subsidies from Pyongyang, and cuts in public subsidies in Japan, are squeezing these institutions, where student numbers have fallen from a peak of 40,000 in the early 1960s to about 8,000. The Japanese government also refuses to extend tuition support given to all other high school students, and Chongryon, the pro-North Korean organization in Japan, lost its headquarters to pay off debts. Changes in Japanese tax laws, harassment targeting students wearing the distinctive uniforms, and the decision by many zainichi to send their children to public schools are increasing financial difficulties for these schools and their future appears bleak. About 75% of zainichi are affiliated with Mindan, the pro-South Korean organization in Japan. Divided ideologically, the two organizations—Chongryon and Mindan—are united in their zeal to sustain a strong sense of Korean identity and oppose assimilation and naturalization.

Koreans in Japan have fragmented identities, living on the margins in Japan and viewed as foreigners in Korea. In recent years there has been an increase in the numbers of Koreans becoming naturalized citizens, some 10,000 a year, due to the advantages this confers, the barriers it lowers, and the inescapable reality for some of having a less resolutely Korean identity rooted in the nation state; identity as a Korean is not, for increasing numbers of young zainichi, a matter of passports. There are some 8,000 marriages annually between zainichi and Japanese (6,000 with Japanese men and 2,000 with Japanese women); their children automatically gain Japanese citizenship under a 1985 law. Most naturalization occurs at time of marriage or employment, suggesting it is mostly a pragmatic decision, as younger generations develop more flexible identity strategies that facilitate their assimilation.

Another reason for zainichi to naturalize is because Japan has become decidedly less hospitable to ethnic Koreans, despite the incredible boom in Korean popular culture in Japan that was sparked by the joint hosting of the World Cup football tournament in 2002. This anti-Korean backlash is due to a series of missile tests by North Korea, its nuclear weapons program, and frenzied media coverage of Japanese nationals' abductions by North Korean agents. This has generated a virulent anti-North Korean groundswell, whipped up by politicians and the media, one that generates pressure on zainichi to blend in.

In recent years there has been an outpouring of hate speech targeting ethnic Koreans in Japan, a disturbing development even if it is not representative. These xenophobic sentiments have sparked a backlash among Japanese, and counter-demonstrations, but the mass media has tapped into this virulent jingoism.

Since 2013 the weekly magazines and manga publishers have regularly featured anti-Korean and anti-Chinese screeds, feeding discriminatory sentiments. Shin Okubo, Tokyo's cosmopolitan hub for the K-pop boom and long an enclave of non-Japanese diversity in Tokyo, was suddenly thrust into the front trenches of jingoism as nationalist right-wingers marched through its streets carrying ominous placards calling for death to Koreans. The Japanese courts have penalized thuggish intimidation of ethnic Korean schoolchildren in Kyoto, and ordinary citizens have organized counter-demonstrations, but Japan's political leadership was eerily quiet on the matter, passively condoning intolerance. Following UN criticism, in 2014 Yoichi Masuzoe, the Governor of Tokyo, confronted Prime Minister Abe, pointing out that the spread of hate speech was embarrassing in the run-up to the 2020 Olympics and reflected badly on the nation. The government hastily convened a committee to prepare relevant legislation, but one LDP lawmaker on this committee told reporters that he wanted to use the new law to prevent protesters from gathering outside the Diet and criticizing government policy, not exactly the hate speech Masuzoe or the UN had in mind.

Koreans resident in Japan are no strangers to prejudice. Indeed, in the aftermath of the 1923 earthquake, thousands were killed in Tokyo by vigilante mobs enraged by baseless rumors that Koreans were setting fires, poisoning wells and looting. In 2000, then Governor Shintaro Ishihara told Self-Defense Force troops to be vigilant about crimes by *sankokujin* ("third country people," a derogatory term for Koreans and Chinese) in the event of an earthquake, a chilling reference evoking the sentiments behind the *senjingari* ("Korean hunting") massacres of 1923.

Contemporary Korea-phobes find a receptive environment in 21st-century Japan. Problems with South Korea over unresolved historical grievances have escalated in recent years as Korean courts have ruled Japanese firms should compensate forced laborers and pressured Korea's government to demand redress for wartime sex slaves who served in Japanese military brothels. President Park Geun-hye amplified this anti-Korean backlash by admonishing Prime Minister Abe to improve his understanding of the nations' shared history and giving him the diplomatic cold shoulder. As the bilateral history wars heat up, Koreans in Japan are paying the price of a rising nationalist backlash.

Okinawa

During the US Occupation of Japan (1945–1952), American forces established a network of bases in Okinawa that remain at the heart of the fraught relations that prevail between Tokyo, Washington and Okinawans. Japan's Cold War bargain meant allowing the US to continue operating military bases in the nation and conceding administrative control over Okinawa, where most of the US bases were located. Making these concessions was a condition for ending the US Occupation, but Okinawans felt abandoned by this accommodation, and thus on the day when Japan celebrates the end of the Occupation (April 26 is National Sovereignty Day),

Okinawans still protest the betrayal. For many years, Okinawans agitated for ending US control, with violent anti-base protests erupting in 1970. Finally in 1972 Washington agreed to a reversion of sovereignty, ceding control back to Tokyo. But the extensive network of bases remained, occupying some 18% of the main island where about 75% of the US military presence in Japan is concentrated. It is also Japan's poorest prefecture, fueling local resentment that their interests are ignored except for base-related issues. Okinawa has been called a Cold War island because the US insisted on keeping it as part of its anti-communist containment strategy, a militarized bulwark for projecting American military power in Asia and preventing the spread of communism. In the post-World War II era, these bases have been used extensively, during the Korean and Vietnam Wars, and in the post-Cold War era in the conflicts in Iraq and Afghanistan.

Overall, the US military bases are relatively uncontroversial in mainstream discourse because Japanese outside Okinawa are not bothered by their presence and the government has convinced the public that they are valuable for the security of Japan. Opponents of the bases suggest that the US presence might make the islands into targets and thus they are more of a danger than a security umbrella. Islanders' identity draws on the traumatic Battle of Okinawa slaughter in 1945 that claimed some 140,000 civilian lives, one-third of the population. Controversy also focuses on the storage of nuclear weapons at Kadena Airbase prior to the 1972 reversion, in violation of Japan's non-nuclear principles. It has also emerged that the US military dumped significant quantities of Agent Orange on the bases, contaminating the land with chemicals used widely in the Vietnam War and subsequently linked to cancer among US military veterans exposed to the defoliant.

US Ambassador Edwin Reischauer, who served in Japan from 1961 to 1966, rationalized the concentration of the US military bases in Okinawa because there they would not become politicized among the mainstream Japanese public (Packard 2010). But this has not prevented them from being a target of sustained anti-base activism by Okinawans concerned about crime, noise and environmental issues. Since the mid-1970s, Japan has covered the local land rental and staffing costs of the bases, rising to some $2 billion a year, as part of its contribution to burden sharing, which makes retaining the bases attractive to US policymakers in times of shrinking military budgets. Tokyo has tried with little success to mollify Okinawans with massive public works projects and other job-generating, economy-boosting subsidies, but anti-base sentiments remain widespread, for very good reasons.

In 1995 three US servicemen kidnapped and gang-raped a 12-year-old Okinawan schoolgirl, sparking massive demonstrations. Okinawans have long resented crimes committed by US soldiers and sailors, and the Status of Forces Agreement (SOFA) that protected them from local prosecution and incarceration for their crimes. In response to this especially heinous incident, the US and Japan modified the SOFA to allow local prosecution and incarceration for certain serious crimes. In addition, they negotiated for a decade to come up with a plan to reduce the US military footprint in Okinawa by shifting, consolidating, closing and handing over bases and returning land that was no longer required.

The 2006 Roadmap, as the plan is called, has hit a variety of snags because redeployment of personnel to Guam and elsewhere was predicated on closing the US Marine Airbase Futenma and relocating it to a less densely populated area in northern Okinawa, adjacent to Henoko, a fishing village which is part of the town of Nago. Futenma is the US Marine Airbase in Ginowan City and it is slated for closure because it is located in a residential community where chances of an accident are unacceptably high. In 2004 a helicopter crash at an adjacent university caused no casualties, but highlighted the urgent need to close the base. The 2006 Roadmap calls for building a V-shaped runway out into reclaimed land in Oura Bay off Henoko, where there is a coral reef in pristine waters. Islanders oppose this plan because it is not immediately obvious why reducing the military footprint requires building an additional new military facility in Okinawa rather than somewhere else.

Okinawans resent shouldering a disproportionate share of the base-hosting burden. In 2013 a delegation representing the "Okinawan Consensus," from all levels of government ranging from village assemblies to the prefectural assembly, formally demanded that the central government close Futenma and not relocate it anywhere in Okinawa. Polls conducted in 2014 indicate that over 80% of the public oppose the Henoko relocation plan, and voters have backed anti-base candidates at the town, prefectural and national levels. Given that democracy is one of the shared values that are ostensibly the foundation of the US–Japan alliance, the decision by Tokyo and Washington to ignore island-wide opposition has fueled accusations of hypocrisy.

At the end of 2013, eager to proceed with the landfill phase of the Henoko project, Prime Minister Abe's government promised a staggering $20 billion over the ensuing eight years if the governor would give his approval. Then Governor Hirokazu Nakaima succumbed to this extravagant inducement, but became the island's most reviled politician and the prefectural assembly demanded that he resign. An anti-base candidate ousted Nakaima in the 2014 gubernatorial elections, based on hopes that he will overturn the decision to proceed with the Henoko base construction.

For Okinawans the situation has not changed much, as central government policymakers see their protests more as a nuisance than a legitimate expression of longstanding, unaddressed grievances. The Henoko plan fuels the anti-base movement as Okinawans stand up to power politics and exercise their democratic rights, a little nationalism that remains a reproach to alliance managers pressing ahead with a roadmap that appears to be a dead end. Based on wartime memories seared into the collective consciousness of contemporary Okinawans, there are shared anxieties about serving as a sacrificial pawn and getting caught in between the machinations of distant powers.

Select Bibliographical Guide to Nationalisms in Asia

I have organized this guide to correspond to the four sections of the book as follows:

I Introduction and National Identity
II Political Economy and Spectacle
III Shackles of the Past
IV Flashpoints and Fringes

This guide is a selective list of relevant sources that are useful and pertinent. I have focused mostly on books, but also include a few relevant journal articles. In most cases I give information on the latest available edition of books, and in general this bibliography features more recent texts because they are more likely to be available. I have annotated the first section which presents background information for what follows, while the subsequent three sections are organized by subject matter covered in each of the chapters. As some of this material is overlapping across chapters in each section, I thought this method of organizing sources by section might prove most useful for further study. In the final section there is a list of some academic journals and Internet sources relevant to Asian nationalism. Clearly, the more one looks, the more one will find, and in this era of search engines there is a nearly inexhaustible supply of resources; the discerning reader must separate the wheat from the chaff and this bibliography is a stab at doing so.

Nationalism in Asia: A History Since 1945, First Edition. Jeff Kingston.

I Introduction and National Identity

This book focuses on how nationalism is embraced, expressed, manifested and manipulated in post-1945 Asia and the various agendas it serves. Nationalism has become a key aspect of politics and society in Asia and as such is key to understanding 21st-century regional dynamics. There are relatively few comparative studies of Asian nationalism that span the region. Michael Leifer (ed.), *Asian Nationalism* (Routledge 2000) is a multi-author collection of vintage country studies that lacks thematic coherence or a common analytical thread. Highly recommended is the astute and sophisticated political economy perspective on several Asian examples presented by Radhika Desai (ed.), *Developmental and Cultural Nationalisms* (Routledge 2009). Desai's collection of Asian country studies is especially useful because of the common critical analysis and thematic coherence.

For a theoretical introduction the best option is Anthony Smith, *Nationalism* (Polity Press, 2nd ed., 2010). The two most useful analytical overviews of theories of nationalism are: Umut Ozkirimli, *Theories of Nationalism: A Critical Introduction* (Palgrave Macmillan, 2nd ed., 2010) and Erika Harris, *Nationalism: Theories and Cases* (Edinburgh University Press 2009). These books present clear summaries of the main theories, key critiques levied against them, and their relation to other literature in the field, and as such are invaluable. For additional readings in nationalist theory see: Benedict Anderson, *Imagined Communities: Reflections on the Origin and Spread of Nationalism* (Verso 2006); Partha Chatterjee, *Nationalist Thought and the Colonial World: A Derivative Discourse?* (Zed Books 1986); Ernest Gellner, *Nations and Nationalism* (Cornell University Press, 2nd ed., 2009); and Eric Hobsbawm, *Nations and Nationalism Since 1780* (Cambridge University Press, 2nd ed., 2012).

Other works cited in the Introduction:

Anderson, B., *Imagined Communities: Reflections on the Origin and Spread of Nationalism* (Verso, 3rd ed., 2006).

Clark, C., *The Sleepwalkers: How Europe Went to War in 1914* (Harper 2013).

Guha, R., *Patriots and Partisans* (Penguin 2012).

Kivimäki, Timo, "East Asian Relative Peace and the ASEAN Way," *International Relations of the Asia Pacific*, 11 (2011), 57–85.

Murakami, Haruki, *Asahi* (September 28, 2012).

Renan, Ernest, "What Is a Nation?" [1882], in Geoff Eley and Ronald Grigor Suny, eds., *Becoming National: A Reader* (Oxford University Press 1996), 41–55.

Smith, A.D., *Nations and Nationalism in a Global Era* (Polity 1995).

In general, the field of Asia studies divides the region into the sub-regions of East Asia, Southeast Asia and South Asia, and cross-regional dialogue between specialists is not well developed. Thus, the literature tends to be sub-regional or country specific. For general background, see Patricia Buckley and Anne Walthal, *East Asia: A Cultural, Social and Political History*, Volume II (Cengage, 3rd ed., 2013); Milton Osborne, *Southeast Asia: An Introductory History* (Allen and Unwin, 11th ed., 2013);

and Sugata Bose and Ayesha Jalal, *Modern South Asia: History, Culture, Political Economy* (Routledge 2011).

Ainslee Embree and Carol Gluck (eds.), *Asia in World History: A Guide for Teaching* (M.E. Sharpe 1997) remains quite useful for general background.

Leaders

There is an excellent compendium on many of the key Asian leaders who are discussed in this study: Ramachandra Guha (ed.), *Makers of Modern Asia* (Belknap Press 2014). There are chapters, *inter alia*, on Gandhi, Nehru, Mao Zedong, Chiang Kai-shek, Sukarno, Deng Xiaoping and Indira Gandhi.

The best biography on Shigeru Yoshida is John Dower's *Empire and Aftermath: Yoshida Shigeru and the Japanese Experience 1878–1954* (Harvard East Asian Monographs 1988). Yoshida is also assessed in Richard Samuels, *Machiavelli's Children: Leaders and Their Legacies in Italy and Japan* (Cornell University Press 2005).

On China's leaders see:

Lampton, David, *Following the Leader: Ruling China, from Deng Xiaoping to Xi Jinping* (University of California Press 2013).
Shambaugh, David (ed.), *Deng Xiaoping: Portrait of a Chinese Statesman* (Oxford University Press 1995).
Short, Philip, *Mao: A Life* (Henry Holt and Co. 2000).
Spence, Jonathan, *Mao Zedong* (Viking 1999).

On Park Chung-hee's mixed legacy see:

Kim, Byung-kook and Ezra F. Vogel (eds.), *The Park Chung Hee Era: The Transformation of South Korea* (Harvard University Press 2011).
Kim, Hyung-A and Clark W. Sorensen (eds.), *Reassessing the Park Chung Hee Era, 1961–1979* (University of Washington 2011).

On Indonesia's leaders see:

Elson, Robert E., *Suharto: A Political Biography* (Cambridge University Press 2008).
Legge, John, *Sukarno: A Political Biography* (Editions Didier Millet, 3rd ed., 2012).

Memoirs and Ideas

The following books are written by these leaders or focus on their thinking and influence.

Adams, Cindy, *Sukarno: An Autobiography as told to Cindy Adams* (Bobbs-Merrill 1965).

Cheek, Timothy (ed.), *A Critical Introduction to Mao* (Cambridge University Press 2010).
Cook, Alexander (ed.), *Mao's Little Red Book: A Global History* (Cambridge University Press 2014).
Hasan, Mushirul, *Nehru's India: Select Speeches* (Oxford 2011).
Nehru, Jawaharlal, *The First Sixty Years; Presenting in His Own Words the Development of the Political Thought of Jawaharlal Nehru and the Background against Which It Evolved* (John Day 1965).
Nehru, Jawaharlal, *Jawaharlal Nehru: An Autobiography* (Penguin 2004).
Paget, Roger (ed. and trans.), *Indonesia Accuses! Soekarno's Defence Oration in the Political Trial of 1930* (Oxford University Press 1975).
Park, Chung-hee, *Major Speeches by Korea's Park Chung Hee* (compiled by Shin Bum Shik) (Hollym 1970).
Soeharto, *My Thoughts, Words and Deeds: An Autobiography* (Citra Lamtoro Gung Persada 1991).
Soekarno, *Nationalism, Islam, and Marxism* (Cornell University 1970).
Tharoor, Shashi, *Nehru: The Invention of India* (Arcade Publishing 2012).
Yoshida, Shigeru, *Yoshida Shigeru: Last Meiji Man* (trans. Kenichi Yoshida and Hiroshi Nara) (Rowman & Littlefield 2007).

Legacies

To get a sense of the impact and long shadow cast by imperialism in modern Asia there is the excellent Pankaj Mishra, *From the Ruins of Empire: The Intellectuals Who Remade Asia* (Farrar, Straus and Giroux 2012).

In addition:

Anderson, Benedict, *The Spectre of Comparisons: Nationalism, Southeast Asia and the World* (Verso 1998).
McMahon, Robert, *Colonialism and Cold War: The United States and the Struggle for Indonesian Independence, 1945–49* (Cornell University Press 2011).
Miller, Manjai Chaterrjee, *Wronged by Empire: Post-Imperial Ideology and Foreign Policy in India and China* (Stanford University Press 2013).
Saller, Sven and J. Victor Koschman (eds.), *Pan-Asianism in Modern Japanese History* (Routledge 2007).
Schell, Jonathan and John Delury, *Wealth and Power: China's Long March to the Twenty-First Century* (Random House 2013).

Identity

Three of our nations are covered in Henry Nau and Deepa Ollapally (eds.), *World Views of Aspiring Powers: Domestic Foreign Policy Debates in China, India, Iran, Japan and Russia* (Oxford University Press 2012). It is an interesting window on the background and politics of domestic discourses in these countries regarding world affairs and how they affect foreign relations.

For a stimulating elaboration of the East Asian national identity syndrome, involving sharp and sudden swings in nationalist sentiments, which offers a multi-dimensional assessment of evolving national identity in China, Japan and South Korea, see Gilbert Rozman (ed.), *East Asian National Identities: Common Roots and Chinese Exceptionalism* (Stanford University Press 2012). National identity and the fraught bilateral relationship between Japan and South Korea in the context of US alliance politics is astutely observed in Brad Glosserman and Scott Snyder, *The Japan–South Korea Identity Clash: East Asian Security and the United States* (Columbia University Press 2015).

For an intriguing, multifaceted discussion of how the idea of Japan resonates in East Asia, see Paul Morris, Naoko Shimazu and Edward Vickers (eds.), *Imagining Japan in Postwar East Asia* (Routledge 2013).

The concept of soft power and how it influences regional relations, including Southeast Asia, is assessed in Jing Sun, *Japan and China as Charm Rivals: Soft Power in Regional Diplomacy* (University of Michigan 2013).

International Relations in Asia

A longstanding proponent of constructive engagement, with extensive service in the US government, shifts to a harder-line perspective in reassessing China's mainstream hawkish nationalists and their strategic ambitions in Michael Pillsbury, *The Hundred-Year Marathon: China's Secret Strategy to Replace America as the Global Superpower* (Henry Holt & Co. 2015).

In addition:

Breslin, Shaun (ed.), *Handbook of China's International Relations* (Routledge 2015).

Dower, John, "The San Francisco System: Past, Present, Future in U.S.-Japan-China Relations," *The Asia-Pacific Journal*, 12:8:2 (February 24, 2014).

Miller, Alice and Richard Wich, *Becoming Asia: Change and Continuity in Asian International Relations Since World War II* (Stanford University Press 2011).

Scott, David (ed.), *Handbook of India's International Relations* (Routledge 2015).

Selden, Mark, "Economic Nationalism and Regionalism in Contemporary East Asia," *The Asia-Pacific Journal*, 10:43:2 (October 29, 2012).

Shambaugh, David and Michael Yahuda (eds.), *International Relations of Asia* (Rowman & Littlefield, 2nd ed., 2014).

Smith, Sheila, *Japanese Domestic Politics and a Rising China* (Columbia University Press 2015).

Tan, Andrew (ed.), *East and Southeast Asia: International Relations and Security Perspectives* (Routledge 2013).

Tan, Andrew, *The Arms Race in Asia: Trends, Causes and Implications* (Routledge 2014).

Tan, Andrew (ed.), *Security and Conflict in East Asia* (Routledge 2015).

Tay, Simon, *Asia Alone: The Dangerous Post-Crisis Divide from America* (Wiley 2010).

Country Studies

For general post-1945 background for individual countries there are many excellent options including: Tamara Jacka, Andrew Kipnis and Sally Sargeson, *Contemporary China: Society and Social Change* (Cambridge University Press 2013); Ramachandra Guha, *India After Gandhi: The History of the World's Largest Democracy* (Ecco 2007); Adrian Vickers, *A History of Modern Indonesia* (Cambridge University Press, 2nd ed., 2014); Jeff Kingston, *Contemporary Japan* (Wiley, 2nd ed., 2012); and Charles Armstrong, *The Koreas* (Routledge, 2nd ed., 2013).

Further recommended readings on each of the focus nations follow.

China

For China, there is an abundance of recent books, and perhaps the best account for our purposes is by the *Washington Post* correspondent Philip Pan, *Out of Mao's Shadow: The Battle for China's Soul* (Picador 2008).

Some of the better options are also written by journalists: Evan Osnos, *Age of Ambition: Chasing Fortune, Truth and Faith in the New China* (Bodley Head 2014); Louisa Lim, *The People's Republic of Amnesia: Tiananmen Revisited* (Oxford University Press 2014); Peter Hessler, *Country Driving: A Chinese Road Trip* (Canongate 2011); and Pallavi Aiyar, *Smoke and Mirrors: An Experience of China* (Fourth Estate 2008).

There is no better source on the Dream question discussed in Chapter 2 than William Callahan, *China Dreams: 20 Visions of the Future* (Oxford 2013). Also useful are: Helen Wang, *The Chinese Dream: The Rise of the World's Largest Middle Class and What It Means to You* (Bestseller Press 2012); Evan Osnos, "Can China Deliver the China Dream(s)?" *New Yorker* (March 26, 2013); Gerard Lemos, *The End of the Chinese Dream: Why Chinese People Fear the Future* (Yale University Press 2012); P. Link, "*He Exposed Corrupt China Before He Left*," *New York Review of Books* (August 2014); and Thomas Friedman, "China Needs Its Own Dream," *New York Times* (October 2, 2012).

On the nexus of nationalism, values and political interests in China, the dangers of Han chauvinism, and efforts to tame popular nationalism, see Suisheng Zhao, *A Nation-State by Construction: Dynamics of Modern Chinese Nationalism* (Stanford University Press 2004). For analysis of the impact on foreign relations 1978–2012, see Jessica Chen Weiss, *Powerful Patriots: Nationalist Protest in China's Foreign Relations* (Oxford University Press 2014).

For a succinct summary of the nature of the Chinese government and the implications of its rise for global politics that makes a case for the onward and upward scenario, see Stefan Halper, *The Beijing Consensus: How China's Authoritarian Model Will Dominate the Twenty-First Century* (Basic Books 2010).

If I had to choose one scholar's book on China for an opinionated and succinct introduction it would be Odd Arne Westad, *Restless Empire: China and the World Since 1750* (Basic Books 2012).

The following scholarly works are also key sources on contemporary Chinese nationalism:

Gries, Peter Hays, *China's New Nationalism: Pride, Politics and Diplomacy* (University of California Press 2004).
Kirby, William (ed.), *The People's Republic of China at 60: An International Assessment* (Harvard University Press 2011).
Link, Perry, Richard Madsen and Paul Pickowitz (eds.), *Restless China* (Rowman & Littlefield 2013).
Osnos, Evan, "Can China Deliver the China Dream(s)?" *New Yorker* (March 26, 2013).
Shirk, Susan, *China: Fragile Superpower* (Oxford University Press 2008).
Unger, Jonathan and Geremie R. Barmé (eds.), *Chinese Nationalism* (M.E. Sharpe 1996).
Wang, Hui, *The End of the Revolution: China and the Limits of Modernity* (Verso 2011).
Wasserstrom, Jeffrey, *China in the 21st Century: What Everyone Needs to Know* (Oxford University Press, 2nd ed., 2013).
Wasserstrom, Jeffrey, "A Mongkok Morning," *Huffington Post* (November 26, 2014).
Zhao Suisheng (ed.), *Construction of Chinese Nationalism in the Early 21st Century: Domestic Sources and International Implications* (Routledge 2014).

India

The first chapter introduces the Idea of nation and draws on Sunil Khilnani, *The Idea of India* (Penguin, 2nd ed., 2003). The best analysis of the intellectual history of modern India is Ananya Vajpeyi, *Righteous Republic: The Political Foundations of Modern India* (Harvard University Press 2012). For further essential reading see: William Dalrymple, *Nine Lives: In Search of the Sacred in Modern India* (Knopf 2010); Akash Kapur, *India Becoming: A Portrait of Life in Modern India* (Riverhead 2013); Perry Anderson, *The Indian Ideology* (Verso 2012); and Pankaj Mishra, "India and Ideology: Why Western Thinkers Struggle with the Subcontinent," *Foreign Affairs* (November/December 2013), 139–147.

The following works are cited in the text:

Dalrymple, William, "India: The War Over History," *New York Review of Books*, 52:6 (April 7, 2005), 62–65.
Doniger, Wendy, "Banned in Bangalore," *International New York Times* (March 7, 2014a), 8.
Doniger, Wendy, "Censorship by the Batra Brigades," *New York Review of Books*, 61:8 (May 8, 2014b), 51.
Mishra, Pankaj, "Modi's Idea of India," *International New York Times* (October 24, 2014).
Panagariya, Arvind and Megha Mukim, "A Comprehensive Analysis of Poverty In India," Policy Research Working Paper 6714 (World Bank 2013).
Sen, Amartya, "India's Women: The Mixed Truth," *New York Review of Books*, 60:15 (October 10, 2013), 24–27.

Tagore, Rabindranath, *Nationalism* (Book Club of California 1917).
Vajpeyi, Ananya, "The Triumph of the Hindu Right," *Foreign Affairs* (September/October 2014), 150–157.

On the rise of Hindutva (Hindu nationalist movement), see: Christophe Jaffrelot, *The Hindu Nationalist Movement and Indian Politics* (Penguin 1999); Christophe Jaffrelot (ed.), *Hindu Nationalism: A Reader* (Princeton University Press 2007); and Radhika Desai, *Slouching Towards Ayodhya: From Congress to Hindutva in Indian Politics* (Three Essays, 2nd rev. ed., 2004).

For poignant background, see Katherine Boo's superb study of contemporary slum life, *Behind the Beautiful Forevers: Life, Death and Hope in a Mumbai Slum* (Portobello 2013). For in-depth analysis of caste, see Anupama Rao, *The Caste Question: Dalits and the Politics of Modern India* (University of California Press 2009).

Japan

For an opinionated, widely ranging and engaging overview relevant to nationalism, see R. Taggart Murphy, *Japan and the Shackles of the Past* (Oxford University Press 2014).

In order to understand contemporary Japanese nationalism the following are especially pertinent:

Bix, Herbert, *Hirohito and the Making of Modern Japan* (HarperCollins 2001).
Doak, Kevin, *A History of Nationalism in Modern Japan: Placing the People* (Brill 2006).
Dower, John, *Embracing Defeat: Japan in the Wake of WWII* (W.W. Norton 1999).
Funabashi, Yoichi (ed.), *Media, Propaganda and Politics in 20th-Century Japan* (trans. Barak Kushner) (Bloomsbury Academic 2015).
Gayle, Curtis, *Marxist History and Postwar Japanese Nationalism* (Routledge 2003).
Hoppens, Robert, *The China Problem in Postwar Japan: Japanese National Identity and Sino-Japanese Relations* (Bloomsbury Academic 2015).
Lie, John, *Multiethnic Japan* (Harvard University Press 2001).
McVeigh, Brian, *Nationalisms of Japan: Managing and Mystifying Identity* (Rowman & Littlefield 2004).
Ozawa, Ichiro, *Blueprint for a New Japan* (trans. Louisa Rubinfien) (Kodansha 1994).
Pyle, Kenneth, *Japan Rising: The Resurgence of Japanese Power and Purpose* (Public Affairs 2009).
Samuels, Richard, *Securing Japan: Tokyo's Grand Strategy and the Future of East Asia* (Cornell University Press 2011).

For a very readable and insightful journalist's account of contemporary Japan, see David Pilling, *Bending Adversity* (Allen Lane 2014).

Indonesia

The most relevant book for this section is Robert E. Elson, *The Idea of Indonesia: A History* (Cambridge University Press 2008).

Regarding the impact of the 1965 mass killings, see Ariel Heriyanto, *State Terrorism and Political Identity in Indonesia: Fatally Belonging* (Routledge 2005).

For more on the New Order under Suharto, these journalists' accounts are especially good: Adam Schwarz, *Indonesia: A Nation in Waiting* (Talisman 2013); Hamish McDonald, *Suharto's Indonesia* (University of Hawai'i Press 1981); and Michael Vatikiotis, *Indonesian Politics Under Suharto: The Rise and Fall of the New Order* (Routledge, 3rd ed., 2013).

On Islamic identity see:

Burhanudin, Jajat and Kees van Dijk (eds.), *Islam in Indonesia: Contrasting Images and Interpretations* (Amsterdam University Press 2013).

Elson, R.E., "Nationalism, Islam, 'Secularism' and the State in Contemporary Indonesia," *Australian Journal of International Affairs*, 64:3 (2010), 328–343.

Fellard, Andree and Remy Madinier, *The End of Innocence? Indonesian Islam and the Temptations of Radicalism* (trans. Wong Wee) (University of Hawai'i Press 2011).

van Bruinessen, Martin, *Contemporary Developments in Indonesian Islam: Explaining the "Conservative Turn"* (Institute of Southeast Asian Studies 2013).

For an illuminating trip through this sprawling archipelago, exploring its diversity, complexities, contradictions and hidden stories, see Elizabeth Pisani, *Indonesia, Etc: Exploring the Improbable Nation* (Norton 2014).

South Korea

The best overview highlighting the sources of nationalism is Bruce Cumings, *Korea's Place in the Sun: A Modern History* (W.W. Norton 2005).

For additional background, see Michael Robinson, *Korea's Twentieth-Century Odyssey: A Short History* (University of Hawai'i Press 2007); and Kyung Hwang, *A History of Korea* (Palgrave Macmillan 2010).

In order to understand the importance of war and colonialism in defining Korean nationalism, see Bruce Cumings, *The Korean War: A History* (Modern Library 2010).

For an excellent scholarly assessment of contemporary nationalism, see Gi-Wook Shin, *Ethnic Nationalism in Korea: Genealogy, Politics, and Legacy* (Stanford University Press 2006).

Further recommended readings:

Kal, Hong, *Aesthetic Constructions of Korean Nationalism: Spectacle, Politics, and History* (Routledge 2011).

Lee, Sook-jong, "The Assertive Nationalism of South Korean Youth: Cultural Dynamism and Political Activism," *SAIS Review*, 26:2 (January 2006), 123–132.

So, Ching-sok, *Korean Nationalism Betrayed* (trans. Han Do-Hyun and Pankaj Mohan) (Global Oriental 2007).

For a recent journalistic assessment, see Daniel Tudor, *Korea: The Impossible Nation* (Tuttle 2012).

Nation Branding and Contemporary Culture

For those interested in exploring these subjects raised briefly in Chapter 3, I recommend the following:

Bestor, Victoria and Theodore Bestor (eds.), *Routledge Handbook on Japanese Culture and Society* (Routledge 2011).

Chua, Beng Huat, *Structure, Audience and Soft-Power in East Asian Pop Culture* (Hong Kong University Press 2012).

Chua, Beng Huat and Koichi Iwabuchi (eds.), *East Asian Pop Culture: Analyzing the Korean Wave* (Hong Kong University Press 2008).

Condry, Ian, *The Soul of Anime: Collaborative Creativity and Japan's Media Success Story* (Duke University Press 2013).

Curtin, Michael and Hemant Shah (eds.), *Reorienting Global Communication: Indian and Chinese Media Beyond Borders* (University of Illinois Press 2010).

Dinnie, Keith, *Nation Branding: Concepts, Issues, Practice* (Butterworth-Heinemann 2008).

Dwyer, Rachel, *Bollywood's India: Hindi Cinema as a Guide to Contemporary India* (Reaktion Press 2014).

Galbraith, Patrick, *The Moe Manifesto: An Insider's Look at the Worlds of Manga, Anime and Gaming* (Tuttle 2014).

Golkusing, K. Moti and Wimal Dissanayake (eds.), *Popular Culture in a Globalised India* (Routledge 2009).

Heryanto, Ariel (ed.), *Popular Culture in Indonesia: Fluid Identities in Post-Authoritarian Politics* (Routledge 2008).

Hong, Euny, *The Birth of Korean Cool: How One Nation Is Conquering the World Through Pop Culture* (Picador 2014).

Ingulsrud, John and Kate Allen, *Reading Japan Cool: Patterns of Manga Literacy and Discourse* (Lexington 2009).

Kasbekar, Asha, *Pop Culture India: Media, Arts, and Lifestyle* (ABC-Clio, 2006).

Kim, Youna, *The Korean Wave: Korean Media Go Global* (Routledge 2013).

Kinsella, Sharon, *Adult Manga: Culture and Power in Contemporary Japanese Society* (University of Hawai'i Press 2000).

Kumar, Shanti, *Gandhi Meets Primetime: Globalization and Nationalism in Indian Television* (University of Illinois Press 2005).

Kuwahara, Yasue (ed.), *The Korean Wave: Korean Popular Culture* (Palgrave Macmillan 2014).

Latham, Kevin, *Pop Culture China: Media, Arts, and Lifestyle* (ABC-Clio, 2007).

McCarthy, Helen and Jonathan Clements, *The Anime Encyclopedia: A Century of Japanese Animation* (Stonebridge Press, 3rd rev. ed., 2015). (The digital edition features numerous hyperlinks that greatly enhance the value of this publication.)

McCray, Douglas, "Japan's Gross National Cool," *Foreign Policy*, 130 (May 2002), 44–54.

Shen, Yipeng, *Public Discourses of Contemporary China: The Narration of the Nation in Popular Literatures, Film, and Television* (Palgrave Macmillan 2015).

Tan, See-kam, Peter Feng and Gina Marchetti (eds.), *Chinese Connections: Critical Perspectives on Film, Identity, and Diaspora* (Temple University Press 2009).

Tudor, Daniel, *A Geek in Korea: Discovering Asian's New Kingdom of Cool* (Tuttle 2014).

Watson, Iain, "Paradoxical Multiculturalism in South Korea," *Asian Politics and Polity*, 4:2 (April 2012), 233–258.

Weintraub, Andrew (ed.), *Islam and Popular Culture in Indonesia and Malaysia* (Routledge 2011).

Wheeler, Mark, *Japanese Visual Culture: Exploration in the World of Manga and Anime* (M.E. Sharpe 2008).

Environment

Asia's enormous challenges of environmental degradation, resource competition and sustainable development are examined in the following:

Chellaney, Brahma, *Water: Asia's New Battleground* (Georgetown University Press 2011).

Clifford, Mark, *The Greening of Asia: The Business Case for Solving Asia's Environmental Challenge* (Columbia University Press 2015).

Geall, Sam (ed.), *China and the Environment: The Green Revolution* (Zed Books, 2013).

Japan Environmental Council (ed.), *The State of the Environment in Asia 2006/2007* (United Nations University Press 2009).

Ma, Damien and William Adams, *In Line Behind a Billion People: How Scarcity Will Define China's Ascent in the Next Decade* (Pearson FT Press 2013).

Managi, Shunsuke (ed.), *The Routledge Handbook of Environmental Economics in Asia* (Routledge 2015).

Money, Elizabeth C., *The River Runs Black: The Environmental Challenge to China's Future* (Cornell University Press, 2nd ed., 2011).

Warren, Carol, *Community, Environment and Local Governance in Indonesia: Locating the Commonweal* (Routledge 2009).

Women

Broadbent, Kaye and Michele Ford (eds.), *Women and Labour Organizing in Asia: Diversity, Autonomy and Activism* (Routledge 2008).

Edwards, Louise and Mina Roces (eds.), *Women in Asia* (4 volumes, Routledge 2009).

Kelkar, Govind and Malthreyi Krishnaraj (eds), *Women, Land and Power in Asia* (Routledge 2013).

Mann, Susan (ed.), *Women and Gender Relations: Perspectives on Asia: Sixty Years of the Journal of Asian Studies* (Association for Asian Studies 2004).

Solotaroff, Jennifer and Rohini Pande, *Violence Against Women and Girls: Lessons from South Asia* (World Bank 2014).

The East Asian Peace

The causes for the absence of inter-state conflict since 1979 are assessed in the following:

Goldsmith, Benjamin E., "Different in Asia? Developmental States, Trade, and International Conflict Onset and Escalation," *International Relations of the Asia-Pacific*, 13 (2013), 175–205.

Goldsmith, Benjamin E., "Domestic Political Institutions and the Initiation of International Conflict in East Asia: Some Evidence for an Asian Democratic Peace," *International Relations of the Asia-Pacific*, 14 (2014), 59–90.

Kivimäki, Timo, *The Long Peace of East Asia* (Gower Publishing 2014).

Weissman, Mikael, *The East Asian Peace: Conflict Prevention and Informal Peacebuilding* (Palgrave Macmillan 2012).

Making a sobering argument about the prospects for war in the region: Christopher Coker, *The Improbable War: China, the United States and the Logic of Great Power Conflict* (Hurst 2015).

II Political Economy and Spectacle

General

Alagappa, Muthiah, *Civil Society and Political Change in Asia: Expanding and Contracting Democratic Space* (Stanford University Press 2004).

Bauer, Joanne and Daniel A. Bell (eds.), *The East Asian Challenge for Human Rights* (Cambridge University Press 1999).

Bridges, Brian and Lok-sang Ho (eds.), *Public Governance in Asia and the Limits of Electoral Democracy* (Edward Elgar 2009).

Cauquelin, Josiane, Paul Lim and Birgit Mayer-Konig (eds.), *Asian Values: Encounter with Diversity* (Curzon Press 1998).
Charlton, Sue Ellen, *Comparing Asian Politics: India, China and Japan* (Westview Press, 4th ed., 2014).
Costa, Antony (ed.), *Globalization and Economic Nationalism in Asia* (Oxford University Press 2012).
de Bary, William Theodore, *Asian Values and Human Rights: A Confucian Communitarian Perspective* (Harvard University Press 1998).
Diamond, Larry and Marc E. Plattner (eds.), *Democracy in East Asia* (Johns Hopkins University Press 1998).
Katzenstein, Peter and Takashi Shiraishi (eds.), *Beyond Japan: The Dynamics of East Asian Regionalism* (Cornell University Press 2006).
Kelly, David and Anthony Reid (eds.), *Asian Freedoms: The Idea of Freedom in East and Southeast Asia* (Cambridge University Press 1998).
Kennedy, Andrew, *The International Ambitions of Mao and Nehru: National Efficacy Beliefs and the Making of Foreign Policy* (Cambridge University Press 2012).
Lee, Rose and Cal Clark, *Democracy and the Status of Women in East Asia* (L. Rienner 2000).
Mietzner, Marcus (ed.), *The Political Resurgence of the Military in Southeast Asia: Conflict and Leadership* (Routledge 2011).
Runciman, David, *The Confidence Trap: A History of Democracy in Crisis from WWI to the Present* (Princeton University Press 2013).
Sen, Amartya, *Development as Freedom* (Oxford University Press 1999).
Weiss, M. and Edward Aspinall (eds.), *Student Activism in Asia: Between Protest and Powerlessness* (University of Minnesota Press 2012).

China

For authoritative academic analysis of how the Communist Party of China (CCP) responded to the collapse of the Soviet Union, see David Shambaugh, *China's Communist Party: Atrophy and Adaptation* (University of California Press 2009).

For an astute journalist's assessment of the CCP and how it wields power and rules, see Richard McGregor, *The Party: The Secret World of China's Communist Rulers* (Harper 2010).

For a handy anthology, see Chris Ogden (ed.), *Handbook of China's Governance and Domestic Politics* (Routledge 2015).

Recommended:

Ai Weiwei, *Ai Weiwei's Blog: Writings, Interviews, and Digital Rants, 2006–09* (ed. and trans. Lee Ambrosy) (MIT Press 2011).
Bell, Daniel, *The China Model: Political Meritocracy and the Limits of Democracy* (Princeton University Press 2015).

Brady, Anne-Marie, *Marketing Dictatorship: Propaganda and Thought Work in Contemporary China* (Rowman & Littlefield 2008).
Brady, Anne-Marie (ed.), *China's Thought Management* (Routledge 2011).
Ching, Kwan Lee, *Against the Law: Labor Protests in China's Rustbelt and Sunbelt* (University of California Press 2007).
Heilmann, S. and E. Perry, *Mao's Invisible Hand: The Political Foundations of Adaptive Governance* (Harvard University Press 2011).
Ho-fung Hung, "Three Views of Consciousness in Hong Kong," *The Asia-Pacific Journal*, 12:44:1 (November 3, 2014).
Kennedy, Andrew, "Red Dragon, Green Energy: Techno-nationalism in China's Search for Renewable Power," *Asian Survey*, 53:5 (2013), 909–930.
Kennedy, Andrew, "Powerhouses or Pretenders: Debating China and India's emergence as technological powers," *The Pacific Review* (January 2015), 1–22.
Mengin, F., *Cyber China: Reshaping National Identities in the Age of Information* (Palgrave Macmillan 2004).
Nathan, Andrew, Larry Diamond and Marc Plattner (eds.), *Will China Democratize?* (Johns Hopkins University Press 2013).
Parker, Emily, *Now I Know Who My Comrades Are: Voices from the Internet Underground* (Farrar, Straus and Giroux 2014).
Shen, Simon and Shaun Breslin (eds.), *Online Chinese Nationalism and China's Bilateral Relations* (Lexington 2010).
Tang, Wenfang and Benjamin Darr, "Chinese Nationalism and Its Political and Social Origins," *Journal of Contemporary China*, 21:77 (2012), 811–826.
Weiss, Jessica Chen, "Authoritarian Signaling, Mass Audiences and Nationalist Protest in China," *International Organization*, 67:1 (2013), 1–35.
Xuecun, Murong, "Beijing's Facts, and Fictions," *New York Times* (April 16, 2014).

India

For a useful anthology, see Paul Brass (ed.), *Routledge Handbook of South Asian Politics: India, Pakistan, Bangladesh, Sri Lanka, and Nepal* (Routledge 2010).

Recommended:

Bhagwati, Jagdish, *Financial Times* (April 16, 2014).
Chibber, Pradeep K. and Sandeep Shashtri, *Religious Practice and Democracy in India* (Cambridge University Press 2014).
Corbridge, Stuart, John Harriss and Craig Jeffrey, *India Today: Economy, Politics and Society* (Polity Press 2013).
Eckert, Julia, "Theories of Militancy in Practice: Explanations of Muslim Terrorism in India," *Social Science History*, 36:3 (2012), 321–345.
Goswami, Ranjit, "India's Ponzi-Styled Economic Reforms Run out of Steam," *East Asia Forum* (June 4, 2013).
Guha, Ramachandra, *Patriots and Partisans* (Allen Lane 2012).

Kennedy, J. and L. King, "The Political Economy of Farmers' Suicides in India: Indebted Cash-Crop Farmers with Marginal Landholdings Explain State-Level Variation in Suicide Rates," *Globalization and Health*, 10:16 (March 26, 2014).

Kohli, Atul, *Poverty Amid Plenty in the New India* (Cambridge University Press 2012).

Mehta, Pratap Banu, "State and Democracy in India," *Polish Sociological Review*, 178 (2012), 203–225.

Mishra, Atul, "India's Non-Liberal Democracy and the Discourse on Democracy Promotion," *South Asian Survey*, 19:1 (March 2012), 33–59.

Mishra, Pankaj, "Which India Matters?" *The New York Review of Books* (November 21, 2013).

Sharma, Prashant, *Democracy and Transparency in the Indian State: The Making of the Right to Information Act* (Routledge 2014).

Sivaramakrishnan, K., "Environment, Law and Democracy in India," *The Journal of Asian Studies*, 70:4 (November 2011), 123–140.

Subramaniam, Arjun, "Challenges of Protecting India from Terrorism," *Terrorism and Political Violence*, 24:3 (July 2012), 396–414.

U.S.-India Policy Institute, "Six Years After Sachar: Review of Socially Inclusive Policies in India since 2006," www.usindiapolicy.org/six-years-after-sachar-review-of-socially-inclusive-policies-in-india-since-2006/

Wilkinson, Steven, *Army and Nation: The Military and Indian Democracy since Independence* (Harvard University Press 2015).

Indonesia

Aspinall, Edward, *Opposing Suharto: Compromise, Resistance, and Regime Change in Indonesia* (Stanford University Press 2005).

Aspinall, Edward, *Islam and Nation: Separatist Rebellion in Aceh, Indonesia* (Stanford University Press 2009).

Aspinall, Edward, "Democratization and Ethnic Politics in Indonesia: Nine Theses," *Journal of East Asian Studies*, 11:2 (2011), 289–319.

Aspinall, Edward and Marcus Mietzner (eds.), *Problems of Democratisation in Indonesia: Elections, Institutions and Society* (Institute of Southeast Asian Studies, Singapore 2010).

Bourchier, David and John Legge (eds.), *Democracy in Indonesia 1950s and 1990s* (Monash University 1994).

Crouch, Harold, *The Army and Politics in Indonesia* (Cornell University Press 1978).

Feith, Herb, *The Decline of Constitutional Democracy in Indonesia* (Cornell University Press 1962).

Feith, Herb and Lance Castles, *Indonesian Political Thinking, 1945–1965* (Cornell University Press 1970).

Honna, Jun, *Military Politics and Democratization in Indonesia* (Routledge 2003).

Horowitz, Donald, *Constitutional Change and Democracy in Indonesia* (Cambridge University Press 2013).

Kunkler, Mirjam and Alfred Stepan (eds.), *Democracy and Islam in Indonesia* (Columbia University Press 2013).

Mietzner, Marcus, *Military Politics, Islam, and the State in Indonesia: From Turbulent Transition to Democratic Consolidation* (Institute of Southeast Asian Studies, Singapore 2009).

Mietzner, Marcus, *Money, Power, and Ideology: Political Parties in Post-Authoritarian Indonesia* (National University of Singapore Press 2013).

Sundhaussen, Ulf, *The Road to Power: Indonesian Military Politics 1945–67* (Oxford University Press 1982).

Van Dijk, C., *Rebellion under the Banner of Islam: The Darul Islam Movement in Indonesia* (Martinus Nijhoff 1981).

Japan

Bowen, Roger, *Japan's Dysfunctional Democracy* (M.E. Sharpe 2003).

Caprio, Mark and Yoneyuki Sugita, *Democracy in Occupied Japan: The US Occupation and Japanese Politics and Society* (Routledge 2007).

Curtis, Gerald, *The Logic of Japanese Politics: Leaders, Institutions, and the Limits of Change* (Columbia University Press 1999).

Estevez-Abe, Margarita, *Welfare and Capitalism in Postwar Japan: Party, Bureaucracy, and Business* (Cambridge University Press 2008).

George, Timothy, *Minamata: Pollution and the Struggle for Democracy in Postwar Japan* (Harvard University Press 2001).

Hook, Glen (ed.), *Contested Governance in Japan: Sites and Issues* (Routledge Curzon 2006).

Imada, Makoto, *Civil Society in Japan: Democracy, Voluntary Action and Philanthropy* (Springer 2010).

Johnson, Chalmers, *MITI and the Japanese Miracle: The Growth of Industrial Policy 1925–75* (Stanford University Press 1982).

Katz, Richard, *Japan, the System that Soured: The Rise and Fall of the Japanese Economic Miracle* (M.E. Sharpe 1998).

Krauss, Ellis, *The Rise and Fall of Japan's LDP: Political Party Organizations as Institutions* (Cornell University Press 2010).

McClelland, Mark, *Love, Sex and Democracy in Occupied Japan* (Palgrave Macmillan 2012).

Mulgan George, Aurelia, *The Politics of Agriculture in Japan* (Routledge 2000).

Mulgan George, Aurelia, *Japan's Failed Revolution: Koizumi and the Politics of Economic Reform* (Asia Pacific Press 2002).

Nagy, Robert, "Nationalism, Domestic Politics and the Japan Economic Rejuvenation," *East Asia*, 31:1 (March 2014), 5–21.

Pekkanen, Robert, *Japan's Dual Civil Society: Members without Advocates* (Stanford University Press 2006).

Ruoff, Kenneth, *The People's Emperor: Democracy and the Japanese Monarchy, 1945–1995* (Harvard University Press 2003).

Sasaki, Fumiko, *Nationalism, Political Realism and Democracy in Japan: The Thought of Maruyama Masao* (Routledge 2012).

Scheiner, Ethan, *Democracy without Competition in Japan: Opposition Failure in a One-Party Dominant State* (Cambridge University Press 2006).

Shibuchi, Daiki, "Emerging Hate Groups in Japan," *East Asia Forum* (July 26, 2013).

Stockwin, J.A.A., *Governing Japan: Divided Politics in a Resurgent Economy* (Blackwell, 4th ed., 2008).

Trevor, Malcolm, *Japan: Restless Competitor; the Pursuit of Economic Nationalism* (Curzon Press 2001).

Korea

Armstrong, Charles, *Korean Society: Civil Society, Democracy and the State* (Routledge, 2nd ed., 2007).

Doucette, Jamie and Se-Woong Koo, "Distorting Democracy: Politics by Public Security in Contemporary South Korea," *The Asia-Pacific Journal*, 11:48:4 (December 2, 2013).

Khil, Young Whan, *Transforming Korean Politics: Democracy, Reform and Culture* (M.E. Sharpe 2005).

Lee, Hyun, "The Erosion of Democracy in South Korea: The Dissolution of the Unified Progressive Party and the Incarceration of Lee Seok-ki," *The Asia-Pacific Journal*, 12:52:5 (December 29, 2014).

Shin, Gi-Wook and Paul Y. Chang (eds.), *South Korean Social Movements: From Democracy to Civil Society* (Routledge 2011).

Suh, Jae-Jung and Taehyun Nam, "Rethinking the Prospects for Korean Democracy in Light of the Sinking of the Cheonan and North-South Conflict," *The Asia-Pacific Journal*, 11:10:1 (March 11, 2012).

Sports

Astill, James, *The Great Tamasha: Cricket, Corruption and the Turbulent Rise of Modern India* (Bloomsbury 2013).

Brady, Anne-Marie, "The Beijing Olympics as a Campaign of Mass Distraction," *The China Quarterly*, 197 (2009), 1–24.

Bromber, Katrin, Birgit Krawietz, and Joseph Maguire (eds.), *Sport across Asia: Politics, Cultures, and Identities* (Routledge 2013).

Chakraborty, Subhas Ranjan, Shantanu Chakrabarti, and Kingshuk Chaterjee (eds.), *The Politics of Sport in South Asia* (Routledge 2009).

Cho, Ji-Hyun and Alan Bairner, "The Sociocultural Legacy of the 1988 Seoul Olympic Games," *Leisure Studies*, 31:3 (2012), 271–289.

Cho, Younghan (ed.), *Football in Asia: History, Culture and Business (Sport in the Global Society)* (Routledge 2014).

Collins, Sandra, "East Asian Olympic Desires: Identity on the Global Stage in the 1964 Tokyo, 1988 Seoul and 2008 Beijing Games," *The International Journal of the History of Sport*, 28:16 (2011), 2240–2260.

Guha, Ramachandra, *A Corner of a Foreign Field: The Indian History of a Foreign Sport* (Pan Macmillan 2003).

Gupta, Amit, "The IPL and Indian Domination of Global Cricket," *Sport in Society: Cultures, Commerce, Media, Politics*, 14:10 (2011), 1316–1325.

Holt, Richard and Dino Ruta (eds.), *Routledge Handbook of Sport and Legacy* (Routledge 2015).

Houlihan, Barrie, "Sport, National Identity and Public Policy," *Nations and Nationalism*, 3:1 (1997), 113–137.

Klein, Alamn, *Growing the Game: The Globalization of Major League Baseball* (Yale University Press 2008).

Macnaughtan, Helen, "The Oriental Witches: Women, Volleyball and the 1964 Tokyo Olympics," *Sport in History*, 34:1 (2014), 134–156.

Maguire, Joseph and Masayoshi Nakayama (eds.), *Japan, Sport and Society: Tradition and Change in a Globalizing World* (Routledge 2006).

Majumdar, Boria, "The 'Accidental Legacy' of Commonwealth Games 2010," *South Asian History and Culture*, 3:1 (January 2012), 126–132.

Manheim, Jarol, "Rites of Passage: The 1988 Seoul Olympics as Public Diplomacy," *The Western Political Quarterly*, 43:2 (June 1990), 279–295.

Menon-Sen, K., "Delhi and CWG2010: The Games Behind the Games," *Journal of Asian Studies*, 69:3 (August 2010), 677–681.

Nair, Nisha, "Cricket Obsession in India: Through the Lens of Identity Theory," *Sport in Society: Cultures, Commerce, Media, Politics*, 14:5 (2011), 569–580.

Qing, Luo and Giuseppe Richer (eds.), *Encoding the Olympics: The Beijing Olympic Games and the Communication Impact Worldwide* (Routledge 2012).

Reporters Without Borders, "Repression Continues Six Months after Beijing Olympics Opening Ceremony, but Media and Dissidents Fight Back" (2009). www.refworld.org/cgi-bin/texis/vtx/rwmain?page=search&docid=498fe055c&skip=0&query=beijing%20olympics&coi=CHN

Tendulkar, Sachin, *Playing It My Way: My Autobiography* (Hodder & Stoughton 2014).

Thakur, R., "Singh: Missing for a Decade", *Japan Times* (March 16, 2014).

Tsutsui, William M. and Michael Baskett (eds.), *The East Asian Olympiads, 1934–2008: Building Bodies and Nations in Japan, Korea, and China* (Global Oriental 2011).

Whiting, Robert, *The Samurai Way of Baseball: The Impact of Ichiro and the New Wave from Japan* (Grand Central Publishing 2005).

Whiting, Robert, *You Gotta Have Wa: When Two Baseball Cultures Collide on the Baseball Diamond* (Vintage 2009).

Ying Yu and Jiangyog Liu, "A Comparative Analysis of the Olympic Impact in East Asia: From Japan, South Korea to China," *The International Journal of the History of Sport*, 28:16 (2011), 2290–2308.

III Shackles of the Past

Memory

Berger, Thomas, *War, Guilt and World Politics after World War II* (Cambridge University Press 2012).

Buruma, Ian, *The Wages of Guilt: Memories of War in Germany and Japan* (Farrar, Straus and Giroux 1994).

Choi, Suhi, *Embattled Memories: Contested Meanings in Korean War Memorials* (University of Nevada Press 2014).

Field, Norma, *In the Realm of the Dying Emperor: A Portrait of Japan at Century's End* (Vintage 1993).

Fujitani, T., Geoffrey White and Lisa Yoneyama (eds.), *Perilous Memories: The Asia-Pacific War(s)* (Duke University Press 2001).

Gardner Feldman, Lily, *Germany's Foreign Policy of Reconciliation: From Enmity to Amity* (Rowman & Littlefield 2012).

Hasegawa, Tsuyoshi and Kazuhiko Togo (eds.), *East Asia's Haunted Past* (Praeger Security International 2008).

Hashimoto, Akiko, *The Long Defeat: Cultural Trauma, Memory and Identity in Japan* (Oxford University Press 2015).

He, Yinan, "The Past and Present of Sino-Japanese Relations: Revisiting the Roles of the US Factor and Historical Legacy," in Caroline Rose and Victor Teo (eds.), *The United States between China and Japan* (Cambridge Scholars Publishing 2013).

He, Yinan, "Remembering and Forgetting the War: Elite Mythmaking, Mass Reaction, and Sino-Japanese Relations," in Jun-Hyeok Kwak and Melissa Nobles (eds.), *Inherited Responsibility and Historical Reconciliation in East Asia* (Routledge 2013).

He, Yinan, "War, Myths, and National Identity Formation: Chinese Attitudes toward Japan," in Gérard Bouchard (ed.), *National Myths: Constructed Pasts, Contested Presents* (Routledge 2013).

Hein, Laura and Mark Selden (eds.), *Censoring History: Citizenship and Memory in Japan, Germany and the United States* (M.E. Sharpe 2000).

Hotta, E., *Japan 1941: Countdown to Infamy* (Knopf 2013).

Kim, Mikyoung, "Human Rights, Memory and Reconciliation: Korea-Japan Relations," *The Asia-Pacific Journal*, 11:10:2 (March 11, 2013).

Kingston, Jeff, "Awkward Talisman: War Memory, Reconciliation and Yasukuni," *East Asia*, 24:3 (2007), 295–318.

McGregor, Katharine, *History in Uniform: Military Ideology and the Construction of Indonesia's Past* (University of Press 2007).

Ryang, Sonia, "Reading Volcano Island: In the Sixty-Fifth Year of the Jeju 4.3 Uprising," *The Asia-Pacific Journal*, 11:36:2 (September 9, 2013).

Saaler, Sven, *Politics, Memory and Public Opinion: The History Textbook Controversy and Japanese Society* (Deutsches Institut fur Japanstudien 2005).

Seaton, Philip, *Japan's Contested War Memories: The "Memory Rifts" in Historical Consciousness of World War II* (Routledge 2007).

Szczepanska, Kamila, *The Politics of War Memory in Japan: Progressive Civil Society Groups and Contestation of Memory of the Asia-Pacific War* (Routledge 2014).
Takenaka, Akiko, *Yasukuni Shrine: History, Memory and Japan's Unending Postwar* (University of Hawai'i Press 2015).
Wang, Zheng, *Never Forget National Humiliation: Historical Memory in Chinese Politics and Foreign Relations* (Columbia University Press 2012).
Yamazaki, Jane, *Japanese Apologies for World War II: A Rhetorical Study* (Routledge 2005).
Zurbruchen, Mary S. (ed.), *Beginning to Remember: The Past in the Indonesian Present* (Singapore University Press 2005).

Reconciliation

Dudden, Alexis, *Troubled Apologies: Among Japan, Korea and the United States* (Columbia University Press 2008).
Funabashi, Yoichi (ed.), *Reconciliation in the Asia-Pacific* (US Institute of Peace Press 2003).
Kwak, Jun-Hyeok and Melissa Noble (eds.), *Inherited Responsibility and Historical Reconciliation in East Asia* (Routledge 2013).
Lam, Peng-er, *Japan's Peace-Building Diplomacy in Asia: Seeking a More Active Political Role* (Routledge 2009).
Mitani, Hiroshi, "Why Do We Still Need to Talk About 'Historical Understanding' in East Asia?" *Asia-Pacific Journal*, 12:32:2 (August 11, 2014).
Shin, Gi-Wook, Soon-Won Park, and Daqing Yang, *Rethinking Historical Injustice and Reconciliation in Northeast Asia: The Korean Experience* (Routledge 2007).
Togo, Kazuhiko, *Japan and Reconciliation in Post-War Asia: The Murayama Statement and Its Implications* (Palgrave Macmillan 2013).

Traumas

Bass, Gary, *Blood Telegram: India's Secret War in East Pakistan* (Random House 2013).
Brooks, Tim, *Quelling the People* (Stanford University Press 1999).
Callahan, William, *China the Pessoptimist Nation* (Oxford University Press 2010).
Caprio, Mark, *Japanese Assimilation Policies in Colonial Korea, 1910–1945* (University of Washington Press 2009).
Chang, Iris, *The Rape of Nanking: The Forgotten Holocaust of World War II* (Basic Books 1997).
Dikotter, Frank, *Mao's Great Famine: The History of China's Most Devastating Catastrophe, 1958–1962* (Walker & Company 2011).
Dikotter, Frank, *The Tragedy of Liberation: A History of the Chinese Revolution 1945–1957* (Bloomsbury Press 2015).

Dower, John, *War without Mercy: Race and Power in the Pacific War* (Pantheon 1987).

Dudden, Alexis, *Japan's Colonization of Korea: Discourse and Power* (University of Hawai'i Press 2006).

Esherick, Joseph, Paul Pickowitz, and Andrew Water (eds.), *The Chinese Cultural Revolution as History* (Stanford University Press 2006).

Fogel, Jishua (ed.), *The Nanjing Massacre in History and Historiography* (University of California Press 2000).

Ganesan, N. and Sung Chull Kim, *State Violence in East Asia* (University of Kentucky Press 2013).

Goto, Kenichi, *Tensions of Empire: Japan and Southeast Asia in the Colonial and Postcolonial World* (Ohio University Press 2003).

Hein, Laura and Mark Selden, *Living with the Bomb: American and Japanese Cultural Conflicts in the Nuclear Age* (M.E. Sharpe 1997).

Hoyt, Edwin, *Inferno: The Firebombing of Japan, March 9–August 15* (Madison Books 2013).

Ikeda, Kyle, *Okinawan War Memory: Transgenerational Trauma and the War Fiction of Medoruma Shun* (Routledge 2014).

Kammen, Douglas and Katherine MacGregor (eds.), *The Contours of Mass Violence in Indonesia, 1965–68* (University of Hawai'i Press 2012).

Katsiaficas, George, *Asia's Unknown Uprisings: South Korean Social Movements in the 20th Century*. Vol. 1 (PM Press 2012).

Khan, Yasmin, *The Great Partition: The Making of India and Pakistan* (Yale University Press 2007).

Kovner, Sarah, *Occupying Power: Sex Workers and Servicemen in Postwar Japan* (Stanford University Press 2012).

Kwon, Heonik, "Korean War Traumas," *The Asia-Pacific Journal*, 38:2:10 (September 20, 2010).

Kyung-Koo, Han, "Legacies of War: The Korean War—60 Years On," *The Asia-Pacific Journal*, 38:3:10 (September 20, 2010).

Lee, Hong Yung, Yong-chúl Ha, and Clark Sorenson, *Colonial Rule and Social Change in Korea, 1910–1945* (University of Washington Press 2013).

Lewis, Linda S., *Laying Claim to the Memory of May: a Look Back at the 1980 Kwangju Uprising* (University of Hawai'i Press 2002).

McCormack, Gavan, "The End of the Postwar? The Abe Government, Okinawa, and Yonaguni Island," *The Asia-Pacific Journal*, 12:49:3 (December 8, 2014).

McCoy, Alfred (ed.), *Southheast Asia under Japanese Occupation* (Yale University Press 1980).

Mitter, Rana, *China's War with Japan 1937–45: The Struggle for Survival* (Allen Lane 2013).

Nair, Neeti, *Changing Homelands: Hindu Politics and the Partition of India* (Harvard University Press 2011).

Nishino, Rumiko, "The Forgotten Victims in the 'Asahi Bashing' Case," *The Asia-Pacific Journal*, 12:49:2 (December 22, 2014).

Nozaki, Yoshiko, "The 'Comfort Women' Controversy: History and Testimony," *The Asia-Pacific Journal*, 3:7 (July 2005).

Nussbaum, Martha, *The Clash Within: Democracy, Religious Violence, and India's Future* (Harvard University Press 2008).

Roosa, John, *Pretext for Mass Murder: The September 30th Movement and Suharto's Coup d'État in Indonesia* (University of Wisconsin Press 2006).

Selden, Mark, "Bombs Bursting in Air: State and Citizen Responses to the US Firebombing and Atomic Bombing of Japan," *The Asia-Pacific Journal*, 12:3:4 (January 20, 2014).

Shin, Gi-Wook and Kyung Moon Hwang (eds.), *Contentious Kwangju: The May 18 Uprising in Korea's Past and Present* (Rowman & Littlefield 2003).

Shin, Gi-Wook and Michael Robinson (eds.), *Colonial Modernity in Korea* (Harvard University Press 1999).

Soh, C. Sarah, *The Comfort Women: Sexual Violence and Postcolonial Memory in Korea and Japan* (University of Chicago Press 2008).

Stetz, Margaret and Bonnie B.C. Oh (eds.), *Legacies of the Comfort Women of World War II* (M.E. Sharpe 2002).

Sukanta, Outu Oka (ed.), *Breaking the Silence: Survivors Speak about 1965–66 Violence in Indonesia* (trans. Jennifer Lindsay) (Monash University Press 2014).

Tanaka, Yuki, *Hidden Horrors: Japanese War Crimes in World War II* (Westview Press 1998).

Tanaka, Yuki, *Japan's Comfort Women: Sexual Slavery and Prostitution during World War II and the US Occupation* (Routledge 2002).

Tanaka, Yuki and Marilyn Young, *Bombing Civilians: A Twentieth Century History* (New Press 2009).

Tarling, Nicholas, *A Sudden Rampage: The Japanese Occupation of Southeast Asia, 1941–45* (Hurst & Company 2001).

Tunzelman, Alex Von, *Indian Summer: The Secret History of the End of an Empire* (Picador 2008).

Wakabayashi, Bob Tadashi (ed.), *The Nanking Atrocity 1937–38: Complicating the Picture* (Berghahn Books 2007).

Yang Jisheng (trans. Stacy Mosher), *Tombstone: The Great Chinese Famine, 1958–1962* (Farrar, Straus and Giroux 2013).

Yoshida, Takashi, *The Making of the Rape of Nanking: History and Memory in Japan, China and the United States* (Oxford University 2006).

Yoshimi, Yoshiaki, *Comfort Women: Sexual Slavery in the Japanese Military during World War II* (Columbia University Press 2000).

Yu Gao, *New York Times* (February 3, 2015).

Yu Hua, "China's Struggle to Forget," *New York Times* (March 17, 2014), 7.

Museums

Allen, Matthew and Rumi Sakamoto, "War and Peace: War Memories and Museums in Japan," *History Compass*, 11:2 (2013), 1047–1058.

Denton, Kirk, *Exhibiting the Past: Historical Memory and the Politics of Museums in Postsocialist China* (University of Hawai'i Press 2014).

Hatch, Walter, "Bloody Memories: Affect and Effect of World War II Museums in China and Japan," *Peace & Change*, 39:3 (2014), 366–394.

Jeans, Roger, "Victims or Victimizers? Museums, Textbooks, and the War Debate in Japan," *The Journal of Military History*, 69:1 (2005), 149–195.

Kingston, Jeff, "Awkward Talisman: War Memory, Reconciliation and Yasukuni," *East Asia*, 24:3 (2007), 295–318.

Kingston, Jeff, "Nanjing's Massacre Memorial: Renovating War Memory in Nanjing and Tokyo," *Japan Focus* (August 22, 2008).

Kingston, Jeff, "Museums, Manga, Memorials and Korean-Japanese History Wars," *Asian Studies*, II:XVIII:2 (2014), 41–71.

Morris-Suzuki, Tessa, "Remembering the Unfinished Conflict: Museums and the Contested Memory of the Korean War," *The Asia-Pacific Journal*, 29:4:9 (July 27, 2009).

O'Dwyer, Shaun, "The Yasukuni Shrine and the Competing Patriotic Pasts of East Asia," *History & Memory*, 22:2 (2010), 147–177.

Yoshida, Takashi, *From Cultures of War to Cultures of Peace: War and Peace Museums in Japan, China and South Korea* (Merwin Asia 2014).

Textbooks

Bhattacharya, Neeladri., "Teaching History in Schools: The Politics of Textbooks in India," *History Workshop Journal*, 67:1 (2009), 99–110.

Dierkes, Julian, *Postwar History Education in Japan and the Germanys: Guilty Lessons* (Routledge 2010).

Friedrich-Ebert-Stiftung (Tokyo), *The Politics of History—History of Politics: Sources Relating to the History Textbook Controversy and Other Debates over History and Memory in Japan and East Asia* (Friedrich-Ebert-Stiftung 2014).

Fukuoka, Kazuya, "School History Textbooks and Historical Memories in Japan: A Study of Reception," *International Journal of Politics, Culture, and Society*, 24:3/4 (December 2011), 83–103.

Guichard, Sylvie, *The Construction of History and Nationalism in India: Textbooks, Controversies and Politics* (Routledge 2010).

Han, Un-suk, Takahiro Kondo, Biao Yang, and Falk Pingel (eds.), *History Education and Reconciliation: Comparative Perspectives on East Asia* (Peter Lang 2012).

Joshi, Sanay, "Contesting Histories and Nationalist Geographies: A Comparison of School Textbooks in India and Pakistan," *South Asian History and Culture*, 1:3 (June 2010), 357–377.

Kan, Kimura, "Discovery of Disputes: Collective Memories on Textbooks and Japanese-South Korean Relations," *Journal of Korean Studies*, 17:1 (2012), 97–124.

Koide Reiko, "Critical New Stage in Japan's Textbook Controversy," *The Asia-Pacific Journal*, 12:13:1 (March 31, 2014).

Kwan-Choi Tse, Thomas, "Creating Good Citizens in China: Comparing Grade 7–9 School Textbooks, 1997–2005," *Journal of Moral Education*, 40:2 (2011), 161–180.

Namiki, Yorihisa, "Japan and China: History and Textbooks," *Social Science Japan*, 24 (October 2002), 25–31.

Nozaki, Yoshiko, *War Memory, Nationalism and Education in Postwar Japan, 1945–2007: The Japanese History Textbook Controversy and Ienaga Saburo's Court Challenges* (Routledge 2008).

Packard, G., *Edwin O. Reischauer and the American Discovery of Japan* (Columbia University Press 2010).

Sakaki, Alexandra, "Japanese-South Korean Textbook Talks: The Necessity of Political Leadership," *Pacific Affairs*, 85:2 (2012), 263–285.

Shin, Gi-Wook and Daniel Sneider (eds.), *History Textbooks and the Wars in Asia* (Routledge 2011).

Sin, Ju-back, "How to Cross the Border of Historical Perceptions in the History Textbooks of Korea, China and Japan: Liquidation of the Asia-Pacific War and Historical Reconciliation," *Korea Journal*, 48:3 (Autumn 2008), 133–165.

Sneider, Daniel, "Textbooks and Patriotic Education: Wartime Memory Formation in China and Japan," *Asia-Pacific Review*, 20:1 (May 2013), 35–54.

Suwignyo, Agus, "Indonesian National History Textbooks after the New Order: What's New under the Sun?" *Bijdragen von de Taal-, Land-, en Volkenkunde*, 170 (2014), 113–131.

Tan, Paige Johnson, "Teaching and Remembering," *Inside Indonesia*, 62 (April–June 2008). www.insideindonesia.org/teaching-and-remembering

IV Flashpoints and Fringes

The following are good sources on the history and geo-politics of regional flashpoints and rivalries.

Bush, Richard, *The Perils of Proximity: China-Japan Security Relations* (Brookings Institution Press 2010).

Camilleri, Joseph (ed.), *Asia-Pacific Geopolitics: Hegemony vs Human Security* (Edward Elgar Publishing 2007).

Drifte, Reinhard, "Territorial Conflicts in the East China Sea—From Missed Opportunities to Negotiation Stalemate," *The Asia-Pacific Journal*, 7:22:3 (May 30, 2009).

Drifte, Reinhard, "The Japan-China Confrontation over the Senkaku/Diaoyu Islands—Between 'Shelving' and 'Dispute Escalation,'" *The Asia-Pacific Journal*, 12:30:3 (July 28, 2014).

Dyer, Geoff, *The Contest of the Century: The New Era of Competition with China—and How America Can Win* (Vintage 2014).

Economist, "Kashmir: The K-Word," *Economist* (November 3, 2010).

Economy, Elizabeth and Michael Levy, *By All Means Necessary: How China's Resource Quest Is Changing the World* (Oxford University Press 2014).

Emmott, Bill, *Rivals: How the Power Struggle between China, India, and Japan Will Shape Our Next Decade* (Mariner Books 2009).

Fenby, Jonathan, *Will China Dominate the 21st Century?* (Polity 2014).
Hara, Kimie, *Cold War Frontiers in the Asia Pacific: Divided Territories in the San Francisco System* (Routledge 2007).
Hayton, Bill, *The South China Sea Dispute* (Yale University Press 2014).
Hong, Zhao, *China and India: The Quest for Energy Resources in the 21st Century* (Routledge 2012).
Hong, Zhao, "The South China Sea Dispute and China-ASEAN Relations," *Asian Affairs*, 44:1 (2013), 27–43.
Kaplan, Robert, *Asia's Cauldron: The South China Sea and the End of a Stable Pacific* (Random House 2014).
Kohno, M. and Francis Rosenbluth (eds.), *Japan and the World: Japan's Contemporary Geopolitical Challenges* (Yale University 2008).
Lee, Seokwoo and John Van Dyke, "The 1951 San Francisco Peace Treaty and Its Relevance to Sovereignty over Dokdo," *Chinese Journal of International Law*, 9:4 (2010), 741–762.
Lim, Robyn, *The Geopolitics of East Asia: The Search for Equlibrium* (Routledge 2003).
Luttwak, Edward, *The Rise of China vs. the Logic of Strategy* (Harvard University Press 2012).
Nathan, Andrew and Andrew Scobell, *China's Search for Security* (Columbia University Press 2012).
Pant, Harsh, *The China Syndrome* (HarperCollins 2013).
Peer, Basharat, *Curfewed Night: A Frontline Memoir of Life, Love and War in Kashmir* (Scribner 2010).
Selden, Mark, "Small Islets, Enduring Conflict: Dokdo, Korea-Japan Colonial Legacy and the United States," *The Asia-Pacific Journal*, 9:17:2 (April 25, 2011).
Smith, Jeff, *Cold Peace: China-India Rivalry in the Twenty-First Century* (Lexington Books 2013).
Tay, Simon, *Asia Alone: The Dangerous Post-Crisis Divide from America* (John Wiley 2010).
Thant Myint-U, *Where China Meets India: Burma and the New Crossroads of Asia* (Farrar, Straus and Giroux 2011).
Wang, Hui, *The Politics of Imagining Asia* (trans. Theodore Huters) (Harvard University Press 2011).
Wang, Hui, *China from Empire to Nation-State* (trans. Michael Hill) (Harvard University Press 2014).
Weiss, E., R. Jeffrey, and A. Regan (eds.), *Diminishing Conflicts in Asia and the Pacific: Why Some Subside and Others Don't* (Routledge 2013).

Foreign Policy

Given leadership transitions in all of our focus nations, a shift in priorities and methods, and intensifying rivalries, foreign policy assessments can be quickly overtaken by events. With that caveat these sources are helpful guides to better understanding the flashpoints in Asia.

China

French, Howard, "China's Dangerous Game," *The Atlantic* (November 2014, online).

Hughes, Christopher, "Reclassifying Chinese Nationalism: The Geopolitik Turn," *Journal of Contemporary China*, 20:71 (2011), 601–620.

Li, Mingjian and Kalyan M. Kemburi (eds.), *China's Power and Asian Security* (Routledge 2014).

Reilly, James, *Strong Society, Smart State: The Rise of Public Opinion in China's Japan Policy* (Columbia University Press 2011).

Reilly, James, "China's Unilateral Sanctions," *Washington Quarterly*, 35:4 (Fall 2012), 121–133.

Reilly, James, "A Wave to Worry About? Public Opinion, Foreign Policy and China's Anti-Japan Protests," *Journal of Contemporary China*, 23:86 (2014), 197–215.

Shambaugh, David, *China Goes Global: The Partial Power* (Oxford University Press 2013).

Suisheng Zhao, "Foreign Policy Implications of Chinese Nationalism Revisited: The Strident Turn," *Journal of Contemporary China*, 22:82 (2013), 535–553.

India

Ganguly, Sumit (ed.), *India's Foreign Policy: Retrospect and Prospect* (Oxford University Press 2010).

Khilnani, Sunil, *Non-Alignment 2.0: A Foreign and Strategic Policy for India in the 21st Century* (Penguin 2014).

Malone, David, *Does the Elephant Dance? Contemporary Indian Foreign Policy* (Oxford University Press 2012).

Ogden, Christopher, *India's Foreign Policy* (Polity 2014).

Pant, Harsh (ed.), *The Rise of China: Implications for India* (Cambridge University Press 2012).

Ray, Jayanta Kumar, *India's Foreign Relations 1947–2007* (Routledge 2010).

Sikri, Rajiv, *Challenge and Strategy: Rethinking India's Foreign Policy* (Sage 2009).

Indonesia

Connelly, Aaron, "Indonesian Foreign Policy under President Jokowi," www.lowyinstitute.org/publications/indonesian-foreign-policy-under-president-jokowi (October 16, 2014).

Kahin, Audrey and George Kahin, *Subversion as Foreign Policy: The Secret Eisenhower and Dulles Debacle in Indonesia* (New Press 1995).

Kurlantzick, Joshua, *Indonesian Foreign Policy* (Pais International 2013).

Leifer, Michael, *Indonesian Foreign Policy* (Routledge 2014, reissue of 1983).

Murphy, Ann Marie, "Democratization and Indonesian Foreign Policy: Implications for the United States," *Asia Policy*, 13:1 (2012), 83–111.

Parameswaran, Prashanth, "Between Aspiration and Reality: Indonesian Foreign Policy after the 2014 Elections," *Washington Quarterly*, 37:3 (2014), 153–165.

Pitsuwan, Fuadi, "Smart Power Strategy: Recalibrating Indonesian Foreign Policy," *Asian Politics and Policy*, 6:2 (April 2014), 237–266.

Sukma, Rizal, *Islam in Indonesian Foreign Policy: Domestic Weakness and the Dilemma of Dual Identity* (Routledge 2003).

Weinstein, Franklin, *Indonesian Foreign Policy and the Dilemma of Dependence: From Sukarno to Soeharto* (Equinox 2007, reissue of 1976).

Japan

Bukh, Alexander, *Japan's National Identity and Foreign Policy: Russia as Japan's 'Other'* (Routledge 2010).

Cooney, Kevin J., *Japan's Foreign Policy Since 1945* (M.E. Sharpe 2007).

Hook, Glenn D. (ed.), *Japan's International Relations: Politics, Economics and Security* (Routledge, 3rd ed., 2012).

Togo, Kazuhiko, *Japan's Foreign Policy 1945–2003* (Brill 2005).

South Korea

Bong, Youngshik, "Built to Last: The Dokdo Territorial Controversy," *Memory Studies*, 6:2 (April 2013), 191–203.

Cho, Sung Hun, "The US Strategy toward Japan after the WWII and the Dokdo issue," *Review of International and Area Studies*, vol. 17, 2 (2008), 41–80.

Heo, Uk and Terence Roehrig, *South Korea's Rise: Economic Development, Power and Foreign Relations* (Cambridge University Press 2014).

Kang, Song-hak, *Korea's Foreign Policy Dilemmas: Defining State Security and the Goal of National Unification* (Global Oriental 2011).

Van Dyk, John, "Legal Issues Related to Sovereignty over Dokdo and Its Maritime Boundary," *Ocean Development & International Law*, 38:1 (July 2007), 157–224.

Internal Conflict

Bhan, Mona, *Counterinsurgency, Democracy, and the Politics of Identity in India: From Warfare to Welfare?* (Routledge 2014).

Fortuna Anwar, Dewi, Helene Bouvier, Glenn Smith, and Roger Tol (eds.), *Violent Internal Conflicts in Asia Pacific: Histories, Political Economies and Policies* (Yayasan Obor 2005).

Lloyd Parry, Richard, *In the Time of Madness* (Jonathan Cape 2005).

Pandita, Rahul, *Hello, Bastar: The Untold Story of India's Maoist Movement* (Tranquebar Press 2011).

East Timor

Kingsbury, Damien, *East Timor: The Price of Liberty* (Palgrave Macmillan 2009).

Nevins, Joseph, *A Not-So-Distant Horror: Mass Violence in East Timor* (Cornell University Press 2005).

Minorities

Allen, Mathew, *Identity and Resistance in Okinawa* (Rowman & Littlefield 2002).

Barabantseva, Elena, *Overseas Chinese, Ethnic Minorities and Nationalism: De-centering China* (Routledge 2011).

Bertrand, Jacques, *Nationalisms and Ethnic Conflict in Indonesia* (Cambridge University Press 2004).

Bhalla, A.S. and Dan Luo, *Poverty and Exclusion of Minorities in China and India* (Palgrave Macmillan 2013).

Bovingdon, Gardner, *The Uyghurs: Strangers in Their Own Land* (Columbia University Press 2010).

Buckley, Alan, *Meltdown in Tibet: China's Reckless Destruction of Ecosystems from the Highlands to the Deltas of Asia* (Palgrave Macmillan 2014).

Castellino, Joshua and Elvira Dominguez Redondo, *Minority Rights in Asia: A Comparative Legal Analysis* (Oxford University Press 2006).

Chung, Erin Aeran, *Immigration and Citizenship in Japan* (Cambridge University Press 2014).

Cooley, Alexander, *Great Games, Local Rules: The New Great Power Contest in Central Asia* (Oxford University Press 2012).

Hansen, Mette Halskov, *Frontier People: Han Settlers in Minority Areas of China* (UBC Press 2009).

Hein, Laura and Mark Selden (eds.), *Islands of Discontent: Okinawan Responses to Japanese and American Power* (Rowman & Littlefield 2003).

Human Rights Watch, "Devastating Blows: Religious Repression of Uighurs in Xinjiang" (Human Rights Watch 2005). www.hrw.org/reports/2005/china0405/3.htm

Lafitte, Gabriel, *Spoiling Tibet: China and Resource Nationalism on the Roof of the World* (Zed Books 2013).

Laruelle, Marlene and Sebastian Peyrouse, *The Chinese Question in Central Asia: Domestic Order, Social Change and the Chinese Factor* (Columbia University Press 2012).

Leibold, James, *Ethnic Policy in China: Is Reform Inevitable?* (East-West Center (Honolulu) 2013).

Lie, John, *Zainichi (Koreans in Japan): Diasporic Nationalism and Postcolonial Identity* (University of California Press 2008).

Lie, John, *Multiethnic Japan* (Harvard University Press 2001).

Lindsey, Tim and Helen Pausacker (eds.), *Chinese Indonesians: Remembering, Distorting, Forgetting* (Institute of Southeast Asian Studies, Singapore 2005).

Mackerras, Colin, *China's Ethnic Minorities and Globalization* (Routledge 2003).

McCormack, Gavan and Satoko Norimatsu, *Resistant Islands: Okinawa Confronts Japan and the US* (Rowman & Littlefield 2012).

Morris-Suzuki, Tessa, *Re-Inventing Japan: Time, Space, Nation* (M.E. Sharpe 1998).

Morris-Suzuki, Tessa, "Immigration and Censorship in Contemporary Japan," in Sayed Javed Maswood, Jeffrey Graham, and Hideaki Miyajima (eds.), *Japan—Change and Continuity* (Routledge 2002), 163–178.

Peer, Basharat, "The Longest Fast," *Aljazeera America* (March 8, 2014), http://america.aljazeera.com/features/2014/3/the-longest-fast.html

Perdue, Peter, *China Marches West: The Qing Conquest of Central Eurasia* (Harvard University Press 2005).

Purdey, Jemma, *Anti-Chinese Violence in Indonesia, 1996–99* (University of Hawai'i Press 2006).

Rashid, Ahmed, *Jihad: The Rise of Militant Islam in Central Asia* (Yale University Press 2002).

Rashid, Ahmed, "Why and What You Should Know about Central Asia," *New York Review of Books* (August 15, 2013), 76–82.

Shipper, Apichai, "Nationalisms of and Against Zainichi Koreans in Japan," *Asian Politics & Policy*, 2:1 (2010), 55–75.

Suryadinata, Leo (ed.), *Chinese Indonesians: State Policy, Monoculture and Multiculture* (Eastern Universities Press 2004).

Thum, Rian, *The Sacred Routes of Uyghur History* (Harvard University Press 2014).

Weiner, Michael (ed.), *Japan's Minorities: The Illusion of Homogeneity* (Routledge, 2nd ed., 2008).

Yi, Joseph and Gowoon Jung, "Debating Multicultural Korea: Media Discourse on Migrants and Minorities in South Korea," *Journal of Ethnic and Migration Studies* (February 2015).

Aceh

Aspinall, Edward, "From Islamism to Nationalism in Aceh, Indonesia," *Nations and Nationalism*, 13:2 (2007), 245–263.

Aspinall, Edward, "Separatism in Aceh: From Social Rebellion to Political Movement," in Michele Ford (ed.), *Social Activism in Southeast Asia* (Routledge 2013), 40–55.

Drexler, Elizabeth, *Aceh, Securing the Insecure State* (University of Pennsylvania Press 2008).

Human Rights Watch, *Policing Morality: Abuses in the Application of Sharia in Aceh, Indonesia* (Human Rights Watch 2010).

Irian Jaya/West Papua

Elmslie, Jim, *Irian Jaya under the Gun: Indonesian Economic Development versus West Papuan Nationalism* (University of Hawai'i Press 2002).

King, Peter, *West Papua and Indonesia Since Suharto: Independence, Autonomy or Chaos?* (University of New South Wales Press 2004).

Kirksey, Eben, *Freedom in Entangled Worlds: West Papua and the Architecture of Global Power* (Duke University Press 2012).

Leith, Denise, *The Politics of Power: Freeport in Suharto's Indonesia* (University of Hawai'i Press 2002).

Kashmir

Ali, Tariq (ed.), *Kashmir; The Case for Freedom* (Verso 2011).

Bose, Sumantra, *Kashmir: Roots of Conflict, Paths to Peace* (Harvard University Press 2005).

Guha, Ramachandra, "Democracy and Violence in India and Beyond," *Public Policy Research*, 20:1 (2013), 40–50.

Malik, Iffat, *Kashmir: Ethnic Conflict, International Dispute* (Oxford University Press 2005).

Peer, Bashrat, *Curfewed Nights* (Random House 2009).

Index

Figures are represented in italics.

Nationalism in Asia: A History Since 1945, First Edition. Jeff Kingston.